HOW TO RESTORE AND REPAIR PRACTICALLY EVERYTHING

HOW TO RESTORE AND REPAIR PRACTICALLY EVERYTHING

LORRAINE
JOHNSON

LONDON
MICHAEL JOSEPH

Very special thanks to Phoebe Phillips whose warmth made this book possible; to Alwyn Bailey who patiently took photographs far into the night; to Mr. B.D. Archibald who answered endless questions about British products; and to the staff at Walter Parrish International for their tireless help.

First published in Great Britain by
Michael Joseph Ltd
52 Bedford Square, London WC1B 3EF
1977

ISBN 0 7181 1629 1

Designed and Produced by Walter Parrish International Ltd., London

Printed and Bound in Great Britain
by Purnell and Sons Limited
Paulton, near Bristol, Avon

This book is dedicated to my parents and grandparents who encouraged me to use my head and hands

CONTENTS

INTRODUCTION

This book came about because I found myself, a native of Ohio, in London with no money and an apartment full of junk. I quickly discovered that fixing that junk, ranging from pieces of furniture to fabrics and floor coverings, required patience above all else: patience to look for further useful items in junk stores, patience in finding matching bits and pieces with which to restore them, and patience in making a good and workable job of restoring them to a condition fit for everyday use. The thing became something of an obsession and my interest turned towards items of less immediate usefulness, even to fairly valuable antiques and more recent examples of lovely craftsmanship—I became a collector, and this book reflects the enthusiasm that grew in me. I hope it proves useful to others.

How to go about it? Well, give yourself plenty of time, and give yourself adequate space in which to work. Happily taste and period preferences need not come into it, for whether you are repairing a chrome and glass table from the "twenties", or an 18th century sideboard, the job needs the same sensible and sensitive approach.

This book is designed for beginners. Its twelve sections each contain a brief sketch of the history, development and characteristics of the subject. Whatever the piece you intend to restore, first make sure that it is not a signed antique, too old and too valuable for your amateur attentions—although as you gain experience you will be able to tackle better pieces with confidence, it is always better, with an object of any value, to be very cautious and to seek expert advice whenever necessary. Before beginning on any piece it is important to date it roughly, by consulting books on decorative styles or by visiting the nearest museum having a collection of appropriate objects. You can recognize pre-19th century pieces, for example, by the absence of metal nails and screws, slightly crude finishing, evidence of much wear and tear, and frequently a soft luster resulting from centuries of loving care. But since all of these characteristics can be faked to simulate age, do not take apparent age for granted. If you think you have a genuine rare piece do not hesitate to consult a museum expert or reputable dealer before laying your hand to it.

A famous furniture restorer, Leslie Wenn, once said, "I have sometimes had to restrain a craftsman, through genuine pride in his work, from re-painting, regilding or re-carving, when a careful job of reviving, cleaning, or refixing would be more appropriate. This tendency again demonstrates the difference between a good craftsman and a good restorer". The latter is what this book is all about.

Today we have access to centuries of man's artistic efforts, and we have become more aware of them as the result of travel and increased exposure through the media and through the efforts of museums and historical societies. These help to develop a healthy respect and understanding of the people about us, and their past. This respect obviously is what makes the restorer "conservative" in the true sense of the word; saving, preserving or keeping from harm or decay something which is worthy and representative of the past, for it is unlikely that artifacts designed and made even as little as thirty years ago will ever be made in that way again. Tastes and techniques change.

So, make a habit of keeping and caring for everything. Store it if it does not appeal to you at the moment; your tastes may change.

HOW TO USE THIS BOOK

It is important to realise that many of the jobs described in this book, especially those concerned with painting, finishing and polishing, are easy and quick to do, but they may take hours or even days of drying time between comparatively short periods of actual work. It is necessary therefore, if restoration work is undertaken frequently, to make a workplace which is large enough, secure from the inquisitive fingers of children (and envious adults), and as dust-proof as possible; somewhere you can work undisturbed, and where your work can be left safe until you return to it.

A point which cannot be emphasized too often or too strongly—keep all chemicals and other dangerous substances clearly labeled, safely packaged and under lock and key.

Remember ventilation too; fumes and smells can arise from some jobs, which are pervasive and unpleasant. If you have a place adequate in other respects but poor in ventilation, install a fan or extractor. And then, plan the layout of your workplace—a strong bench large enough for any job, with adjacent storage facilities like shelves, drawers, ledges; sufficient containers for small objects, like screws, nails, nuts, bolts etc; bottles and jars for liquids, cans for paint brushes; boxes and bins for "spare parts" and clean rags; and of course the means of racking your tools so that they are kept clean, sharp and readily available.

The sections of this book have been arranged in such a way as to make it easy for the reader to find exactly what is needed, with a brief sketch of the development of the object, the materials from which it is made, the preparations and materials needed for restoration, step-by-step descriptions of how the job should proceed, and hints, alternative methods and materials. Each section is fully illustrated to show the detail of a technique, with drawings and many photographs.

The book starts with Tools (although tools are again mentioned in the different sections in conjunction with descriptions of their use on the different projects), for work with wood, metal, fabrics, etc. Then follow sections on Wood and work associated with wood or like wood, such as Bamboo and Cane, Lacquer and Special Effects such as antiquing, gilding and so on. Textiles follow, with Leather and Carpets and Rugs. Glass and Pottery and Porcelain precede the section on Stone and Stoneware, and then All Kinds of Metals, and a short section on miscellaneous items not covered previously. The vast majority of subjects which will crop up before the beginner are dealt with, and the materials, tools and objects mentioned are commonly available. Where references to techniques and materials apply to more than one section, a cross-reference is made, and there is a full index to enable the reader to trace details of particular interest.

TOOLS AND SUPPLIES

A handyman's guide of 1902 offers the opinion that without tools the hand would be powerless. It was some 500,000 years ago that the first implements were used by early man, probably of stone or bone, and possibly just picked up off the ground and used in a moment of frustration.

These days good tools are costly, but you will do better if you buy the best you can afford. It *is* possible to take short cuts in the jobs you have in mind, but with bad tools, bad work is more likely to be the result. Once you become familiar with the brand names of well made tools, watch out for them in second-hand stores or special-offer sales, and buy if the price is right because, more often than not, the implement may need only to be cleaned and sharpened to restore it to its former efficiency.

The chapters which follow deal in a more specific way with tools appropriate to the job in hand, but this section on Tools should enable you to identify some of the implements lying around your home, like the pinking scissors that have always been referred to as "the zig-zag cutters with the blue handle".

Tools are here divided into groups according to their use—tools for hammering, gripping, sawing and sewing—so the alternative tools are shown in close proximity. It is important that you learn the name of each tool. Everybody knows what a hammer is, but if you want to *remove* nails as well as knock them in, you want a *claw* hammer; if you wish to knock the dents out of a piece of silver, a *ball peen* hammer is the one to use.

Also included in this section is a list of basic supplies, supplemented by a list of textile supplies. These lists are separate because, while fabrics can be stored and repaired in the home, the materials used for other jobs require specially planned storage, and are used in a special area away from the living rooms of your home. This area can range from a closet shelf to an elaborate work bench surrounded by pegboards. If you work in such a way as to have to find and lay out your tools and materials specially before each job, and to have to put them away again afterwards, together with the half-finished job, the whole project will tend to become a tedious time-consumer. Then there are the jobs which require hours of interim drying time, when the object being restored should lie undisturbed until ready for the next stage; this is difficult to achieve if you are working on the kitchen table.

The most elegant storage area is surely one of these old pharmacy counters with wide wood top and dozens of small drawers, often sold at country auctions. If you are lucky enough to find one intact, and the price is right, buy it—such things are becoming valuable in their own right.

Your tools should be kept clean and sharp, in a suitable container (a tool box) or hung in proper order on hooks on the wall of your work place, adjacent if possible to your bench. Pegboard is useful for arranging the hooks. But at first you may have to settle for tackle boxes for the small stuff and a drawer or a strong box for the larger tools.

If you are just beginning, or space is scarce, possibly the most important items, after a few essential tools, are clean cotton rags and containers with lids—it seems you never have enough of either. Get the habit of saving all scraps from clean sheets, towels etc., and keep them in a small plastic laundry basket. Save all coffee cans, glass jars, yoghurt containers with lids. Containers without tops can hold brushes and pencils. But do remember that some chemicals, like the petroleum-based ones, will react with plastic, while some strong acids will react with metal—so glass jars and containers are usually safest. You should also keep heavy paper sacks for soiled rags. But when disposing of them be very careful, for there are certain chemicals and paints which, in conjunction, can be very inflammable, and somewhat explosive! Such disposables should be burned in an open space—and stay well away; be sure not to annoy the neighbors.

Finally, keep all tools and materials properly labeled. A horrible accident could be caused if something dangerous was labeled as something innocuous, and it was not stored securely. On the dark side, in case of emergency, you will at least be able to tell the doctor the name of what was swallowed if the container is clearly labeled.

Care of Tools

When storing metal and wooden tools, always spread a film of light machine oil evenly over the surface to prevent rusting and deterioration; for this purpose keep an oiled felt pad in a sealed container near the work table and, if possible, keep them in a dryish atmosphere.
Always store tools away from children.

Brushes

The illustration shows the parts of a brush. Always clean brushes thoroughly when you have finished using them unless returning to the project within a short time (if so, wrap the brush head tightly in tinfoil or plastic to prevent it drying out). Don't leave brushes standing in water or brush-cleansing liquid thinking that you'll take care of them later. If you forget, the paint will harden on the bristles, the ferrule will have been covered and only a strong paint remover will save the brush; even so it will never be the same.

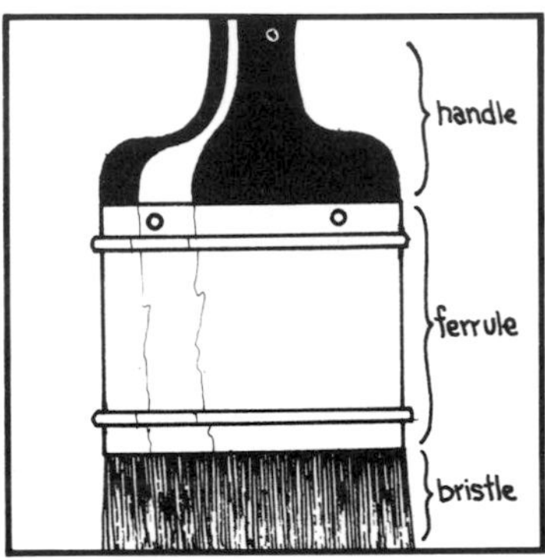

The parts of a brush.

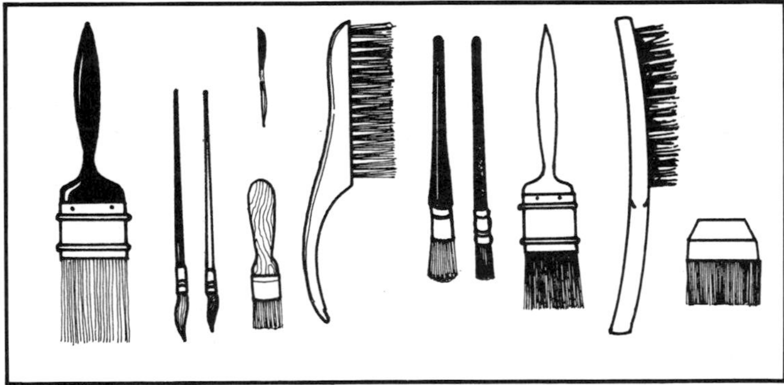

Brushes, from left to right: varnish brush, long-hair white bristle, red sable brush, striping brush (top), stencil brush (bottom), dusting brush, oval sash brush, camel-hair brush, $1\frac{1}{2}''$ (3.75cm) general purpose paint brush, wire brush, gilder's tip.

Removing Oil-Based Paints: Fill a glass jar two-thirds full with brush cleaner or turpentine substitute. Agitate the brush in the liquid, pressing against the sides of the jar to force out the excess. When the liquid has become very discolored and the brush looks clean, fill another jar half full and repeat until most of the paint is removed. To test, part the bristles and see if they are clean near the ferrule. Wash the brush in warm soapy water, rinse and repeat again with cleaner if necessary. Shake or blot out the excess water and leave it to dry naturally. Wrap brushes in newspapers when dry to keep out moths and store them lying flat if possible. It is a good idea to keep the brushes used for both types of paint separate. Also keep a separate $1\frac{1}{2}''$ (4cm) oxhair bristle brush for applying varnish and another for shellac.

Small Oil-Painting and Detail Brushes: After cleaning as above and blotting to remove moisture, oil the bristles with linseed oil to keep the hairs supple. "Point" the brush by putting a drop of oil on the brush and slowly rotate it between your thumb and index finger. The handiest small brush for cleaning and applying some faux finishes is the old toothbrush—never toss used ones out, but keep them with your other brushes for future use.

Removing Water-Based Paints: Clean the bristles under warm running water, swishing the bristles out with soapy solution and forcing the paint out from the ferrule. Then rinse the brush thoroughly until the water runs clean, shake or blot out the excess water and leave it to dry (but not over a hot radiator, which will dry the bristles unnaturally quickly).

Carving Tools

Purchase chisels and gouges as needed because there are many types, each suited to a particular job, and even new chisels will need sharpening or honing before use. Chisel blades are flat across but arched in length and all have a honed angle of 30° and a ground angle of 25°. Bevel-edge chisels will do most jobs but all chisels are designed for cutting with or across the grain.

Gouges are used for less drastic action on wood. For example, a firmer gouge will cut shallow indents and curved grooves, while a scribing gouge can be used to trim curves (see pages 16-7 for sharpening instructions).

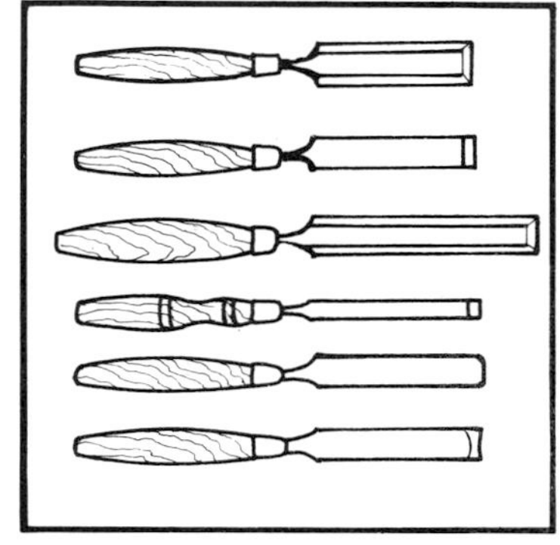

Chisels, from top to bottom: bevel edge, firmer, paring, mortise, firmer gouge, scribing gouge.

Cutting Tools

- Heavy duty scissors—for cutting heavy fabrics, leather, etc.
- Cuticle scissors—perfect for rounding the edges for découpage.
- Embroidery scissors—for fine needlework and awkward areas.
- Cane cutters
- Side cutters—for removing the short ends of cane from difficult places.
- Metal shears (tin snips)
- Pinking scissors—to minimize raveling.
- Knife with replaceable blade—for cutting thin leather, paper, etc. (also available with saw blades).

The blunt edges of scissors can be sharpened by running a fine slipstone held at right angles to the face of the blade, and damaged edges can be repaired by running a fine slipstone, moistened with a little light oil, over the inner face of the blade.

If scissors don't cut after they have been sharpened, make sure that they haven't lost their slight inward curvature. If this happens, hold the blade in a vise between three equally spaced blocks. Then tighten the vise slowly.

To tighten a loose pivot screw, put the head of the screw on a metal surface (like the flat top of a vise) and hit the bottom end of the screw sharply with the rounded end of a hammer.

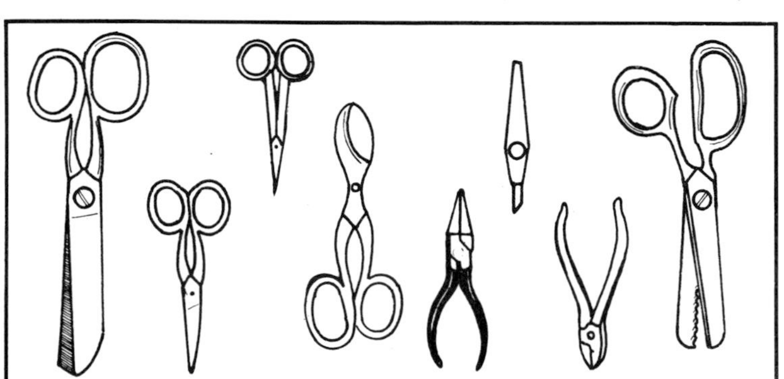

Cutting tools, from left to right: heavy duty scissors, embroidery scissors, cuticle scissors, cane clippers, round-nose pliers, knife with replaceable blade, side cutters, pinking scissors.

Drilling Tools

Swing brace—a hand-drill used with bits to make a hole of more than $\frac{1}{4}''$ (7mm) diameter. Often has a hollow handle to store bits. It is available with a ratchet mechanism to drill in confined quarters where it is not possible to make a full turn with the handle.

Hand-drill—a basic and indispensable drill used with twist bits to drill holes up to $\frac{1}{4}''$ (7mm) diameter in both metal and wood.

Push drill—a one-handed tool for light drilling, particularly useful for starting screw holes and driving screws in place.

Electric drills—can be used for all drilling purposes, but although very useful they are not essential unless you are doing a large number of do-it-yourself projects. Various attachments are available for sanding, sawing, buffing and polishing.

Bradawl—looks like a squat screwdriver with a sharp point, and is used to start holes in wood for screws and nails. Work it by moving it back and forth.

Gimlet—looks like a wine bottle opener and is worked clockwise to start holes for screws.

When drilling try to keep the pressure constant at a reasonable speed. If the drill wobbles, the hole may be oversize and the drill bit may snap. When drilling into metal, select the appropriate bit and oil it lightly before starting. It may help to bang a small hole in the metal first with a punch.

Drilling tools, from left to right: hand drill and bit, electric drill top), bradawl (bottom), swing brace and bit, push drill (top), gimlet (bottom).

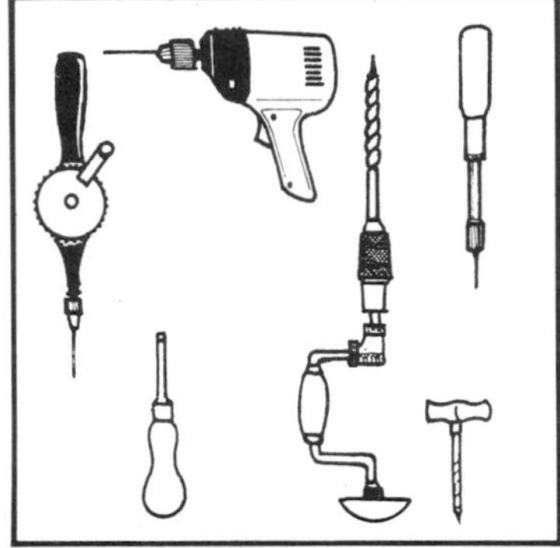

Files and Rasps

The rasp is a coarse file for cutting wood quickly, and is usually followed with a finer file such as the half-round. There are two kinds of rasp, the wood rasp and the cabinet rasp. The wood rasp is coarser. The rat-tail file is perfect for smoothing hollow curves while the open file is available flat or shaped like a plane.

Care of Files and Rasps: Always oil after use to prevent rusting.

Files and rasps, from top to bottom: flat rasp, half round rasp, needle file, open file (Surform), round file.

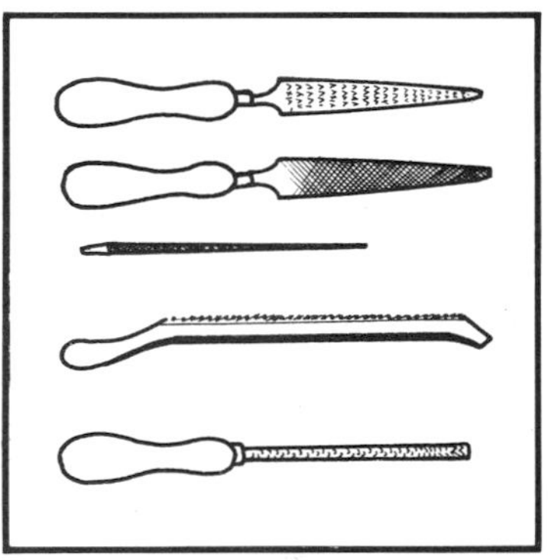

Gripping Tools or Holding

Bench vise—an invaluable clamp which ideally is fixed permanently to a work bench, but portable ones are available which can be fixed to any stable tabletop.

Combination pliers—6″ (15cm) is a handy size. Used to unfasten small nuts and for cutting wire. High quality pliers are the best purchase since it is important that the jaws meet perfectly. Oil the jaw and pivot occasionally.

G-clamp—used to hold pieces of wood together during measuring or while glue dries. The thumb screw is a smaller version for holding smaller components together. Always keep the screw shank well oiled.

Needle or taper-nosed pliers—pointed tip pliers for gripping small objects like screws, chain links, etc. Commonly 6″ (15cm) long although jeweler's snipnose pliers are $4\frac{1}{2}''$ (11cm).

Pincers—used to take out nails and tacks from places inaccessible to a claw hammer. Tower pincers have a fine claw at the end for this purpose.

Round-nosed pliers—used for curling wire to make chain links. The size of the curve depends on the placement of the wire in the jaws of the pliers. A small curve is made when the wire is positioned at the front of the pliers.

Spanner—the adjustable variety is the handiest and is perfect for loosening tight nuts.

Wrench—available in several sizes and shapes to fit specific nuts, and adjustable as pictured.

Gripping tools, top row from left to right: G-clamp, thumb screw, adjustable wrenches; bottom row from left to right: slip joint pliers, combination pliers, needle-nose pliers, pincers, bench vise.

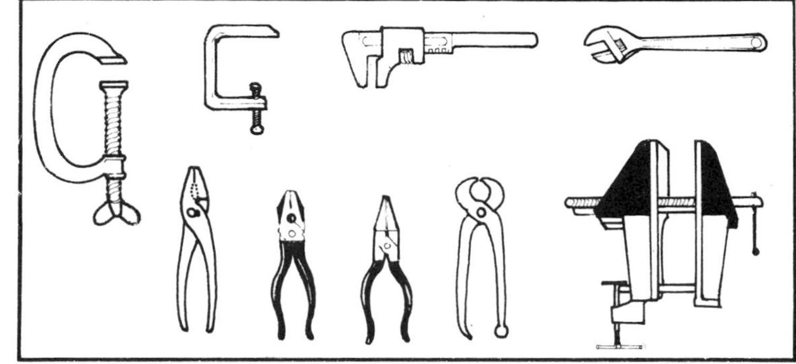

Hammers

Claw hammer—has claw for removing unwanted nails (always protect the surface with a block of wood under the front end of the hammer).

Upholsterer's hammer—has magnetized tip for picking up tacks.

Wooden mallet—for carpentry and cabinet work, knocking joints together and for hitting the ends of chisels.

Ball peen hammer—the rounded ends used for working with metal.

Soft-face hammer—for striking finely finished surfaces; has renewable tips.

Hammers, from left to right: claw, ball peen, upholsterer's jack hammer, wooden mallet, soft face hammer.

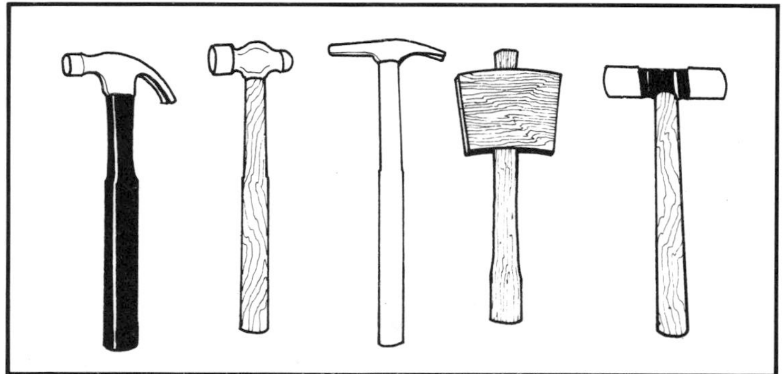

To fit a new wooden handle to a hammerhead: When buying a new handle choose one with an even, straight grain in the wood, which indicates strength.

● Grip the old hammerhead in a vise with handle down. Drill several holes into the handle with $\frac{1}{4}''$ (7mm) bit, on each side of the wedge. Pull off the head. If it sticks, punch it out with another hammer and screwdriver.

● If steel wedges were used, keep them for the new handle but, if the new handle is not cut to take wedges, grip it in the vise and saw cuts into the handle top. The cuts should be $\frac{1}{4}''$ (7mm) deeper than the wedge length.

● Put the head onto the handle, making sure that it is down on the handle as far as it can go. A bit of handle should stick out at the top. Saw this excess off with a small handsaw.

● Drive the wedges in with another hammer until they are flush with the face of the handle top. If there are no wedges, make some from bits of hardwood.

Lamps/Torches

Blowtorch or blowlamp—a kerosene or gas-fired blowtorch is used to remove very thick paint which resists chemical strippers. Use flexible scraping knives to scrape off the bubbled paint. CAUTION: It is easy to burn the wood underneath the paint, so always keep the blowtorch moving. STOP before you come to the raw wood. Chemical stripper can be used to remove stubborn patches.

Soldering iron—used when repairing metal in conjunction with solder and flux. Some have adjustable thermostats to make the job easier and these are recommended if lots of metalwork is to be done. Do not leave the soldering iron unattended while it is on and obviously avoid touching the hot end or the hot solder.

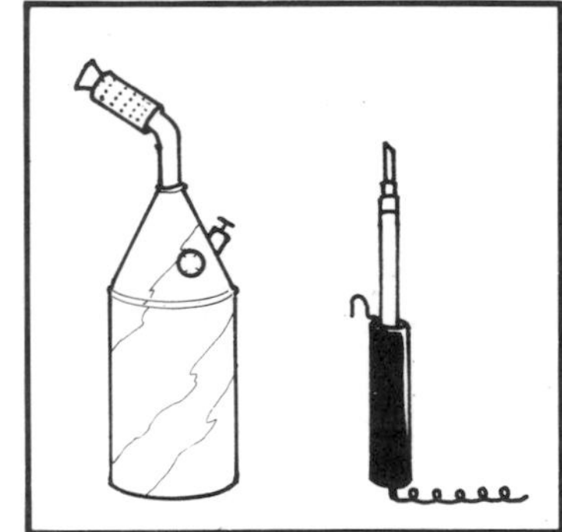

Left, blowtorch or blowlamp; right, soldering iron.

Measuring Tools

Compass—available with pencil clamp for drawing circles and marking equal distances.

Spirit level—a bubble will center in the curved glass tube if your work is perfectly horizontal or vertical. This glass tube can be bought independently and inexpensively, or purchased already mounted in a wooden case.

Zig-zag rule—handy for measuring up to 6 feet (2 meters). Collapses to 6″ (15cm). Try to purchase one marked in both inches and millimeters.

Metal rule—6″-3′ (15cm-1 meter) for using as a straight edge with a knife when cutting linoleum, paper, leather, etc.

T (or Try) square—for use when a perfect right angle is required.

Tape measure—metal (for carpentry) or plastic-coated cloth (for needlework) with metric units up to 152cm on one side and inches up to 60″ on the other.

Measuring tools, left, top to bottom: tape measure, zig-zag rule, compass; right: T or try square, metal rule, spirit level.

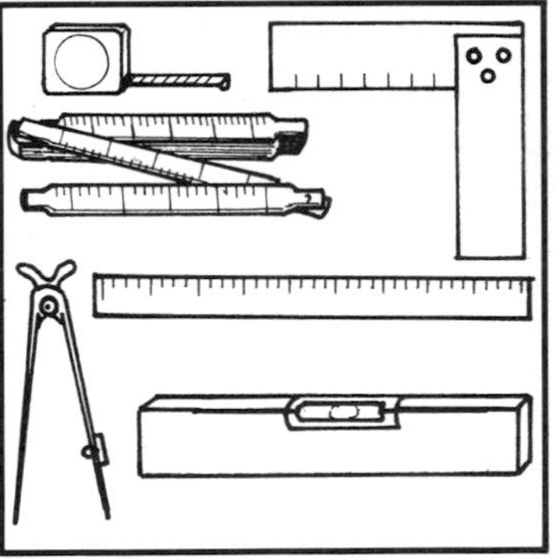

Sharpening Tools

Oilstones and Slipstones

Always oil both oilstone and slipstone before use with a few penny-size dots along the surface. Also try to use the whole surface, to prevent uneven wear. If the stone becomes oil-clogged (rare), put it on a metal tray or rack in a warm oven set at 300°F (150°C) to dry out excess oil. Buy the longest stone, to make handling easier, and keep stones in a hardwood box with a lid, or immersed in liquid paraffin or kerosene.

Oilstones come in three grades: coarse, medium and fine, and are of either natural or artificial stone. Natural oilstones give the best edge but are more expensive than artificial ones. If a stone becomes dirty or gummy scrub it with a stiff brush dipped in a solvent like gasoline or kerosene. Combination stones usually have medium and fine grit—one on each side.

Sharpening the blade of a plane and/or chisel: Both of these tools used for cutting have two angles forming their cutting edge: a smaller ground angle of 25° and a sharper honed angle of 30°. The ground area needs only occasional sharpening but the honed edge needs to be kept sharp all the time.

● Hold the blade flat on an oilstone (which has been moistened with a few drops of light oil) and raise it to an angle of 30°.

● Rub back and forth diagonally across the surface of the stone, until a burr or rough edge is built up along the flat side and then turn it over and rub the burr off with a single stroke. Honing guides are available for holding the blades at the correct angle.
● Test for sharpness by drawing the blade down a held piece of paper—a properly sharpened blade will make a smooth cut, with no tearing.

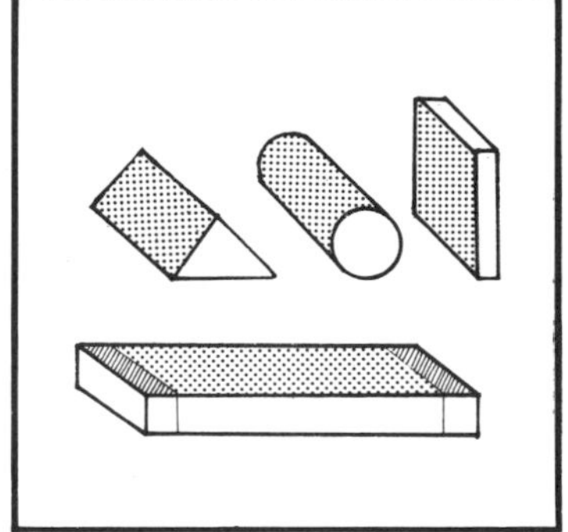

Top, slipstones; bottom, oilstone.

Planes

The basic use of a plane is to reduce the wood, leaving it flat and smooth. There are several kinds of planes, each designed for a special use, but only two are pictured here—the jack and the block. Always adjust the blade in the plane before using it and sharpen if necessary.

The plane is correctly set when the blade protrudes about the thickness of a hair on the plane bottom. You can adjust this by turning the nut. The cutting edge must also be parallel with the plane bottom. Look at it from the bottom and adjust it with the lateral adjustment lever. The wood to be planed needs to be supported, so that it does not vibrate or move with the action of the plane.

Jack plane—gets its name from its all-around versatility. It is best for general use, especially for trimming long boards.
Block plane—can be held with one hand and so is very useful when planing small pieces of wood.

Planes: top, jack plane; bottom, block.

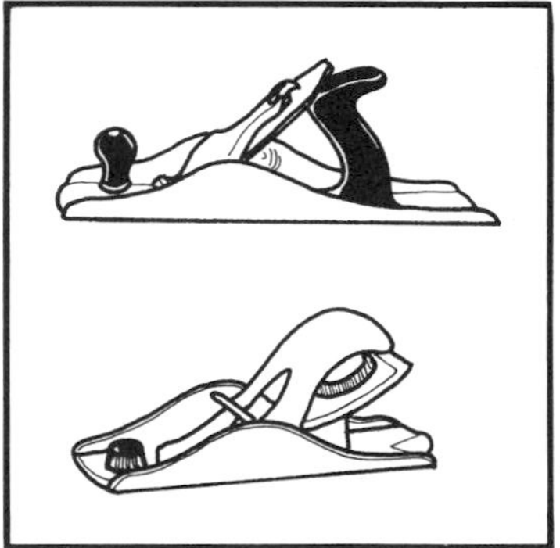

Hints

Always push with the grain.
If grain is ripped, reverse direction for next stroke.
Don't plane painted wood—it needs to be stripped first.
Wipe all metal parts with an oil rag before storing on its side.
A candle rubbed on the base of the plane will lubricate it when in use.
Use a long plane when smoothing a long edge as a short plane will tend to create undulations.

Sawing Tools

There are three main kinds of saws—large handsaws, stiff-backed saws for cutting joins and other fine work, and special purpose saws. The greater the number of teeth or points per inch, the finer the cut.

Before storing wipe the blade with oil to prevent rusting and hang all saws upright if possible to prevent damage to teeth. If the blade is rusty, clean it with steel wool dipped in white spirit (turpentine substitute).

Handsaws include:
Panel saw—for cutting with and across the grain.
Cross-cut saw—for cutting across the grain.
Rip saw—for cutting with the grain.

These saws look very similar—to distinguish them count the number of teeth or points to the inch (2.5cm). The panel saw has ten, while the rip has only four. All handsaws should cut freely under their own weight and your forward pressure. If sticking occurs while in use, rub the blade with a candle, but if it persists the blade may need sharpening, resetting or replacing.

Stiff-backed saws include:
Tenon saw—for joint cutting both with and across the grain.
Dovetail saw—a smaller version of the tenon, for making finer cuts.

Special purpose saws include:
Coping saws—for cutting curves.
Fret saw—for cutting intricate shapes from thin plywood.
Hacksaw—for cutting metal.
"Nests"—consisting of a handle and the following blades: 14″ (35.5cm) compass blade, 10″ (25.5cm) panel blade, 16″ (40.5cm) blade with pruning teeth on one side and cross-cut teeth on the other. Some "nests" include a keyhole saw.

Knives with replaceable blades can also be fitted with saw blades, if only light sawing is to be done.

TOOLS AND SUPPLIES

Sawing tools, left row from top to bottom: panel saw, hacksaw, dovetail; middle, coping saw; right row from top to bottom: compass saw, knife with replaceable blades and saws, tenon saw.

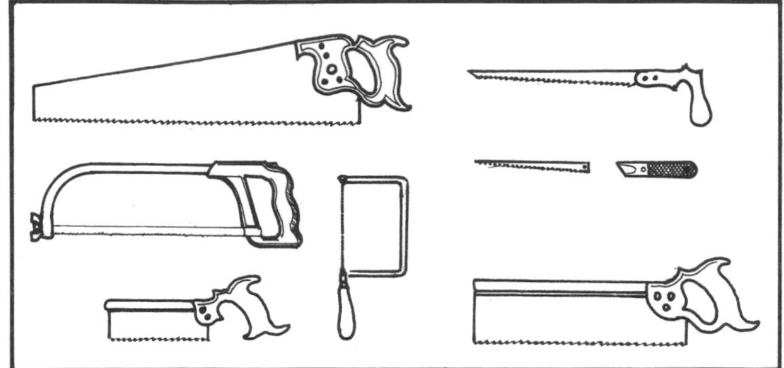

Hints

Hold saw at 45° to the piece you are sawing.
Cut on the waste side of marked line.
Support piece near the end to stop it falling and prevent splintering.
Watch for hidden nails in old wood, which could damage your saw.
When fitting new blades to coping saws and hacksaws give the blade enough tension so that when plucked a musical note sounds.

Scraping Tools

Cabinet scraper—a thin flexible sheet of toughened steel used to remove layers of unwanted finish, used either alone or with chemical strippers; also for correcting irregular surfaces after planing and before rubbing with abrasive papers. It is held in both hands and tilted forwards as it is being pushed away from you, and if in good repair should take off shaving after shaving of uniform thickness nearly as wide as its cutting edge.

Broad scraper—semi-flexible knife with 3″ (7.5cm) blade for removing paper, paint, etc.

Combination shave hook—an extremely useful tool combining curves, points and angles for removing paint etc. from crevices and curved surfaces.

Filling knife (or putty knife)—more flexible, and sharper. Useful for applying malleable substances like fillers, etc.

Palette knife—small, oil-color artist's tool, very flexible.

Skarsten scraper—a blade mounted in wood, also for scraping off old paint.

Scraping tools, from left to right: skarsten (top), cabinet scraper (bottom), broad scraper, filling knife or putty knife, combination shavehook, palette knife.

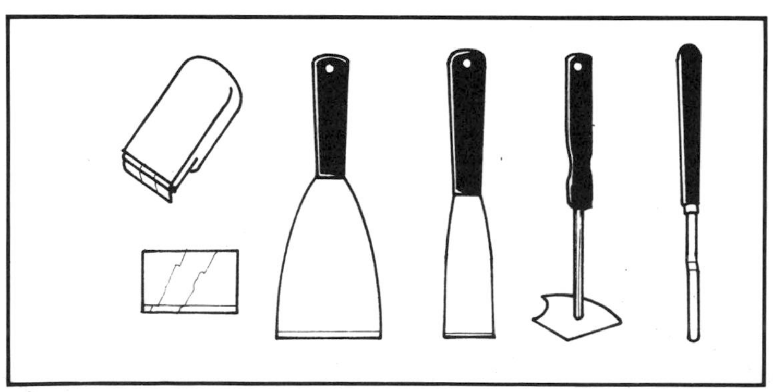

Screwdrivers

It hardly matters what type of screwdriver is chosen, but remember that the blade should fit the entire width of the slot in the screw head. Screwdrivers with fluted handles are easier to grip than those with smooth handles. Also buy the best you can- -it is very frustrating for the blade to wiggle in the handle after only brief use.

Spiral ratchet—made for hanging doors so one hand is free—a good basic screwdriver. The blade works in a hollow handle which allows it to twist in place, using only a small wrist motion.

Cabinet—long handled.

Electrician's—for small screws (don't use a flat-ended bradawl).

Stubby or pocket pattern—with stubby blade especially suitable for driving large screws in awkward areas.

Offset or rightangle—for screws which a normal screwdriver couldn't reach.

Phillips—for driving Phillips head screws.

Engineer's—can be struck to loosen screws.

Screwdrivers, from left to right: engineer's, cabinet, ratchet, offset or rightangle (top), stubby (bottom), Phillips head.

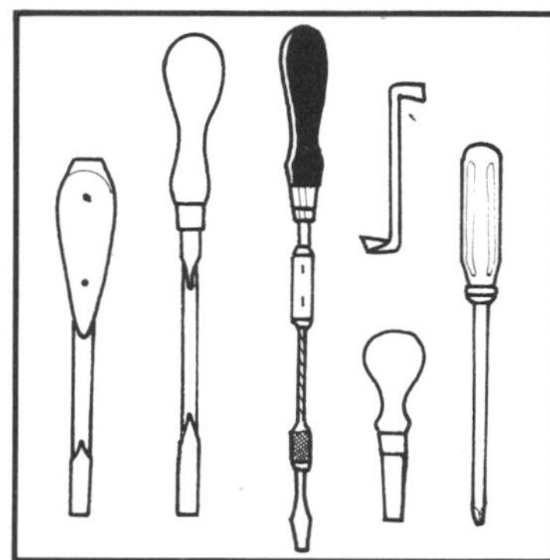

Hints

● The handles of tools are now usually available in wood or plastic. Plastic handles are stronger but wooden handles are more comfortable, as they absorb perspiration.

● Try out all new tools on a sample piece of wood or metal.

● All tools with metal parts should be covered with a film of oil after use and before storing.

● Wipe all tools clean after each use.

A Basic Tool Kit

Abrasive paper sanding block, and assorted abrasive papers.

Combination pliers, 6″ (1.5m) square nosed type, with side cutters.

Folding rule, or steel tape, 6′-10′ (2-3 meters).

Knife with replaceable blades, also taking saw blades.

Metal ruler 12″-18″ (30-46cm), for use with knife when cutting along straight edge.

Screwdriver—6″(15cm) and bradawl for starting holes.

T (or Try)-square—6″ (15cm) to ensure right angles.

The following tools are nice to have, but are not essential for beginners:

Bench vise (portable, so that it can also be used for clamping).

File, general purpose, for use on wood or metal.

Hand drill, bit brace and countersink bit for sinking screws beneath the surface.

Panel saw or tenon saw, depending on the type of work you plan to do.

Power drill and attachments (sanding and buffing wheels, masonry bits, etc.)

Jack plane and combination oilstone for sharpening the blade.

Wood chisels, $\frac{3}{4}$″ (2cm) firmer beveledged, and mallet $4\frac{1}{2}$″ (11cm).

Abrasive Papers

Store abrasive papers in a warm, dry place and never attempt to use them on damp wood. Always use at least two grades when trying to get a really smooth finish; coarse paper, worn smooth, will not give the same effect as a finer paper. While working "snap" abrasive paper to unclog it. Incidentally, there is no such thing as "sand-paper" and although these papers feel gritty, sand has been replaced by more effective smoothing agents.

Below are the five types of abrasive papers used for smoothing woods, while the chart shows comparative grades.

Glass paper—has grains made from crushed glass (once reputedly derived from crushed port bottles!). It is available with a base of cloth or paper and is commonly used for hand smoothing.

Garnet paper—has grains made of crushed garnet stone, so it costs a bit more but it is very durable and recommended for smoothing by hand.

Aluminum oxide paper—is used when really heavy cutting action is desired—its synthetic grains are very tough.

Silicone carbide paper—is also known as "wet-and-dry" paper because it can be used damp (not wet) for fine smoothing of paint-work or dry like other abrasive papers. When damp it leaves a black-gray "gravy" which has to be washed off, but when lubricated with water, it lasts a long time. It can be used on both metal and wood and is also available on a cloth base.

Flint paper—is rarely used any more and although it is inexpensive, it is not recommended because its grains are softer than glass or garnet, and it has a short life.

Hints

Emery paper is available for sanding metal but it is rarely used for sanding wood.

Both garnet and aluminum oxide papers come in "open coat" and "close coat"—with "open coat" there is more space between the grains, making it less likely to clog and therefore better for smoothing softwoods; while in "close coat" the grains are more closely spaced and are best for hardwoods.

Steel wool can also be used for smoothing wood and the finer grades are recommended after smoothing with fine abrasive paper to give a final perfect finish. As with abrasive papers, always work with the grain. Wear a handkerchief tied "bandit-style" to protect your throat and lungs when sanding.

Abrasive Paper Gradings

American	*British*	*Continental*	*Also called*
80	M2 coarse	4	"Cabinet" for preparing the wood
120	F2 medium	3	
150	1 extrafine	1	
150	1 extrafine	1	"Finishing" for use during the final smoothing process
240	Flour	00	

Steel Wool

000 —finest: for rubbing down paint, varnish or shellac before final coat.

00 —very fine: used between coats of varnish, lacquer, etc., dulling varnish, removing tar and dirt from chrome.

0 —fine: used for cleaning and polishing metal, also to remove paint and spots from fired ceramics and glass.

1 —standard: for cleaning and preparing for first coat of paint and smoothing woodwork.

2 —medium: for removing rust and dirt from metal and tools, and paint from surfaces in combination with a chemical paint remover.

3 —coarse: for heavy abrasive action when smoothing rough surfaces; also removes rust crust.

Glues and Gluing

Gluing must be the simplest repair to do! Strangely it is often neglected which is unfortunate, because a little glue applied after slight damage can prevent more extensive problems. The section below deals with glue suitable for porous materials like wood, paper, textiles, some plastics, and rubber. A wooden matchstick is often perfect for applying non-water-soluble glues. Always save even the smallest splinters and chips and glue these in place after the main piece has set. For gluing glass and pottery, see the detailed chapters concerned.

There are six basic types of glue in common use today:

Traditional glues like animal and fish glues, casein glue and scotch glues are gradually being superseded as they are neither heat- nor waterproof. Although they are not generally recommended some craftsmen prefer them—such as gilders, who use rabbit glue.

General purpose glues—cellulose- or acetate-based, and usually sold in tubes—are water-resistant, free from staining and excellent for fixing plastics, metals, and most inlays to wood. Do not work with these near an open fire—they are inflammable, and avoid inhaling the fumes.

Epoxy resins—are modern, synthetic-based glues. They are strong and versatile, perfect for home use, and usually come in two part kits—a glue and a hardener. Most take about six hours to set but a warm room will speed the setting. Follow directions on the package as the mixtures vary slightly. Caution: synthetic resin glues become rubbery if kept unused. They should not be used for gluing wood as they are harder than the wood itself and allow no natural movement and thus may cause splitting.

Polyvinyl acetate glue—is a thick, white cold-setting inexpensive resin-based glue and can be used extensively, although it is not waterproof. It will keep for several months (though not in a cold place) but may stain the lighter woods and tends to creep a bit. PVA is a good general purpose glue and is often sold in a squeeze bottle with a handy pointed nozzle. It is water-soluble.

Contact adhesives—which are usually rubber-based, are only recommended when clamping is difficult but a strong bond is desired. The glue is applied to both surfaces and, when tacky, they are brought together. The two pieces are immovable upon contact, so adjusting is impossible. They are very useful when bonding other materials to wood.

Latex glues—are derived from the milky fluid of the rubber tree, although synthetic latex is now manufactured. They can be applied either to one surface or both and are thinned with water. Their odor is slightly objectionable. Latex glues are perfect when working with textiles, although some fabric dyes seem soluble, so test an inconspicuous spot before application.

	Fabrics	Glass, China Porcelain, Pottery	Hardboard	Leather	Metal	Paper	Plastics soft	Plastics hard	Stone	Wood
Fabrics	6	2	5	6	2	6	2	5		4
Glass, China Porcelain, Pottery	2	3	3	2	3	2	2	2	3	
Hardboard	5	3	4	4	5	5	2	5	3	4
Leather	6	2	4	5	5	2	2	5	5	6
Metal	2	3	5	5	3	2	2	3	3	3
Paper	6	2	5	2	2	2	2	2	2	4
Plastics soft	2	2	2	2	2	2	2	2	2	2
Plastics hard	5	2	5	5	3	2	2	3	3	3
Stone		3	3	5	3	2	2	3	3	3
Wood	4		4	6	3	4	2	3	3	4

This chart shows what kind of adhesive is best for any combination of materials. The numerals correspond to the adhesives described more fully above:

1 Traditional animal-based glues
2 General purpose glues
3 Epoxy resins
4 PVA glues
5 Contact adhesives
6 Latex glues

Nails

Nail points are slightly wedge-shaped so that they break through the fibers of the wood easily and are held in place by the same elastic fibers of which wood is composed, which try to regain their original composition, and so grip tightly on the nail.

● To drive a nail, tap it lightly with a hammer at first but if the surface is hard or the correct placement is crucial, use a bradawl of suitable size to start your hole.

● Put the bradawl across the grain and turn to left then right until the hole is $\frac{1}{4}$″ (7mm) deep.

● After the first light tap which sinks the nail, continue striking it with sharp, accurate blows until the nail is set.

Hints

Hold the hammer near the end of the handle, especially when driving large nails.

Keep your eye on the nail head as you strike.

When trying to sink small nails or tacks, it will save your fingers if you push them first through thin cardboard and hold that instead. When the nail or tack is almost sunk, pull the cardboard away, then give a final tap. When putting a nail into thin wood, wet the nail first.

● To sink a nail beneath the surface, use a second square or round nail, or nail punch.

● Center the point on the nail head and hit squarely, driving it beneath the surface.

● Fill the indentation before proceeding. Obviously the larger the nail's head, the easier it is to hit and sink.

If the nail begins to split the wood or go in crookedly, remove it at once before it is too difficult to remove. Take it out by grasping it with pliers (pincers), and lever down towards the wood. Protect the wood by putting a small block of wood between it and the surface of the pincers. (A claw hammer can also be used in the same way.)

Never re-use a bent nail, or a nail hole.

Invisible nails: Raise a chip in the surface of the wood with a chisel or gouge. Start a hole with a bradawl underneath the chip and drive the nail in. The chip is then glued in place and later the glue is cleaned off.

Cleaning rusty nails and screws: Put a small amount of oil on them, place them in a heavy paper bag with emery powder or any fine abrasive and shake. Keep nails in a sealed glass jar to discourage rust.

Screws

To place a screw, start the hole with a bradawl or a gimlet drill bit one size smaller than the screw size. Before inserting the screw, dip the shank in oil—this assists insertion and also keeps it rust-free.

Use a screwdriver whose tip fits the entire slot in the screw-head. It is also advisable to enlarge the top of the opening with a countersink bit to keep the head of the screw flush with the surface.

To remove a stubborn screw: Brush head of screw with wire brush to remove rust and dirt. Put drop of oil around the surface of screwhead. Use a long-handled screwdriver and try to turn the screw counter-clockwise. If that fails, turn it clockwise to tighten it more and then counter-clockwise.

● If the screw still won't move, keep the screwdriver firmly in the slot and strike the handle of the screwdriver with a hammer or mallet. Try to turn again clockwise.

● If this again fails, hold the screwdriver blade at an angle against the edge of the screw slot. Tap it around counter-clockwise with a wooden mallet. Again try to turn screw.

● If all else fails, heat the head of the screw with a hot soldering iron. This will cause the screw to expand and compress the lumber. When the screw cools, undo it.

Screws with broken heads: Gouge around the area and, using pliers, try to dislodge the screw from the base, but it is sometimes actually necessary to cut out the wood holding the screw.

Basic Supply List

Small wire mesh kitchen strainer
Thermometer (cooking)
Chamois
Masking tape
Jeweler's rouge or pumice powder
Soft pure cotton rags
Empty glass jars, tin cans and atomizer spray bottles
Double boiler
Camphor
Denatured alcohol (methylated spirits)
Small can shellac
Small can varnish
Benzine
Sharp, hard pencils
String
Spray fixative
Powdered pigments, especially raw umber
Linseed oil
Turpentine substitute
Kerosene (Paraffin)
Ammonia
Vinegar
Beeswax
General purpose glue (or PVA)
Latex glue
Tweezers
Cotton wool or absorbent cotton
Spar varnish
Chalk (powdered or stick form)
Distilled water
Turpentine
Japan paints
Wooden matches
Pieces of white cardboard

Basic Sewing Kit

(for upholstery, rugs, embroidery, etc.)
Good solid thimble
Cloth measuring tape in mm and inches
Needle threader
Assorted scissors
- embroidery
- tailor's shears
- pinking shears
- cuticle

Assorted needles
- lacing
- curved upholstery
- straight upholstery
- large rug (blunt)
- crewel (blunt)
- tapestry (blunt)
- sharps

Assorted threads in neutral tones
- heavy linen
- button
- heavy cotton
- light cotton
- embroidery floss
- embroidery wool
- silk

Special Sewing Tools and Supplies

Hand hook for repairing rugs
Latch hook
Knitting needles in 2 or 3 sizes
Crochet hooks, one fine, one thick
Embroidery frame
Assorted canvas pieces
Bias binding tape

WOOD

In these times of environmental pessimism, it is comforting to think that there will always be wood if only man can be bothered to plant the trees, for unlike coal and diamonds, harvested timberlands can be replenished.

Incredibly, twelve million years ago our planet was covered with a homogeneous mass of trees, descendants of mosses and ferns, spreading from pole to pole. In fact these trees made life possible by exuding oxygen into an unbreathable atmosphere. There are roughly two types of trees: broad-leaved trees or hardwoods, and cone-bearing trees with needle-like leaves, known as softwoods. Hardwoods include: oak, beech, mahogany, ash, walnut, plane, elm, birch, maple, cherry and teak. The main attractions of hardwoods are variety of tone, closely figured grain, strength and weight, but they are more expensive than softwoods. When worked they move less, join and finish better. Some common softwoods are: yellow or white pine, white fir, pitch pine, spruce, redwood, and cedar. The generally lighter softwoods have been preferred in their native Scandinavia for years, a preference which is spreading and encouraging us to strip and bleach our stained, heavy-looking woods. The more exotic hardwoods used mainly for veneers (thin layers of wood used for facing other woods) include bird's-eye maple, satinwood, rosewood, zebrawood, ebony and pearwood.

The grain and pattern in woods runs up the tree trunk and along the branches; wood is more likely to split along the grain than across it.

Converting timber to furniture involves rather unnatural processes. First, trees (some of which may have been growing for 60-120 years) are felled. Then they have to be seasoned—strengthened by a gradual drying-out process. Seasoning takes place in slow kilns or drying sheds where the timber is stacked and the sap or natural tree juice is allowed to evaporate of its own accord. A freshly cut tree contains about 50% sap by weight and needs to dry for no less than one month. In the good old days of the 18th century, timber would not be used for 8-10 years after felling. (Incidentally, the Dutch laid their trees in water with their heads up for two years until all the sap was driven out by water and only then allowed the wood to dry.)

After drying, logs are planked or machine-sawed into boards in one of several ways. Obviously considerable skill is exercised by the sawer who must cut the logs while removing defects like knots or excessive insect damage. After sawing, the planks will shrink slightly in width and thickness but not in length. If warpage occurs at this stage, the timber has been hastily or improperly seasoned. Over a period of time, exposure to air gradually hardens the surface and changes its appearance.

Happily, the unique characteristics of wood have been respected by craftsmen throughout history and their efforts continue to give us pleasure today. Unfortunately though, all wooden furniture has not been given the tender loving care it deserves and you may encounter one or more of the problems listed later.

Learn to give your wood pieces the best treatment and they will reward you with gleaming beauty for a lifetime.

On pages 28/29 are diagrams showing a few of the ways that wood can be sawn for use, and some of the common man-made boards.

SOFTWOODS

Pine

Red Baltic pine
Scots fir
Scots pine

Yellow Pine

Canadian pine
Ottawa pine
White pine
Pitch pine
Parana pine

Douglas Fir

British Columbian pine
Oregon pine
Yellow fir
Hemlock
Larch
Manio
Podo
Sequoia or redwood
Sitka spruce (also called silver spruce)
Spruce
Western red cedar
Yew

HARDWOODS

Abura
Afara
Afrormosia
Agba
Alder
Amboina
Antaris
Apple
Ash
Aspen
Avodire
Balsa
Basswood
Beech
Birch
Bird's-eye maple
Blackbean
Blackwood
Boxwood
Camphor
Canary (American whitewood)
Cedar
Cherry
Chestnut
Cocobolo
Coigue
Cottonwood
Courbaril
Crabwood
Dahoma
Ebony
Elm, British
Elm, Wych
Eucalyptus
Gaboon
Greenheart
Hickory
Holly
Hornbeam
Iroko
Ironbark
Jarrah
Jelutong
Kokko
Krabak
Laburnum
Lacewood
Laurel
Lignum vitae
Lime
Magnolia
Mahogany, African
Mahogany, Central American
Mahogany, Cuban
Makore
Maple
Meranti
Nyankom
Oak, American
Oak, British
Oak, European
Oak, Japanese
Oak, silky
Obeche
Olive
Opepe
Padauk
Palado
Pearwood
Plane
Plum
Poplar
Primavera
Purpleheart
Ramin
Rauli
Rosewood
Sapele
Satinwood, East Indian
Satinwood, West Indian
Sycamore
Teak
Thitka
Tulipwood
Tupelo
Walnut, African
Walnut, American black
Walnut, European
Walnut, Japanese
Walnut, Queensland
Willow
Zebrawood (Zebrano)

WOOD GRAINS

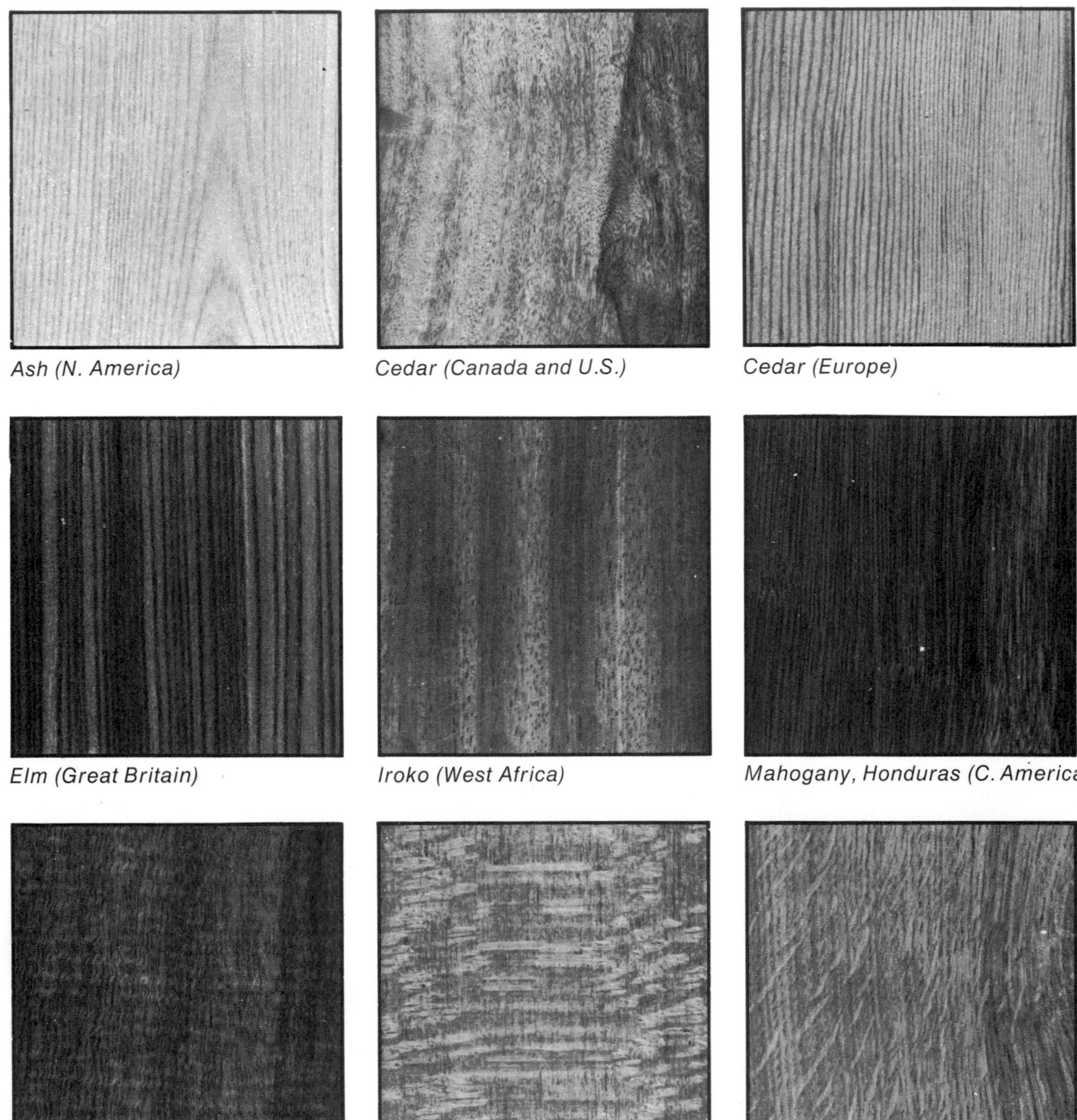

Ash (N. America)

Cedar (Canada and U.S.)

Cedar (Europe)

Elm (Great Britain)

Iroko (West Africa)

Mahogany, Honduras (C. America)

Mahogany, African (W. Africa)

Oak, silky (Australia)

Oak, British

Oak, brown (Great Britain)

Rosewood (Madagascar)

Rosewood (Brazil)

Sycamore, weathered (Britain)

Teak (S.E. Asia)

Tulipwood (Brazil)

Walnut, American Black

Walnut, African

Walnut, Queensland (Australia)

Walnut, European

Willow (Europe)

Zebrawood (W. Africa)

WOODS, NATURAL AND MAN MADE

Sawn Logs

The first method of sawing wood produces a board with a beautiful grain in the length section [1].
The second method, sawing radially, is intended to highlight the beauty of the annual rings when cut obliquely [2].
The third method of cutting isolates the central weaker piece [3].
In the fourth method, quartered logs can be cut without too much waste [4], while a variation on quarter-sawing produces more waste [5].

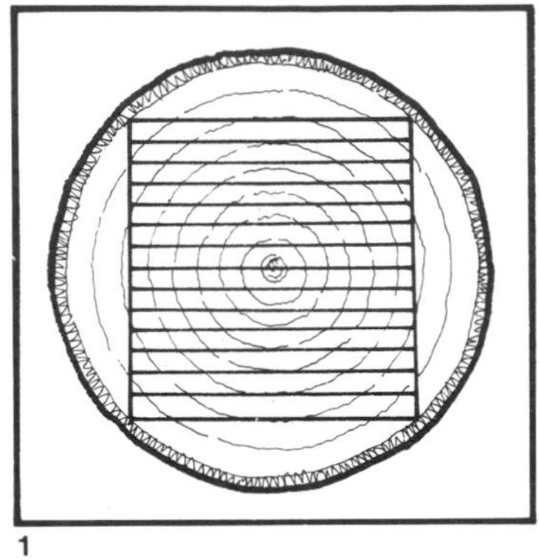
1

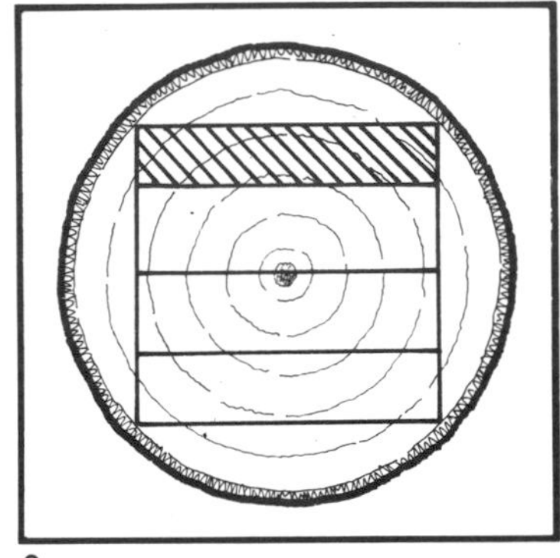
2

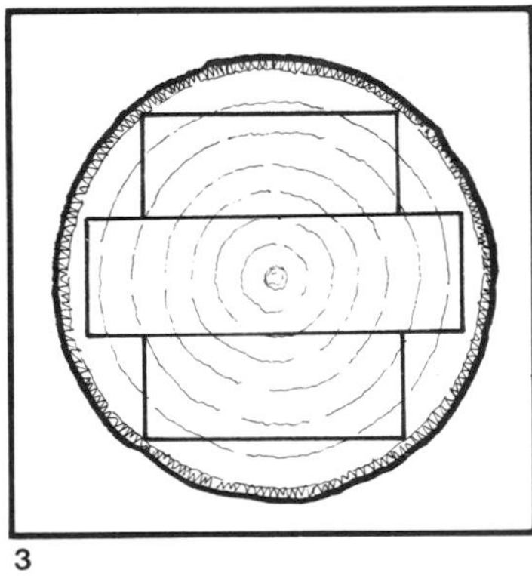
3

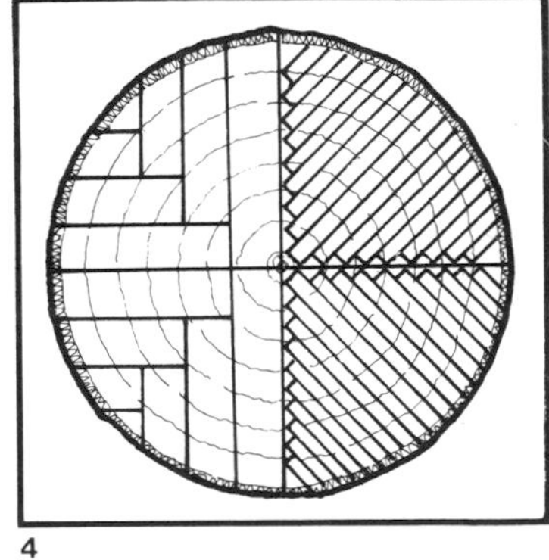
4

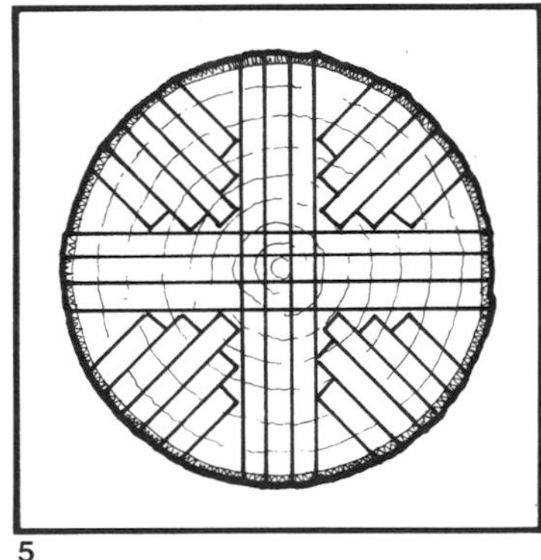
5

All the following new boards have the same advantage—they are strong and will not warp or shrink and are easier to purchase than most "solid" wood. Often you will come across an inexpensive but lovely table base with no top, and finding a matching top of solid wood can be very difficult. Settle for laminboard or faced plywood, strip the table base, and stain them both to match.

Alternatively paint either the table base or top with gloss paints and enjoy your bargain.

Man-made Boards

There are also several kinds of man-made boards; battenboard, blockboard, chipboard, fiberboard, hardboard, laminboard and plywood.
Battenboard is a lower grade of built-up board, similar but inferior to blockboard and rarely used now [6].
Blockboard is made from thin strips of softwood laid edge to edge, sandwiched between veneers and pressed into sheets [7].

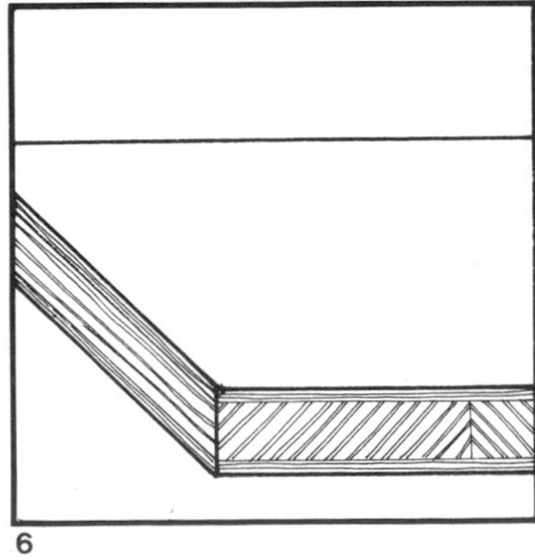
6

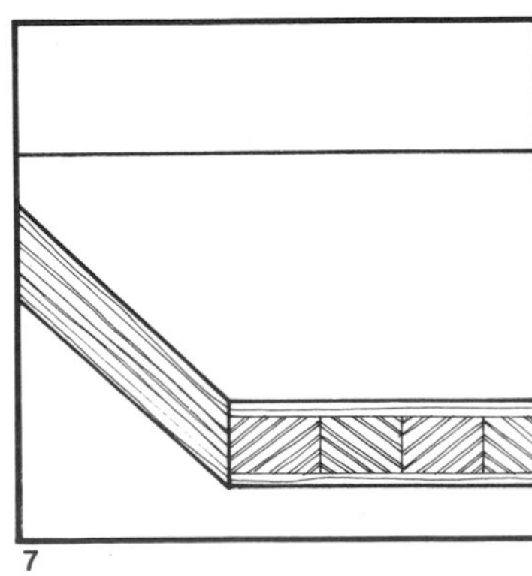
7

Chipboard is made from machined wood chips bonded together with a synthetic resin under heat and pressure. It is cheaper than blockboard and can be used in most do-it-yourself projects but needs to be supported by a wooden framework. It is available in thicknesses of $\frac{1}{8}$″ (2.5mm) to $\frac{1}{2}$″ or $\frac{3}{4}$″ (13 or 18mm) [8].

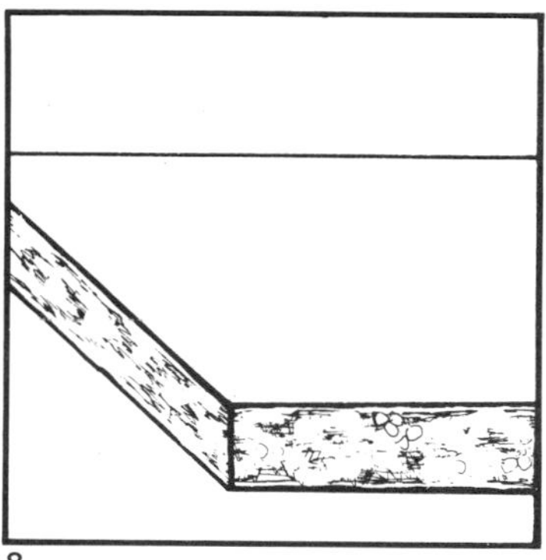
8

Fiberboard, sometimes called Masonite, is formed from wood pulp on fiber and a bonding agent, used most often for wall insulation and bulletin boards. It is available in thicknesses from $\frac{1}{8}$″ (3mm) to $\frac{1}{4}$″ (7mm) [9].

Hardboard is softwood pulp pressed into sheets $\frac{1}{12}$″ (2.4mm) to $\frac{1}{2}$″ (13mm) thick, usually with one smooth face and one rough, textured face [10].

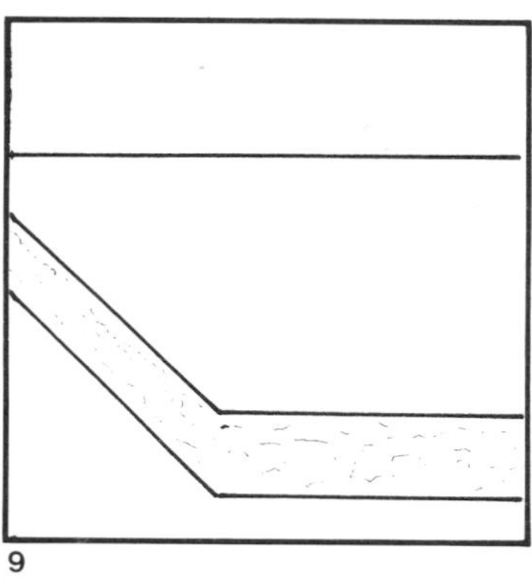
9

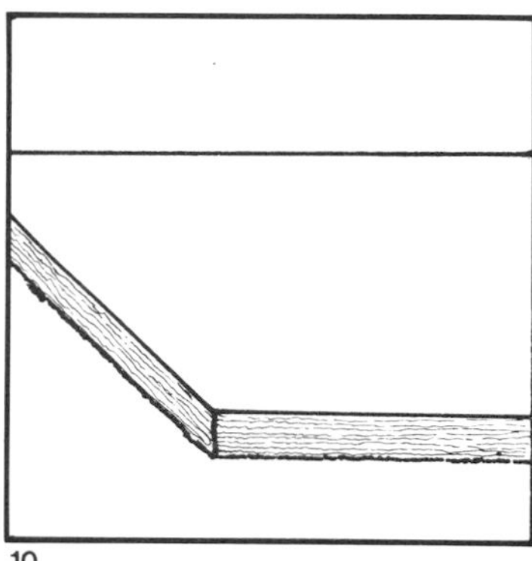
10

Laminboard (laminated board) is used in the manufacture of modern veneered furniture. It is similar to blockboard but the core is made of several $\frac{1}{4}$″ (7mm) strips glued together. The veneers commonly used are birch, poplar and gaboon. Its advantage over blockboard is that the pattern of the core is less likely to show on the surface of the veneer [11].

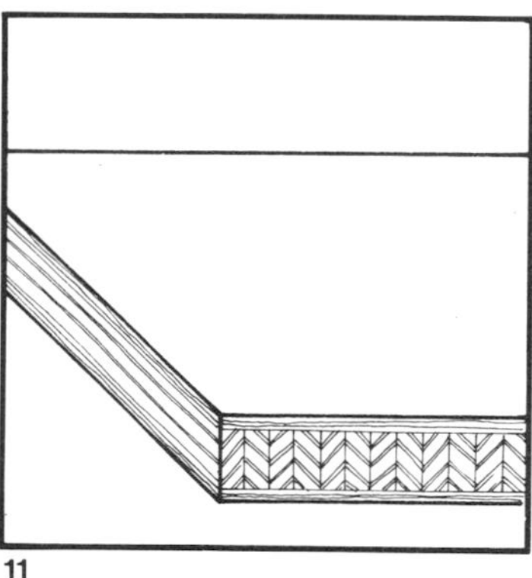
11

Plywood is made of three or more thin layers of wood, usually birch, alder, ash, gaboon or douglas fir, with the grain of each piece at right angles to the layers above and below it. When glued together under pressure, this reduces most shrinkage and splitting; obviously the more layers glued together, the stronger the ply is. It is available in thicknesses of $\frac{3}{4}$″ (2cm) to $\frac{1}{4}$″ (7mm). Faced plywood has one surface veneered with a more expensive hardwood like oak and is used where this surface matters [12].

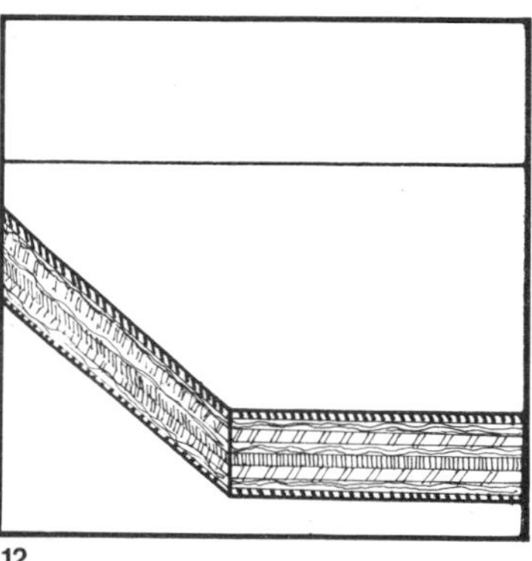
12

SIMPLE REPAIRS

Dry rot is a fungus which grows and feeds in warm, moist conditions. The affected wood is powdery to the touch and you may eventually recognize its musty smell. It may be prevented by keeping all furniture in well ventilated rooms, i.e. attics are better for storage than damp cellars, provided they don't get too hot during the summer, as heat and lack of humidity causes cracks. Dry rot can be stopped from spreading by spraying adjacent areas with a commercial fungicide or mercuric oxide in methyl alcohol [13]. (Hint: for this purpose always keep refillable spray bottles). But the only safe treatment is to cut out and burn all affected wood.

Salts: If an object has been found buried, salts from the soil have probably caused white blotches. The only remedy is careful bathing with water, followed by gentle and slow drying.

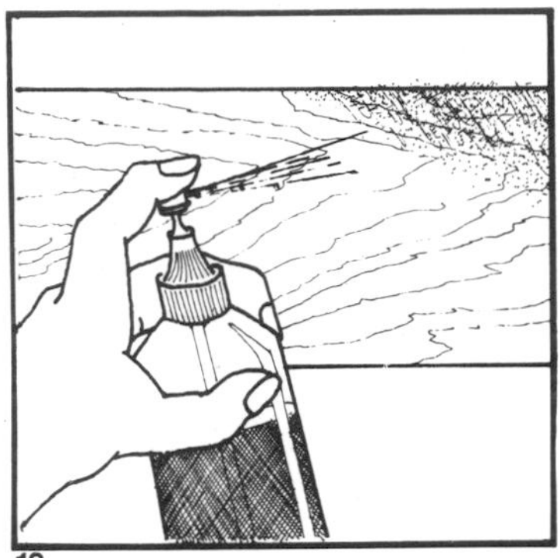

13

Immersion in water or damp: This is for entire pieces, not for damp patches (see White Spots or Rings, and Black Spots).

- If an object is found in a very damp place, sudden drying will cause warping; so place it on a rack, inside a vessel containing paraffin oil or kerosene (weight down if necessary), and keep it there until the water absorbed by the wood has been replaced by it [14].
- Next soak it in petroleum spirit or benzine until this replaces the oil.
- Drain, dry carefully and apply paraffin wax by the following method: warm the object and wax to room temperature and apply the wax with a soft rag. If you notice excess wax staying on the surface, remove it with another soft cloth soaked in petroleum spirit or benzine: Note: this treatment will darken the wood slightly and you cannot paint over it, although you can apply varnish.

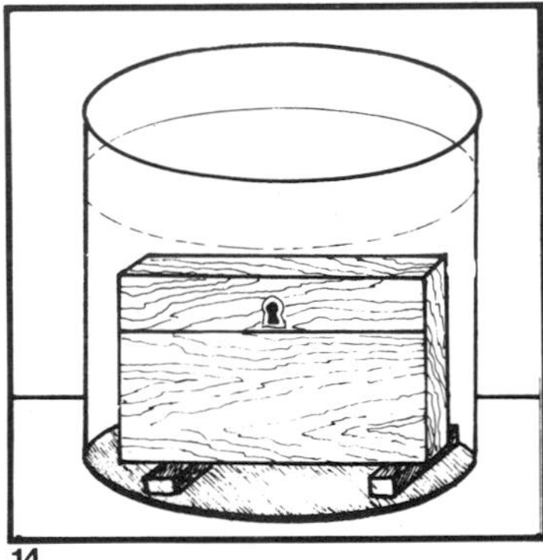

14

Dents: it is always best to remove dents as soon as possible.

- First try letting hot water sit in the hollow, which swells the compressed fibers [15].
- If that fails, place a dampened cotton cloth over the dented area and heat it with an electric iron, causing steam [16]. Use the tip of the iron for smaller dents, the whole iron for larger ones. Be sure to let the wood dry *thoroughly* afterwards before re-waxing or re-polishing the area.

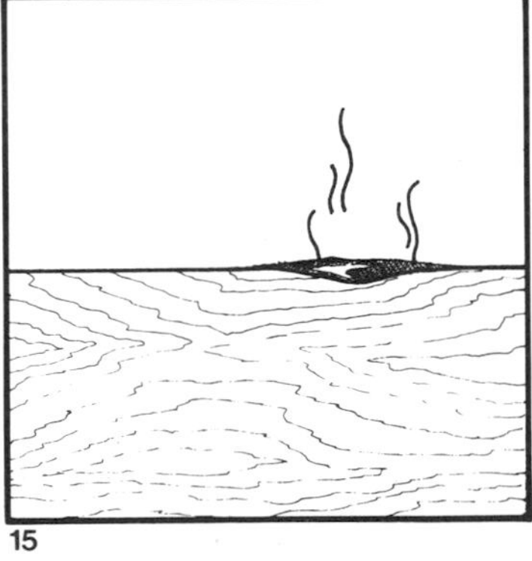

15

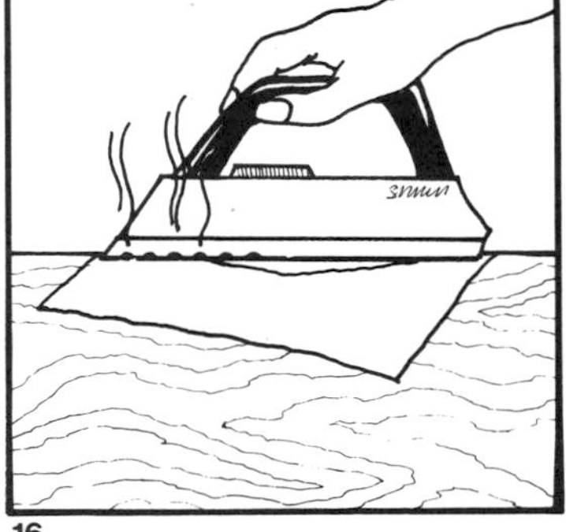

16

Deep burns (e.g. from a cigarette):

- Slowly and carefully sand with the finest abrasive paper (garnet paper is perfect).
- If this causes a slight indentation, fill with stick shellac and smooth out with soft cotton rag.
- If the indentation is very deep after sanding, you may have to fill it with tinted beeswax. You will need 2-4oz (60-125gms) beeswax and a vegetable or wood dye which blends with the polished wood surface.
- To make this, carefully melt the beeswax in a double boiler over low heat and gradually add small quantities of the dye to the molten wax [17]. Do not over-tint; remember you can always darken but not lighten. You may have to mix two dyes to get close to your present finish.
- Pour into an empty, clean, tin can and leave wax to set. When it is hard, pry it out of the can with a putty knife [18]. Roll a bit between your fingers to soften it.
- Warm the blade of a palette knife, place the wax on it and let it drip into the damaged area until it is overfull (to allow for shrinkage) [19].
- When the wax has set, carefully shave off the excess.

17

18

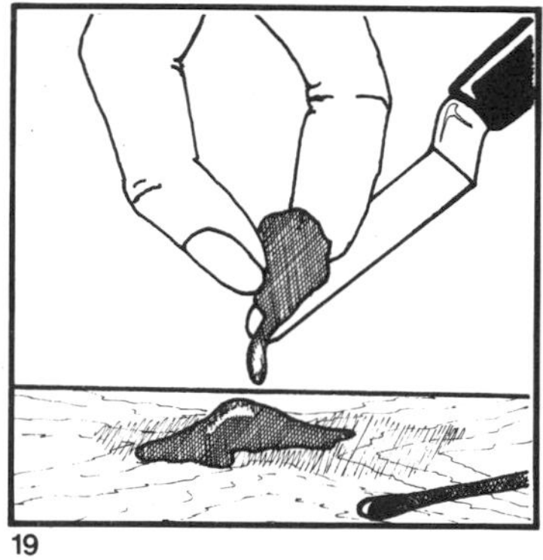
19

● If the burn is on a very glossy French polish finish, build up the hole with layers of French polish (see formula and technique for French polishing on page 52) until it is level with the adjacent surface and continue polishing until the edges are well blended.

White spots or rings: These are formed by water or by the bases of hot dishes. Rub the spot lightly with a piece of soft cotton dampened with spirits of camphor; or with a solution of one part ammonia or one part turpentine mixed with one part linseed oil [20].

Black spots: are usually caused by water penetrating a French polished surface. There is not much you can do. If there are several, remove the finish with methylated spirits and steel wool as directed on page 43, bleach the spots, if necessary using a small brush, and refinish.

20

Small scratches and gouges: Use woodturner's cement, also called stick shellac, stick filler, furnisher's wax. It looks like a thick crayon and is applied by simply "pencilling" along the line of the scratch [21]. For deeper scratches, melt a bit of the crayon with a match, dropping it on to a warm palette knife. Spread this onto the area, and remove the excess by polishing with a cotton rag. Alternatively, make your own filler from beeswax and dye as instructed under Deep Burns.

Dirty, dull finish: A formula for cleaning emulsion which also polishes and can be kept in a sealed glass jar, shake jar to mix:
1 part linseed oil
1 part white vinegar
1 part turpentine
$\frac{1}{4}$ part denatured alcohol
(methylated spirits)

21

Woodworm The grub or larva of a wood-boring beetle is usually introduced by bringing an infested wood or wicker article into the house. The insects then fly to infest other pieces, so always check recently purchased articles for a sprinkling of pinhead-size holes. The attack often starts in the cheaper softwood at the back or bottom. These holes are the result of the adult beetle hatching inside the wood and boring out to escape from its nest in July or August [22]. If the holes appear to show clean wood inside, with sharp edges, or if wood-dust is found under the piece, it will have to be treated.

● Inspect carefully, turning upside down if possible. If a valuable upholstered piece is affected, consult a firm specializing in insect treatments. They will probably recommend fumigating in a sealed chamber with a gas which does not damage the covering.

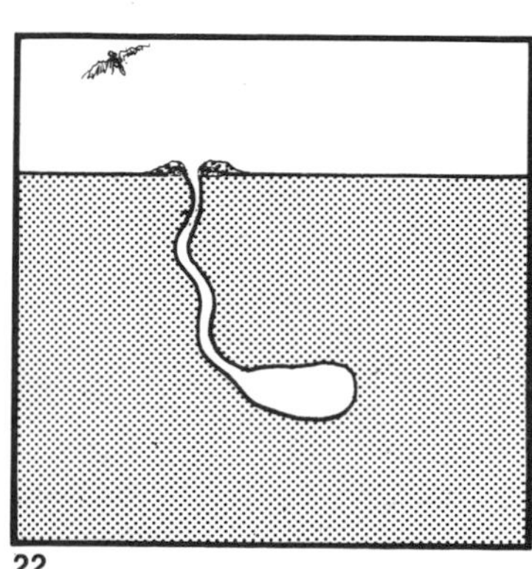
22

● If treating the item yourself, isolate it in a workroom or garage to prevent further infestation and then saturate the affected area with a commercial woodworm solution, or use kerosene or paraffin and then wood naphtha or liquid ammonia. It is best to place the liquid in a pointed nozzle can (a small, clean oilcan will do) and squirt into EACH AND EVERY HOLE to penetrate to the larvae [23]. Just wiping woodworm killer on is ineffectual and will simply form an air bubble. Leave on for 24 hours and wipe off the excess if there is any. Unfortunately this will destroy most polished surfaces so try to keep the treatment confined to infested areas.

● If the infestation is really bad, you may have to cut out the área and insert a new piece. Remember to check constantly after discovery to make sure the larvae have not moved on to another piece.

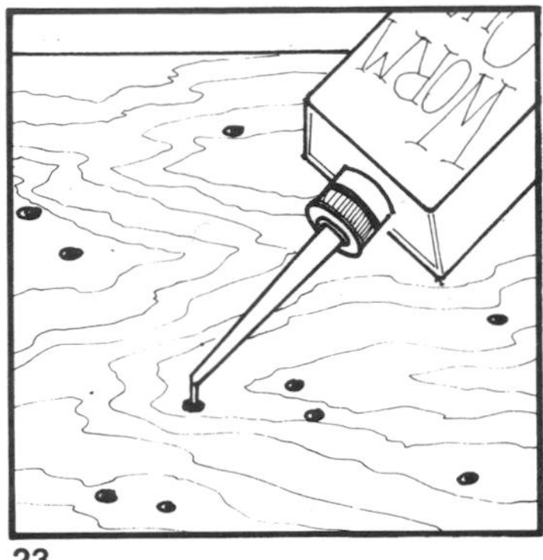

23

Knot holes: Usually these are only troublesome on unseasoned new wood but sometimes they appear after stripping a piece down to base wood [24]. To "seal off" knots that ooze resin, dissolve 5oz shellac and 1oz sandarac in 1pt denatured alcohol (methylated spirits). Strain this through a wire mesh strainer and apply it with an old brush, to the knot and surrounding area.

24

Chips and small holes: Cracks, splits, enlarged pores and knot holes all require filling. Use proprietary wood filler like plastic wood or make one up by mixing fine sawdust with a wood-working glue until the mixture is slightly stiff. Cabinet makers used to save sawdust from each kind of wood for this purpose. If the mixture appears too light, add a bit of powdered pigment from the sienna or umber range. On pieces to be clear finished, matching the filler to surrounding wood is critical.

● Apply the filling with a filling knife, so that it projects slightly above the surface [25]. This will contract in drying. Sand the area if necessary.

● An alternative wood filler can also be made from glue, tissue paper, linseed oil and chalk.

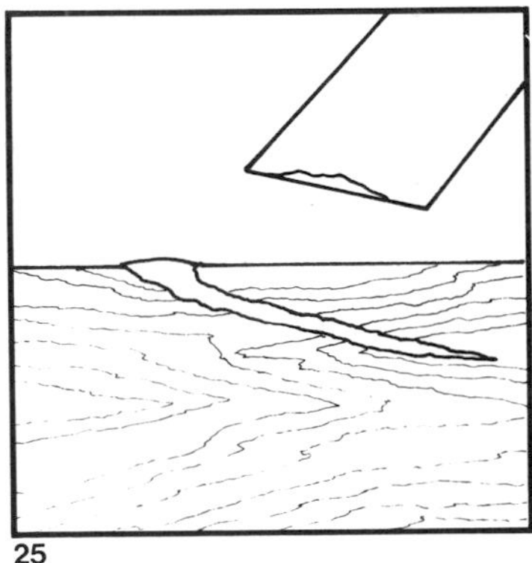

25

Just thin the glue over low heat in an old pan, add the tissue paper torn into pieces, then add the linseed oil, stirring the whole time until it becomes thick. Add a bit of powdered chalk and use for filling holes and cracks. Once applied it sets hard in two to three days.

● Another filling which is not so attractive, so use it only for surfaces which will be painted: mix one part whiting with three parts plaster of Paris. Tint with powdered pigment if desired. Add water to form a paste and apply with a putty knife or small palette knife. (Hint: I find the palette knife perfect for the small filling jobs because of its flexibility [26]).

26

Stains

Before attempting to remove a stain, remember: ALL STAIN REMOVERS ARE POWERFUL SO USE THEM WITH CAUTION, and follow the manufacturer's instructions. If mixing your own be sure they are accurately labeled before putting them away.

After removing most stains, it will be necessary to touch up the bleached area to match the surrounding finish. Use several coats of thinned French polish or varnish applied with a small brush. Sometimes you may also find it necessary to apply a wood stain to the bleached area before polishing or varnishing. In this instance, match the wood with commercially available oil- or water-based stains, mixing two shades together if necessary to get a perfect match.

Grease, fats and oils: Benzoline or benzine will remove these stains. Failing that, try cigarette lighter fluid. The drawback is that all of these may affect the glue which holds veneer. For veneered or inlaid pieces use talc instead: spread a thick layer of it on the spot, place several layers of white tissue paper on top of this and warm the paper gently and slowly with a hot iron (wool setting, don't use steam—Fig. 27). Both the talc and paper will soak up the grease. Repeat if necessary. Alternatively, use fuller's earth instead of talc.

27

Alcohol: Drink, perfume or medicine leave a white mark on French polished surfaces and the only treatment is to apply new French polish. (See page 52 for French polish formula). On varnished furniture the damage is worse, because most varnishes are soluble in alcohol. In this case sand the spot with very fine abrasive paper and touch up varnish as described above. (See Hints page 44).

Wine or fruit stains: These are seldom very deep. Clean the surface by light sanding, and with a cotton swab, dab on diluted hydrochloric acid, followed by a few drops of hydrogen peroxide. This method also works well with very old red ink.

Blood: Use ordinary hydrogen peroxide or get some sodium thiosulphate (diluted to 5%) from a pharmacist. Apply as above.

Ink: The removal of ink is a trial and error effort. On a fresh stain, wash with water, then apply lemon juice to bleach it, using absorbent cotton or cotton wool or paint brush [28]. Unfortunately the area may then need to be treated for water damage. An old ink stain will need to be sanded lightly to expose the wood. Then place a piece of cotton that is just the right size over the stain and pour sulphuric acid onto the cotton [29]. Wait 2-3 minutes and inspect. Repeat if necessary. Alternatively use diluted oxalic acid with warm water. This also works best on red ink stains.

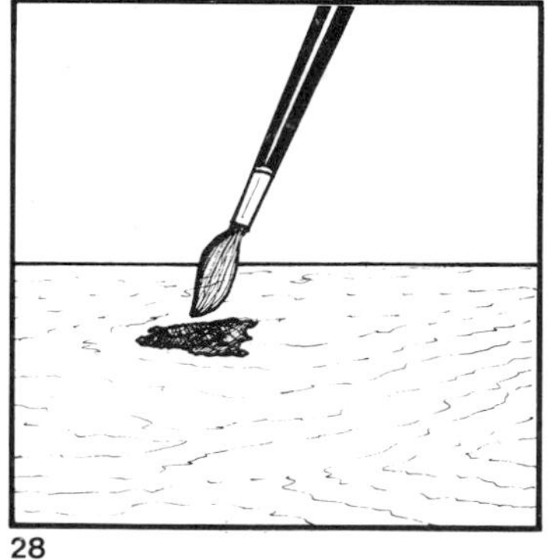
28

29

AA–C

Loose Screws

These are commonly found on hinges and handles either because the screw hole has become enlarged or the wood surrounding the screw has been damaged.

- First make sure that the wood surrounding the hinge or handle is not split [30].
- If it is, remove the hinge or handle, fill the split with a wood filler and let it dry before continuing [31].

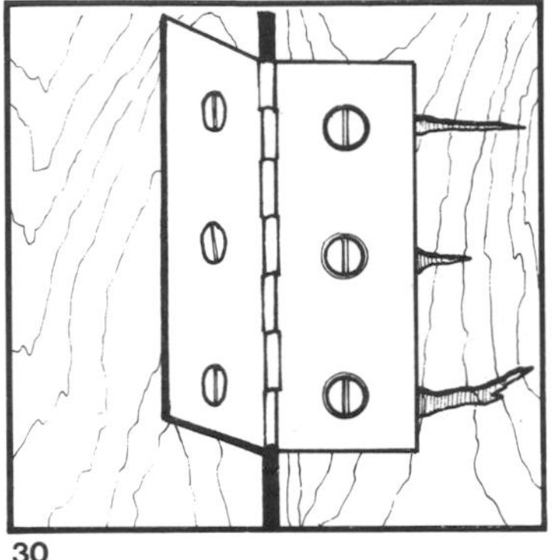

30

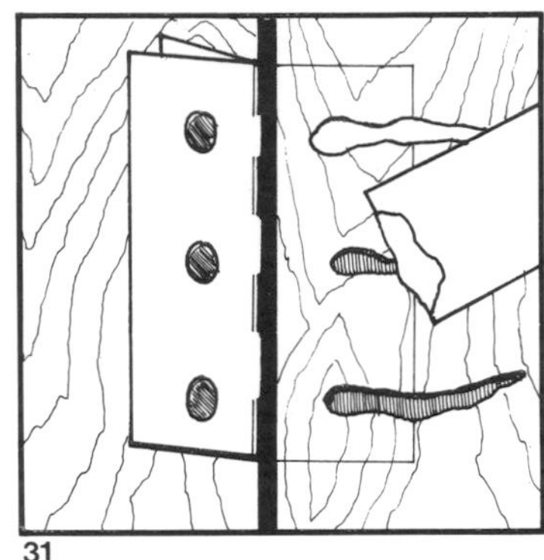

31

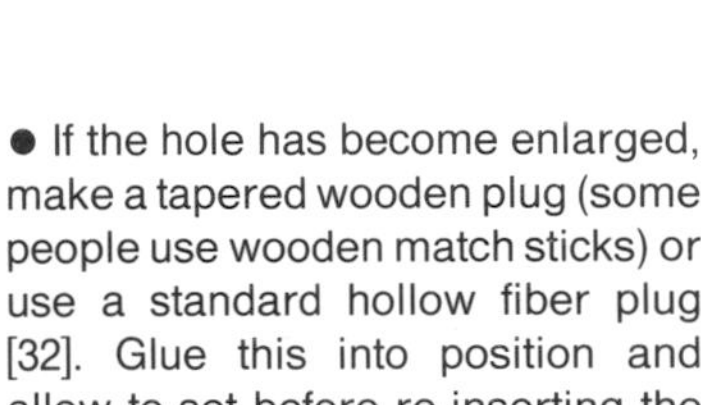

- If the hole has become enlarged, make a tapered wooden plug (some people use wooden match sticks) or use a standard hollow fiber plug [32]. Glue this into position and allow to set before re-inserting the screw.

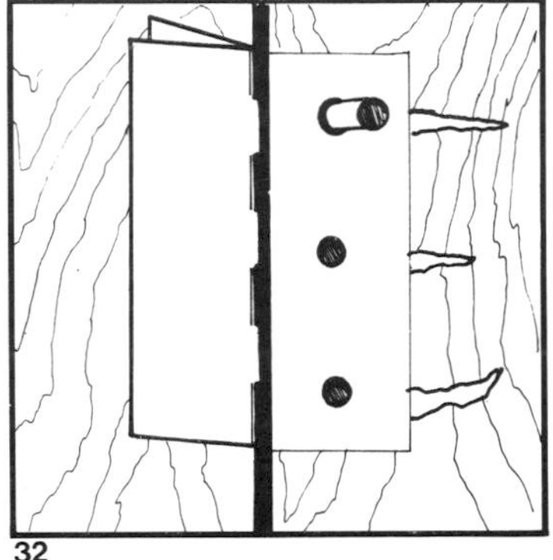

32

Doors That Won't Close

This problem is probably caused by a hinge which is too deeply set so that the door tends to spring open. Remove the hinge and trace around it with a sharp pencil onto a piece of cardboard [33]. Cut out the cardboard, place it under the hinge and reset the screws. This will raise the hinge. If the hinge jams make sure that the screws are flush with the hinge and not protruding.

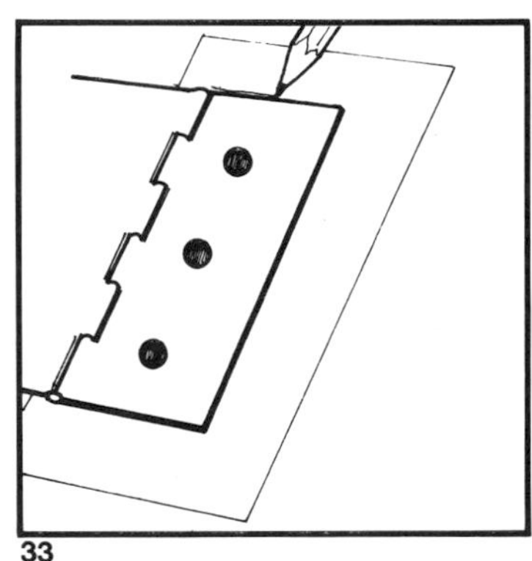

33

Chair or Table With Wobbly Legs

A wobble is caused by unevenness in either the floor or chair legs.

- Place the chair on a piece of chipboard or flatboard [34]—if it still wobbles one or two of the legs will probably be shorter than the rest. (If it doesn't wobble on a stable surface, then it's the floor that is uneven and you can either repair the floor or move the chair!)
- While the chair is still on a level surface determine which legs are shorter. Push thin pieces of cardboard or thin scraps of wood under the short leg to see how much needs to be cut from the other chair legs [35].
- Once the chair seems steady remove the wood or cardboard from under the shorter leg and use it to mark how much has to be cut from the others [36].
- Saw off the excess with a small saw. If the legs are angled as shown in illustration [37], cut the ends so they are horizontal.
- Smooth the legs with fine abrasive paper and refinish if necessary. (See pages 40-45.)

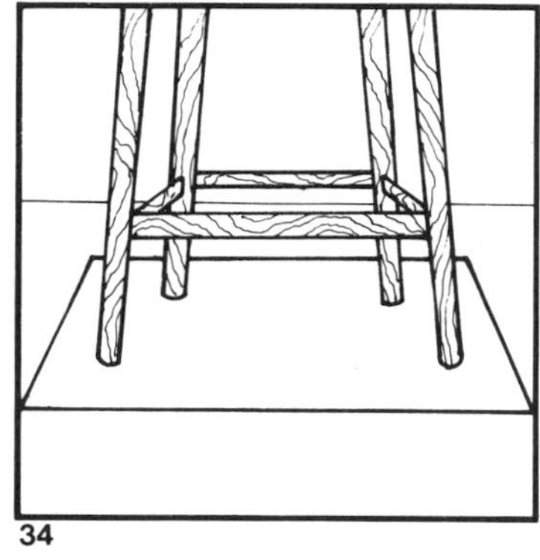
34

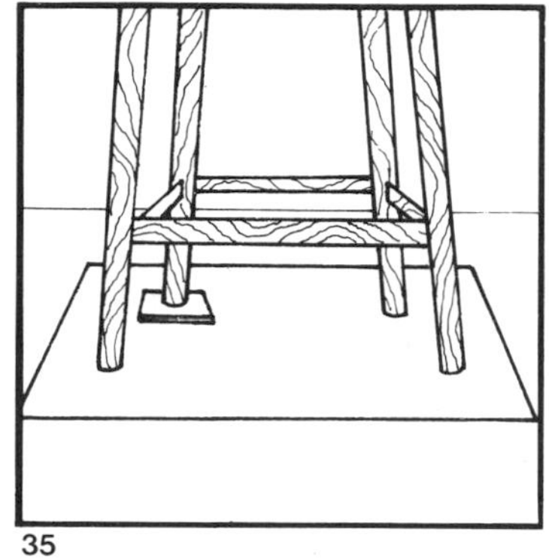
35

36

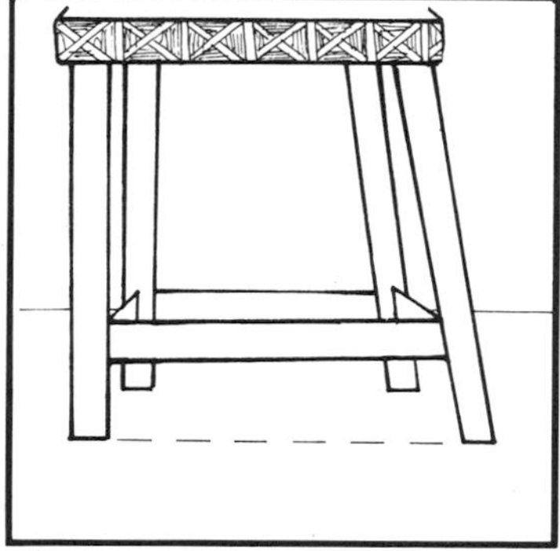
37

Stiff Drawers

In wet weather, drawers tend to stick more because the wood fibers have expanded. To remedy, try rubbing the outside of the drawer with soap or a candle [38]. If this fails remove a bit of the wood from the side of the drawer with coarse abrasive paper, sanding with the grain. Old paint drops often clog up the runners—obviously these can be removed with a scraper and with paint remover.

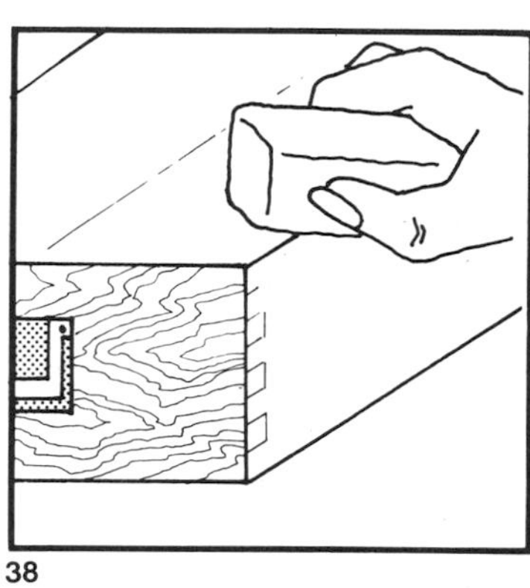
38

Drop-Leaf Table

These tables often need repairing because the drop-flaps, sometimes called leaves, tend to droop towards the floor.

- Just open the leaves, pull out the stays and check if the tops of the stays are in even contact with the leaves [39]. (A T-square or right angle is useful here.)

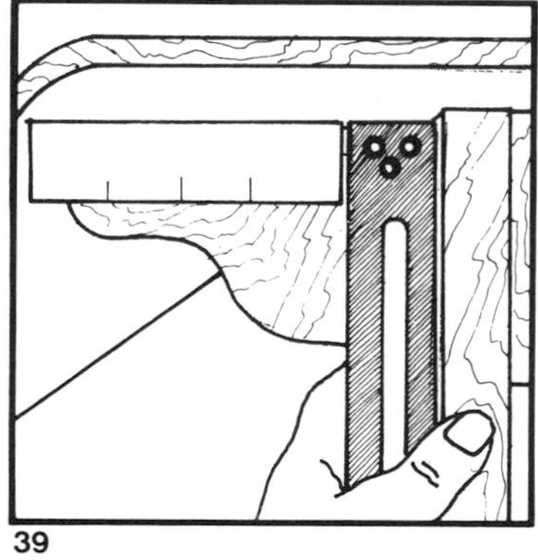
39

- If not, insert a small hardwood wedge, until the angle is perfect and the table top flat [40].

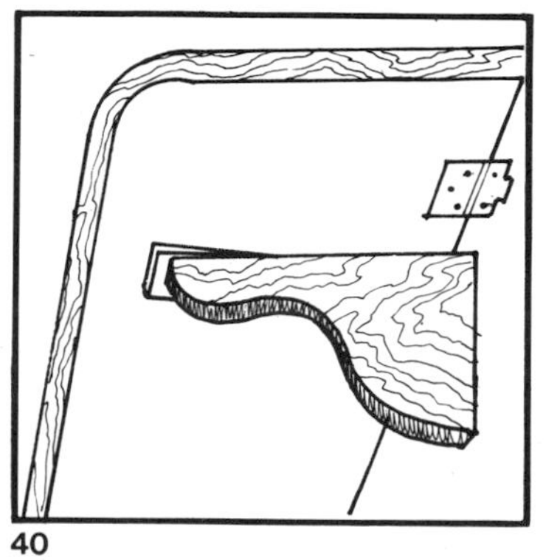
40

- If the table gets heavy use, you may need to make a longer wedge so that the leaf is more firmly supported, and then screw the wedge into place [41].

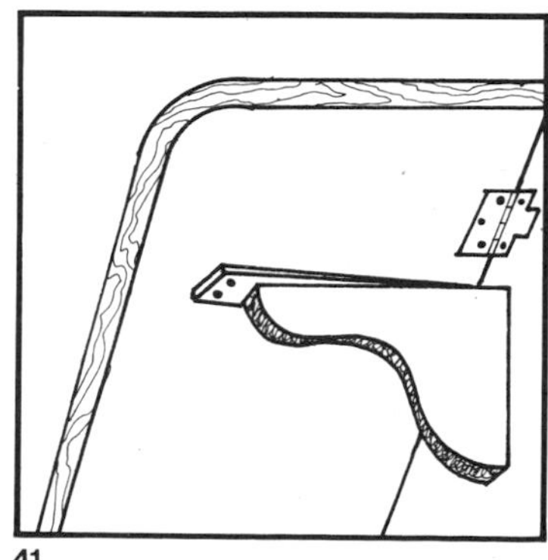
41

Repairing Joints–General Advice

There are literally dozens of ways of joining one piece of wood to another. Some of these are simple enough for the amateur making a bookcase; others involve skilful carpentry, but a joint only comes to the attention of a restorer when it has become "unjointed" and then the job most often simply involves glues, clamps and a bit of care. Eight of the common joints used in furniture construction are illustrated here so you can see how the components work as a joint and recognize them before attempting repairs.

Those pictured are: bridle joint [42], common housing joint [43], dowel and stub tenon joint [44], halved angle joint [45], lapped dovetail [46], mortise and tenon joint [47], simple miter joint [48], and the rebated or rabbeted joint [49].

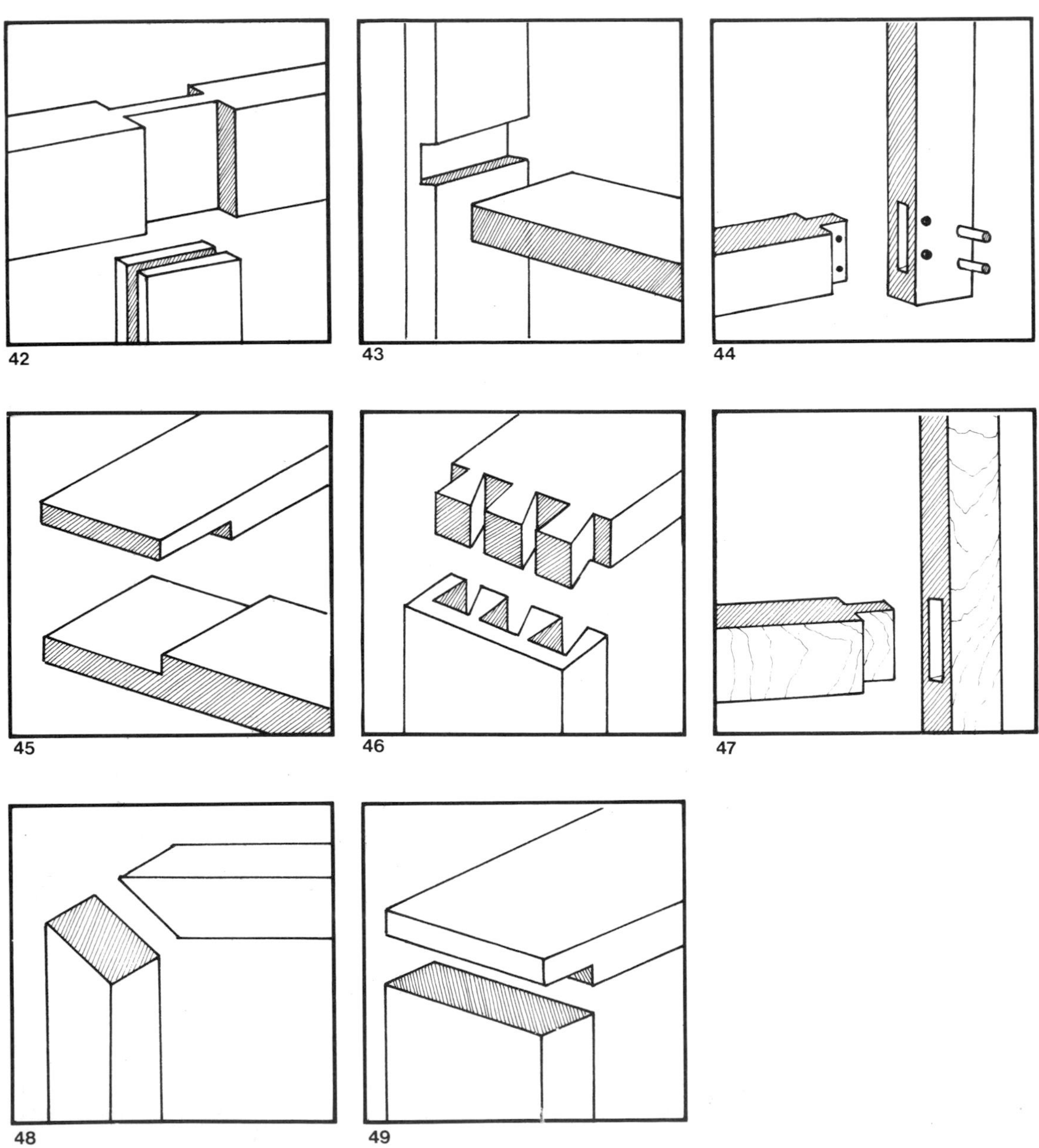

Gluing Joints

When applying glue, take care not to use so much that it oozes out and damages the surrounding finish, nor so little that the bond is weak. Cellulose based or polyvinyl acetate glues are suitable for most jobs—they are strong, waterproof and will allow you to adjust the bond if necessary. On the other hand, when instant permanent bonding is desired, as in butt joints, use an urea formaldehyde or rubber-based glue. See glue chart in the chapter on tools and materials for details.

- When starting don't rip the loose joint apart but ease one part from the other very carefully.
- Remove any old glue with a blunt knife or scraper [50], using warm water or alcohol-based solvent to dissolve any that remains.
- When working with non-water soluble glues, a wooden matchstick eases application [51].

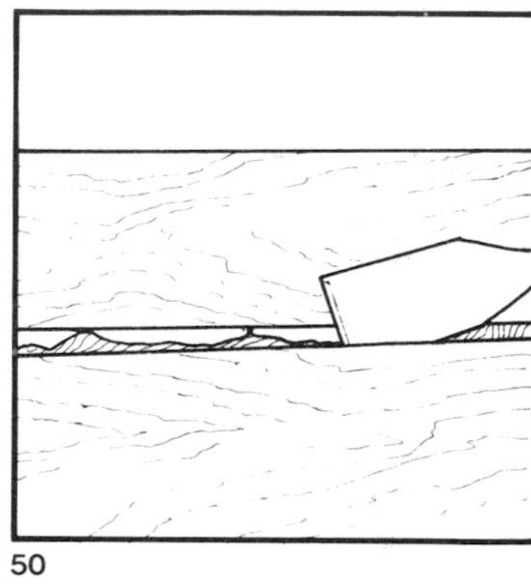
50

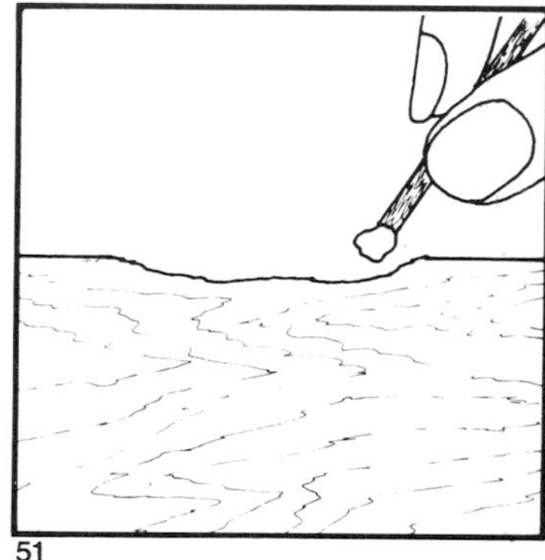
51

- Always save even the smallest splinters or chips, and glue these in place after the main joint has set [52].
- Most glues are completely set in 24 hours—consult the container to be sure. You can encourage drying by keeping the room temperature at 70°F (20°C).
- Avoid cheap vinyl glue which seperates into layers—this indicates poor quality ingredients and/or mixing.

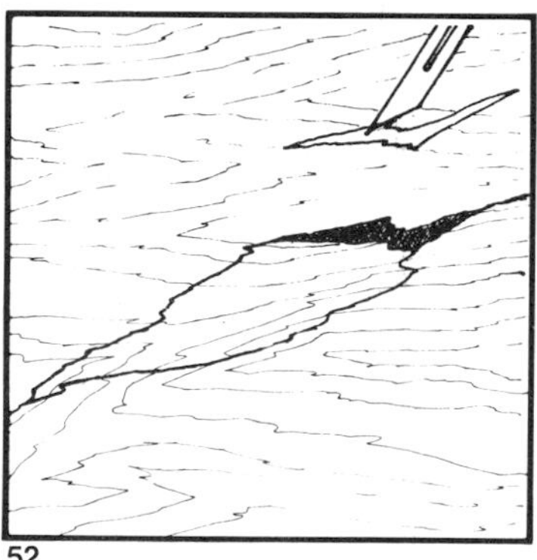
52

Doweled Joints

These sometimes present a special problem as the dowels not only come out but also break off. In this case saw off the remaining dowel ends, then drill out the dowel stubs (usually $\frac{1}{8}''$-$\frac{1}{4}''$, 3-7mm) [53].

- Cut dowels from a purchased length to fill the depth of the holes just drilled plus the depth of the hole it is to be inserted into.
- Cut slits in one end of the dowel [54], the ends having been tapered with a chisel.

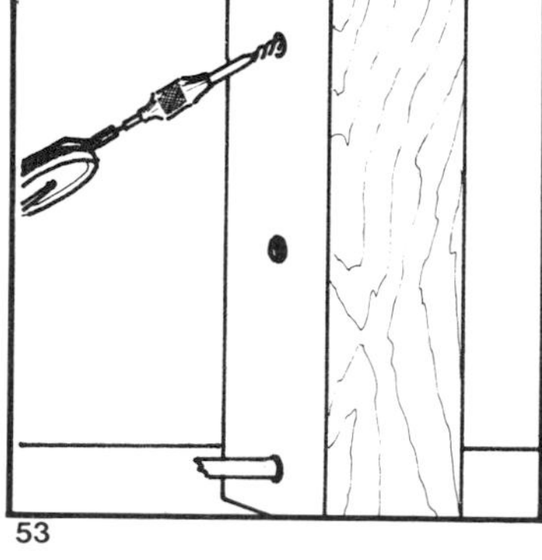
53

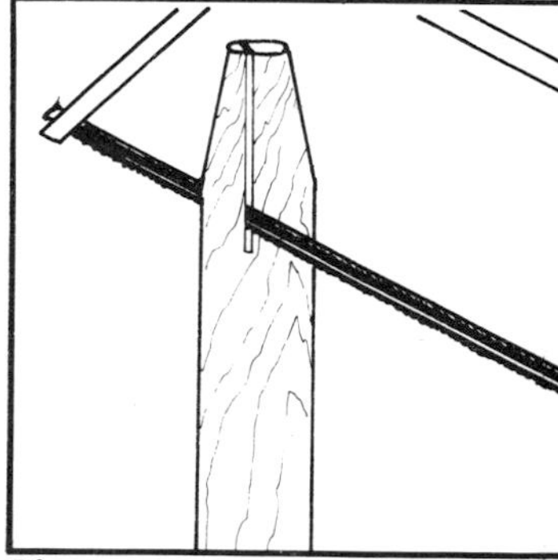
54

● Apply a household cement to the dowels and insert firmly [55].
● If a sound dowel remains, simply clean away the old glue on the dowel and hole with a scraper and warm water, and apply the new glue. A G-clamp may be necessary to hold the gluing for a few hours; alternatively bind it with string.

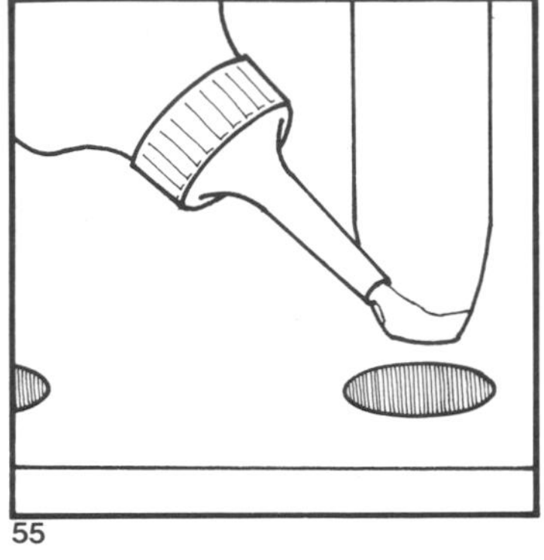
55

Tenon Joints

Tenon, or mortise and tenon, joints are often found joining the cross rails to the side legs of tables. They can be recognized as an oblong shape of contrasting grain on the outside of the table leg. Gluing will often solve the problem of a loose joint and if that fails, wedges should be cut from hardwood without pronounced grain such as ramin, beech, mahogany or jelutong.

● The wedges are sawn or chiseled to the desired length and width from the end of a piece of wood. The end section of the tenon is slotted in two or three places with a sharp chisel [56].
● Cover the wedges with PVA wood glue and tap them into the slots of the inserted tenon with a hammer [57]. The wedges may stick out slightly and this excess can be removed with a chisel once the glue is dry.

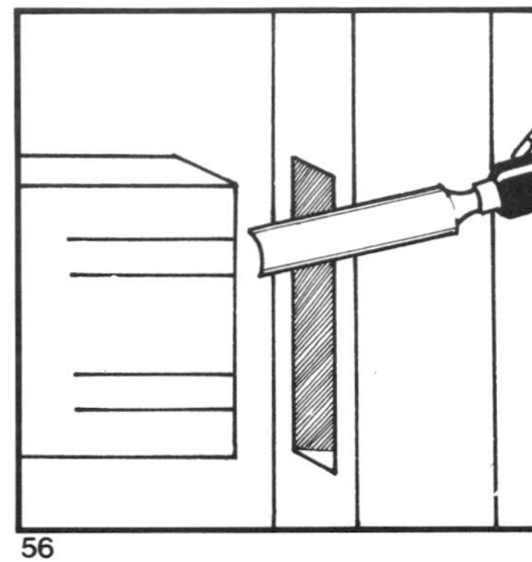
56

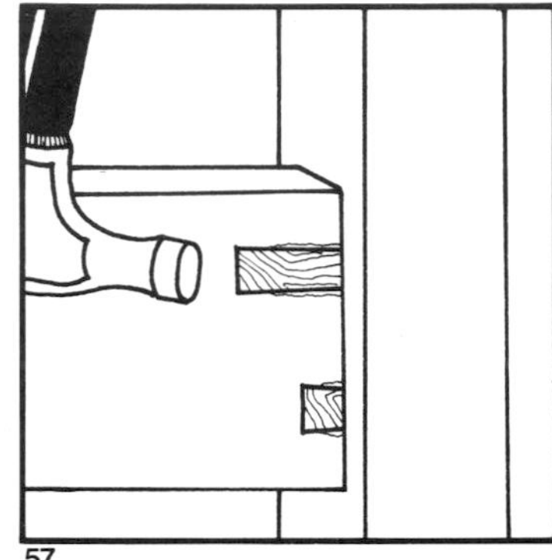
57

● With bridle and halved angle joints clamping may be necessary while, with a common housing, it is important that the two parts are "square"—test with a right angle to be sure.
● The lapped dovetail, commonly found on drawers, presents another problem—one side may be loose, while the other remains intact. In this instance use the nozzle of the glue container to reach hard-to-get-places, rather than taking apart the entire drawer.

Broken Chair Backs

When the fretwork in chair backs breaks, glue it immediately if possible to prevent further damage to the chair or the person sitting in it! If a piece is actually missing try to match the thickness and grain of the rail and then stain the new piece to match (see page 48). Taper the end of the new piece to increase the gluing surface [58].

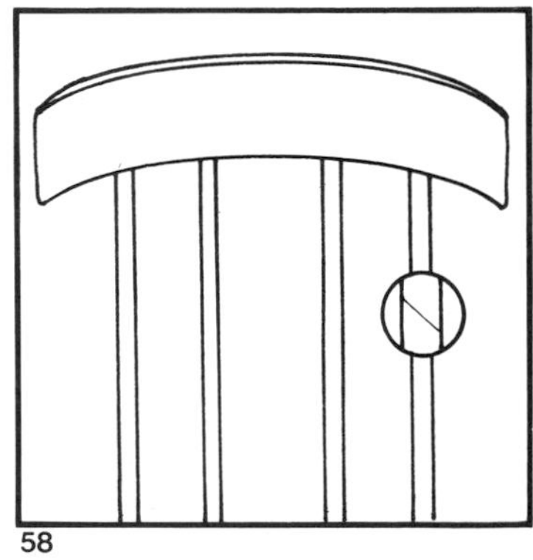
58

● If the fret is perfectly round make or purchase a dowel with the same diameter. A square fret can be made by gluing pieces of wooden slatting together to get the desired dimension. Get your wood yard to order the necessary type of wood and cut it for you. To replace a piece completely, cut off the old rail with a coping saw [59] and drill or pick out any wood that remains in the hole.
● Re-drill the hole so the diameter is slightly wider than the new fret or slat. If a square hole is desired then use a chisel. Cut the new piece to length but be sure to add the depth of each hole at either end.
● Taper the ends to fit snugly in each hole, apply a drop of cellulose-based glue and set in place, supporting the new piece if necessary.

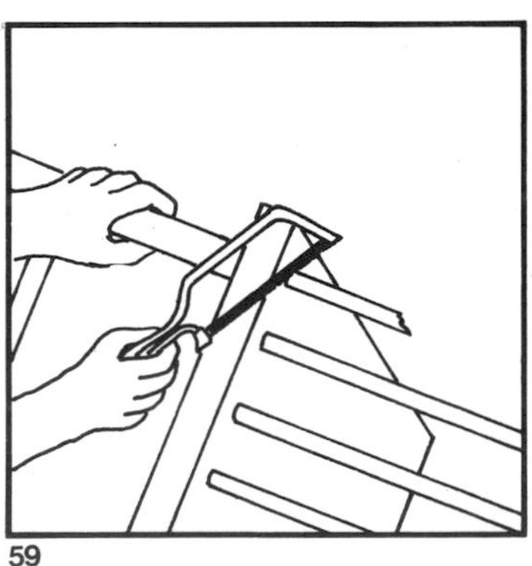
59

● If the chair backs and legs are in one piece as they often are in period furniture, or if there are no slats between the joint and back-legs, then the back may work itself away from the chair seat. On the underside you will probably see triangular blocks holding the legs to the seat [60]. On chairs with upholstered seats you may have to remove the bottom cover and webbing. This will probably expose dowels holding the chair seat in place.

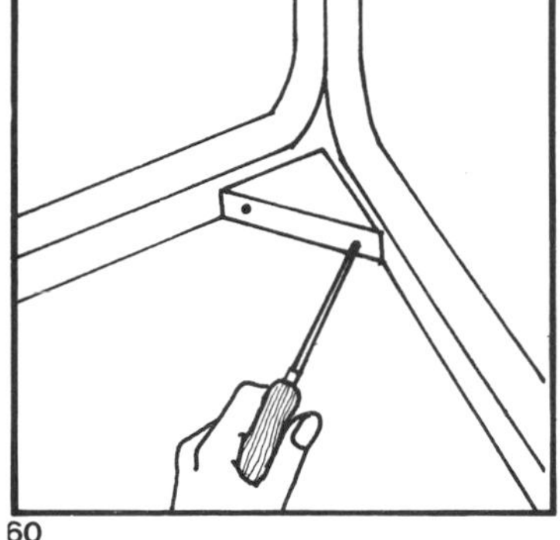
60

● Drill them out from the back or from inside the seat frame [61].
● Measure the depth of the holes with a pencil [62]. Cut new dowels a bit longer, tap them in place and clamp or tie the chair together.

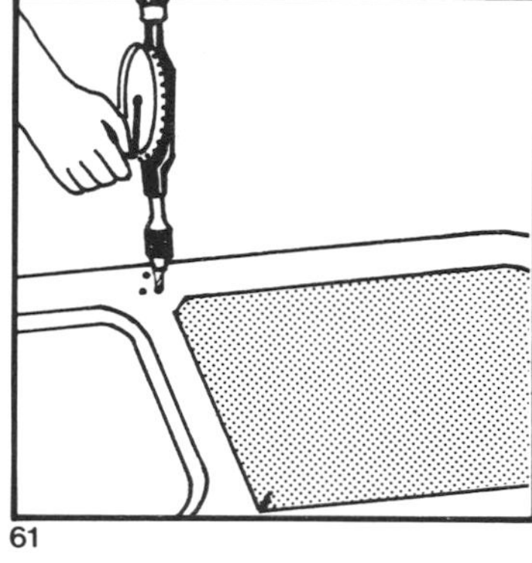
61

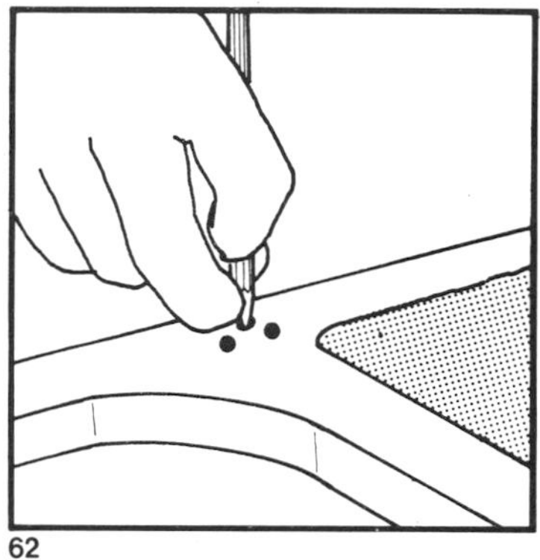
62

Replacing Panes of Glass

In antique furniture, glass is often fixed by a mixture of putty and gold size. Once the glass breaks, a soldering iron must be used to remove the putty. DO NOT attempt to cut or chisel it away—it is rock-hard. Instead proceed as follows:
● Remove as much of the broken glass as possible.
● Move the soldering iron over a small area of putty at a time [63]. When soft, lift it out, a little at a time, with a dull kitchen or putty knife [64].

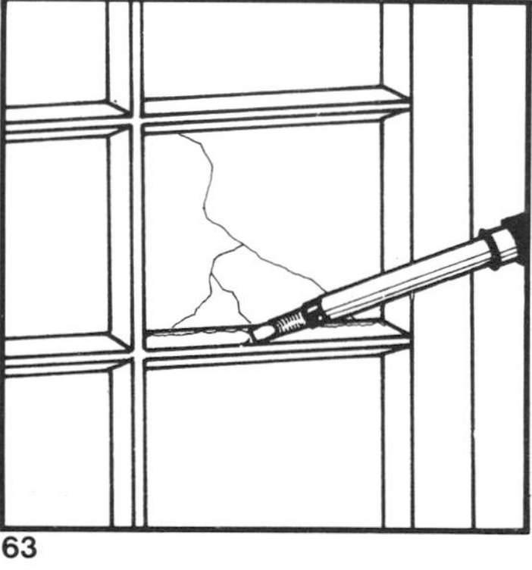
63

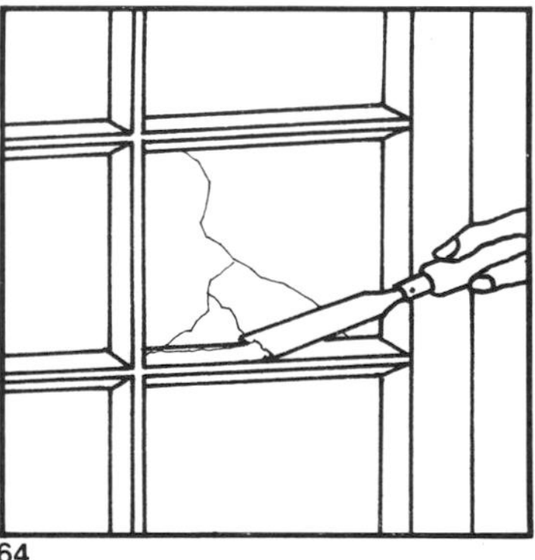
64

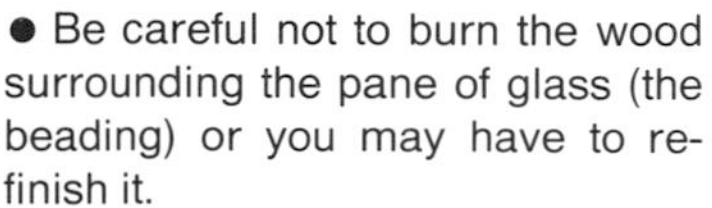

● Be careful not to burn the wood surrounding the pane of glass (the beading) or you may have to refinish it.
● Remove all remaining bits of glass, tapping them out gently with handle of putty knife. Wear gloves to protect your fingers [65].
● To replace the glass, cut a piece of cardboard to fit inside the wood and then mark off $\frac{1}{16}''$ (2mm) around the edge. Get new glass cut to this size—take a piece of broken pane with you for thickness. Then:

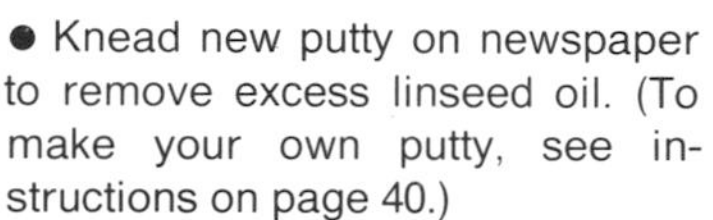

● Knead new putty on newspaper to remove excess linseed oil. (To make your own putty, see instructions on page 40.)

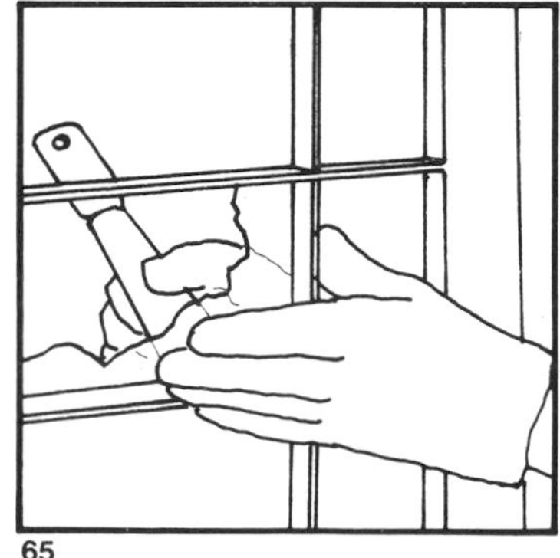
65

● Press hole in centre of putty and fill the hole with gold size. Knead the putty and size together until the size is absorbed [66].
● Press small rolled amount of putty along the inside of the beading, eventually going all the way around [67]. Place the new pane of glass into the putty, making sure it sits straight and there are no gaps in the putty holding it.

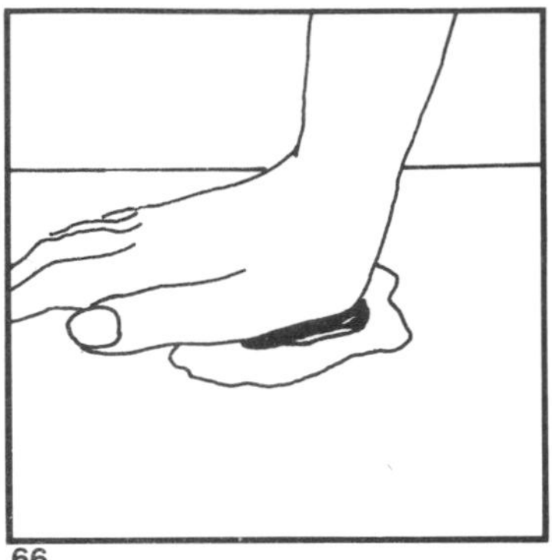

66

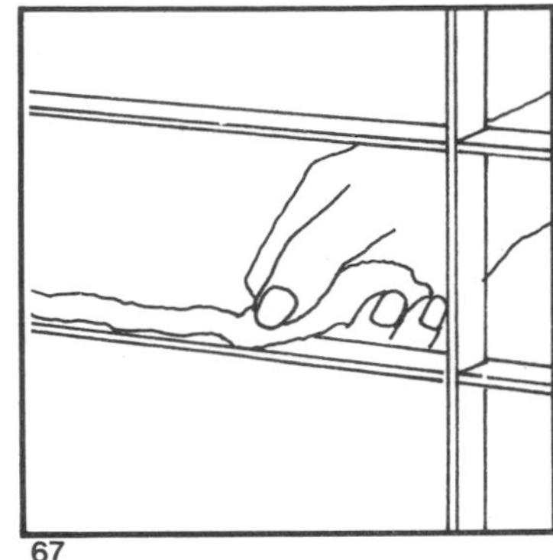

67

● While supporting the glass from the inside with one hand, scrape the excess from the outside with a putty or scraping knife [68].
● Take another roll of putty and press it against the glass on the inside, shaping the correct slant between the glass and the wooden beading. Make sure the putty doesn't show on the outside.
● Paint the putty with artist's oil paints to match the wooden beading as closely as possible.

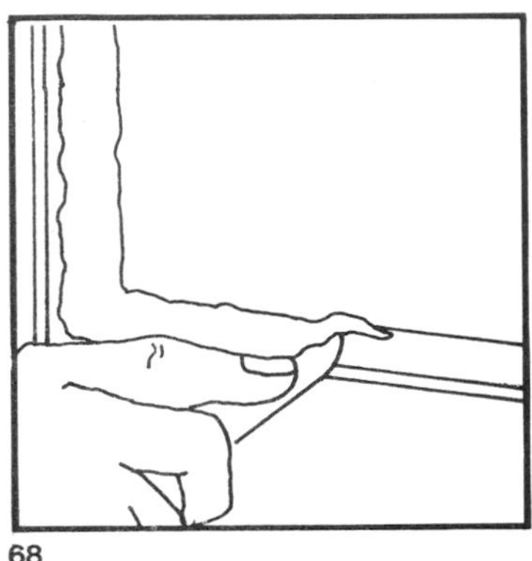

68

To Make Putty

Mix whiting with enough raw linseed oil to give it a dough-like consistency. This, without the addition of gold size, can be softened with paraffin oil or kerosene.

PREPARING WOOD FOR REFINISHING

Before you begin stripping and refinishing, do any necessary repairs, consulting pages 30-9 for advice. Once the object is repaired, remove all handles, knobs etc. (except hinges), and look closely at the existing finish. Today the trend is to remove the heavy finishing and polishes of the 19th century, letting the natural grain and color of the wood show. Fashions change, though, and if that glossy, French-polished mahogany table is in perfect condition, think hard before stripping it. Remember you may have to do eight matching chairs as well. On the other hand, a coat of opaque paint (most probably enamel) may have been applied to cover a bad stain, damage, or crude workmanship. Obviously it's impossible to tell what is underneath until the finish is removed. You can try a tiny section first at the back or side, but even if that looks all right, you may find after the messy job of paint removal that it really looks better painted.

Remember that old decorated pieces have a charm of their own—there may be figures, flowers, or designs which are far too pretty to destroy. In that case, see the section on lacquer work, and concentrate merely on touching up the most damaged areas. On the other hand it may be covered with a black paint, which was often used in the early 19th century to imitate expensive ebony, and later in England signified mourning for the death of Prince Albert, Queen Victoria's husband, in 1861. Sometimes this dense varnish hides atrocious workmanship but it *is* removable: try denatured alcohol (methylated spirits) first, if that fails use a chemical stripper containing acetone, and brush it on. Proceed as for chemical stripping (below). Once you decide to strip and refinish, gather up lots of old newspapers, cotton rags, paper towels, rubber gloves, old clothes and some of the following tools:

- Filling knife or putty knife
- Shave hook or combination shave-hook for curves and awkward parts
- Abrasive paper (medium and fine)
- Steel wool (fine)
- Old paint brush
- Goggles to protect your eyes from fumes and strong chemicals.

Always work in well-ventilated conditions with the piece standing on a few scraps of wood over a thick layer of newspaper.

Cleaning Wood

- Cleaning is necessary before stripping. If the piece is just slightly dirty, washing it with vinegar or stale beer should do the trick, but if it is really dirty use a strong detergent; 2oz (50gms) to 2 pints (1 liter) warm water.
- Sponge over the entire surface, leaving it on about ten minutes.
- Repeat the application but don't let it soak for more than ten to fifteen minutes at a time, or the water may penetrate cracked or broken finishes and damage the wood underneath.
- Dirty carvings can be cleaned with an old toothbrush or shaving brush [1].
- Rinse and dry off the piece with the cotton rags.

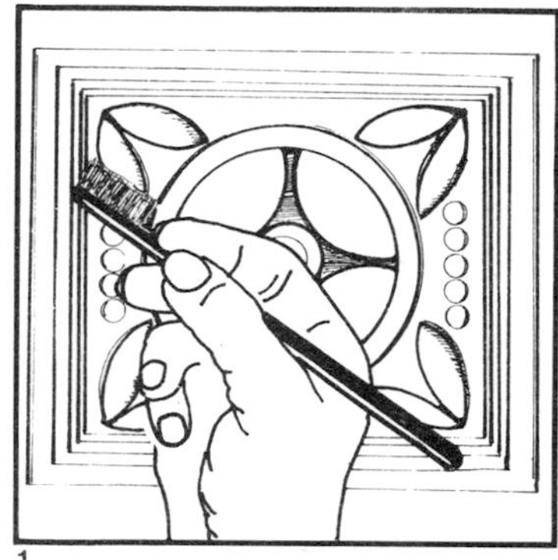
1

Stripping Wood

To remove opaque finishes (paints, enamels, etc.) and some clear finishes, the following methods can be used:

Mechanical: A cabinet scraper or double-edge scraper can be used but is not recommended. Unless you are an expert it removes the finish very unevenly, dulls the cabinet, and often scrapes and gouges the wood.

Chemical Stripping: The action of a proprietary paint stripper (liquid or jelly) reacts with the paint, causing it to dissolve and bubble up. It is also perfect for intricately carved areas, beadings and crevices which are hard to reach with a scraper.

- Spread papers under the piece; wear old clothes and rubber gloves.
- The stripper is applied with an old paint brush [2] and scraped off with a stripping knife after the bubbling begins [3]. Don't "paint" the stripper back and forth over the same section but do be sure to cover all areas of the object.

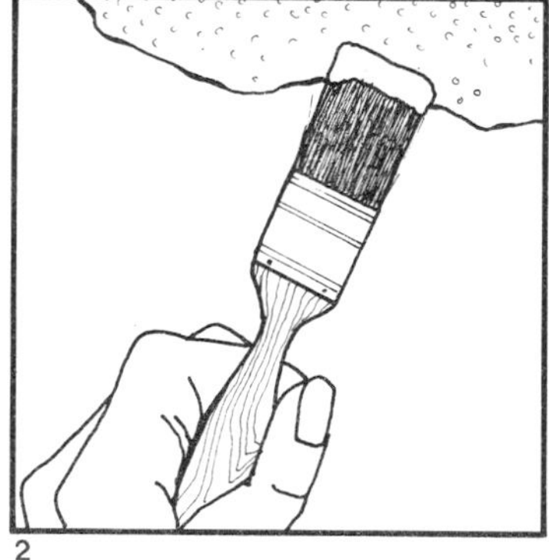
2

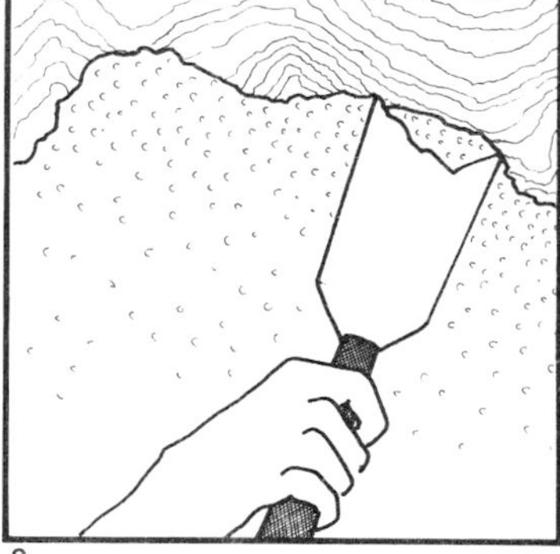
3

- Use a combination shave hook, chisel or a piece of broken glass with an end taped to protect your hand when removing paint from carved details, beading or crevices. (If there are several layers of paint to be removed, several applications of the stripper may be necessary.) Caution: work in a well ventilated room or outdoors—the fumes are unhealthy and the smell pervasive! Also protect your eyes with goggles. The paint scraps that fall on the newspaper are caustic and will burn the skin, so after you have finished, wrap up the paper carefully and throw it away. *Do not* throw it onto an open fire.

Heat Stripping: This is the quickest way of stripping paint, but it also easily damages the wood underneath if the blowtorch (sometimes called a blowlamp) is held in one place for too long. Another disadvantage is that it can't be used on intricate areas or near glass because of the high temperature of the flame, so glazed bookcases or cabinets should be stripped with chemicals. Practice on scraps of wood before working on a good piece—different fittings are available to regulate the size of the flame. You will need the following equipment:

Blowtorch—an investment well worth making if you plan to do a lot of renovation. Butane gas torches available with refill cans are increasingly popular.

Asbestos sheet to protect floor (don't use newspaper)

Container for the paint scraps (not plastic)

Broad (3″ or 7.5cm) stripping knife.

● Move the flame back and forth across the surface to "melt" the paint. As the paint bubbles and shrivels, scrape it away, holding the scraper at an angle to prevent the hot scraps from burning your hands [4]. Caution: Turn the blowtorch away from your work while you scrape, to prevent accidental burns, and NEVER let the flame stay long on any one area. Do not use a blowtorch near any flammable object—it is a potentially dangerous tool and shoul be used with the greatest of care.

4

Caustic Soda Stripping: Caustic soda or potash ("lye"), or alternatively one of the caustic products sold for unblocking drains, can be used. By far the most spectacular, this method is particularly suitable for large pieces, but it must be done outdoors, with a garden hose nearby. Wear goggles, heavy clothes and plastic gloves (not rubber ones which will dissolve).

● Add a handful of potash to 2 pints (1 liter) of water [5] for a fairly strong solution.

5

● Apply the mixture with a large sponge, mop or squeegee mop [6]. Don't rinse off the froth as it appears—froth is a sign that the stuff is working.

● To treat carvings, lay the object down and work at it with a toothbrush and/or dull knife, trying not to gouge the wood.

6

Drain Clearing Soda: If you use the drain-clearing crystals, sprinkle them dry over the surface of the piece, distributing them evenly.

● Then pour very hot water over them from a watering can with a fine rose sprinkler [7]. The result is instantaneous effervescence. Caution: stand back and keep children and pets away from these procedures.

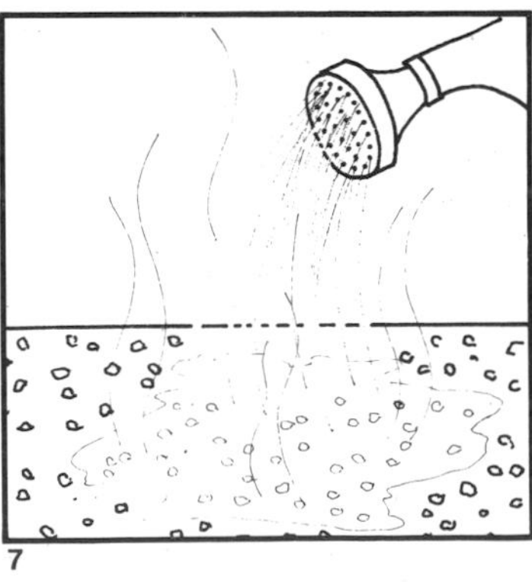
7

● Rinse the piece down and rinse again. The hose is most useful and effective in removing the soda from the tiniest crevices. If you don't rinse thoroughly, the potash will cause a "bloom" or slight film to appear on the surface.

● It will probably be necessary to "bleach" most wood after this type of paint removal (see p. 44). Unfortunately potash will also darken oak and some chestnut, while cherry reddens.

Removing Clear Finishes

If the grain is visible, one of many clear finishes has been employed. These finishes have several names, various ingedients and numerous solvents. The main categories are waxes, natural oils, French polishes, varnishes and shellacs.

Waxes, such as beeswax, and oils, such as linseed, can be removed by saturating a soft cloth with turpentine. If the piece is well coated, fine steel wool and turpentine will be more effective. This will expose bare wood, if the piece has had no other finish applied. If this process doesn't reveal bare wood, then one of the following treatments will be necessary.

Removing French Polish: If the object has been French polished, spread papers, put on rubber gloves, open the windows, and apply a drop of denatured alcohol (methylated spirits) [8].

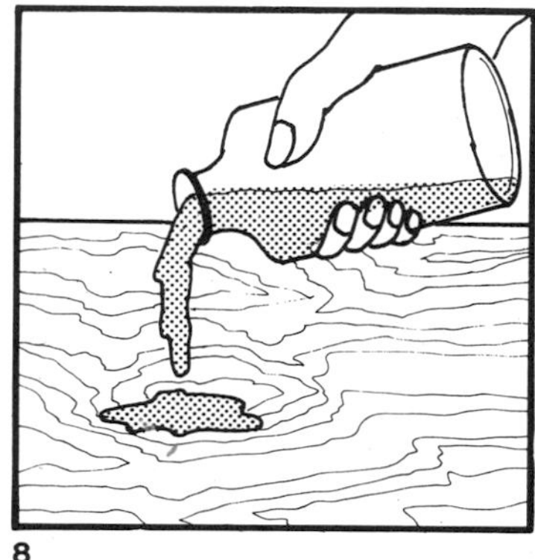

8

● Rub the finish with a finger-sized piece of fine steel wool, until a "light gravy" seems to appear [9]. REMEMBER: WORK WITH THE GRAIN, NOT ACROSS IT OR IN CIRCLES. Once this happens, the polish is yielding and should be mopped up quickly with absorbent cotton or cotton wool, paper towels, or toilet tissue. Toilet tissue seems the easiest as as you can put your gloved fingers in the hole and unwind lots of it easily and quickly.

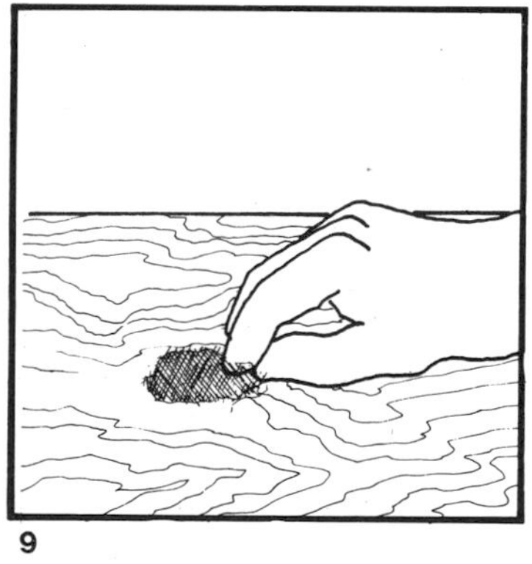

9

● Continue until the paper or cloth no longer shows any signs of this brown stain. It is best to go over the piece once, let it dry and go over again. (Strong liquid ammonia and proprietary paint removers can also be used for removing French polish but these fumes are even more unpleasant than those from methylated spirits).

Removing Varnish: Varnishes tend to attract dirt and become more opaque as they age, obscuring the grain of the wood beneath. This is the main reason for removing them. This, however, is a more complex problem than taking off French polish as there are about 200 known varnish formulae and unfortunately it is impossible to distinguish one from the other. Basically they are a solution of a resin in a solvent and it is this solvent which softens them for removal. There are basically three kinds of varnish: cellulose, alkyd and plastic. Try the following solvents in an inconspicuous spot in this order: Turpentine, denatured alcohol (methylated spirits), reliable commercial strippers, acetone (extremely volatile, so slightly dangerous, but fast acting), ammonia which darkens the wood, and caustic soda (or "lye"). Shellac is soluble in methylated spirits or strong borax and water solution. The modern "plastic" varnish is very hardwearing and widely used on furniture less than thirty years old. Chemical strippers will remove it.

● Always spread papers. Work in a well ventilated room, and wear rubber gloves and protective clothing.
● Apply the solvent with an old paint brush then rub or scrape off the old varnish with steel wool and/or a stripping knife. Again, work with the grain, not across it or in circles [10].

10

Bleaching Wood

Once bare wood is reached and all traces of the former finish are removed, the object is ready for refinishing. But if the wood still seems too dark or if there is a local stain [11], it will be necessary to use strong bleach. You can try either commercial wood bleaches, sodium-hypochlorite or crystalline oxalic acid. ALWAYS ADD CRYSTALS TO WATER in the proportions 1oz (30gms) to $\frac{1}{2}$ pint (0.3 liter). Rinse off with 1oz (30gms) borax to $\frac{1}{2}$ gallon (2 liters) of water followed by a clear rinse.

CAUTION: These bleaches are variously poisonous and much stronger than domestic bleaches. If you are bleaching the whole piece, first try the bleach on an inconspicuous place to see its effect. Spread newspapers and wear rubber gloves. Then apply the bleach with an old paint brush either to the whole piece or to the local stain. Let dry for 24 hours before proceeding to refinish.

11

Alternative: Add 1 part .880 ammonia to 5 parts water; apply with an old brush and rinse with 1 part 100 volume hydrogen peroxide mixed with two parts water. This mixture is quite a powerful bleach—it will take the redness out of mahogany leaving it very light.

Sanding Wood

Both stripping and bleaching will raise the grain of the wood slightly, necessitating a light sanding with a medium fine abrasive paper, followed by a fine grade. Remember, NEVER SAND IN CIRCLES OR ACROSS THE GRAIN. SAND ONLY WITH THE GRAIN.

Hint: For smoothing flat surfaces use a sanding block—a hand size block of cork, rubber or of wood with felt on one side; it is inexpensive and invaluable. Wrap it with the abrasive paper [12]. If the flat surface is very large, wrap a brick with a cotton cloth, then the abrasive paper; the weight and size of the brick makes a large job easier. Caution: don't round the corners of wood, but sand them lightly with fine abrasive papers. After fine sanding the piece is ready to be refinished.

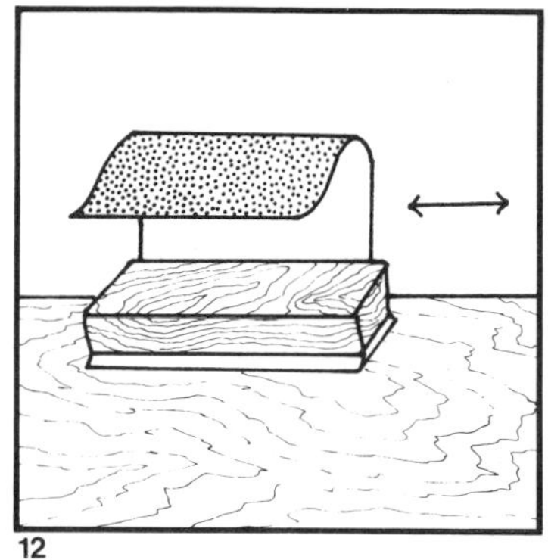
12

TYPES OF ABRASIVE PAPER

Store abrasive papers in a warm, dry place and never attempt to use them on damp wood. Snap paper on a corner to "unclog" it when working. Always use at least two grades when trying to get a really smooth finish; coarse paper, worn smooth, will not give the same effect as a finer paper. Incidentally, there is no such thing as "sandpaper" and although these papers feel gritty, sand has been replaced by more effective smoothing agents.

Below are the five types of abrasive papers used for smoothing woods.

Glass paper has grains made from crushed glass (once reputedly derived from crushed port bottles!). It is available with a base of cloth or paper and is commonly used for hand smoothing.

Garnet paper has grains made of crushed garnet stone so it costs a bit more but it is very durable and recommended for smoothing by hand.

Aluminum oxide paper is used when really heavy cutting action is desired—its synthetic grains are very tough.

Silicone carbide paper is also known as "wet-and-dry" paper because it can be used damp (not wet) for fine smoothing of paintwork or dry like other abrasive papers. When wet it leaves a black-gray gravy which has to be washed off, but when lubricated with water, it lasts a long time. It can be used on both metal and wood and is also available on a cloth base.

Flint paper is rarely used any more and although it is inexpensive, it is not recommended because its grains are softer than glass or garnet, so it has a short life.

Hints: Emery paper is available for sanding metal but it is rarely used for sanding wood. Both garnet and aluminum oxide papers come in "open coat" and "close coat"—with "open coat" there is more space between the grains, making it less likely to clog and therefore better for smoothing softwoods; while in "close coat" the grains are more closely spaced and best for hardwoods. Steel wool can also be used for smoothing wood and is recommended after smoothing with fine abrasive paper to give a perfect finish. Try to purchase 00 or 000 grade and as with abrasive papers, always work with the grain. Wear a handkerchief tied "bandit style" to protect your throat and lungs if they are normally sensitive.

CHOOSING A FINISH

Once a wood piece has been cleaned, stripped and sanded smooth (see pages 44-5), a new clear finish must be applied. The choice between finishes is really a matter of taste and life-style. (If you will have young children with grubby, sticky fingers, spilling milk on to your dining table, then obviously a French polished surface is not practical.) An everyday kitchen table should be oiled and waxed, or varnished with a clear sealer; on the other hand in a formal dining room complete with candelabra and oriental carpet, gleaming French polished wood is ideal. Young children enjoy brightly painted furniture and here durable enamels and quick-drying polyurethanes come into their own.

The piece itself should be looked at very carefully; weigh the original finish against what you feel will show it off best. Heavy Victorian pieces were almost always stained and then highly polished, but they actually look lighter and more "comfortable" stripped or painted a light clear shade, while a simple table, square and low, takes on new life and elegance with a deep stain and gleaming surface.

Filling the Pores of the Wood

Staining will raise the grain of the wood so you need to fill the grain or pores of the wood before staining, French polishing and/or varnishing to ensure an even surface, although today this is often omitted to leave the texture as natural as possible. DO NOT fill before applying a linseed oil, teak oil, beeswax polish or petroleum jelly finish. You can purchase tinted ready-made fillers or make your own from instructions below. This method will fill even the largest pores.

- Tint plaster of Paris (unless a "whitened" grain is desired) with Vandyke brown powdered pigments for use on dark oak or walnut; use red ocher for mahogany [1].
- Dip a water-dampened rag into the tinted plaster and apply it working in circles so that it fills the grain [2]. Finish off by stroking with the grain.
- Allow the filler to dry completely.
- Make sure the pores look and feel sealed; rub your hand across the surface and it should feel smooth.
- When dry smooth with fine abrasive paper, with the grain [3].

Alternative: method ideal for filling the pores before French polishing.

- Purchase pumice powder and sieve it. Dip a clean cotton pad in denatured alcohol (methylated spirits).
- Dip the wetted pad into the sifted pumice powder and coat the entire surface using a small circular motion so that you completely cover the grain in every direction [4].
- Don't push on the pad but shake it out or fold it over as necessary.

Staining Wood

Sometimes newly stripped wood looks too light or too yellow, in which case you may decide to stain it with either a natural wood color or a bright primary stain. If so, use one of the varieties below, and follow the manufacturer's instructions. All of these stains are translucent, and highlight the grain.

Water Stains: The most inexpensive are water stains. Advantages include deep penetration of wood fibers, easy mixing of different shades, brushes that can be rinsed out in water, and quick-drying wood. Disadvantages are that after mixing, straining through a fine wire mesh sieve is sometimes necessary; water often loosens glues holding veneers; and it is difficult to get even results over large surfaces (a 4″(10cm) or larger paint brush helps here). In trying to achieve a particular tone, it may be necessary to purchase a variety of stains, and experiment.

- Mix as directed, but always start with a light application—remember wood can always be made darker by applying additional coats, but lightening is very difficult.
- Stand the piece on a thick layer of old newspaper.
- Apply the stain with a clean paint brush, stroking with the grain [5].
- Tilt the object slightly and begin application at the top so that gravity assists spreading. Avoid loading the brush with too much stain—this causes blotchiness.

5

Oil Stains: Oil stains are made by grinding pigments into a drying oil and turpentine. These are available in wood shades and several bright hues.

- They are brushed onto raw wood [6], then wiped off [7] and allowed to dry for 24 hours. Sand with fine abrasive paper, wipe with white spirit or turpentine substitute, let dry, and repeat application if a darker tone is desired.
- Protect afterwards with a clear varnish.

6

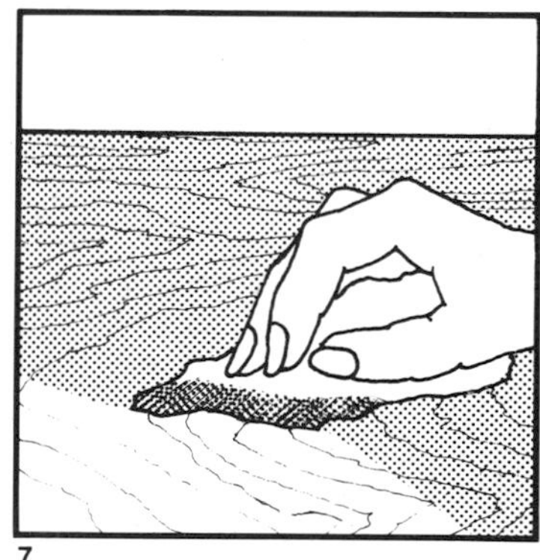
7

- Alternatively you can make your own stain by grinding 1–$2\frac{1}{2}$lbs (450–1100gms) of artists' pigment (do not use dry pigments) into 110fl oz (3.125 liters) of boiled linseed oil. Mix in 2% turpentine and 10% japan drier, and apply as above.
- A quicker-drying stain can be made by grinding 1–$2\frac{1}{2}$lbs (450–1100gms) of pigment into $\frac{1}{3}$ gallon (1.5 liters) of boiled linseed oil and then adding $\frac{2}{3}$ gallon (3 liters) of pure turpentine. The advantages of all these oil stains are that they are easy to prepare, don't raise the grain, are suitable for veneers and cheaper woods, and protect the wood. The disadvantages are that penetration is not deep, so they are worn off if not protected by a sealer, like varnish, and re-staining is difficult, as the wood is already saturated (so the first application must be even).

Note: oil stains become slightly more opaque after drying for several days.

Homemade Stains

If you can find some of these "old time" ingredients, the result will be the same as with prepared stains but less expensive.

To strain the mixtures, when advised, fit a stocking over an old kitchen wire-mesh strainer [8]. Mix only as much as you need and always add crystals to water [9] until no more dissolve, *not the reverse.* Always wear protective clothing and rubber gloves and test on an inconspicuous area first!

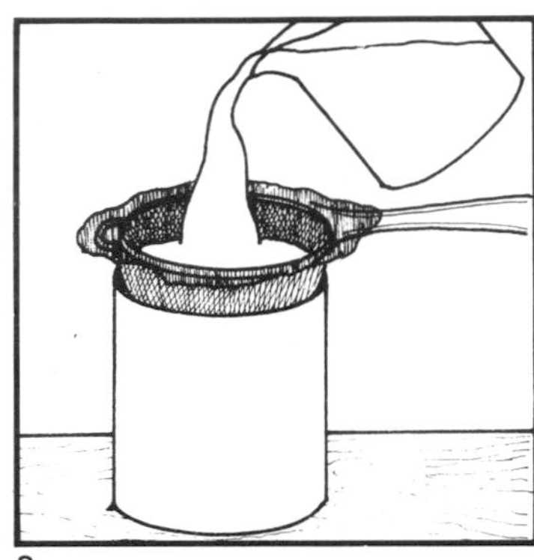

8

9

1) Vandyke crystals or walnut crystals or potassium permanganate—these give a rich brown color to oak, mahogany, or walnut, but use a weakened solution for the latter two woods.

- Dissolve crystals in warm water.
- Apply stain with an old brush; repeat if necessary.
- Add drop of .880 ammonia, which fixes the stain to the wood. Caution: its fumes and touch are noxious.
- Keep stain tightly sealed after addition of ammonia.

2) Green copperas, sometimes called sulphate of iron—imparts a blue-gray tone to oak, will dull the redness in mahogany and, when applied to sycamore, produces a gray tone, becoming what is known then as "harewood". Note: this is *poisonous.*

- Dissolve crystals in warm water, which becomes a muddy green.
- Apply evenly with an old brush.
- The effect begins to show as the wood dries.

3) Aniline dyes are powdered colors most easily applied when mixed with water, but they are also soluble in turpentine or oil. They are *poisonous.*

- For reddish-brown mix Vandyke brown with Bismarck brown.
- For dark brown mix Vandyke brown with black.
- Mix each powder in warm water separately first.
- Add $\frac{1}{2}$ tablespoon of glue and a drop of vinegar to each.
- Mix as desired, remembering the more water added, the lighter the stain.

4) Ammonia-.880 mixed with water will slightly darken oak and mahogany. Avoid inhaling the fumes and don't let the liquid touch bare skin. Work outdoors if possible. After an hour or so it loses its strength when exposed to air.

5) Bichromate of potash, commonly used to darken mahogany; on oak it imparts a greenish-brown tone.

- Dissolve the deep orange crystals in water until the water will take no more.
- Dilute if necessary after testing on an inconspicuous place and let dry.
- Remember, although the mixture itself is a deep orange, the final results depend on the type of wood: some woods are not affected.
- Apply with a brush in daylight.

6) American potash, sometimes called crude caustic potash, dissolved in water until the water will take no more, will "weather" oak, turning it deep brown, and causing the grains to blacken.

PROTECTIVE CLEAR FINISHES

On a piece of furniture which has been filled and stained, or one which has been stripped down to the bare wood, it is advisable to apply a protective finish. If the wood is left raw it will collect dust, stain easily and look grimy in a short time. If you prefer the natural look and feel of raw wood, one of the natural finishes described below is advisable.

Linseed Oil

The easiest and one of the oldest finishes is linseed oil, which hardens and darkens even the softer woods when exposed to air. It is particularly suitable for old oak furniture, but do not use it on Cuban mahogany, rosewood, ebony or other close-grained woods. It is sometimes mixed half and half with pure turpentine when applying to light woods; but it will even darken these slightly.

- First slowly warm the boiled linseed oil in a china cup placed in a pan of hot water until hot to the touch [10].
- Then apply it with a clean cotton pad or a clean 2″ (5cm) paint brush. Rub with the grain [11].
- Keep applying the warm oil until the wood rejects it—you will notice the excess staying on the surface.

10

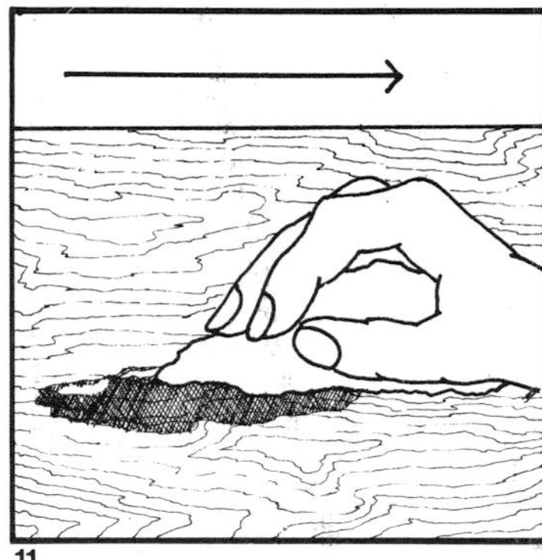

11

- Let it stand for a few hours, wipe off the excess, and leave the piece until it is completely dry; repeat if necessary. Drying will take several days, even in a warm room—the main disadvantage of the process.
- Finally, rub hard with a soft cotton cloth and then apply a furniture wax (optional), for a lasting shine. After application, keep the piece well dusted.

Alternatives: Petroleum jelly can be rubbed into teak and rosewood. Remove the excess 24 hours later, and buff with a soft cloth.

Teak oil can be applied to most woods as well as teak; some people prefer it because it dries quicker and is more resilient than linseed oil. Apply with a soft cloth or 2″ (5cm) brush. Wipe off the excess after half an hour, and apply a second coat. Rub down 36 hours later, or when dry, with very fine steel wool lubricated with a furniture wax. Buff with soft cloth. A new product called "Danish oil" can be used in the same way.

Beeswax

Another natural, clear finish is the classical beeswax and turpentine polish beloved by dealers and collectors. It is quicker to use than oil, once you have made the mixture. The beeswax penetrates the outer layer of the wood, while the solvent turpentine is partially evaporated. This can be applied directly to all bare woods except the naturally oily teak and ebony. It can also be used afterwards as a basic furniture polish and is particularly favored for treating mahogany. Over a longer period of time, polishing with beeswax produces the best "patina"—a beautiful low gloss finish, warm to the touch. Take the time to make this as directed below and you and your furniture will be happy. You can sometimes find this already made in furniture stores but NEVER apply any silicone based polish to wood—it will eventually cause "bloom" or a film to appear.

Classic beeswax polish gives a soft matt sheen but is slightly tacky and also attracts dust. The addition of even a small amount of carnauba wax or powdered resin (1:4) will give a higher gloss and make the beeswax harder and less tacky.

- Use 4oz (100gm) beeswax (either bleached for lighter woods or unbleached for darker woods) to ½ pint (250ml) pure turpentine.
- Grate the beeswax into flakes, using a flat cheese-grater [12].

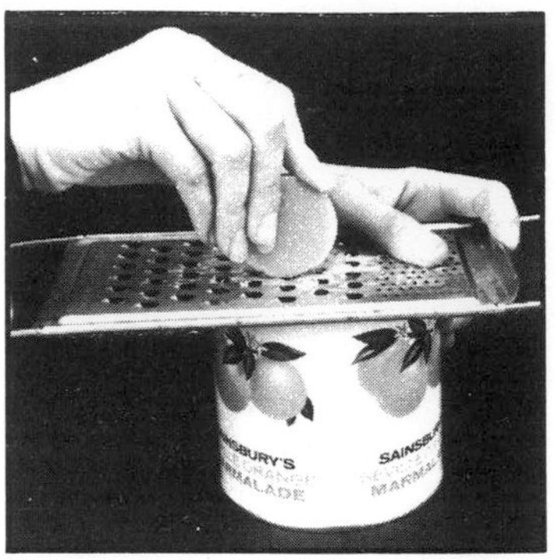

12

- Put the flakes into a bowl or clean tin can and cover with pure spirits of turpentine. DO NOT use turpentine substitute.
- Place the container in a larger outer vessel and pour boiling water into the outer vessel—being careful not to get any water into the beeswax and turpentine.

CAUTION: KEEP TURPENTINE AWAY FROM HEAT SOURCE.

- The flakes will dissolve into the turpentine, encouraged by the surrounding heat. You can stir with a wooden spatula. If the flakes do not dissolve completely, simply renew the boiling water in the outer vessel [13].
- Pour the pale golden liquid into a clean jar or can, but do not put on the lid for 24 hours.
- Apply a thin coat of polish to any clean dry surface of metal or wood and buff with a soft cloth.

13

- Repeat as often as desired, remembering that several thin layers are more effective than the occasional thick one.

Alternative: Brown polish can be produced by adding burnt or raw umber dry pigment to the liquid before it sets. This will obviously gradually darken any surface it is applied to. The addition of lamp black powder to the basic mixture will produce a black polish.

These polishes are not only suited for wooden furniture, but also for wood block floors and old-fashioned linoleum. They are not for modern vinyl tile floors or furniture with synthetic finishes.

Painted-on Clear Finishes—Mat and Gloss

To give a more modern protective coat to raw or stained wood, use one of the many kinds of varnish. Applying several coats gives a French polished "look" but the effect is not really the same. Nevertheless, on furniture or surfaces that will be well-used, a varnish is easier to apply and look after than either oil finishes or French polishing. Each has its virtues. When applying varnish observe the following hints:

- Work in a clean room, 70°F (20°C) ideal temperature, with a *clean* brush.
- Strive for ventilation without drafts—fresh air helps the oxidation of drying oils. That means keeping the door of the room open if you can bear the smell spreading through the house.
- Wear synthetic materials and dampen newspapers under the piece to keep the dust down.

self by dissolving 8oz (225gm) of shellac, ¼oz (7gm) benzoin and ½oz (15gm) sandarac to 2 pints (1 liter) of high quality methylated spirits or denatured alcohol. French polish manufacturers use industrial methylated spirits—try to purchase "methylated finish" or methylated spirit white lac, in which case you leave out the sandarac.

- Mix it in a large tinted glass jar and let dissolve.
- Shake the polish well before using each time.
- Apply it in elongated figure eight movements, working with a very light pressure [22]. Examine your polishing occasionally to make sure that the work is even, turning the outer cover of the pad occasionally. You should notice that every stroke of the pad leaves a thin film of polish. Don't polish continuously and give the drying-out process a chance. After a while you will see that the polish is taking visible effect.

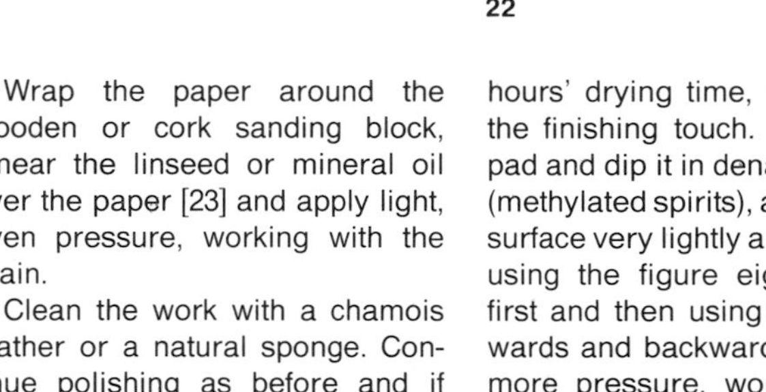
22

- If sticking occurs, lubricate with a drop or two of boiled linseed oil. After a few layers, little flaws may appear, caused by the uneven distribution of the polish. These can be smoothed out by buffing, a combination of sanding and polishing, using abrasive paper or wet-and-dry paper. Buy the finest grade available and lubricate it again with linseed oil or white mineral oil, instead of water.
- Wrap the paper around the wooden or cork sanding block, smear the linseed or mineral oil over the paper [23] and apply light, even pressure, working with the grain.
- Clean the work with a chamois leather or a natural sponge. Continue polishing as before and if necessary buff again: a high gloss finish will develop. When this seems even and thick, it's nearly completed.
- After allowing the final coat 24 hours' drying time, you can apply the finishing touch. Make a clean pad and dip it in denatured alcohol, (methylated spirits), and go over the surface very lightly and very quickly using the figure eight movement first and then using a straight forwards and backwards motion, and more pressure, working with the grain [24]. This should impart a perfect gloss to the piece.
- A French polish reviver can be made from the following ingredients shaken together in a glass jar. It is used as a furniture polish as often as necessary. You can also use most commercially available furniture polishes.

1 part linseed oil
1 part white vinegar
1 part denatured alcohol (methylated spirits)
or
4 parts linseed oil
1 part terebine (a drying medium)
12 parts white vinegar

23

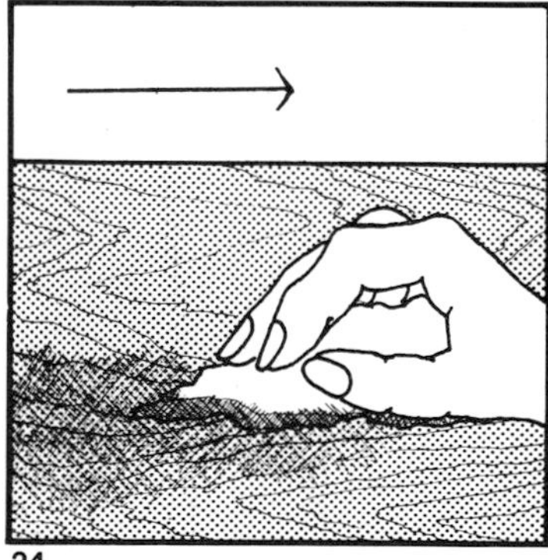
24

OPAQUE FINISHES

Sometimes after stripping a piece and exposing bare wood, badly grained or blotched wood will appear and you will *have* to apply an opaque paint. These are basically of two kinds, the older and tougher enamels and the new, durable, polyurethane or plastic paints which are easier to apply. Both are suitable for furniture, in kitchens and children's rooms, which will have to put up with hard treatment.

If you want contrasting tones on a single project, it will be cheaper to purchase enamels as these are usually available in small cans. On the other hand, if you are painting a large piece in a single shade, don't be afraid to buy a large can, because if it is kept tightly closed, the paint will keep for years. Note: If you are repainting an already painted piece without stripping, begin after the priming stage. The earlier steps are for treating bare wood.

● Spread newspapers, put on old clothes, assemble brushes, rags, a clean jar, turpentine substitute, and fine and medium grade abrasive paper.
● Clean the brushes first with turpentine substitute (or white spirit) and when no traces of paint seem to remain, wash with warm (not hot) water and soap.
● When painting mirrors and frames, always remove the glass or canvas first. Upholstered chairs should have top cover removed, and lift out drop-in seats. Alternatively cover the fabric or leather with plastic bags taped securely into place. Take off any glass or other tops, on tables, unless they are to be painted as well.
● When painting a chest of drawers, remove hardware (fittings) and drawers, and paint them top up; prop bottom of chest off floor with slats of wood [25], painting top, then front and sides, starting at the top.

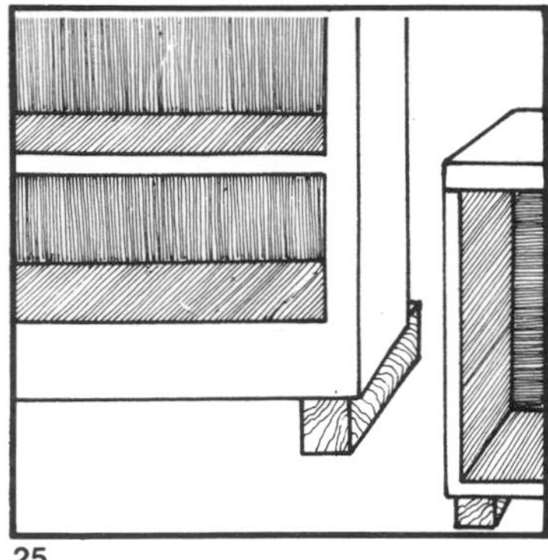
25

● First sand the piece thoroughly with medium, then fine abrasive paper, dust, and wipe with turpentine substitute, let dry.
● Prime the piece with a manufactured oil-based primer. You can use a slightly thinned water-based paint, often called emulsion. Always prime with a paint the same shade or lighter than the final one [26].
● Let the primer dry completely.
● Sand lightly, with the grain, using a fine abrasive paper [27]; dust, then rub down with turpentine substitute.

26

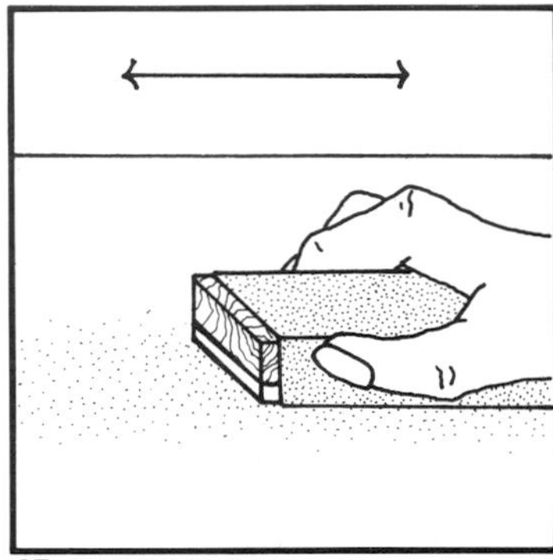
27

● Stir the undercoat and thin if necessary with the recommended solvent until it is the consistency of cream.
● Apply undercoat with a clean brush, stroking first one way and then the next to blend in the brushstrokes.
● When dry sand lightly with very fine abrasive paper, dust and wipe with turpentine substitute [28].
● Apply first coat of enamel or polyurethane-based opaque paint.
● Sand as before with very fine abrasive paper, dust, wipe with turpentine substitute and apply final coat.

For chairs:
● Prop up off the newspapers with slats of wood under the legs.
● Do the underside of the seat first, and top of chair legs, rotating the chair as necessary by holding on to the back.
● Paint the bottom of the legs.
● Do the back of the chair, both sides.
● Do the seat last.

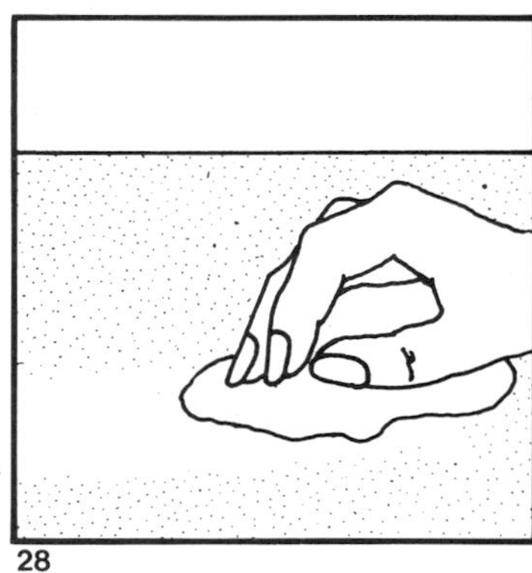
28

Spray Paints

Aerosol spray paints are ideal for objects with awkward shapes or intricate parts difficult to get at. When applied properly they give a very professional effect, and are perfect for spraying wicker furniture. The only disadvantage is that they are more expensive because the spray wastes a certain amount. To start, spread old newspapers everywhere, put on protective clothing and tie a handkerchief over your nose and mouth, as the fumes can be irritating. Shake the can and hold it 6-8″ (20cm) away from the piece, press the nozzle and apply an even film in short bursts. The first coat won't cover, but let it dry and apply another for complete coverage. if the paint runs, you are spraying too long in one place.

Painting Hints

- Work in a clean room, with a clean brush.
- Wear synthetic fabrics, and dampen the newspapers with water to keep down dust.
- Clean new brushes in turpentine substitute before use.
- Brush first one way and then the other to blend and smooth the application.
- Use large brushes for large areas, small brushes for smaller areas.
- Shake or stir the can before using to ensure that the paint is mixed.
- Strive for ventilation without drafts—fresh air helps drying so keep the door of the room open if possible, though unfortunately the smell will spread through the house.
- Keep children and pets AWAY from wet paint. You can put up a net to let air in and keep out pets and children.

General Problems with Clear and Opaque Painted Finishes

1. Bleeding: if the stain, filler or primer spreads into the succeeding coat. This is usually encountered when using older stains and primers. If it really looks awful, there is no choice but to remove it (see p.40-5) and start again. Purchase a recommended non-bleeding paint.
2. Blistering: caused by exposure to excessive heat from the sun or a radiator while the paint is drying. Sometimes this happens when you are sealing "green" or young wood. Remove the finish and apply a coat of shellac or white polish before the varnish or opaque paint.
3. Blooming: bluish or whitish film which appears on the dried surface of varnish or enamel. There are many causes of this. To remove it rub with liquid soap and a fine abrasive, like pumice powder or rottenstone, rinse with clean water and dry with a chamois.
4. Blushing: a whitish film which starts to appear when lacquer or shellac is drying in too humid an atmosphere, or when the coat underneath was not allowed to dry completely. Raise the temperature of the room to 70 F (21 C) and immediately apply a coat of thinner with a little shellac in it. If this fails, flood the entire surface with the recommended solvent to remove *all traces* of the shellac or lacquer and start again.
5. Bubbling: occurs when applying varnish which is too heavy or not brushed in, or when the can has been agitated causing air bubbles. Sand with the grain using very fine abrasive paper to remove the bumps and apply another coat; otherwise strip off the bubbled coat completely.
6. Checking, crazing or hard-lining: irregular lines on the surface of paint. When dry, sand well and rinse with turpentine substitute. Let it dry and apply next coat.
7. Chipping: occurs when top coat cannot adhere to a smooth underneath coat. Rough up the surface with medium-grade abrasive paper, wipe with turpentine substitute and apply another coat. Enamel paints especially need a rough surface or "tooth" to hold the first coat.
8. Crawling: paints seem to shrink or avoid a certain area because that surface is greasy, wet or waxy. Rinse area with turpentine substitute, let dry and resume painting.
9. Wrinkling: when too much varnish has been applied and piles up on itself. Sand the area very well with fine abrasive paper and apply another thinned coat.

VENEERS

Veneering is the art of fixing thin sheets of rare and decorative woods to a base wood called the carcase. Usually the base wood is cheaper, a softwood or even a laminated board, which has the advantage of not warping or cracking, but occasionally a solid oak chest, for example, may have a veneered top. Marquetry and parquetry are decorative veneer techniques. Marquetry (from *marqueter,* French for "to variegate") usually employs pictorial or floral motifs [1], while parquetry is distinguished by purely geometric patterns [2]. Both are usually inlaid into a larger surrounding veneer. Early examples of veneer have been found in Tutankhamen's tomb, but it was not until the 16th century in England, Italy and France that it came into its own; during Louis XIII's reign, ebony veneers were used on cabinets.

1

2

By the 18th century, European trading companies were traversing the globe and bringing back new species of timber, used as ballast. Spanish mahogany (actually from the West Indies) caught the eye of many cabinet-makers, who were keen to work with this new red satiny wood. Charles Cressent and Andre Boulle were among these experimenters; both used mahogany with great success. Boulle (1642-1732) refined the technique of marquetry, as well as inlaying semi-precious materials such as brass, pewter, ivory, ebony, tortoiseshell and mother-of-pearl, and his name has become synonymous with richly ornamented furniture distinguished by double inlays of tortoiseshell and brass. It was the heyday of inlaid cabinet-making and these craftsmen used such exotic woods as bird's-eye maple, pearwood, Brazilian rosewood, boxwood, ebony, zebrawood, purpleheart and palado.

During the early 19th century veneering took on a different style. The classical, light furniture of Sheraton, Hepplewhite and the French Empire craftsmen was usually of a finely-figured light wood, particularly satin wood, veneered over the entire carcase. Inlaid simple border lines of box wood or ebony followed the edge, decoration was mostly of simple natural flower and ribbon designs, either as marquetry for the expensive pieces or painted for the cheaper versions. From about 1840 onwards, Victorian furniture relied less and less on veneer as a decoration, and returned to solid wood construction—heavy and durable. Dark woods were the fashion again, and veneer was used in sheets to cover whole tables, often built of the same wood, but from pieces without the lovely grain and feathering found on the best veneers. Slowly imperfections like slightly uneven motifs and tiny chisel marks disappeared. Today veneers are used on 90% of all manufactured furniture, and can be machined to an incredible thinness of $\frac{1}{24}$″ (1mm). During the 18th century, it was not possible with handwork to reduce the sheets of wood to much less than $\frac{1}{6}$″ (4mm) thick.

When restoring furniture, the first thing to determine is whether a piece is "solid" wood or veneered. Look for the edges that are hidden against the wall, underneath or inside—the veneer won't be used all over, and it will be easy to see the difference between the veneer and the base wood. Also, the run of the grain on a veneered surface will often run in different directions. Obviously you must make sure that the piece is really wood—there are some fairly successful plastic imitations around. On the other hand, if the piece is valuable, take it to an expert restorer—fine veneering is a real art.

Blisters and Swelling

Often veneers are glued on with a water-soluble and antiquated animal glue. Insufficient gluing or damp sometimes causes small blisters to develop. If so, first try using a cork pad and rubbing back and forth vigorously. Sometimes the friction heat will level the blister and the chief advantage is that the finish is less likely to be harmed. If that fails the following process should work.

- Place a piece of cardboard over the swollen area and move a hot iron with great pressure slowly back and forth over the cardboard, until the glue under the swelling has softened [3].
- A heavy object left on the cardboard for 24 hours should restick the veneer [4].

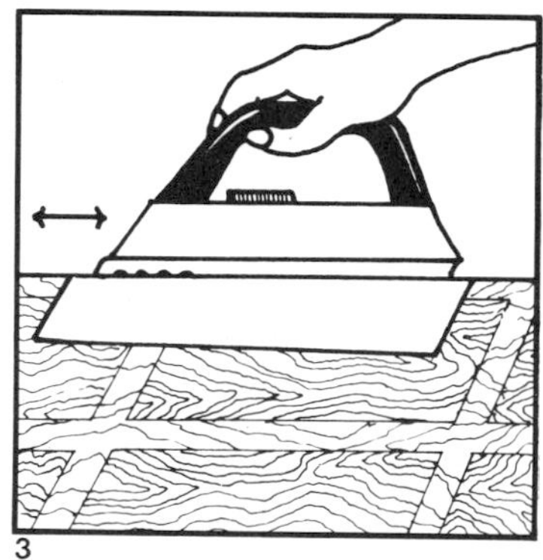
3

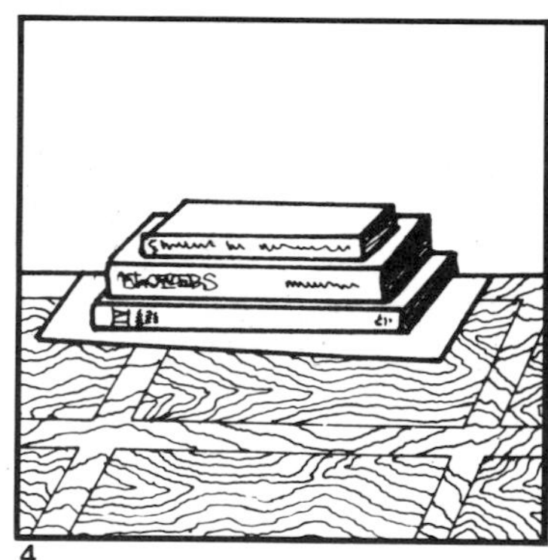
4

Larger or Persistent Bumps

If the above method doesn't work, a bit more glue may need to be applied, underneath the veneer:

- Slit the blister in the middle and along the grain, with a single-edged razor or a knife with replaceable blades [5]. If the carcase wood under the blister is gritty or dirty, try to brush out the dirt.
- Press down on one side of the slit blister: this should open up the other side so that a dab of wood glue (cellulose-based) can be inserted either with the container's nozzle [6], or a pinhead dipped in glue, depending on the size of the slit.

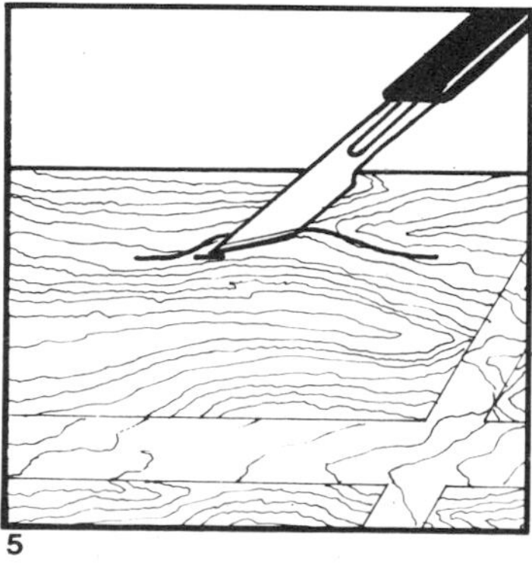
5

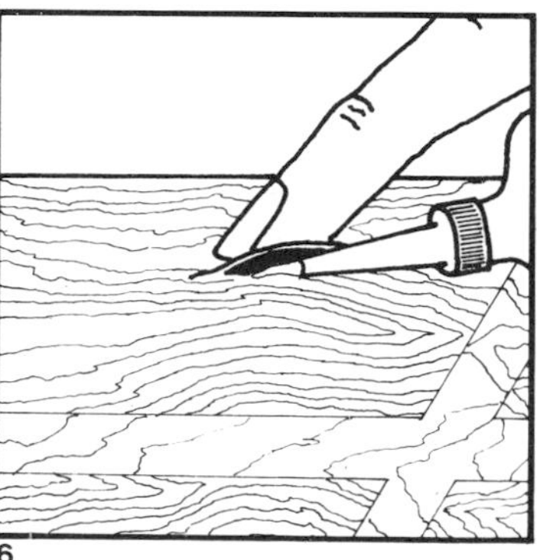
6

● Treat the other side of the blister in the same way.
● Squeeze out excess from both sides and wipe away with a slightly damp, clean rag.
● Put a piece of tissue paper over the glued area if weighting with books, or, if using clamps, use tissue and cardboard first.
● Alternatively, if using a vinyl glue, use the household iron method, but after working the glue in and squeezing out the excess lay tissue paper over the area and iron with a warm iron, applying pressure for as long as necessary. Then switch off the iron and leave it to cool in place. The glue will adhere as the iron cools.

Missing Pieces

If a piece or two of marquetry or parquetry is missing, the solution is easier than if a loose corner or area of the surrounding veneer is missing. Exact matching is critical when re-laying large areas of plain veneered surfaces, slightly less so when replacing parquetry or marquetry. A regular shape is easier to reproduce than an irregular missing area which is virtually impossible to match. If you have a jagged edge, which often happens on drawer corners, trim to give it a regular edge [7]. Try to work out what kind of wood(s) were used and then enquire among the suppliers in your area.

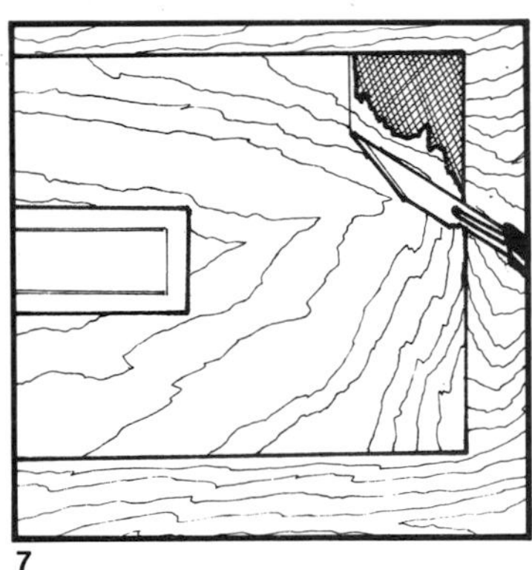
7

● Trace the area to be replaced with a sharp pencil and tracing paper. Tape the paper in place with masking tape if necessary [8].
● Rub the back of the paper with soft pencil lead until it appears dark gray.
● Place the paper, with the traced outline uppermost, on new veneer wood and go over the shape with the pencil again, thus transferring the outline to the wood [9].

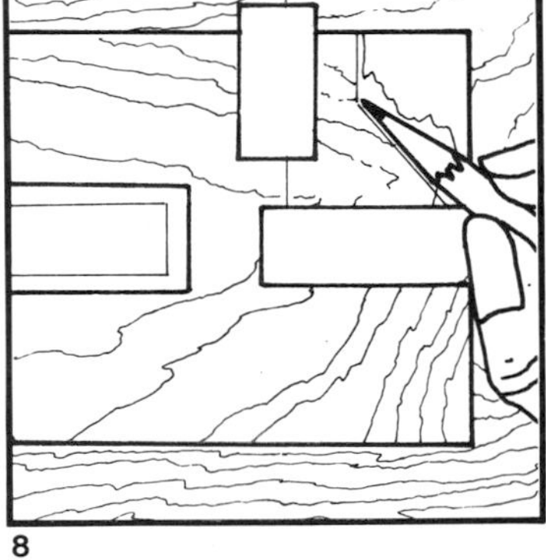
8

9

● CAREFULLY cut around the shape with a single-edged razor, or a knife with replaceable blades, and a steel rule [10].
● Glue the shape carefully into place with wood glue (cellulose-based) or general-purpose glue. If the other shapes have dark lines around them, use a dark felt marker to outline the new shape.
● Be sure the grain on the new pieces is going the same direction as the old piece or matching area.

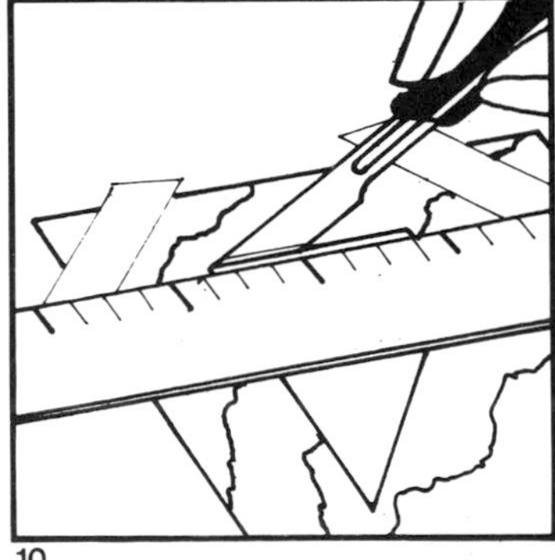
10

If a piece of parquetry or marquetry is completely missing, look at the design to see if a similar part of the motif is still intact to determine whether the missing piece was dark, light, plain or figured etc.

Removing Veneers

● To take off a small area or a single piece of veneer, use a knife with replaceable blades and steel rule to score around the area. Press lightly on the knife at first, then apply more pressure until you encounter the carcase wood.

● For larger areas or stubborn veneer removal, score around the area first, then lift an edge with the knife [11].

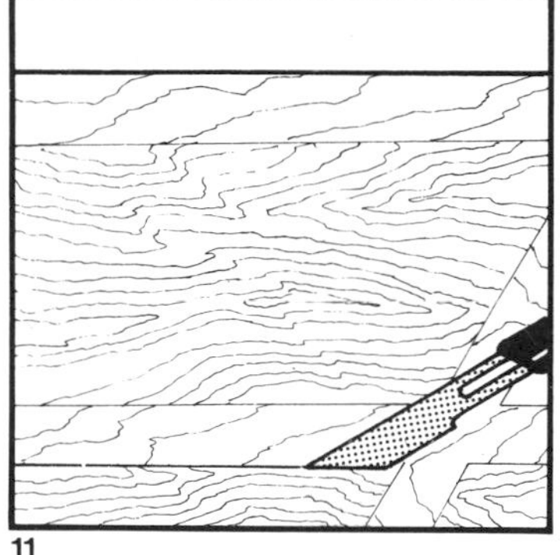
11

● Cut around the area and lift the piece off gently. Work a firmer chisel under the piece [12] and tap the chisel gently with a hammer. This should lift the veneer for removal.

● Clean off old glue (probably animal) with warm water and small sponge or cotton swab [13], but don't let any moisture get under the remaining veneers.

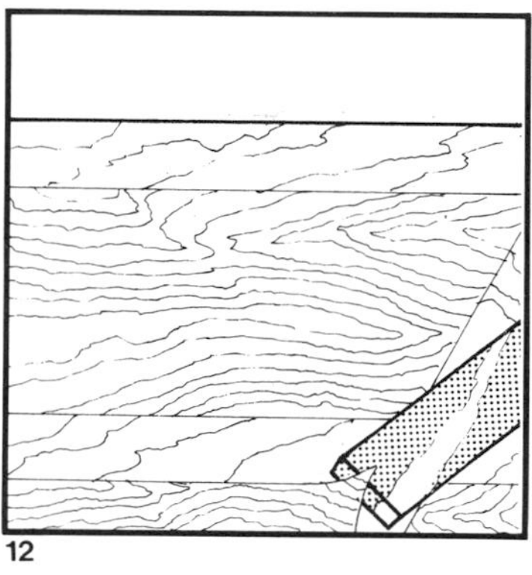
12

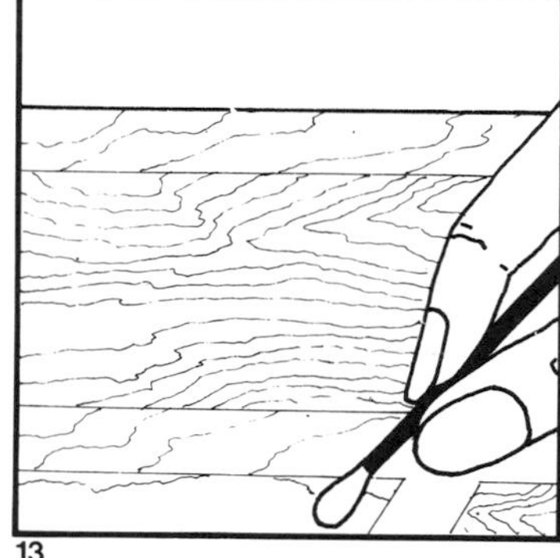
13

● If removing a section with marquetry or parquetry, try to remove these intact, or they will need to be re-cut. Modern veneers are very thin, so if the new piece of veneer lies lower than the surrounding veneers, cut a piece of tissue paper slightly smaller than the new piece, and glue in place. Let it dry, then glue in the new piece [14]. (If there is a large difference, use two pieces of veneer or balsa wood underneath).

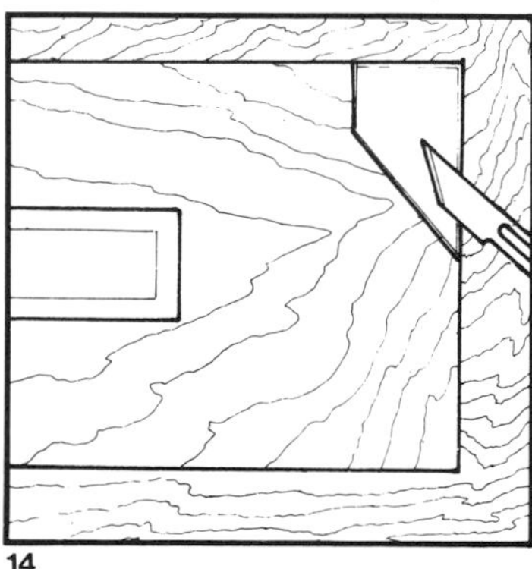
14

● If a new piece is too thick, before you glue it in place, sand underneath it until the surface is flush with the surrounding area. To determine how much needs to be removed, attach the veneer temporarily to the object by means of a ring of Scotch tape [15].

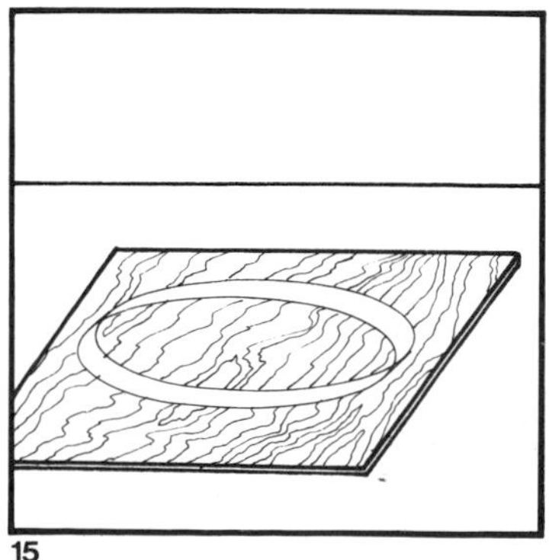
15

● Measure the amount to be removed, and sand with fine abrasive paper wrapped around a sanding block; of course sanding with the grain [16].

● If the piece is too small to smooth with a sanding block, cut a small, e.g. $1\frac{1}{2}'' \times 1\frac{1}{2}'' \times 1\frac{1}{2}''$ (40mm × 40mm × 40mm) cube of wood and wrap the abrasive paper around this miniature sanding block.

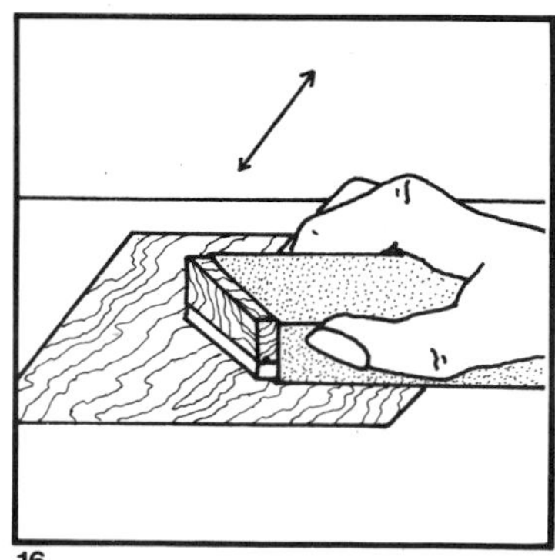
16

Repairing Dents

If the carcase wood seems intact but a veneered surface is dented, try the following remedy:

- Soak in water a piece of cotton fabric, such as a man's handkerchief, wring and place it over the dented area.
- Apply a really hot iron to the cotton so that a lot of steam is produced [17].

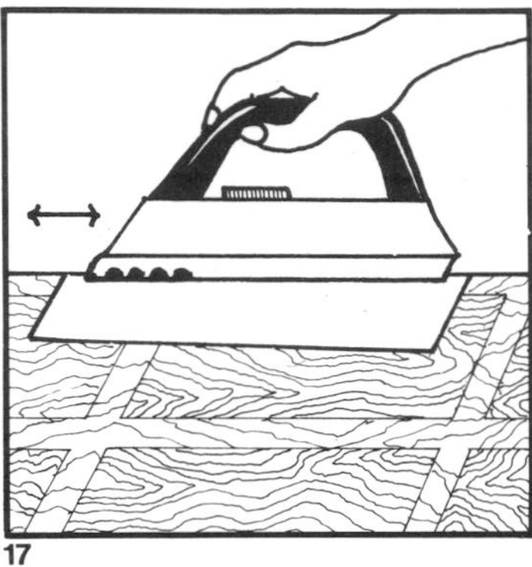

17

- Remove iron after a few seconds, look under the cotton and see if the dent is gone (the steam should swell the fibers of the wood, removing the dent). If you keep the iron on too long the steam may affect the French polish finish or the glue underneath. If the finish is affected, see page 52.

If this fails, the carcase wood under the dent has probably also been dented. If so, try the following method:

- Lift the veneer by slitting it above the dent and with the grain [18].
- Fold the veneer back carefully (if any pieces or fragments break off, save them).
- When the soft carcase wood is exposed, fill the dent with a wood filler (see page 32 for recipes), using a palette knife for small areas [19].

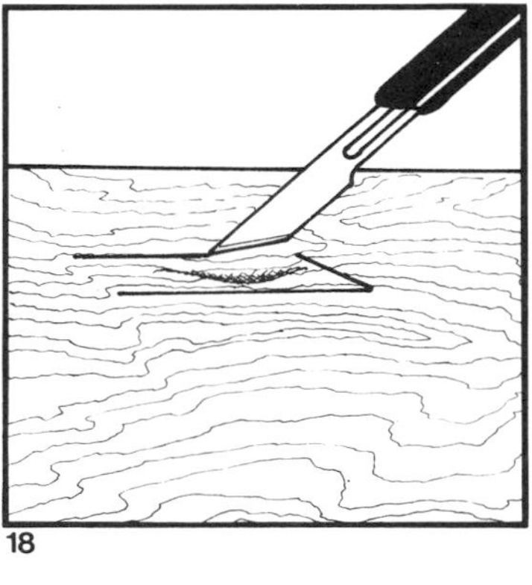

18

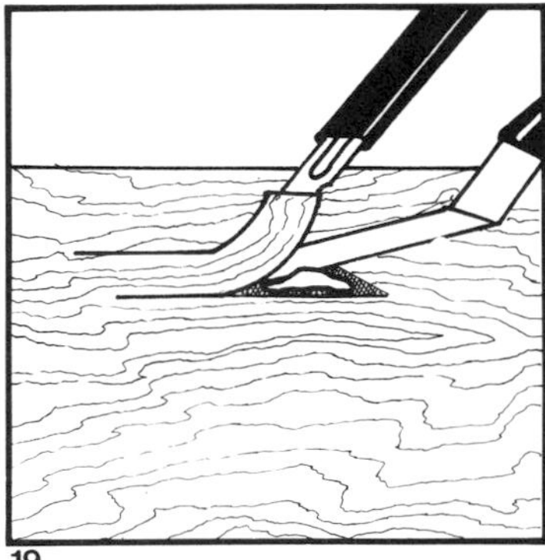

19

- Then let it dry thoroughly.
- The filler will shrink slightly as it dries, so leave a slight excess.
- Glue the veneer back onto the carcase with wood glue, and place a weight over the area (use cardboard with any clamp to protect the veneer) [20].

Repairing the Carcase

If the carcase wood is split, the veneer covering the split will have to be removed, so that the carcase can be looked at and filled [21].

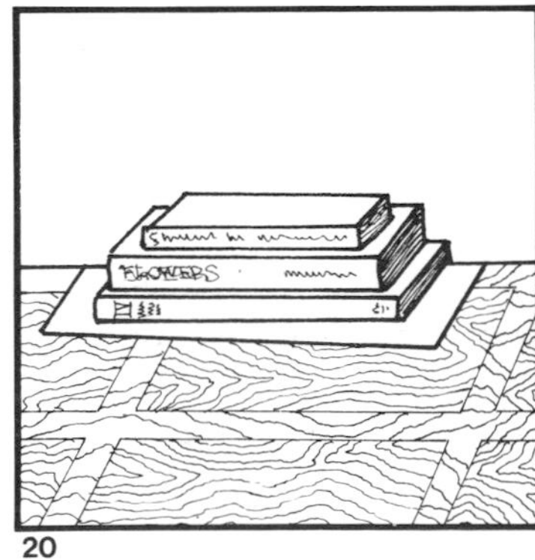

20

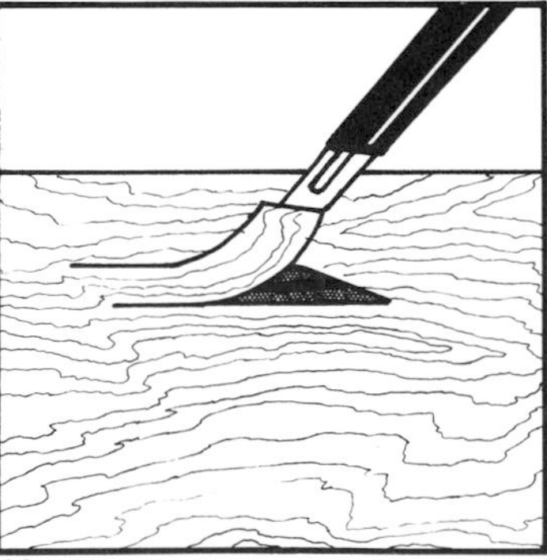

21

Before re-gluing the veneer, it must be thoroughly dry and clean. Clamp large areas of reglued veneers under a sheet of plywood, trying to force out excess glue beginning at the center.
For replacing a veneer on a convex or concave base use a contact cement (2-part glue). The adhesion will be instant and difficult to change so lay the new piece on slowly. For larger areas, apply a cellulose-based wood glue and then wrap wet ropes closely around and around the glued piece (these tighten upon drying and hold the new piece in place [22]).

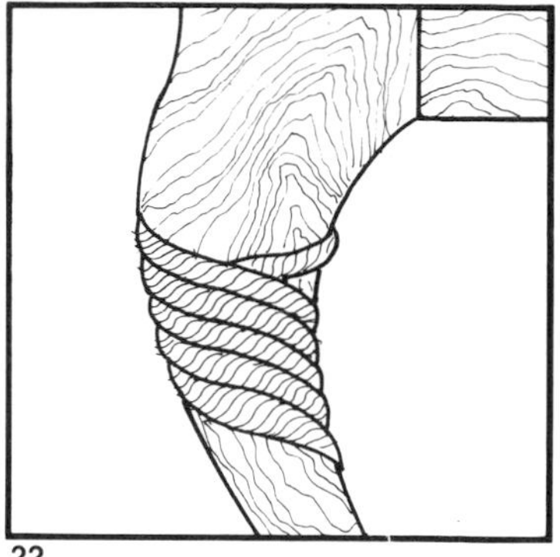
22

Crazing

Quite often the whole surface of older furniture will be covered with a network of tiny cracks, called crazing. If a "crazed" piece needs replacing, you can duplicate the effect by one of the following procedures:

● Wet the new piece of veneer by weighting it under water for 15-30 minutes, or until it seems saturated [23].

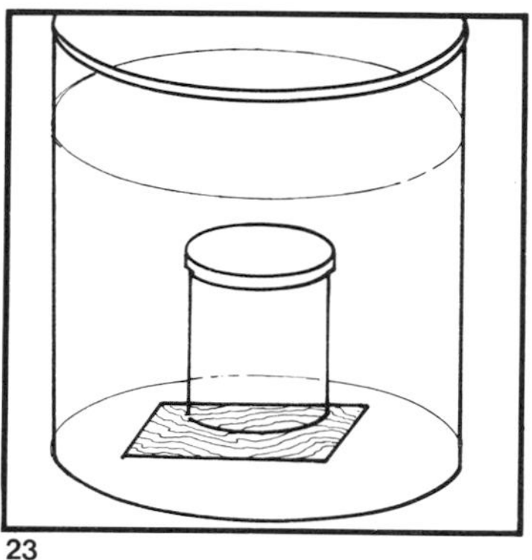
23

● Iron it with a very hot iron—this will singe it and produce tiny cracks [24].
Cut the shape with a mat knife or scalpel and glue into place.

24

Alternative: Wet the veneer, then hold it in tweezers and drop into hot sand; use clean sand heated in an old pan over low heat. Leave the piece in the sand until it "crazes". N.B. Pollard, oak, burr, walnut and bird's-eye maple require previous dampening and placing between two flat boards which are then heavily weighted down.

Hints: When refinishing veneered surfaces you must be very careful. Oil-based varnishes are unsuitable because oil and turpentine can soften the glue, so it is advisable to use quick-drying, volatile spirit polish—French polish is perfect (see p. 52 for instructions).

If the damage is slight, touch up with several coats of thinned varnish or French polish, but if the entire surface needs refinishing, see p. 52.

BAMBOO AND SIMILAR MATERIALS

Twenty years ago we were tossing out household articles made from these natural materials, today they are collectable. In fact, the last time a vogue occurred for articles made of these materials was just before the turn of the last century, when all things oriental were extremely fashionable, just as they are now—clothes, fine art, furniture and interior design were all influenced. This revival could in part be credited to Commodore Perry who opened up trade with Japan in 1853. The first oriental art boutique, Porte Chinoiserie, opened in Paris in 1862 and soon became the gathering place for artists and connoisseurs such as Bracqemond, Degas, Monet and Baudelaire. This second wave of interest reached its peak about 1880 and then declined, although Japanese prints remained a highly important influence in the art world.

At the same time, the graceful curves of bentwood furniture were popular—the Austrian, Michael Thonet (1796-1871) was the best-known exponent of this medium—as they blended well with the delicacy of ''Japonaiserie''. ''Japonaiserie'' is a misnomer because bamboo furniture was never made in Japan, although the components—lacquer panels, rolls of matting and bamboo poles—were.

By the middle of the 19th century, rooms were palm-filled, incense burned, conservatories blossomed, parrots fluttered, silks rustled, and the Victorian era was in full swing. In 1870 there were 150 producers of ''Japonaiserie'' in England alone, manufacturing an incredible 5,000 objects a week—a range that included everything from penholders to entire bedroom suites. Most of the secondhand bamboo, lacquer and cane pieces you can find today were produced during a period lasting from 1840 to 1930, but many of the bargains you may come across will need repairing.

Basketmaking is a much older craft. Nine thousand years ago early civilizations used cane, rush and willow not only for baskets but also for walls, doors, roofs and boats and scaffolding. Although the craft is more ancient than the weaving of cloth, it has never been perfectly mechanized. Rush and willow were used by more northern communities but cane is native to the Malay Peninsula where it grows wild as a thorny creeper 200-600 feet (60-80 meters) long and 1″-1½″ (2-3.75cm) in diameter. There are over 300 species of this creeper-producing rattan or cane palm. When the thorny bark is removed during harvesting, underneath lies a hard, shiny bark which is cut into lengths and split.

Cane seats were popularized by their use with bentwood, although their use in seating dates from earlier times. Tutankhamen's daybed was caned, but the art reached a height in France during the 18th century, while in England, Adam and Heppelwhite both used it extensively.

These beautiful natural materials require little care and incredibly life on earth for over half the human race depends on the cultivation of one or more of these grasses.

FURNITURE

BAMBOO: Repairing and Finishing

Bamboo objects are often found painted with oriental motifs; to restore this lacquer base and handpainted detail see p. 77-89. But first it is advisable to repair the bamboo.

● If a bamboo piece is actually missing you should be able to purchase the correct diameter of pole from a hardware store or crafts supplier. Failing that, try to match it with a cheap fishing pole, slitting it with a sharp knife if necessary.

● Use a wood glue to secure missing or loose bits and a panel or veneer pin if necessary for reinforcement [1]. To prevent the bamboo splitting, moisten the pin slightly.

1

● Bamboo objects are often slightly rickety and it may be necessary to even out the legs at the bottom, as described on pages 34-5.

● Instead of lacquer, manufacturers often used grass matting for surface tops, as a short cut, and this is often damaged or painted over. Carefully lift off the bamboo slits holding it in place, and slowly ease off the matting with the help of a paint scraper [2].

2

● If stubborn pieces remain, soften the glue in warm water.

● If it is in perfect condition and just painted over, apply paint remover and scrub gently with a wire brush to remove the layers of paint; rinse with turpentine substitute and apply two coats of spar or marine varnish or other clear varnish. Wear goggles to protect your eyes when using the highly caustic paint remover, and protective gloves for your hands.

● If the matting is only slightly damaged but stained, brush on wood bleach as many times as necessary to remove the stains [3] and when dry, apply two coats of clear gloss varnish.

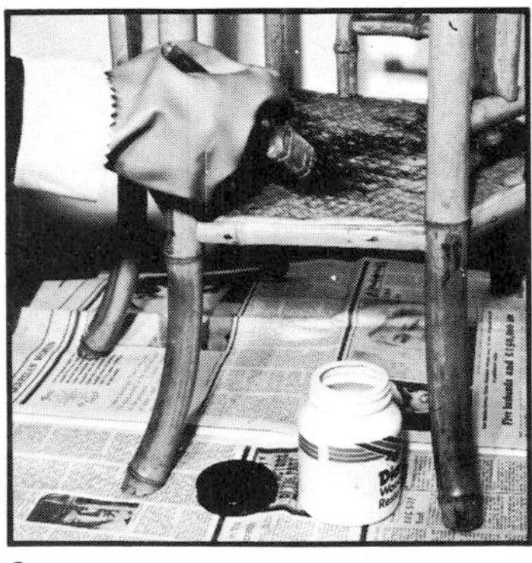

3

● Cut a new top from purchased matting $\frac{1}{32}''$-$\frac{1}{8}''$ (0.75-3mm) thick; small pieces may be cut from place mats of raffia. Glue in place with a clear-drying fabric glue or water-soluble white glue, applying it rather thickly to the surface top and not the matting. Alternatively, cut a new table top from the thicker and stiffer mattings available (using a paper pattern as a guide) [4] and cover it with $\frac{1}{8}''$-$\frac{1}{4}''$ (3-6mm) glass, cut to size (get the edges buffed as well). This will protect and keep the new top in place.

● If the original matting is simply grimy, brush it with warm soapy water but be sure to rinse well because soap is not really good for natural grasses, and then apply two coats of clear gloss varnish [5].

● If the bamboo is intact, inspect its varnished finish. If this is damaged remove the remnants with methylated spirits and fine steel wool—*keep both away from any lacquer work,* working over newspapers and absorbing the gravy-colored liquid with paper towels or toilet paper [6]. Repeat until all the varnish seems removed and then apply a fresh, thinned coat of clear varnish.

● Sand with the finest steel wool, dust and apply second coat. Your bamboo piece should now be gleaming and ready to have its lacquer attended to if necessary.

4

5

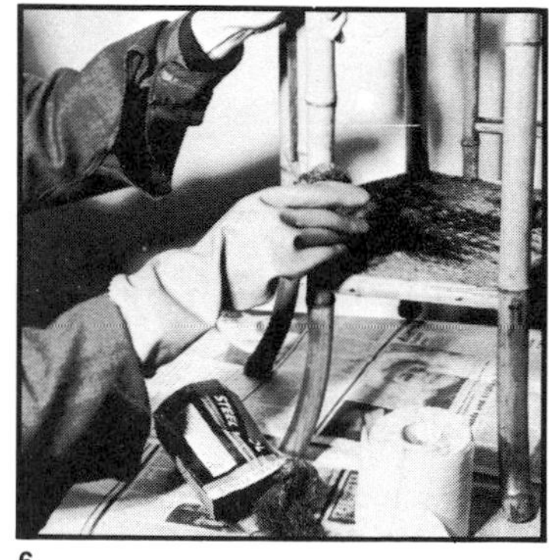
6

BENTWOOD: Repairing and Refinishing

Before repairing or restoring bentwood, turn the piece over and look for a manufacturer's stamp. If it is marked "Thonet" [7], consult a reputable auctioneer or dealer before doing anything which may lessen its value. Michael Thonet's factories produced 20,000 objects a week, but the identifiable pieces are becoming valuable. On the other hand, he had many imitators: but these pieces are usually not as valuable.

7

● Often bentwood has been covered with several layers of paint or varnish by well-meaning decorators. If so, liberally apply a commercial paint remover and scrape off the bubbled stuff over newspaper with a combination shavehook — the curved end is ideal for using on bentwood [8].

8

● Alternatively the piece may be covered with a heavy dark brown varnish which can be removed with fine steel wool and denatured alcohol (methylated spirits) [9].

● After this rather messy job you will be rewarded by the beautifully grained surface of beechwood, always used by Thonet and often by other makers.

9

● At this point, decide whether to stain, repaint, revarnish or simply polish with a furniture wax. I personally prefer stripped bentwood polished with a non-silicone furniture wax or a homemade beeswax and turpentine polish (see recipe p. 50) and buffed to a sheen with a soft cloth. If a high gloss finish is preferred, apply two coats of a thinned clear gloss varnish.

Legs: The most common problem with bentwood, especially chairs, is their wobble. The back legs are usually fastened to the chair seat by nuts and bolts, often complicated by a rounded top bolt; these sometimes become loose. To remedy, grip the nut with a pair of pliers or a wrench and the edge of the bolt with pliers and hold the bolt still with one hand, while you turn the nut with the other [10]. It may help to rest the chair seat on a table top. If the nut and bolt seem immovable add a drop of oil and a drop of turpentine.

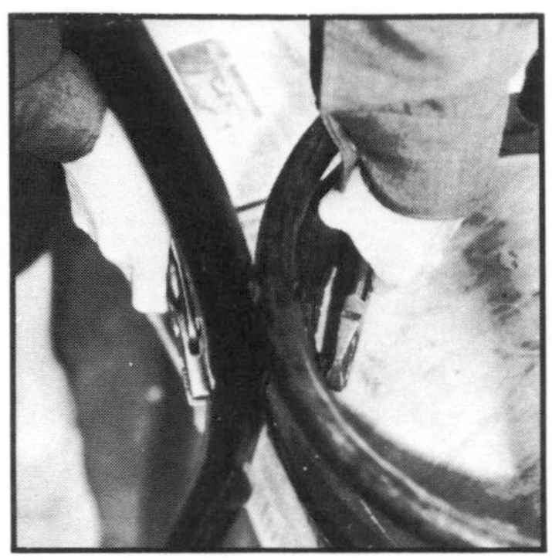
10

BASKETS

Basic Construction

Baskets are usually made from one of four materials, either used alone or in combination: cane, raffia, rush or willow. Illustrated are the parts of a basket and some weaving techniques [11, 12 and 13]. The basket maker uses only the few tools listed opposite, plus his or her hands. Basically they are constructed of different-sized rods or weavers—the thickest ones are used for the base, the next thickest for the side stakes, and thinner ones for the side weavers. Very long thin ones, often of cane split down the middle, are used for wrapping handles.

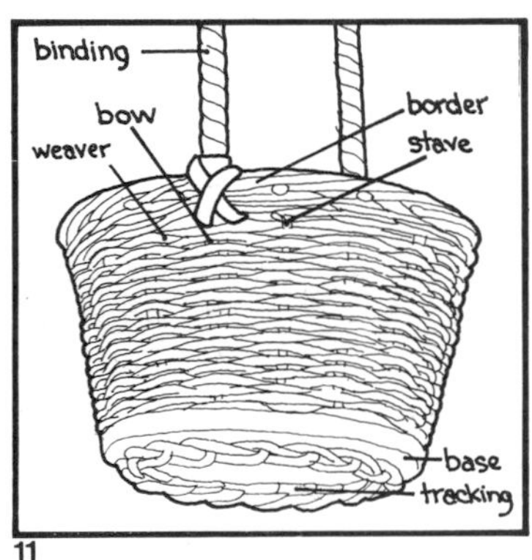

11

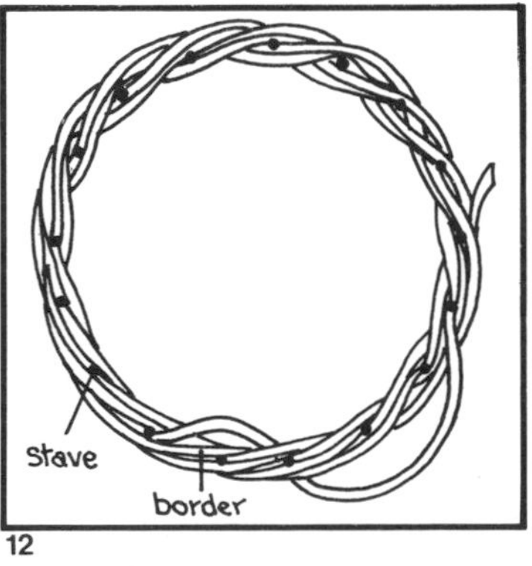

12

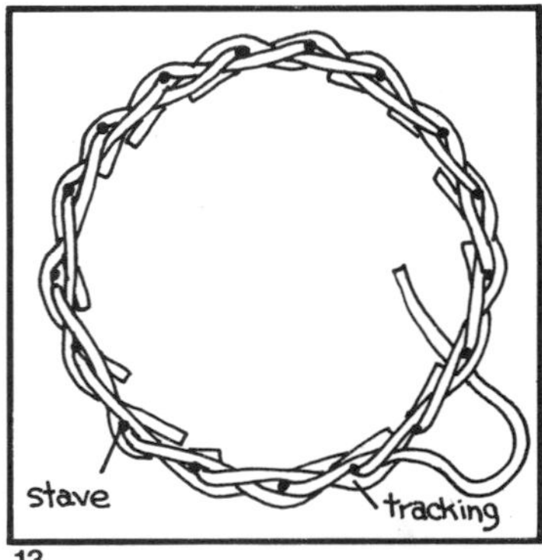

13

Repairing Basketry

- To repair a damaged basket first remove all damaged pieces. Then simply copy what has already been woven, inserting the thickest rods first (often called the bows) and weaving with the thinner more pliable ones. Unfortunately it would be impossible to describe all the styles in basket-weaving here, but all the restorer really needs is a sharp eye.
- Determine the type of material used and try to buy only as much as you need for the job, unless you plan to do some basketmaking. Sometimes you can use string to mend broken handles or fasteners on baskets [14]. If the basket has been attacked by woodworm, unfortunately it is best to burn the basket because the worm will quickly infest other objects in the house. Some basic repairs have been described and illustrated below, followed by specific instructions and hints. You will only need a few of the following tools, depending on the repair to be done:

14

Knife with replaceable blades, for cutting canes, willows and rushes—cane and willow are always cut at an angle as shown in illustration 15.
Pruning shears
Bodkin and screwblock.
Rapping iron or small hammer or old metal file—makes work tighter and levels work before weaving the top border.
Bradawl.

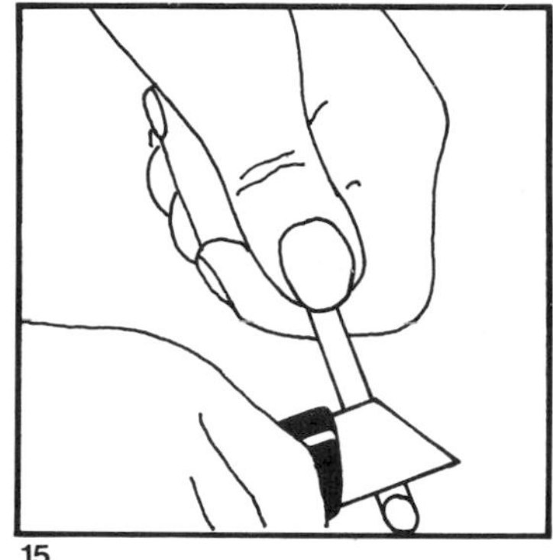
15

Repairing the Handle and Binding: A basket handle is usually made from two different weights of material—a stout rod, called the bow, forms the handle itself, which is wrapped with a thin binding called lapping. This lapping is often split cane but can also be raffia or plastic.

● First remove the damaged binding and examine the bow.
● If this is damaged, remove the whole thing and soak a new rod for at least an hour. Insert the new one, with its cut face outwards about 2″ (5cm) deep next to a stave going through the border [16].
● Carefully bend the bow and insert the other end, cut face outwards, opposite the first.
● Put the lapping in next to the bow about three rows down and cross it over as shown [17].

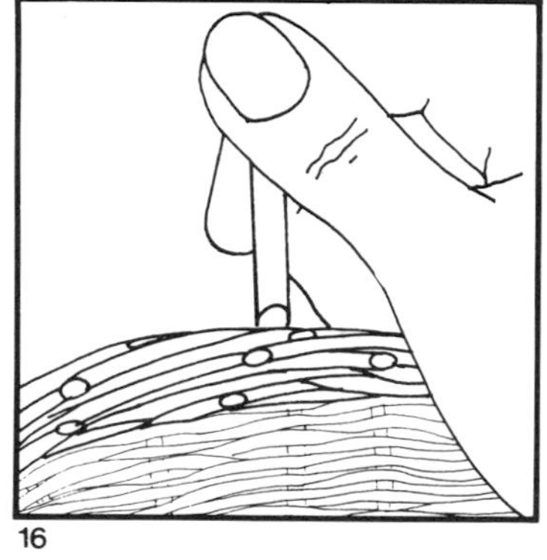
16

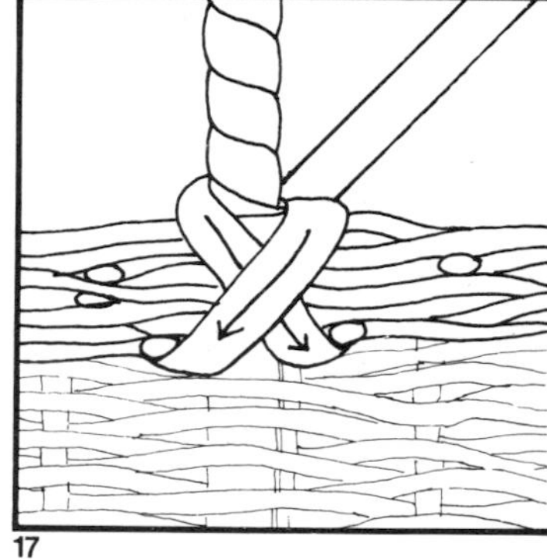
17

● Wind the lapping tightly around the bow, so that its edges touch and at the other end finish by crossing over the lapping in the same way as you started [18].

Repairing a Hole:
Follow the steps shown below:
● Remove the damaged weavers keeping the rods intact, cutting each one off at the center of the nearest stave as shown [19].
● Prepare the material used for the weavers as directed on the next page.

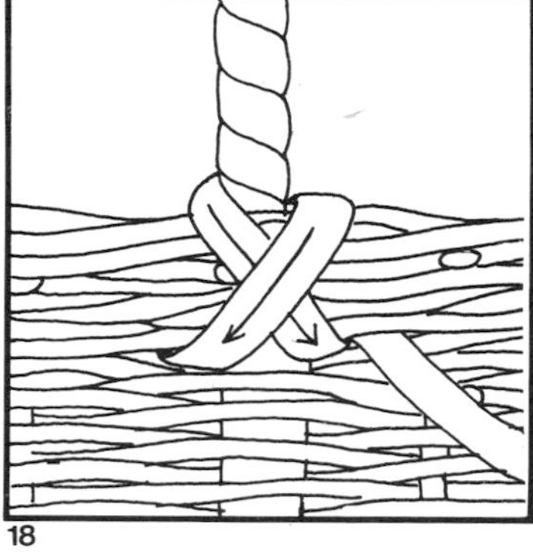
18

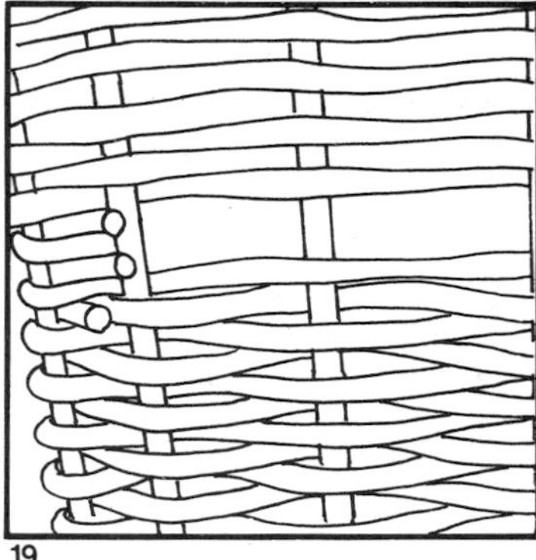
19

● Insert the weaver between the cut end and stave leaving a 2″ (5cm) tail on the inside and weave across the damaged area as shown [20].

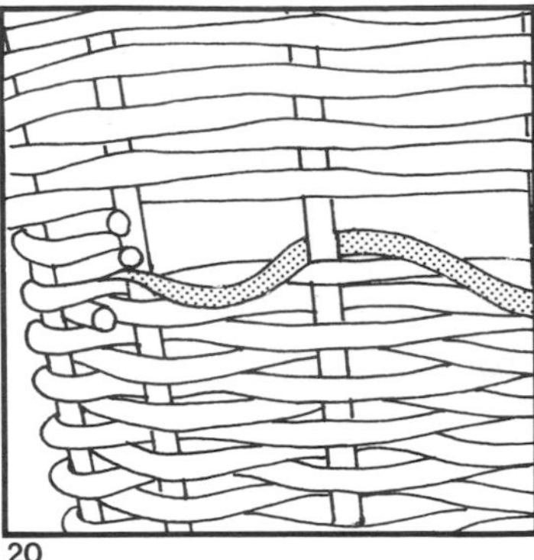

20

Opposite: *A selection of baskets showing what variety of pattern and texture can be achieved with simple weaving materials.*

● Press the weaving down occasionally with your fingers, a bodkin or bradawl, depending on the material used.

● Continue weaving until the hole is patched by the new weaving. If the weaver starts to run out, tuck the last few inches into the inside of the basket and join in a new piece from the inside.

● When finished, cut all the tails on the inside of the basket as close as possible [21].

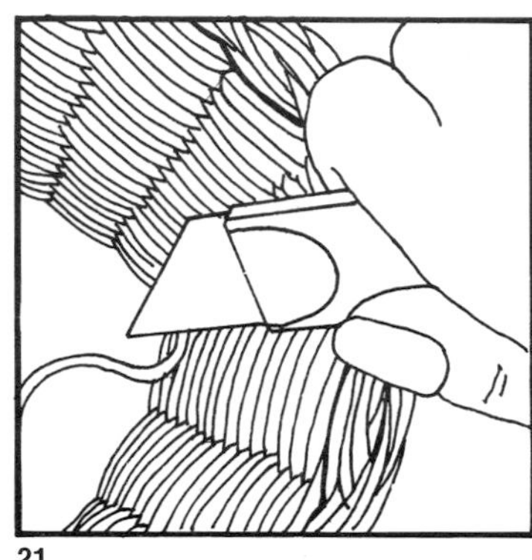

21

COMMON BASKET-WEAVING MATERIALS

Cane

Cane comes in two qualities: red tie used for antique chair seating and blue tie used for more general work. Both are available in six sizes numbered from one to six. Number 1 is the thinnest, numbers 2-4 are suitable for weaving and numbers 5-6 are used for the stakes of baskets. ''Wrapping'' cane is strong $\frac{1}{4}''$-$\frac{1}{2}''$ (6mm-13mm) diameter glossy cane, also called kootoo, used for handles; while for decorative effects, both enameled and painted cane are also available. If possible take a sample of cane from the object you are repairing to the suppliers in order to match it accurately. HINT: When weaving don't use a length more than 3 feet (1 meter) long or it tends to become dirty and tangled. To store after use, dry the cane completely or it will rot. Then stack it in upright bundles or in 12″ diameter coils.

To start, simply soak the cane in water for 5-15 minutes (a bathtub works nicely), remove it from the water and lay it aside under a porous covering (old blankets or sacking) until it becomes soft and pliable. If necessary, dampen the flat side of the cane with a sponge if it becomes dry as you work. Thick or enameled cane will probably need half an hour's soaking.

Willow

Willow is stronger and lighter than cane, and costs less, but it is more difficult to work with. The most commonly cultivated type is the withy or osier willow which is cut in the winter when the sap is down and then graded as follows:

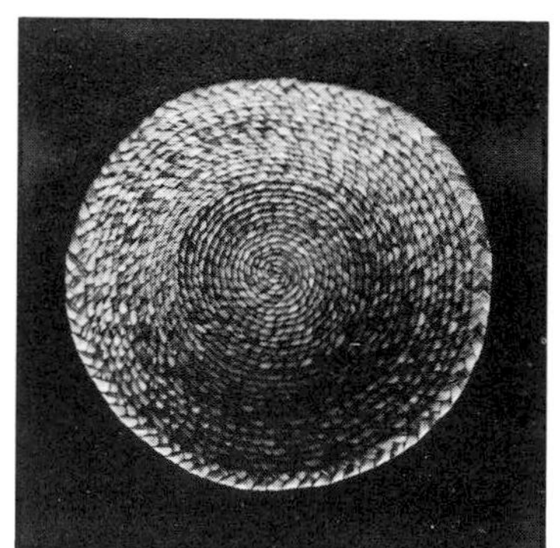

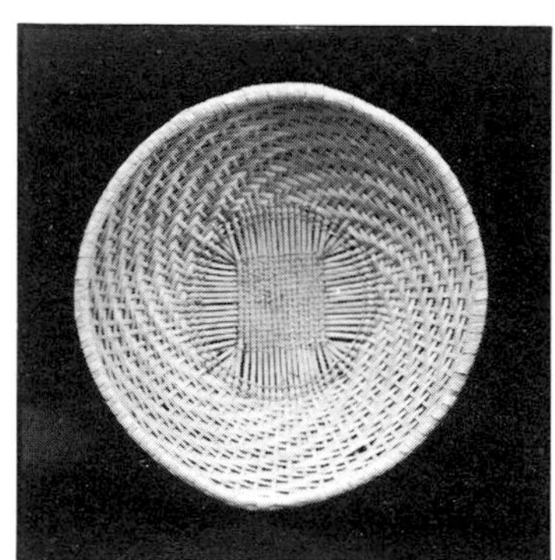

- Brown willow, left to dry with the bark intact.
- White willow, which has its bark peeled and is then left to dry.
- Buff willow, which is boiled for several hours to be stained from the tannin, or dye from the bark, which also acts as a preservative. This is the easiest grade to work with. It is sold in standard lengths each with a traditional name: 3′ (1 meter) lengths are tacks, 4′ (1.20 meters) are short-small, 5′ (1.5 meters) are long-small, 6′ (2 meters) are threepenny. Try to get the 3′ (1 meter) or 18″ (46cm) length if possible, unless there are several repairs to make.

To prepare, soak the willow in water for two to three hours and then wrap the rods in a wet cloth, old blanket or burlap sacking for 12-24 hours—after this it should feel velvety and soft. They will "keep", if kept covered at all times, for about 48 hours, when the willow will begin to feel greasy. At this point it will have to be thoroughly dried out and soaked again for re-use.

When working with willow, notice that it has a curving tendency of its own—use this to your advantage. It also kinks naturally, instead of bending as cane does, and weavers must plan the occurrence of this and not let it "kink" between the wide stakes but against them. Discard any willow that gets bent in the wrong places as it can't be re-dampened like cane. HINT: Slice willow at an angle with a sharp knife to ease insertion of the rods. Cane is joined as it runs out, but in willow all the weavers are joined in at the same time, so they are the same thickness but different lengths.

Raffia

Raffia comes from the leaf of a tropical palm and because it is both tough and supple it has been used in many ingenious ways. It can be woven over a cardboard base, used for embroidering straw handbags and other objects and even knitted or crocheted. It has been most beautifully worked by the natives of North America and Africa.

In basketmaking it is usually braided (plaited) and then either coiled flat and overstitched into place [22] or rolled and tack-stitched into place [23], with stitches about $\frac{1}{4}''$ (7mm) apart. It may also be used for stitching another material, like cane, into place. (After braiding, flatten the raffia with a hot iron, protecting it with a damp rag, and leave to dry before sewing it together with raffia strands or string.)

Raffia is purchased by the hank in natural or tinted shades, from craft suppliers, although a cheaper grade is available from gardening stores. Synthetic raffia is also sold—its advantages are that it comes in continuous lengths and brighter shades and is of an even thickness. Both are worked with a large-eyed blunt needle, available at craft stores. Alternatively a No. 14 tapestry needle or a fine rug-making or carpet needle will do.

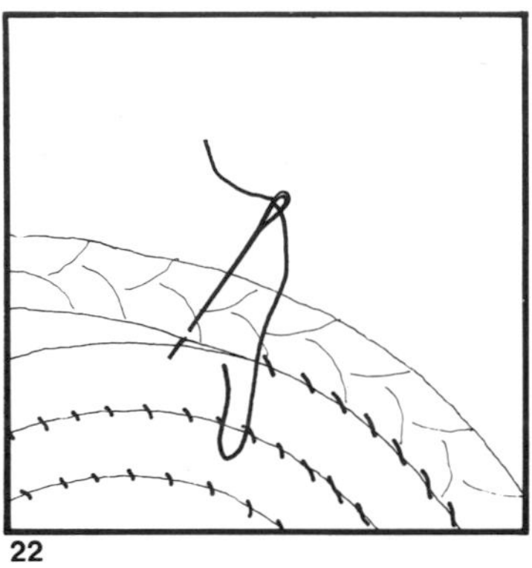
22

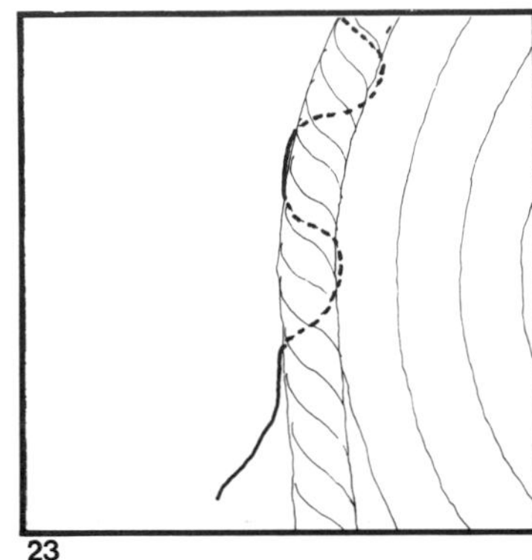
23

Rush Weaving

Rush has been used since Saxon times in England as a floor covering, when it was simply strewn about. Today it is woven into floor mats and other household items. Rushes are also used for seating, a form which was very popular in 17th century England. Its advantage is its availability—it grows abundantly on marshy land near water, so you can just go and pick it. (But if you cannot find any, most craft suppliers stock it.) If gathering it yourself, preferably in July or August, cut as close as possible to the roots with a sharp knife, and tie into armful-sized bunches (called bolts), taking care not to bend any. After cutting, spread them out to dry in the open air and turn them occasionally so that they dry evenly. Store the bolts upright and covered with an old blanket or burlap sacking in a well ventilated position. They can be kept outside if they are protected against rain and strong light. Rushes can be used either twisted, braided (plaited) or woven. When braided they are sewn together either with raffia or brown twine (for thicker work). The sewing will be easier if the needle is pushed into a bar of soap occasionally.

Using Rushes

- Draw them out of the bundle by the thick end.
- Lay them on a flat surface, even in a bathtub, and water them, making sure the excess water can drain away.
- Turn them over as you water to ensure even wetness until they are thoroughly dampened.
- Roll them in an old blanket or burlap sacking and leave for $2\frac{1}{2}$ hours. The cloth prevents them from drying out.
- Use within 48 hours or they will become sticky and will have to be dried off and re-watered. The base of rushwork is usually woven as illustrated [24].

The side weavers are threaded through the needle to ease weaving and the ends are tucked down into the previous rows.

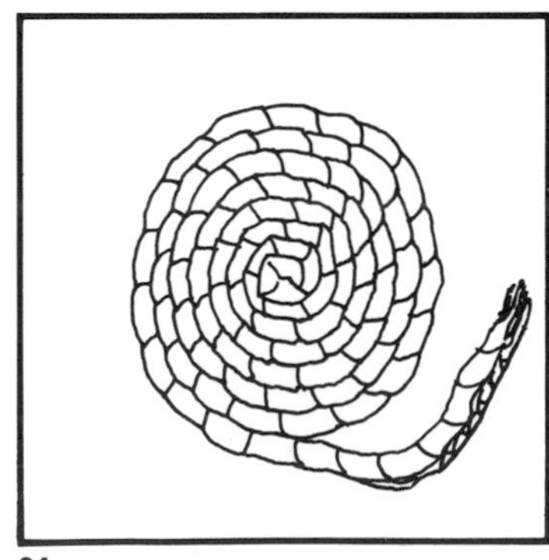
24

Tools required are:
- Needle with a large eye, sometimes called a sacking needle.
- String
- Pliers
- Scissors or pruning shears [25]
- Wooden mallet

HINT: If repairing a fairly large area, inspect it for evenness as you go.

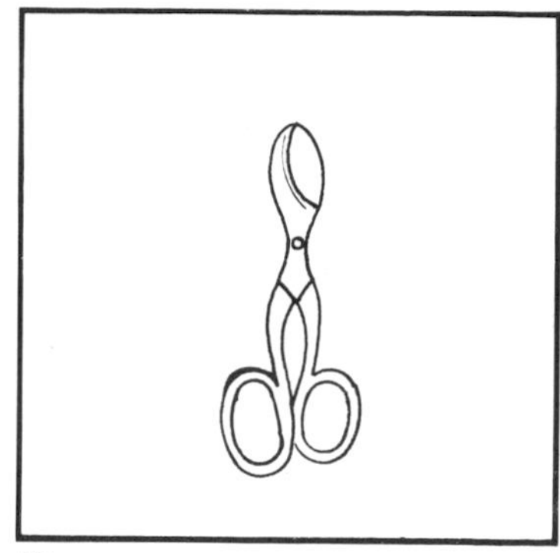

25

SEATING

Repairing Cane Chair Seating

Purchase two sizes of cane, Nos. 2 and 4, but if possible take the old pieces of cane to a craft supply store to match the dimension. (The size depends on the distance between the holes on the chair frame, usually about ½″ (12mm)—if holes are closer than that, purchase Nos. 2 and 3). One bundle will be more than enough for a chair seat.

The chair must be refinished as desired before caning and the old cane must be removed. But first make a sketch of any caning still intact, noting the numbers of canes from each hole and their direction. Knock out old pegs with the hammer or drill them out with a bit one size smaller than the existing holes. Sometimes you will find a "blind hole" (not drilled through) at the corners, which must be drilled clear.

Tools required are:
- Pegs 2″ (5cm) long to hold the cane while weaving. Some are left to hold loose ends or plug empty holes. Rawlplugs will also do temporarily.
- Scissors to cut the cane.
- Knife with replaceable blades to cut the cane where it is difficult to use scissors and also to sharpen the peg points.
- Cleaner—a metal knitting needle or screwdriver with a diameter not more than ⅛″ (3mm). Used to clean holes on the chair frame. A 3″ (7.5cm) nail will do if the pointed end is smoothed over with a metal file.
- Small hammer for flattening the knots, to give a professional finish; also for tapping the pegs in [26].
- Bodkin to help the cane through tight spaces; a large hatpin or sacking needle will also do.
- Bowl of hand-hot water.

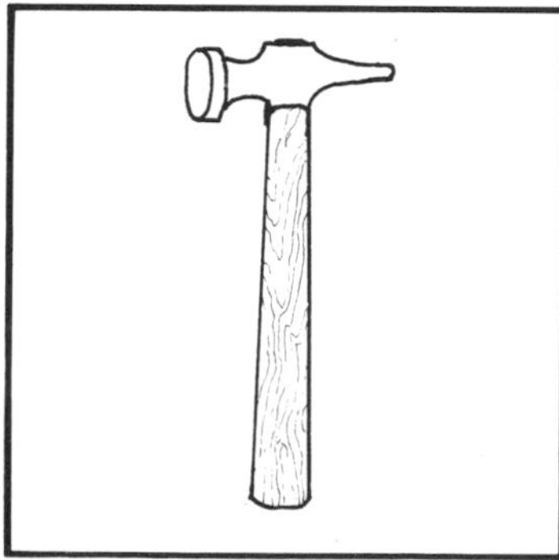

26

Preparation

- As you work dip the cane in the hand-hot water for a moment just before starting to work with it. Keep the cane wet while working, by passing it through this bowl (sometimes best placed just in front of the chair and slightly under).
- Stroke the underside (not the glossy side) with wet fingers to help absorption [27]. Don't soak the cane or it will discolor and don't step on it or it will crack up the entire length. Discard any damaged lengths. The following instructions are for the common seven-step pattern.

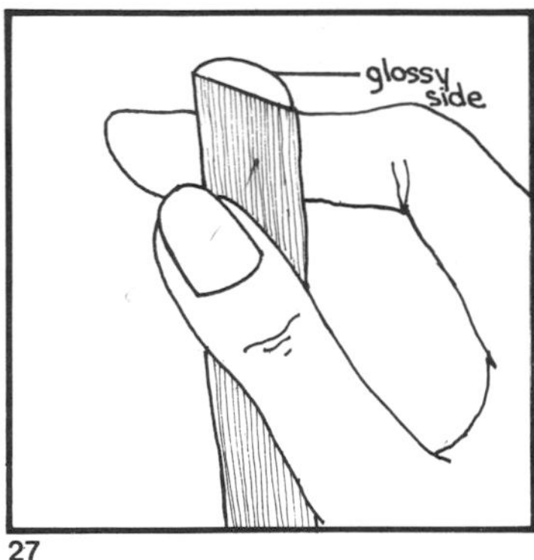

27

CLASSIC CANE SEAT

Step One: Start at the left side of the back and insert one end of the thinner cane into the hole nearest the corner held. Let 4″ (10cm) hang down below. Arrange the cane glossy side up and peg the hole, so that the cane is firmly held in place [28]. Take the long end straight down to the hole next to the corner hole at the front. Make sure the glossy side is up and don't let it twist as it goes through the hole. Pull the cane down tightly, peg it and bring it up through the next hole, glossy side always out even on the underside of the chair frame, and peg it. Now the cane goes across to the back side of the chair again into the hole next to the starting one; pull tight, again making sure glossy side is up. Then peg it in place with the second peg [29]. (Don't move the first peg until later, but the other pegs can "travel" with the weaving.) Continue in this way until the cane runs out or the seat is completely crossed over. If the cane does run out, leave the end hanging on the underside, peg it to hold it securely and begin with a new cane in the next hole, leaving at least 4″ (10cm) of cane hanging to tie up later [30].

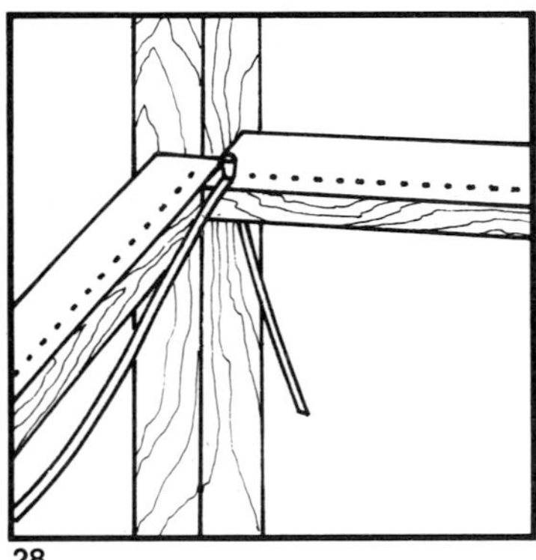
28

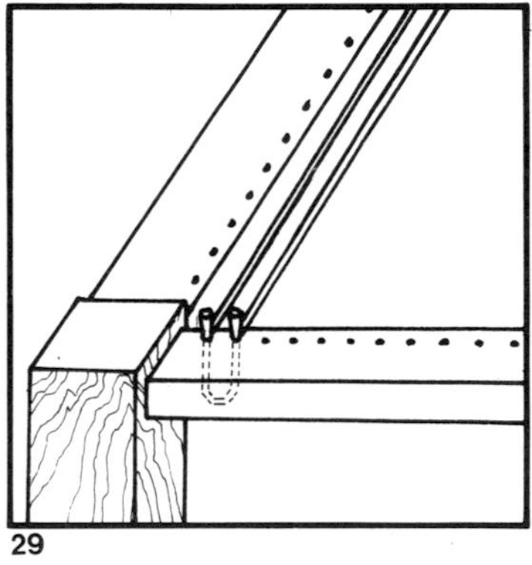
29

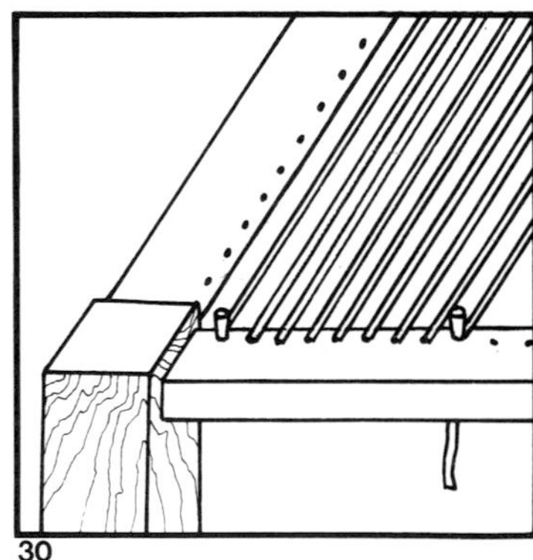
30

Hint: The tension of the cane is very important. Try to keep it fairly tight, but not too tight for later weavings and not so loose that it sags.

Step Two: Started and worked exactly as Step One, keeping the glossy side up, but crossing over Step One as shown [31].

Step Three: This is really a repeat of the first step but don't put the cane in this step directly over the first; insert it parallel and to the right of it [32].

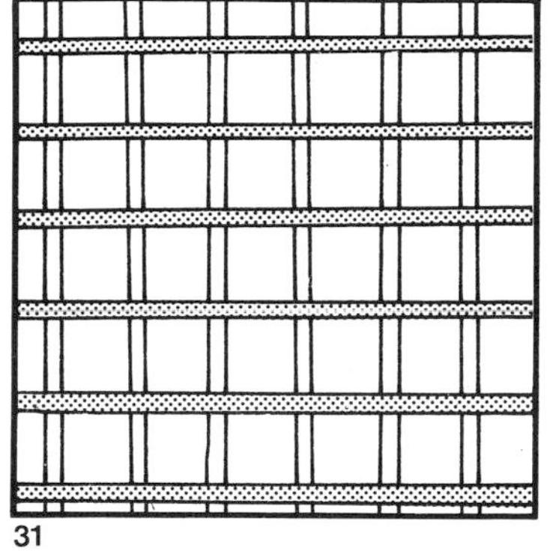
31

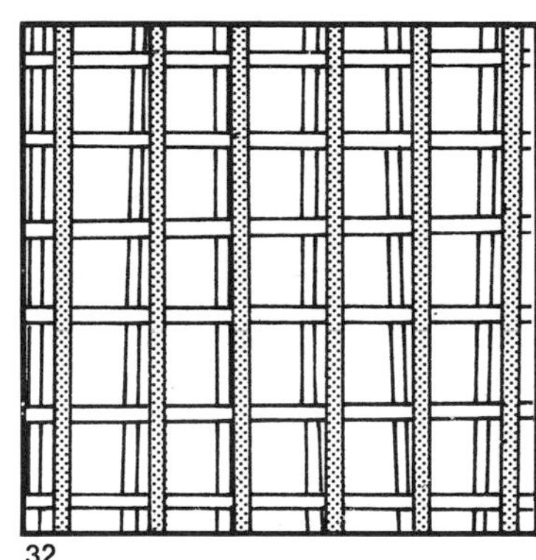
32

Tying in End: By now quite a few loose ends may be hanging from the underside. Just dampen the ends with wet fingers to make them pliable, cut each end to a point with the scissors and pass the end twice over and under the short strands that go between the holes on the underside [33]. Use the bodkin or similar tool to ease the end through untwisted and with the glossy side out. Tap it with a hammer to flatten it down, and finally twist the end off as close as possible. Try to avoid several canes ending at the same hole.

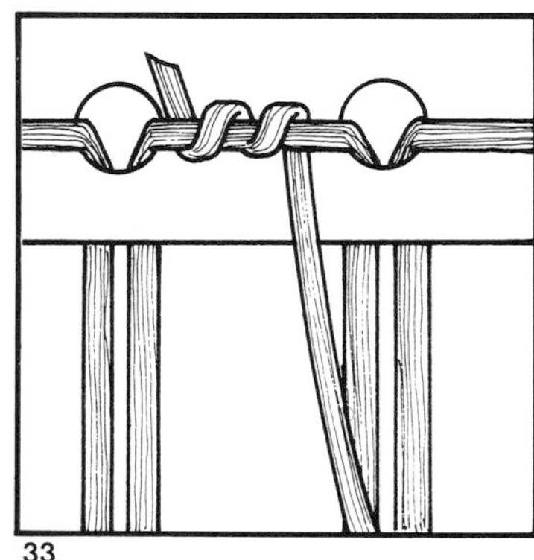
33

Step Four. Similar to Step Two but this time the cane must be woven under then over the vertical canes [34]. This will probably take longer than any other step. Weave in the direction that the cane feels smoothest when you run your fingers along it. Start as in Step Two and peg one end—remember the cane must still be untwisted with the glossy side up. HINT: untwist the length of cane before starting or the entire step will have to be undone if it is crooked. Don't pull the cane tight until you have gone under and over six pairs of vertical cane. Don't worry if the weaving doesn't look too perfect—the next two steps will produce the desired regularity.

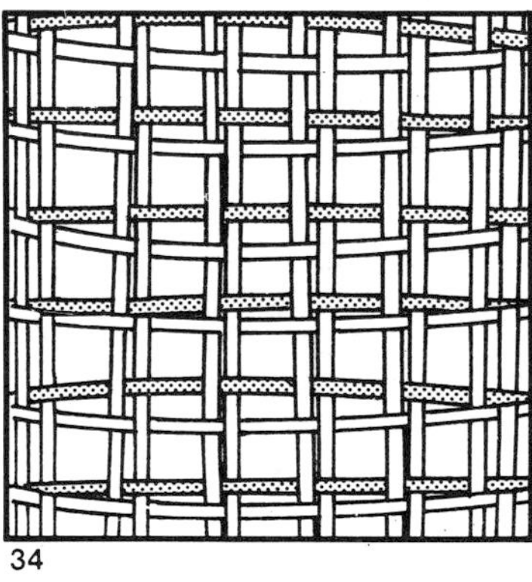
34

Step Five: This is the first diagonal and the first step to use the wider cane (No. 3 or 4) [35]. Begin by pegging the end of the cane in the back lefthand corner. Start weaving over the first pair of horizontals, then under the first pair of verticals, then over the next horizontals and so on until reaching the opposite corner (if the chair is square-framed). Now bring the cane, making sure it is untwisted and glossy side up, through the next hole in front to the left and weave backwards. Weave like this until finishing off in another corner and then go back to the starting hole and start another cane to complete the other half. This time go under the vertical pair first then over the horizontals and continue. It should look like illustration No. 35 if correct. If it is wrong, the only way to correct it is to unpick the mistake carefully. (If the unpicked cane is not dirty or broken, re-soak it for 2-3 minutes or until pliable and re-use).

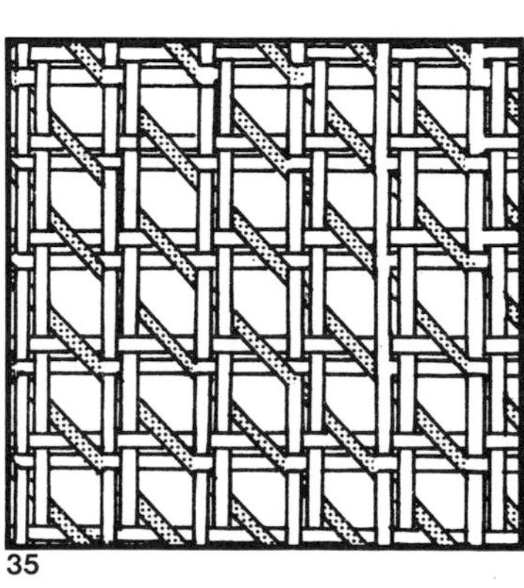
35

Step Six: This is the opposite diagonal and begins in the opposite back corner. It should be woven at right angles to the Step 5 diagonals [36]. But now go under the horizontals and over the verticals. Finish off all hanging ends after this step.

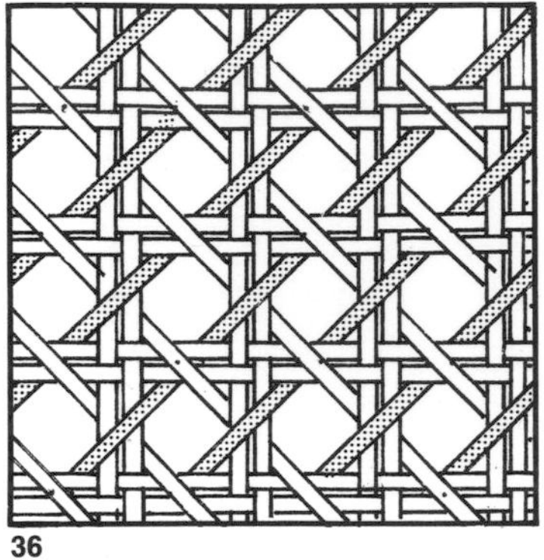
36

Step Seven: An optional finishing touch is a border of cane outlining the weave. (No. 2 and No. 4 canes can be used, though professionals often use Nos. 2 and 6). Start by inserting a No. 2 cane into a hole next to a corner and allow the end to stick up $1\frac{1}{2}''$ (3cm) [37]. Bend this short end into the next hole and bring the long end up through this same hole which should hold the short end in place [38]. The thicker cane is laid over the top of the holes on the chair frame and "stitched" down with the thinner cane, as shown in cross-section [39].

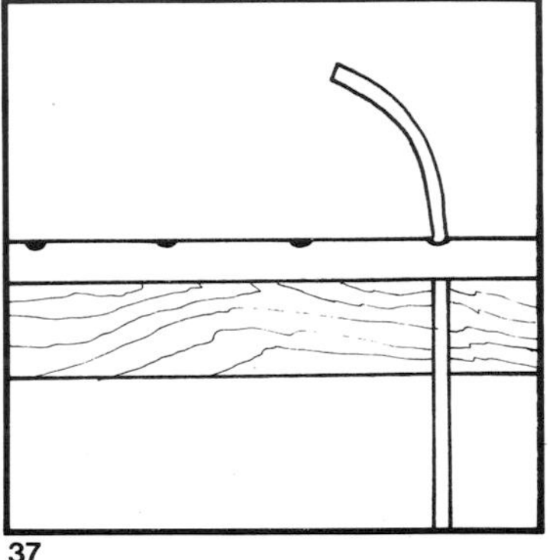
37

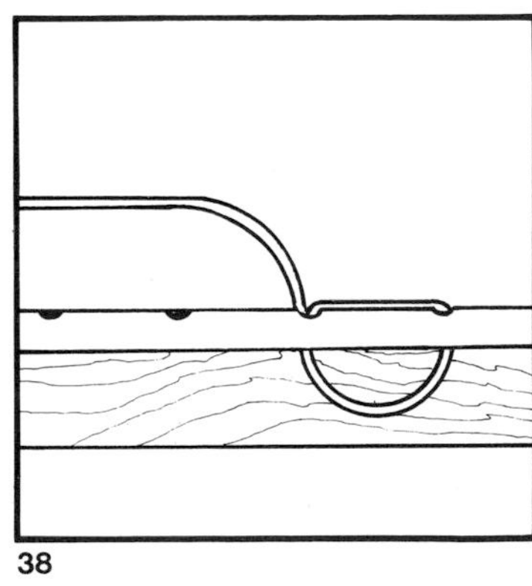
38

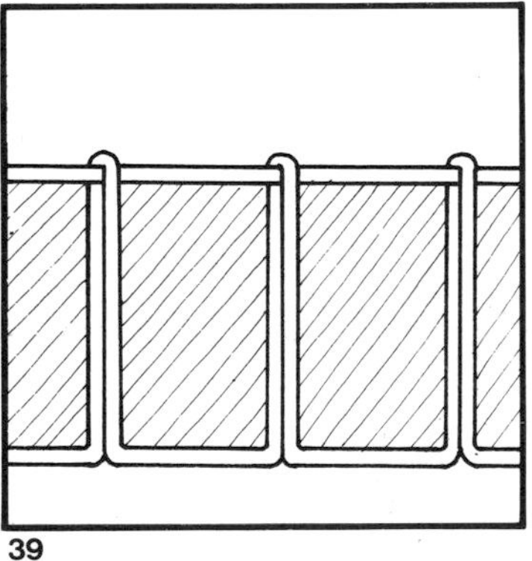
39

AGAIN: remember to keep the cane untwisted and glossy side up. Insert the thicker cane into this same hole, and lay its long end over the holes along that side of the chair frame. Pass the thinner cane over the thicker and take it down into the same hole and up through the next hole on the underside. Then take it back out, over the thick cane and back down. In this way the thicker leading cane will be secured over the holes and the stitches of the thinner cane will produce a decorative border. When the corner hole on this first side is reached, insert both canes and start them both in the first hole on the adjacent side before pegging the ends. Tie and peg all ends underneath upon completion and trim. HINT: The holes are very close together—less than $1\frac{1}{2}''$ (3.75cm), so use every other hole for stitching with No. 2 cane.

Repairing Rush Chair Seating

Approximately $1\frac{1}{4}$lbs (550gm) or three-quarters of a bolt are required for an ordinary chair seat. Prepare the rushes by soaking (see p. 70) and then draw out one or two at a time and twist them together (sometimes two or more twisted together) in a motion away from and not towards you.

The rush must be tightly twisted as it passes along the top side of the seat, but is left untwisted under the seat (see photo 40).

40

- Start at corner A as illustrated [41] passing the long end under the frame, up and around the side bar near corner A, thus securing the short end of the rush. Then pass it across the frame to corner B, securing it similarly there; go on to corner C, then to corner D and back to corner A, passing over the first crosswise strip to corner C, and back to near the starting corner A.
- When the rush runs out, pack it under already woven rushes with a wedge-shaped piece of wood, called a "packing stick". This packing will help keep the rows in position and strengthen the work. When the seat is completed, secure the final end of rush by knotting it round one of the rushes on the underside and tuck the end under.

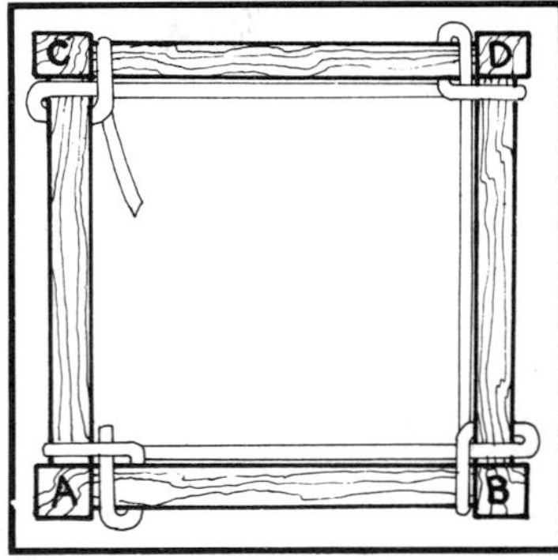

41

- In working oblong seats the sides of the seat will be completed before the back and front, so the center space must be filled by a figure eight weaving as shown in [42].
- If the chair seat is irregular, start as before at corner A and work once around the seat.
- When beginning the second round, wrap the rush once around the side bar but twice around the front bar at corner A and also at corner B. Proceed around the seat to corners C and D in the ordinary way.
- When corner A is reached again, repeat the double wrapping in every alternate round until the remaining space between the rushes is equidistant between A-B and C-D, and then complete as before [43].

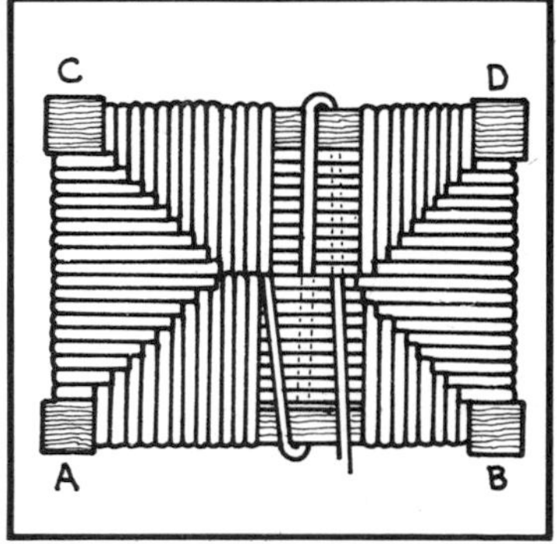

42

43

LACQUER

The Chinese invented it. The Japanese perfected and then exported it. Western Europe and America admired it, copied it, and finally produced their own. As far back as the sixth century, incisions made in the poisonous lac tree (*Rhus vernifica*) produced thick, graybrown sap. It was collected in wooden pails, stirred under the hot sun for many hours until all moisture had evaporated, strained through hemp, tinted with organic pigments, and mixed with egoma oil. The wooden object to be lacquered was covered in linen and several layers of gesso, and taken to as damp and as dust-free an environment as possible.

This oriental finish was so deep and highly lustrous that the exotic plant and animal configurations seemed to float in a shiny sea. Marco Polo noted that the Chinese palaces were filled with this "wonderful painting" and his descriptions aroused the interest of European royalty. Meanwhile, secret Japanese envoys had "borrowed" and refined the process so that eventually the Chinese were importing Japanese lacquerware!

During the 17th century, trade was affected by a shipping ban, so Europeans imitated the style by painting their furniture with glossy finishes, and decorating with gold leaf in an "oriental" pattern.

It is generally agreed that the production of Western lacquer began in Spa, Belgium, during the 1720's. Alder or linden wood was shaped and then soaked in the water from the Poulon spring. Rich in tannin, this water imparted a brownish tone to the wood and fortified it against woodworm. A wide variety of objects from sedan chairs to snuff boxes was produced and sold to the elite clientele of this famous watering place. By 1730 the Martin brothers were using the notable *vernis Martin,* the best facsimile of oriental lacquer at the time. Unfortunately no formula survives, although it reputedly contained garlic juice! The French Revolution put a halt to such frivolity, but by 1815 interest in the orient had again blossomed and it is said that even George Sand tried her hand. Slightly earlier in England Chippendale and Halfpenny were also inspired by the eastern motifs they saw on oriental lacquer and blue and white porcelain. They incorporated several different forms into their furniture designs during the early 1720's "chinoiserie" style, but China-ing is a difficult word, so Japanning became the popular term for an upper-class pastime.

This enthusiasm for lacquered wood was superseded to some extent by a craze for hand-painted motifs on papier mâché and metal, since papier mâché was cheaper, and metal stronger than wood. By the latter part of the 18th century, many household objects were embellished with orientally inspired decoration. In fact "japanning" became a general term for this style, as well as for the technique of lacquering and the *genre* eventually included Elizabethan, rococo, moorish, neo-classical and naturalistic motifs. In Britain this colorful, mass-produced tinware (really tinned sheet iron) became known as "Pontypool ware", although factories were also located in Birmingham, Wolverhampton and Usk. A Quaker, Thomas Algood, opened the first tinware factory in Pontypool, Wales, and by 1801 had patented a completely black varnish of excellent luster and durability, incorporating a quick-drying agent (his secret) but it still had to be hand-rubbed and baked in a slow-drying oven. In Birmingham, John Baskerville developed a better varnish, but Usk and Pontypool produced the finest work. (Uskware is noted for an unusual chocolate brown varnish).

Even Philadelphia newspapers carried advertisements for this "japanned tinware" and encouraged admirers to send for breadbaskets, tea kettles, coffee pots, trays, urns, lamps, tea-caddies, toast racks, chafing dishes, snuffboxes, Dutch ovens and clockfaces. *Tole peinte* was the name given in France to a kind of work which was similar, but more elaborate and finely executed. Often gold leaf and metallic powders were chosen for portraying fountains, birds of paradise and countryside scenes depicting castles, churches, people and villages. This was the origin of the name Toleware given to the objects in America. In 1850 a factory opened in Litchfield, Connecticut, and employed craftsmen from Wolverhampton. They were better paid in the new country and the factory was "modern". The Litchfield factory's most popular items were clockcases marked with the company's name, but their varnish was said to be bubbly, and the firm closed in 1854. In fact after 1850 the quality of the work had generally declined—stencils and transfers were used—so much of the handpainted charm was gone. By 1870 the last English tinware factory had also closed.

Brightly painted tinware continued to be made in the countryside, however, long after it had gone out of fashion in the town. Bargemen and gypsies carried their flowered coal buckets and household goods all over the countryside. The "Pennsylvanian Dutch" style, a kind of countryfied japanning, was strongly affected by the symbols and patterns of middle-European decoration—early Amelung glass was one of the earliest examples in America of its kind.

Papier mâché has earlier origins—archeologists have found "poor men's coffers" of pressed paper in Egypt. In 1772, Henry Clay, an apprentice of John Baskerville, took out a patent for a type of laminated paper which was heat- and water-resistant. Clay made a fortune from the manufacture of trays and other small articles, but was bought out by A. Jennens and T. H. Betteridge of Birmingham, England, in 1816, who introduced mother-of-pearl inlay and gave the already enthusiastic public larger household objects, such as bedsteads, chairs, sofas and even casings for pianofortes. A huge array of articles made of this new material was displayed at the Great Exhibition of London in 1851, which was prepared with the active patronage of Prince Albert. But the height of its practical and futuristic use came in 1853 when C. E. Biefield of Birmingham designed and made a prefabricated life-size papier mâché village consisting of ten cottages and a large hall.

In France, papier mâché had been made since at least the seventeenth century when the ever-popular snuffboxes were made of pulped theater posters; while in Russia, 30 kilometers from Moscow, craftsmen in Palekh, Fedeskimo and Mysteria also produced household articles painted in egg tempera and speckled with tiny flecks of gold or silver. Sadly, by the 1870s European papier mâché had become *passé* and was despised for several decades, but it must be respected for its lightness, ingenuity and eccentricity. Stenciled furniture and pseudo-oriental painted decoration have remained popular ever since. It should be remembered that real lacquering is far more complex than simple "paint and polish". It demands a long time, careful attention to detail, and a lot of patience. If you are in a hurry to refinish a new piece, buy one of the new enamel lacquer paints in a spray can. They will do quite well for most everyday purposes, but if you ever set a piece of real lacquer on top of your spray-painted table you will appreciate the difference.

Caution: never attempt to restore a valuable lacquer antique without expert advice—this is especially true of early signed pieces, or the delicate vases and bowls of the 19th century.

LACQUER

Types of Lacquered Finish (Definitions)

Lac: hence "lacquer": a substance obtained from the sap of the poisonous oriental sumach, *Rhus vernifica,* and refined to produce seed lac or grain lac, a crude granular substance further refined to obtain garnet lac and then button lac and tongue lac from which you get flake lac and finally a white lac—a very shiny but brittle lacquer.

Shellac: a substance derived from the hardening secretions of insects which swarm on trees in India and Thailand. This is melted, purified, and chipped into small pieces and called orange flake shellac or French shellac. A bleached shellac is also available. Both are soluble in denatured alcohol (methylated spirits) and dry to a clear finish with slight orange-peel effect.

Varnish: a solution of resin (copal, mastic, damar, sandarac) in a solvent. There are two types: simple solution or spirit varnish where the resin is dissolved directly in a solvent such as denatured alcohol (methylated spirits) or turpentine; and oil varnishes where the resin is cooked or melted with a drying oil and then thinned with a solvent. Coach- and spar-varnish were once made by this process.

All the finishes rely on the following principle: as the liquid is applied and exposed to the air, the volatile solvent evaporates, leaving a thin film of sap or resin on the object.

Cleaning Lacquered Wood

To clean and polish a lacquered object use any non-silicone furniture wax or the beeswax polish recipe given on page 50. Alternatively, mix olive oil and fine white flour into a paste, apply with a soft rag then gently rub it off.

Cleaning Lacquered Papier Mâché or Tinware

Give objects a gentle wash with a pure soap and water solution and when dry apply any non-silicone furniture polish or a beeswax polish with a soft rag or chamois. Do not rub any of the decorated area very hard. Do not apply the polish if any handpainting needs retouching.

General Advice

If you have a lacquered object with only slight chipping, it is probably easiest to try to match the various tones from small jars of enamels available at hobby shops, because the authentic process described below is quite lengthy. You could even use enamels in place of the japan or artist colors below, but the effect is much cruder and less authentic. If the damage is really extensive, and only traces or much-faded designs remain, better start from scratch and follow the instructions below. Of course, be sure that the object is not extremely valuable, by doing a little research at a museum or by consulting a few books devoted to the subject.

If the old design is too faded, or you are decorating a new piece, select a similar motif from a pattern book, although it may be necessary to alter the motif to fit the object as shown [1 and 2].

On the other hand if you wish to restore the piece, retaining the original hand-painted motif, then proceed according to the following instructions.

1

2

● Before starting, trace any remaining design with a sharp pencil and tracing paper, making notes on the tracing paper of the hues and shades used, so you can duplicate them later.
● Work slowly and accurately looking at the piece in both daylight and artificial light. Many details are "invisible" under one or the other.
● Then take accurate and lengthy notes. For example, don't simply write "yellow flower" but "mustard yellow flower with white center".
● Also try to ascertain if the paints have been applied thinly or thickly and note any striping or highlighting and whether it is in "gold" or paint. The tracing paper should be covered in descriptive adjectives. Alternatively, place a second piece of tracing paper over the first and write the descriptions on this.
● If only minute traces of the hand-painted design remain, it is probably best to lightly sand the surface and then select a motif from a pattern book.
● When selecting an appropriate motif, remember that each period and place had its own style of decoration. Similarly, tin, wooden and papier mâché designs are not interchangeable if you want to be authentic. Many oriental pieces will have motifs in light relief, worked in gesso under the layers of lacquer.

Repairing and Repainting Tinware

Don't begin here until you have made a trace of the previous design or a new one is selected. Follow the steps below to prepare damaged or new tinware for the lacquer base coat and subsequent decoration.

● Pound out any dents with a length of cotton wool wrapped around a hammer with a rounded end [3].
● Sand with fine abrasive paper before applying one coat of a flat, rust-preventive paint (usually gray or burnt-sienna red).
● When this is completely dry, sand again with wet-and-dry paper under running water as shown [4]. HINT: try to sand lightly and evenly.

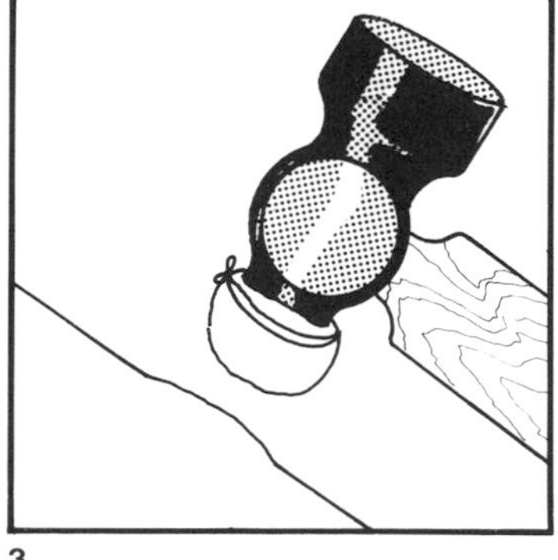
3

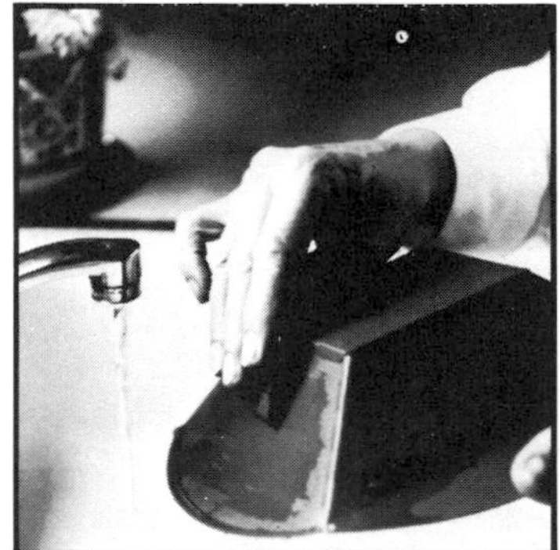
4

● Apply a second coat of the rust preventer; when dry, sand again under running water.

● Dry with a rag. Professional painters use a dustcloth sometimes called a "tacrag" similar to a fine cheesecloth; even old stockings will do. The item is now "primed" and ready to be lacquered.

Repairing Papier Mâché

● To repair a chipped or otherwise damaged piece, first build up layers of synthetic wood filler.

● The photographs show how a papier mâché Victorian doorplate was repaired using a matchstick for support [5].

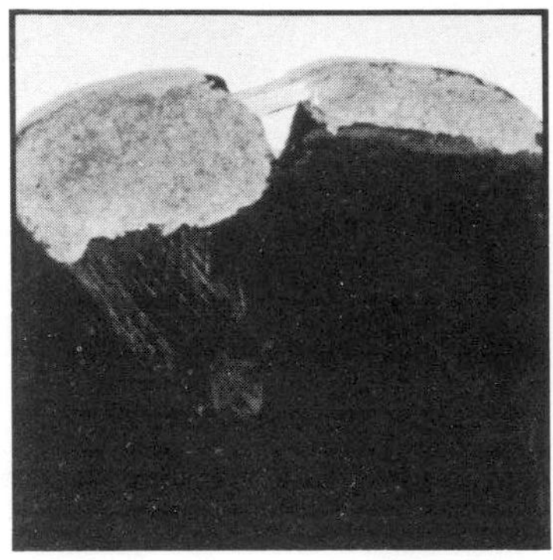

5

● Always overfill slightly, as these tend to shrink when drying [6 and 7].

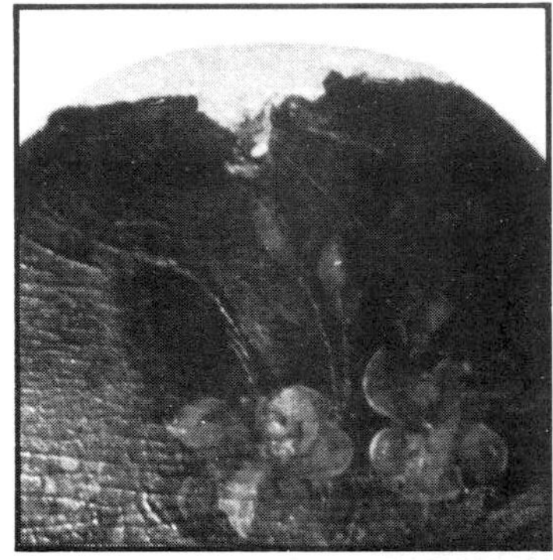

6

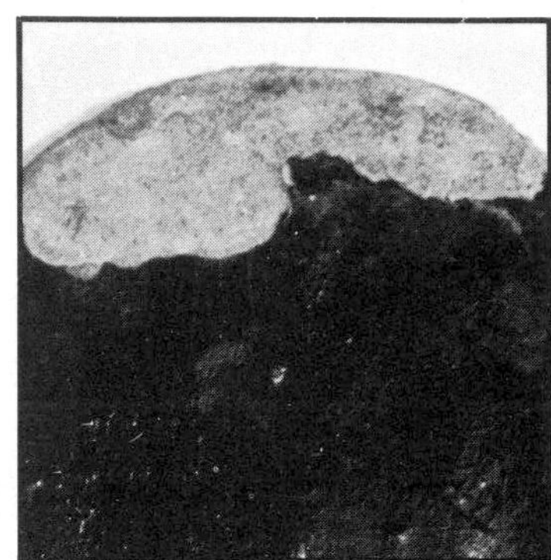

7

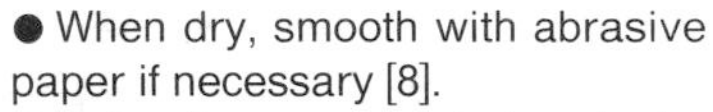

● When dry, smooth with abrasive paper if necessary [8].

● Naturally, any repair has to be touched up to match the surrounding shade. Only then can relacquering and re-decorating begin; if you are only touching up a small area, as shown here in Fig. 9, spend your time blending paints to match the existing shade—here black.

8

9

● Note: e.g. black is rarely pure black straight from the tube; it will need to be tinted with brown, blue, green or red. To check, place a black swatch from a paint store next to the article as shown [10].

10

Repairing Lacquered Wood

This actually presents a more difficult problem than repairing papier mâché or tin, because the wood used under the lacquer, especially in the Victorian era, was cheap and tends to crack and move, thus flaking the paint. This flaking troubles even expert restorers.

● First repair from the underside or wrong side of the lacquer using proprietary wood filler with care [11].
● If the paint has flaked away, leaving a sort of plaster exposed, mix powdered gesso with enough water to form a stiff paste and remold the chipped part.
● For deep chips or serious damage it is better to apply several layers of this rather than trying to mold a great lump. If the damage is less severe you can use a small brush to paint it on but always build it up a bit higher than the surrounding raised work to allow for considerable shrinkage during drying.
After repairing you are ready to apply the first coats of lacquer as directed below. When lacquering a newly stripped piece, apply two coats of wood primer of a shade close to the lacquer shade and when dry sand until smooth.

11

Supplies for Repairing the Lacquer Base (for Papier Mâché, Tinware and Wood)

Try to get this shade as close as possible to the existing one, adding to the following formulas to lighten or darken if necessary. Use only japan paints which are flat, opaque pigments ground in an oil-free resin varnish; this distinguishes them from artist's oil paints which tend to be more translucent. Choose your paints from the list below and, after mixing, test the dried shade for accuracy on white posterboard or palette paper by placing it next to the original shade. Each formula approximates traditional combinations. You can use these mixtures either for restoring an already lacquered object or for giving an impeccable gloss to primed wood.

To apply this base coat, you will need the following supplies.
● Japan colors (purchase only the ones you need, although if you plan to do a lot of lacquering, this is a good basic list).
Liberty red medium (red-purple).
Signcraft red (orange-red).
Chrome yellow light.
Chrome yellow medium.
Cobalt blue.
C.P. green light.
C.P. green medium.
Raw umber.
Burnt umber.
Raw sienna.
Burnt sienna.
French yellow ocher.
Lampblack—a flat black.
● White lead paint—often sold as flake white. To be sure you are getting white lead, purchase it in powder form if possible.
● Turpentine—sealed turpentine, pure gum spirits or rectified. Avoid wood turpentine which is less costly, but less durable.
● Japan drier—a quick drying agent, used at 10% of the lacquer base mixture.
● Use 1″ (2.5cm) oxhair primer brush [12] for applying the base coat, and $1\frac{1}{2}$″ (3.75cm) white bristle brush for applying varnish.

12

● Palette knives—for mixing and stirring paint. Have two if possible.
● Pieces of white posterboard, on which to test shades and brush strokes.
● Shellac—purchase orange flake or white, in small quantity.
● Denatured alcohol (methylated spirits). Always use this for diluting shellac and cleaning shellac brushes.

Applying the Lacquer Base

After these supplies have been assembled, place the object in front of a light source (daylight is best) so that imperfections are obvious. All of the lacquers should be applied as described below. When lacquering large objects place them on a support over damp newspapers which will attract dust away from the object.

● Mix the ingredients as given in the formulas below, strain through a nylon stocking supported by a wire mesh strainer [13].

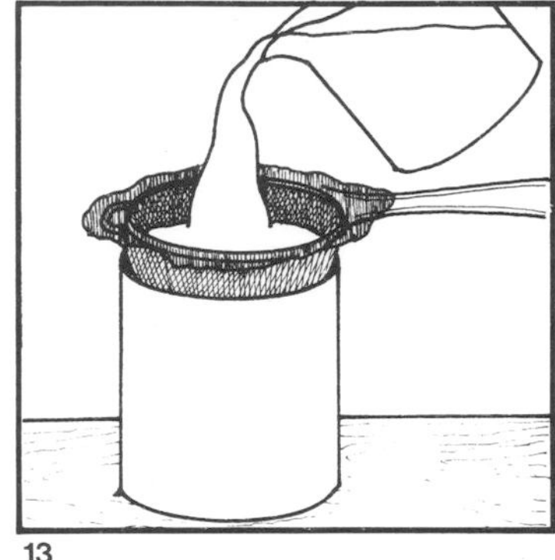

13

● Dip the brush (usually a $1\frac{1}{2}''$ (3.75cm) oxhair bristle) into the lacquer mixture halfway up the bristles and press it on the inside of the jar to remove the excess [14]. Wiping brushes on the rim causes uneven pressure resulting in bubbles. (When just touching up chips, also dip sable hair brush only halfway in lacquer). Alternatively, wrap a wire around the top of the jar as shown [15].

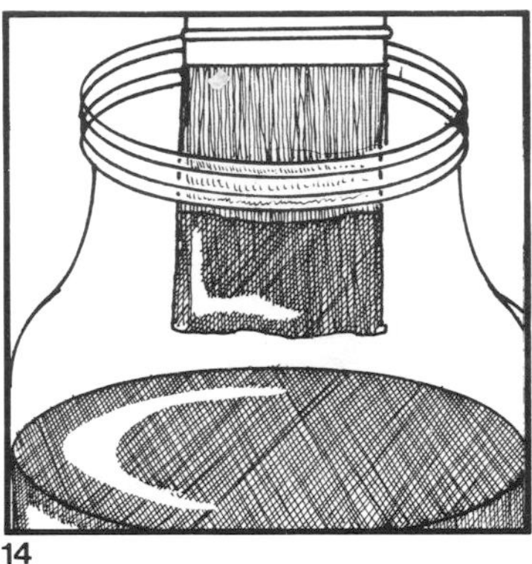

14

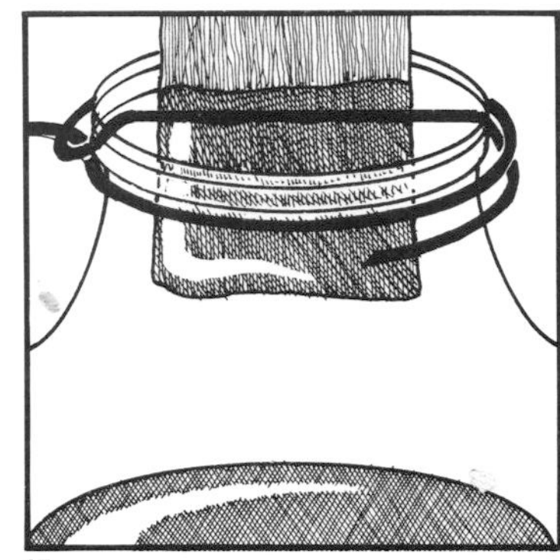

15

● Start "lacquering" in the middle of the object [16] and lightly move the varnish brush to one end, overlap that middle starting point, and brush along to the opposite end.
● Brush from end to end with the grain, then across it, then with it again.

16

● Apply two coats in this way, letting the first dry *thoroughly* before applying the next. Complete drying takes between 24-48 hours, depending on the temperature and humidity of the room—70°F (21°C) is ideal.

● After the second coat has completely dried, the surface is rubbed lightly with the finest wet-and-dry abrasive paper and with non-detergent soapsuds as the lubricant.
● Apply another two coats of lacquer.
● Protect finally with mixture of 50% shellac and 50% denatured alcohol (methylated spirits) [17]. Apply two coats of this, smoothing between each one with the very finest steel wool.

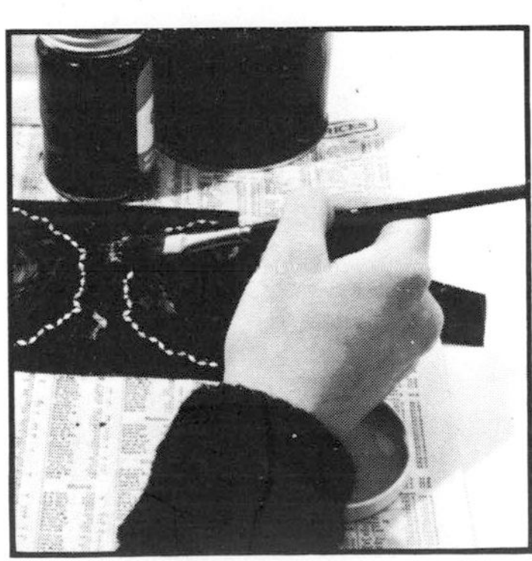

17

Lacquer Formulas

The quantity of lacquer mixed from the following formulas depends on the number and size of articles to be painted; remember that each article needs four coats of the lacquer.

Black Lacquer Undercoat (Negro Nuri): Apply four layers of this finish followed by the red or yellow top coat. These two were often used by Chippendale and seem to suit all kinds of "chinoiserie" very well.
Mix: 5 volumes flat black paint
$\frac{1}{2}$ volume burnt umber japan
$\frac{1}{3}$ volume japan drier
$\frac{1}{4}$ volume spar varnish

Red Lacquer Topcoat: Apply one coat after the black undercoat has dried. To give the antiqued effect, smooth with fine wet-and-dry abrasive paper lubricated with non-detergent soapsuds to reveal the black underneath. Try to work evenly.
1 volume true red japan (purple red)
$\frac{1}{2}$ volume orange red japan
$\frac{1}{4}$ volume flake white paint
$\frac{1}{2}$ volume turpentine

Yellow Topcoat Variation: Apply as with red topcoat above.
1 volume chrome yellow medium japan
$\frac{1}{4}$ volume raw sienna japan
$\frac{1}{2}$ volume turpentine
$\frac{1}{10}$ volume japan drier

Coromandel Lacquer: This formula is a facsimile of the lacquer used on Coromandel screens, so called because they were shipped from the Coromandel coast of India to Europe during the 17th and early 18th centuries. They were usually about eight feet (2.5 meters) high, up to twelve panels in length and combined carving, lacquering and painted scenes. The base coat can be made as follows:
1 volume true red japan (purple-red)
$\frac{1}{2}$ volume burnt sienna japan
$\frac{1}{4}$ volume orange red japan
$\frac{1}{10}$ volume japan drier
$\frac{1}{4}$ volume turpentine

● Apply 4-5 coats over the gesso or casein base (see "Italian lacquer" if this casein needs replacing), and smooth the final coat to a satin smoothness with fine wet-and-dry abrasive paper and soapy solution.

● Protect this with two coats of diluted orange shellac, letting each dry for one hour before rubbing lightly with the finest steel wool.

● Over that apply one coat of the following in a broad streaked manner.
1 volume raw umber japan
$\frac{1}{4}$ volume lampblack japan
7 volumes glazing medium made from:
1 part flatting oil (soybean)
1 part undiluted gloss varnish
1 part thinner (refined mineral spirits)
1-2 parts japan drier

Hint: Store the glazing medium after use in a dark green or brown-tinted glass jar.

English Lacquer: Topcoat:
5 volumes flat black (lampblack)
$1\frac{1}{2}$ volumes burnt umber japan
$\frac{1}{2}$ volume japan drier
$\frac{1}{2}$ volume clear gloss varnish
mineral spirits for thinning
This is smoothed with fine wet-and-dry abrasive paper and soapy solution, dried with soft cloth, and then covered with the final topcoat of the mixture below, heated to room temperature—70°F (21°C).
$\frac{3}{4}$ volume raw umber japan
$\frac{1}{4}$ volume lampblack japan
2 volumes asphaltum
1 volume spar varnish
1 volume mineral thinner
$\frac{1}{4}$ volume japan drier
Allow 48 hours to dry and then rub with rottenstone and allow 24 additional hours before smoothing with fine wet-and-dry paper and soapy solution. Then apply one coat of shellac mixed with denatured alcohol (methylated spirits) 50/50, and rub with the finest steel wool before applying the design, which is usually in gold leaf.

LACQUER FINISHES

Italian Lacquer: This lacquer was usually painted over a gesso (or, nowadays, casein) support which hid poor workmanship, or bad wood or plaster. It's a very long process; only attempt it if the piece is damaged extensively and is worth the trouble. Otherwise fill chips and cracks after tracing design, with a fine already prepared filler or see page 32 to make your own.

- Soak 2/3 rabbit skin glue sheets overnight in 14 fl oz (400cc) water.
- Dissolve gently over heat by placing pan in another larger pan of boiling water. Combine 2 fl oz (55cc) of this with 1qt (1 liter) boiling water.
- Apply resulting size with a stiff bristle brush and let dry overnight.
- Casein mixture.

1qt. (1 liter) white casein paste, often called "deep white" commercially.
2½oz (70gm) casein emulsion
6oz (170gm) kaolin powder
3 drops pine oil
¼ tsp. ox gall
¼ tsp. fungicide crushed in ½ tsp. of water
12 fl oz (340cc) mains water

- Stir kaolin powder into the white casein paste, then add casein emulsion, pine oil, ox gall, fungicide and water. Strain through nylon stocking into glass jar with the help of stiff brush. The mixture should be the consistency of heavy (double) cream.

- Coat the object with the casein mixture and brush it to an even film. Allow it to dry for one hour and apply the second coat stroking the other way. Apply five coats in this manner, sanding lightly between every two coats with very fine abrasive paper. Sand again after final coat.
- Dissolve white aniline powder in hot water. If light tones are required, cold water is added. Rub this over the casein with fine-grained natural sponge and wipe off instantly with an absorbent cloth.
- When this dries (2 hours) coat the piece with thinned white shellac (50/50) five times, letting it dry overnight each time, then rubbing down with the finest steel wool.
- When the last shellac coat has dried thoroughly, two coats of gloss varnish are applied.
- Rub down topcoat with rottenstone and lemon oil.

French Lacquer *(vernis Martin):* During the seventeenth century the French version of lacquer was a tinted varnish over a base. This is a modern approximation of the Martin brothers' famous formula.

- Apply five coats of thinned japan pigment of a middle hue, allowing 24 hours between applications.
- Sand every second coat lightly with fine wet-and-dry abrasive paper and soapy solution.
- Apply white shellac thinned (50/50) with denatured alcohol (methylated spirits) using a soft shellac brush.
- Rub with fine steel wool when dry.
- Apply a glazing medium (see p. 83) tinted with ½oz (14gm) japan in hue slightly darker than base coat. Use brush or natural sponge (fine-grained).
- Let dry for one week and then apply coat of thinned clear varnish. Let dry overnight.
- Apply second coat, but spatter with metallic powders or crushed gold leaf speckles when tacky. To be authentic crush sheet leaf with a gilder's tamper. Cut tube of cardboard or heavy paper diagonally at one end and cover the other end with fine cheesecloth fixed with a rubber band to act as a sieve [18].

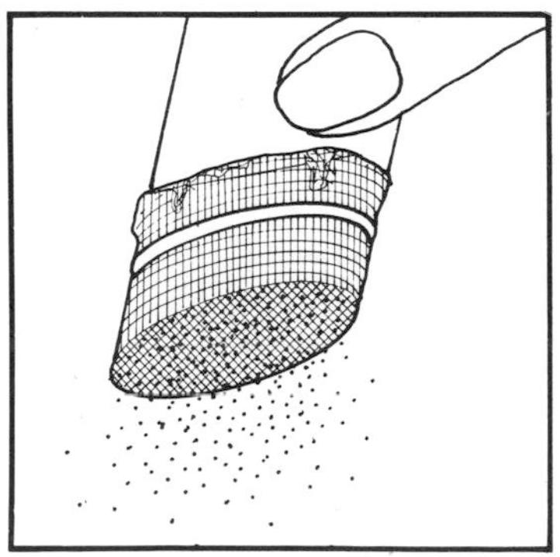
18

With folded paper tip particles into the tube and then disperse the particles lightly over the tacky varnish by tapping the tube with your finger [19]. When dry, smooth the speckled surface very lightly with the finest wet-and-dry paper and soapy solution. Apply several additional coats of varnish, each one smoothed until the desired translucency is achieved.

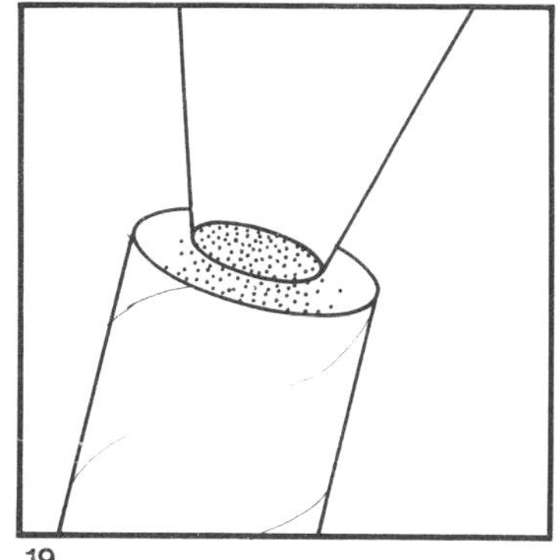

19

To Transfer a Design

After applying the base coats of lacquer and a sealer, you are ready to apply the decorations. First transfer the traced design in the following manner:

- Turn over the tracing you have made and rub with soft rag dipped with ground chalk when transferring to dark objects [20]; when transferring to light objects, rub with a soft pencil.
- Tape the tracing design, chalk or pencil side down, to the object in several places [21]. Scotch tape will do, but masking tape is best. (Here a berry bucket is shown).

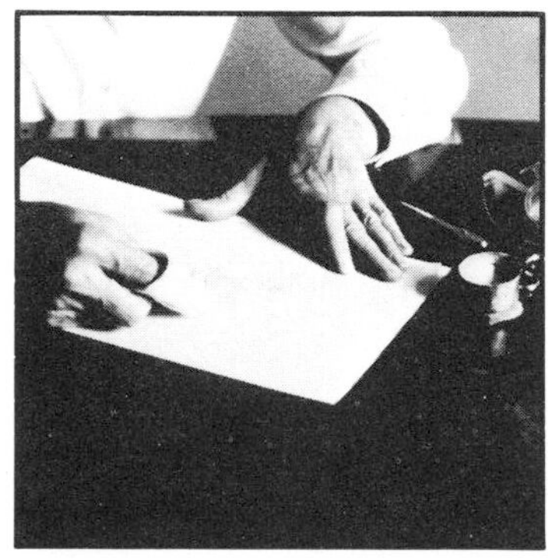

20

21

- Again using a hard, sharp lead pencil, go over each part of the design *very carefully* so that it transfers clearly and completely to the object, as shown at right of Fig. 21. Finally remove the tracing paper and you should see the transferred design and can begin applying the paint [22].

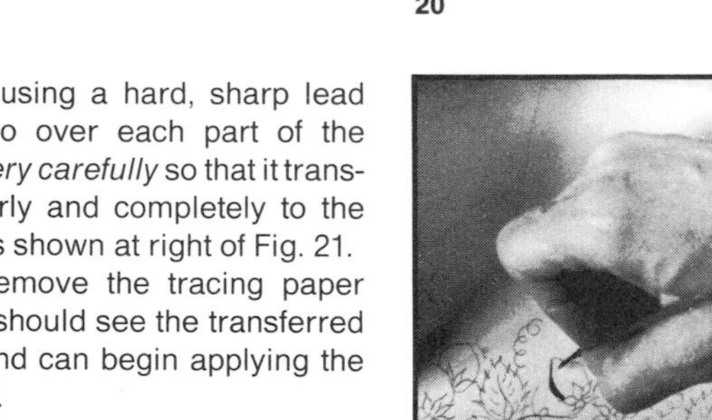

22

The Hand-painted Decoration

When the transfer is completed you are ready to apply the hand-painted motifs, striping and/or gilding which give lacquer its charm. Artist's oil paints are recommended for this work, although casein paints (water-soluble) can be used. The oils lend a more authentic "floated look".

LACQUER FINISHES

Paints: Basically, there are ten pigments used in these decorations and they are listed below under supplies; but always purchase the paint closest to each surviving hue, bearing in mind that paint pigments darken over the years. If gold has been used, purchase a liquid gilt from an art store. Buy the highest quality available. It is applied as directed below. If you are restoring stencilwork see page 97.

Opaques
Titanium White
Chrome Yellow (medium or light)
Vermilion

Transparents	**Semi-transparents**
Alizarin Crimson	Yellow Ocher
Prussian Blue	Burnt Sienna
Yellow Lake	

Toning pigment
Raw Umber—used with blues and greens in mixing as a toner.
Burnt Umber—used with red and yellow in mixing as a toner.
GREENS are obtained by mixing the chrome yellows with Prussian blue and dulling with a bit of raw umber.

Gilding (Optional)
Gold paints and metallic dusts were sometimes used to "highlight" the hand painting on lacquer. Always purchase the best quality gilt paint or dust, because very cheap varieties will darken quickly. See pages 100-2 for further notes on gilding; refer to page 97 for stenciling with gold dust.

Other supplies: Fig. 23 illustrates the following brushes—fine sable hair brushes, sometimes called "French quills", to start, numbers 1-6. For striping, an extremely long-haired striping brush is used; for scrolling, a long-haired red sable brush which is very flexible.

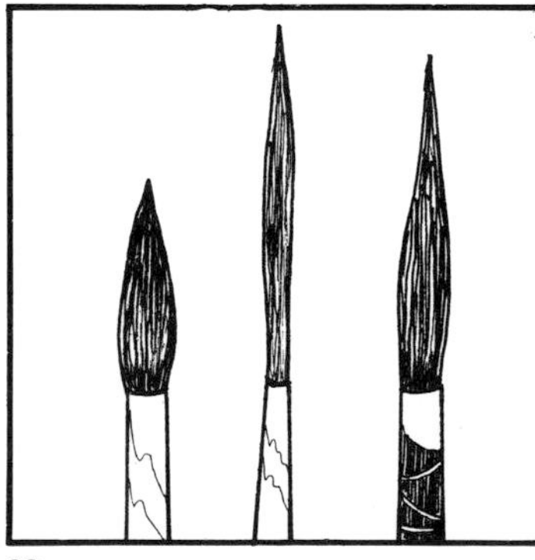
23

- Small jars of pure turpentine (or water if using casein)
- Newspapers to protect the work surface
- Palette paper on which to mix paints
- Spar varnish—a high gloss varnish, easily obtainable at marine supply stores, which allows the wood underneath to breathe a little, thus reducing cracking. Mix with pure turpentine when thinning oil paints.
- Clean cotton rags for wiping brushes, fingers etc.

Mixing and Applying the Paint

The paints can be used straight from the tube or shaded with a toning pigment from the list above.

● To start, place a drop of paint on the palette paper with a drop of spar varnish to one side and a drop of turpentine to the other. Mix these together with the palette knife to obtain a flowing consistency [24].

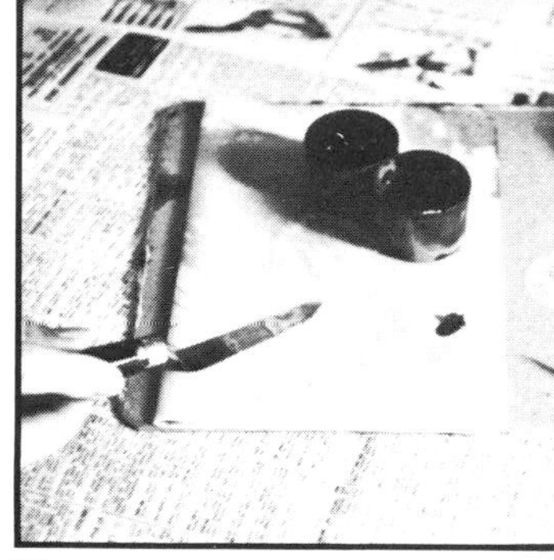

24

● When adding a toning color, again use the palette knife for mixing. Always wipe the knife clean before mixing another pigment, to avoid contamination.

● Apply one pigment at a time, mixing shades according to the notes you made on the trace.

● Paint in a logical order; for example, if the design shows a blue flower with a red center the blue would obviously be applied first [25, 26, and 27]. Allow each application to dry thoroughly and clean the brush with turpentine before applying the next.

25

26

27

● Professionals obtain most shapes with a single movement. This one basic stroke is varied by the size of the brush, the use of the stroke to fill the traced shape, and by the amount of pressure applied to the brush. *Always* practice on a sheet of palette or tracing paper before starting [28].

28

Striping

Striping is achieved only by using the proper striping brushes.

● To stripe make sure that the brush is well loaded, start at the edge or corner, and with your little finger as a guide, glide the brush in one complete movement down the edge, keeping a straight edge [29].

● Avoid using the broad side of the brush. If you make a mistake when applying the paint dip a clean absorbent cotton or cotton wool swab in clear turpentine, dab the area, then wipe with a clean cotton rag. It may help to draw a line with a straight edge before starting, to act as a guide.

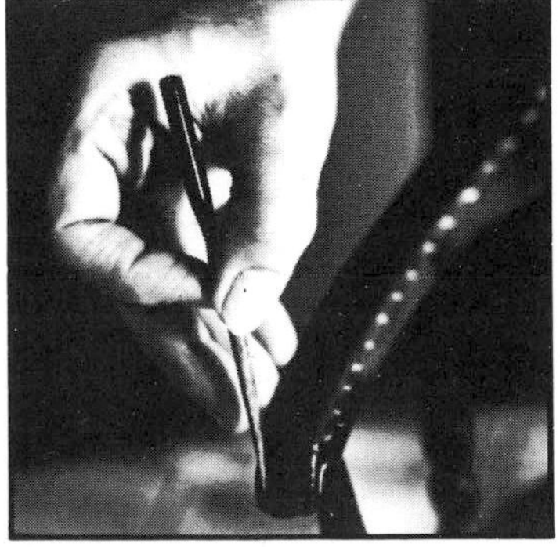

29

Antiquing

This is an optional treatment used on tinware and wood but almost never on papier mâché. It is applied when all the paint is completely dry and gives a lovely mellow effect. Apply two coats of spar varnish, smoothing between coats with fine abrasive paper and follow the instructions on page 92 in the special effects section.

Repairing Inlay on Papier Mâché

The main problem with inlay is that the tiny surrounding crevices trap dirt and polish, which eventually dull it. Try cleaning each piece with a cotton swab dipped in soapy water, then rinse and dry, but never use a strong cleaning solution or apply much pressure. If a piece becomes dislodged, clean it gently and apply a dab of clear celluloid adhesive to the back. in any event, always save even the tiniest piece that comes unstuck because finding a correctly shaped replacement is difficult.

Mid-19th-century papier-mâché chair. Papier-mâché could be molded into elaborate shapes, and was cheap, light, and very strong, although old pieces are rarely found in good condition.

HINTS ON LACQUERING

- Wear synthetic materials to keep down dust.
- Lacquer flakes, due to the movement of the carcase or basewood, so try to keep lacquered pieces away from extremes of temperature and humidity.
- Store japan colors upside down in a can or jar which keeps them moist and easier to mix. Tighten cap securely first.
- When japan pigments are mixed, if the tonal value is above middle, it will appear darker when dry; if below middle value, it will appear lighter when dry.
- When cleaning shellac brushes, NEVER use soap and water. DO use denatured alcohol (methylated spirits).
- When you have finished for the day, sable brushes should be cleaned in turpentine, washed in soap and water and then shaped to a point by rolling them in a drop of linseed oil placed on palette paper, or between your finger and thumb. This will keep these expensive brushes soft and pliable for years. Rinse the brush in clean turpentine before using it again. If brushes are allowed to dry vertically with the bristles up, moisture will seep down into the handle, eventually dissolving the glue holding the brush hairs—so always let brushes dry lying flat.

- Varnish brushes should be cleaned in the specific solvent mentioned on the can.
- Gloss varnish should be diluted 40% with dilutent mentioned on the can. If too thick, it can be warmed in pan of water over a LOW flame.
- Shellac should be stored in a warm place, away from light in a glass container, and purchased in very small quantities.
- Petroleum jelly around the top of glass jars, and a bit of turpentine on top of the paint inside, will help prevent scum forming.
- After each sanding, dust the surface with a soft rag dipped in turpentine.
- Remove all hardware from the object, except the hinges.
- A sharpened typewriter "pencil" eraser is useful for sanding tiny or awkward places.
- Keep an old coffee can with a plastic top for a "slush" can—perfect for depositing used turpentine or varnish, instead of dumping them down the drain.
- Clean the palette knife with turpentine and wipe with rag each time before mixing paints.
- Always use genuine rectified turpentine for thinning paints—never synthetic substitutes; similarly *do not* use plastic-based (polyurethane) varnishes instead of spar varnish.
- When touching up gilding, don't use a cheap gold paint, but an artist's gold powder and the appropriate medium. If the gold leaf is damaged, repair as on pages 103-7, but look closely, as silver leaf was often used as a "cheaper" alternative and then "browned" with tinted varnish to look like gold.
- If touching up BLACK, remember that black is rarely pure black and may need to be tinted with brown, blue green or red (to check, place a pure black swatch from a paint store next to the object).

SPECIAL

This section is devoted to exotica. It is not for beginners at using their hands but for those who have worked with paint for a while and are now interested in the unusual. All special effects require a sensitive eye and plenty of time.

The first two, antiquing and distressing, have no history to speak of, but "fake" their history. "Antiquing" is the art of imparting an antique look to tinware or wood. If properly applied, it shouldn't look grimy but rather suggest that the object has been lovingly dusted a thousand times so that nothing hard, shiny or obvious remains—ideally the piece "ages" before your eyes. The process of "distressing" can be carried out in two ways: there is physical distressing, which employs virtually anything to damage or deface, and thus give a used look to the piece; and distressed paintwork, a more noble way of imparting an antique look. The latter is often done before antiquing.

The "faux" finishes (from *faux,* French for false) have much earlier origins. "Faux marble" occurs on Mycenean pottery made two thousand years before Christ and is mentioned again in a formula from the 7th century. The French and Italian interior artisans used it where real marble never could be—on window shutters and doors—after all, if the walls and floors are the real thing, why let the doors and windows break form? It can be seen at the Borghese Palace in Rome and at Fontainebleau and Versailles in France. In England, Adam used faux marble on ornamental pedestals and it can be seen extensively at the Royal Pavilion in Brighton. Remnants from colonial American floor coverings have also been found.

"Faux porphyry" has a geological origin—porphyritic rock is an aggregate of detached crystals, often feldspar or "fool's gold" embedded in a finer stone ground. It has been used for centuries as a building material and occurs almost worldwide; red porphyry comes from Egypt, green from Greece, brown from Scandinavia and violet and light green from France. Italian craftsmen at the Pitti Palace in Florence were inspired to imitate its rich appearance, and by the 18th century this faux finish was commonly used for desk and table tops, ornamental vases and inlay; it can be varied to achieve a coarse or smooth effect.

Stenciling became popular in America in about 1820 when the Sheraton "fancy chair" was in vogue—it combined stencil work and freehand bronze painting as a substitute for expensive gold-leaf decoration. The best-known of the New England stencilers was Lambert Hitchcock who had a chair factory at Rivertown, Connecticut (it still produces reproduction chairs) but others like W. P. Eaton and James Johnson are less well known. These highly decorated chairs were sold in stores or peddled around the countryside from carts for $1.00! Unfortunately the quality of the stencilwork had declined by 1840 but we have a good idea of the most common designs from the discovery of a whole box of long-forgotten stencils at Dyke Mill, Montague, Massachusetts.

EFFECTS

The Japanese have used stenciling for centuries, cleverly cutting their stencils from disused documents, to decorate lengths of silk, crepe and cotton.

Collage from the French *coller,* to glue, involves arranging and then gluing anything from wire to newspaper, to a background. It is really a fine art technique used by Picasso and Braque, among others, but it is often confused with découpage. Découpage, the art of gluing cut-out decorations to surfaces, is from the French word *couper,* to cut. It probably began in Italy when frustrated Venetian decorators of the 12th century tried to imitate the fashionable "Chinoiserie" or oriental-style lacquer which was more common and more obtainable in northern Europe. In fact, découpage has been called the poor man's lacquer, but like lacquerwork, it really was a hobby of the fashionable classes as evidenced by the publication of *The Ladies' Amusement Book* of 1760 which contained several motifs to color and cut. It was a French engraver, Pillement, who produced the first extensive range of appropriately rococo prints to adorn the already ornate furniture of this period. Interest was renewed in the early 1900's and respected découpers of the day included Caroline Duer, Carl Federer, Maybelle and Hiram Manning. Nursery screens adorned with an assemblage of romantic prints became very popular in England at this time.

In the ancient world, the Chinese, Japanese and Egyptians adorned their temples, palaces, tombs, murals and household furnishings with pure gold. Later Greek and Roman sculptors embellished their statuary with the wondrous stuff, and later still the monks in European monasteries added interest to their austere lives by illuminating the vellum pages of their holy books. The only difference in the manufacture of leaf today is that it can now be beaten much thinner—up to 1/1000″ (0.025mm) thick. Pure gold is not only prohibitively expensive for chairs and tables, it is too soft to be really useful, so wood and base metal pieces were covered with a thin layer of gold metal.

This fashion for gilt decoration comes and goes over the ages, but in the early 18th century the French, in particular, fell in love with the effect of rococo curves, dancing and glinting under their layer of gold and silver. Whole rooms were furnished and decorated floor to ceiling, with not a square inch of wood or plaster to be seen.

Such glitter left its mark even after the fashion died away, and its connotation of opulence has continued to inspire craftsmen. When the White House was rebuilt after the War of 1812 much of the new furniture, ordered from France, was of this "gilt wood" in the new lighter version. The luxuries of that era are long since gone, and less happily, the once common gilders have also nearly disappeared. Today they are usually employed as restorers by art galleries and museums. Unfortunately gold leafing is not for beginners but if you want a similar effect, see pages 100 to 102.

ANTIQUING

This technique is used to give an antique-looking patina to tin or wood, and needs great skill and taste to achieve an authentic effect. To start, the base coat of paint must be protected with two coats of a clear gloss finish, sanding between coats with very fine abrasive paper. When the second application has dried completely, mix a brownish antiquing shade from the following formula and then decide upon the method of application.

- $1\frac{1}{2}$ teaspoonfuls raw umber or you may prefer to mix a shade much darker than the base coat (e.g. if the base coat is light blue you might mix 1 teaspoonful of cobalt blue and raw umber plus the turpentine and spar varnish as below, to get a dark blue antique shade). If your base coat is very light, add $\frac{1}{2}$ teaspoonful of flake white to the raw umber.
- 3 tablespoonfuls turpentine
- 1 tablespoonful spar varnish

Mix the pigments and turpentine together, then add the varnish to this mixture until it coagulates properly. Seal and store in a tinted glass jar.

Stroking Technique

- Dip a ridgy old paint brush into the antiquing formula and go over the surface of the object lightly and in one direction only [1]. If the paint is too runny, stroke out the excess onto some sheets of newspaper.
- Do not go back over your first brush strokes or the effect will be too dark. There should be an even tone with few obvious brush strokes.

1

- Wipe off some of the antiquing with a piece of old denim [2]. Try to work evenly and quickly as the antiquing dries quite fast.
- After the first application some experts "re-touch" edges, crevices and carvings, with a small brush and additional antiquing liquid to give these areas an even more worn look.
- Leave the "antiqued" object for 36 hours and apply another three coats of spar varnish. Obviously let each coat dry between applications and sand lightly between coats.

Alternative: For a lovely dull luster use a satin finish varnish as the final coat, or mix pumice powder or another fine abrasive with a light machine oil to a pasty consistency, and rub over the object after a final coat of spar varnish.

2

Pouncing Technique

- Use a $1\frac{1}{2}''$ (3.8cm) oval sash brush held high up the handle and perpendicular to your work. Dip the brush into the antiquing formula, tap excess out onto newspaper and tap or "pounce" lightly over the surface so that the brush bounces along [3].
- Cover the entire surface once, then repounce edges, crevices and carvings.

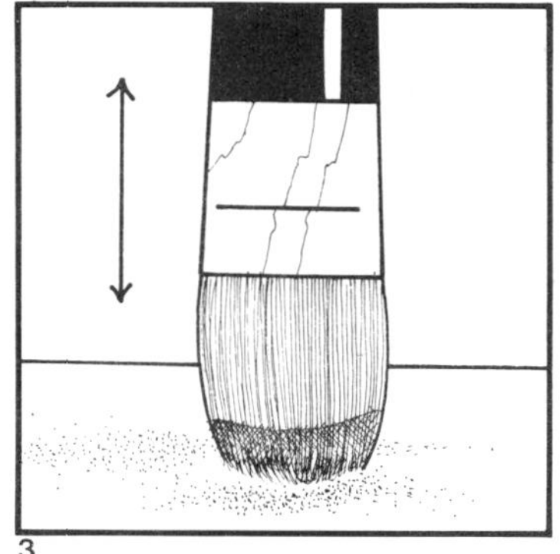

3

Spattering Technique

- Cut the bristles off an old stiff brush to 1″ (2.6cm) [4].
- Dip the brush halfway into the antiquing formula.
- Run the index finger (protected by a stenographer's rubber finger guard) slowly over the bristles so that when loaded an even spray is directed onto the surface below [5].

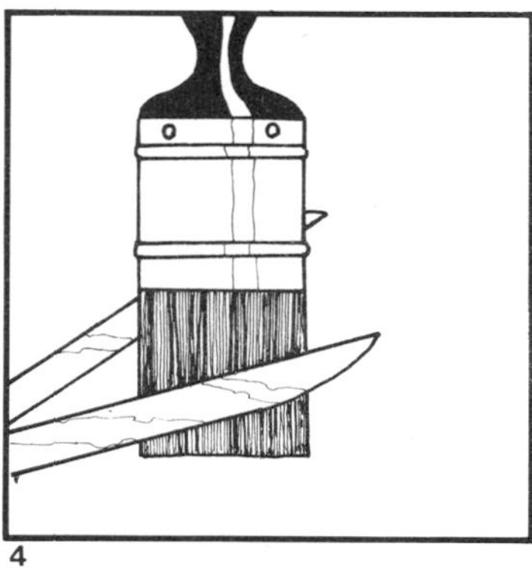

4

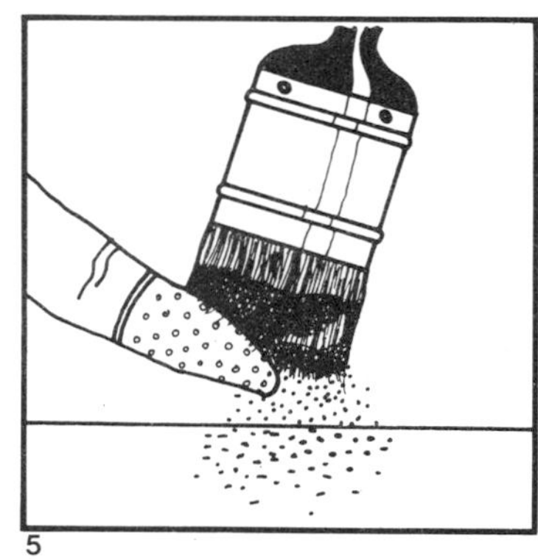

5

- Experiment with the kind of spatters you can obtain by running your finger slowly or quickly over the bristles, but aim for even spattering—you may find it necessary to repeat the process a few times over an area to get an even effect.

Alternatives: For other effects the spatter can be brushed across with a clean dry brush or spattered with turpentine for a softer effect. You could also combine the two "antiquing" techniques.
Stroking is usually recommended for furniture with rustic or simple lines, like early American or early English. Pouncing seems to be the best choice for 18th century French or Italian or any piece with delicate carving, e.g. Adam, Sheraton, or Heppelwhite in style; while spattering is more suitable for Regency, French Directoire and Chippendale. Of course these are only guidelines—so don't be afraid to make your own selection.

FAUX FINISHES

Faux Marbling

This must be applied over three coats of background color which have been sanded with very fine wet-and-dry abrasive paper and a soapy solution. If these base coats are applied with a flat paint, protect them with two coats of thinned shellac, sanded with the finest abrasive paper between coats. It is very important that the surface to be marbled is satin smooth. Assemble the following tools and practice each of the techniques on a piece of scrap white cardboard to see which you feel most comfortable and happy with. It may help to have a picture or a piece of marble nearby for reference and inspiration.

Tools and supplies for the application of floating paint:

Stiff brush and turkey feathers clipped as shown [6].
Two oxhair brushes, $\frac{1}{4}''$ and $\frac{1}{2}''$ (7mm and 13mm).
12″ (30.5cm) squares of cheesecloth.
Small, coarse natural sponges.
Crumpled newspaper.

6

Marbling—First Steps

● First make a flatting oil from one volume boiled linseed oil mixed with six volumes turpentine or paint thinner.
● Then make the floating paint: Mix one volume japan paint with a solution of equal parts of flatting oil and mineral spirits to the consistency of water.
● Dilute an equal portion of the base hue.
● Brush the surface first with some flatting oil then immediately with the diluted base hue.
● Dip any "tool" from the list above into mineral spirits and then the floating japan paint while the surface is still wet, following the instructions below.

Ways of Marbling

Six alternative methods:

The oxhair brushes, each dipped into a different shade of floating paint are held at the top of the handles and used as one brush [7]. Pat on the paint, letting the shades flow together.
Each 12″ (30.5cm) square of cheesecloth is twisted into a coil [8] and then each section of the coil can be loaded with a different floating shade and rolled over the wet surface again and again, reloading each section as necessary.
Clipped feathers are dipped into the mineral spirits, combed with a fine comb and then each loaded with a different floating shade and used on the broad side to "paint" on the shade [9].
The clipped brush is used so that each group of bristles is loaded with a separate floating shade and then is turned and twisted over the surface [10].

7

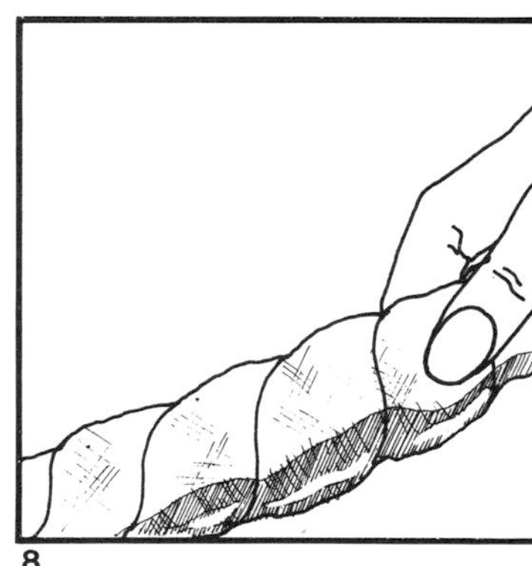
8

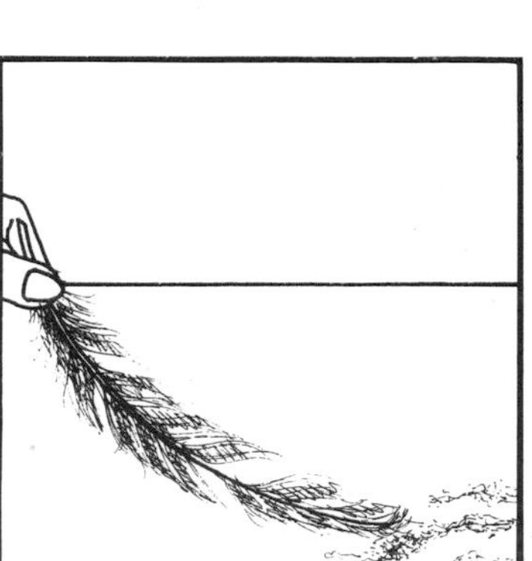
9

10

Several small natural sponges can each be loaded with paint and rolled over the surface [11].
Newspaper can be crumpled up, saturated with paint and dabbed over the surface [12].

11

12

Any of these methods should produce interesting and irregular effects but if they are not satisfactory, or the surface dries too quickly, try dipping a small natural sponge into turpentine or paint thinner and squeezing it out over the surface [13]. Try not to flood it, as many of the effects will then dissolve. If the spirit collects in pools, dab up the excess with absorbent cotton or cotton wool. All areas that resemble marble can now be left to dry, but inadequately decorated areas may need further treatment. You can use another clipped feather, crumpled newspaper, or cheesecloth, dipped again in the "floating" paint, to touch up. Eye-droppers could also be used.

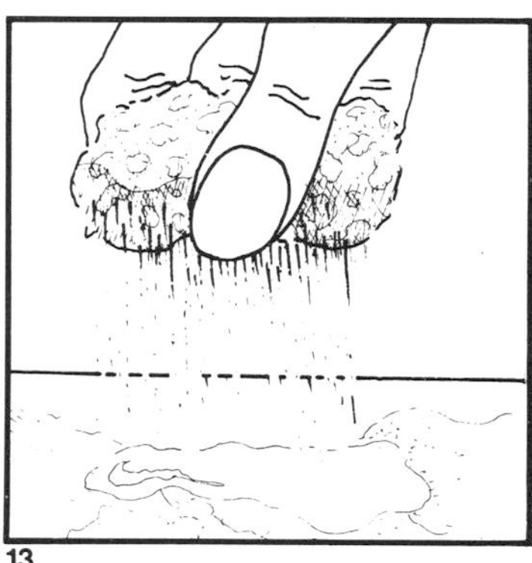
13

Veining: An additional final touch to faux marble is veining. In a natural state these veins are really impurities in the marble; to achieve this, dip a fine brush into the mineral spirits and then a darker shade of japan paint, and hold as shown [14]. This should be done when the ground is still slightly damp and the stroke should be varied. When satisfied with the marbling and veining, let the surface dry for several days and then protect it with two coats of thinned gloss varnish.

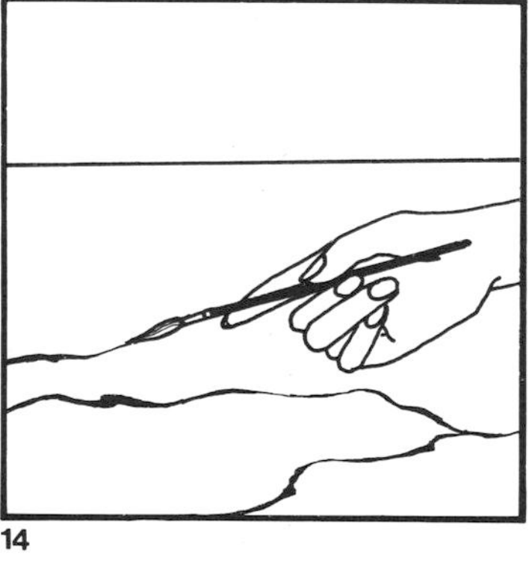
14

Faux Porphyry

This special effect is really a variation of the spattering technique used in antiquing but gives a much more stony effect.

- Apply two coats of the following mixture for a gray-beige base hue:
  6 volumes flat white paint
  1 volume raw umber
  1 volume yellow ocher
- Sand lightly after application to remove brush strokes.
- Use japan paints for spattering, mixed with the following values in mind. These can be whatever strikes your fancy but obviously they should go with or complement the base hue.

a) dominant hue, light value
b) dominant hue, middle value
c) dominant hue, dark value
d) 1st contrasting hue, light value
e) 2nd contrasting hue, middle value
f) 3rd contrasting hue, dark value

● Mix one volume japan paint (this can be flat white tinted with the selected hue), three volumes pure turpentine and 1/10 volume japan drier for each spattering hue.

Applying Faux Porphyry

● Dip a short, coarse bristled brush halfway into the first spattering hue of light value [15], and rap the side of the ferrule on a wooden block as it is swung over the surface—this will release largish spatters [16].

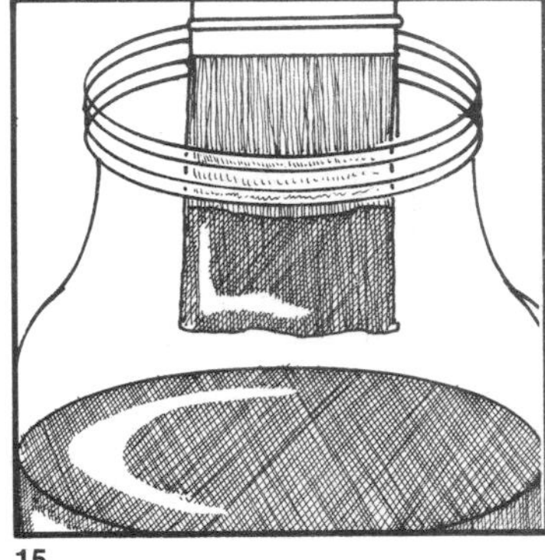

15

16

● For fine specks run your index finger (protected with a rubber finger guard) slowly over the bristles so that when loaded an even spray is directed to the surface below [17].

● If a large or unwanted spatter occurs accidentally, scrape it off when dry with a single-edged razor blade [18].

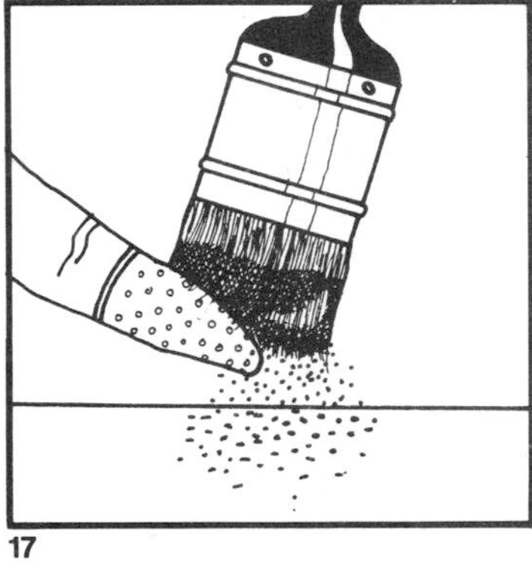

17

18

● Another touch (optional) is a rich gold fine spatter applied as above and prepared from the following formula:

$\frac{1}{4}$ volume rich gold powder
1 volume quick size
$\frac{1}{4}$ volume turpentine

● This can be followed by black and/or white spattering depending on the desired effect.

● Finally the surface must be protected with two coats of clear varnish, sanding with finest abrasive paper between coats if necessary.

STENCILING

Stenciling

This technique can be used on walls or furniture using gold powders or any other powdered pigment. In any event, do a bit of research and try to select a pattern which is appropriate in period and style. You will need the following supplies:

Masking tape
Architect's linen or stencil paper, sharp pencil
Piece of glass
Piece of cardboard
Knife with replaceable blades
Piece of denim
Powdered pigment (gold leaf powder is used here)

To Stencil

- Tape the linen or stencil paper over the design and carefully trace it [19].
- Tape the completed traced pattern to a piece of glass big enough to accommodate the entire stencil.
- Very carefully cut out the stencil, using the knife (it is sometimes helpful to place the glass over a piece of colored paper to make cutting easier) [20].

19

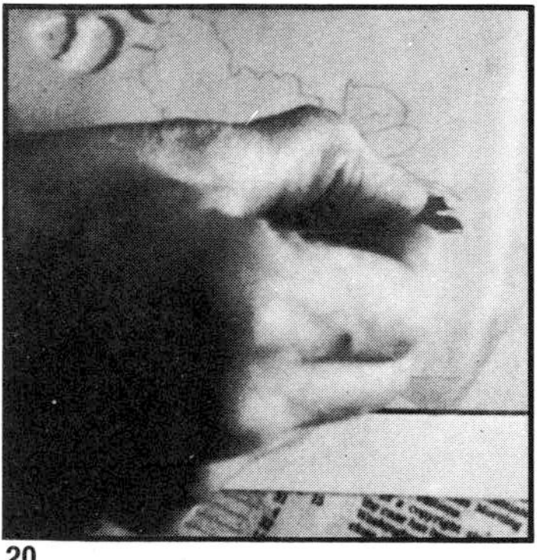
20

- Carefully place the stencil on the piece of furniture and hold it in place with masking tape.
- Shake a bit of gold powder onto the cardboard and with your denim-wrapped index finger, dab the powder until the denim feels well saturated [21].
- Very quickly and carefully dab the powder over the holes in the stencil starting at one end and moving gradually across each hole [22].
- Try not to allow the "gold" to slip under the stencil—this will cause a sloppy edge. (If this happens, after completing the dabbing, use turpentine and a cotton swab to even the edge.)

21

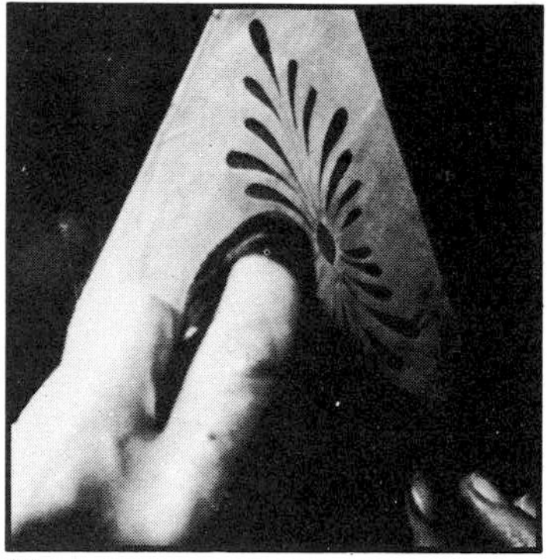
22

● When you have dabbed the entire stencil, carefully untape and peel back the cut stencil [23].
● Let the "gold" dry for 36-48 hours before applying two coats of protective clear varnish.
● Sand lightly after the first two coats with fine wet-and-dry abrasive paper and a soapy solution.

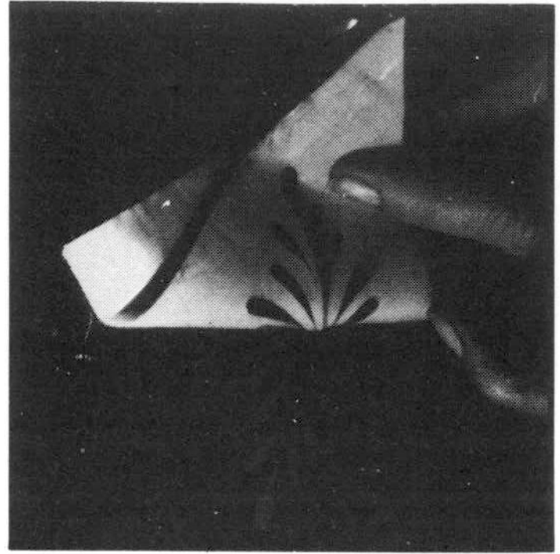
23

Alternative: Other pigments can be applied after the first coat of varnish. If you want a silver and gold effect, purchase aluminum powder instead of silver powder, which darkens upon being varnished. Bronze powders can also be used.

PHYSICAL DISTRESSING

This is a "cheat" used to give objects a look of battered old age by means of scars, stains, simulated wormholes etc. It is rather a brutal process and cannot really be recommended. You can use a rubber or wooden hammer to soften edges; to scar, use lengths of chain or keys on a hanger; to "wormhole", heat a sharp pointed metal tool to red hot and ram it into the wood holding it with pliers. The stain formula below is applied to darken wood, as age might, and is used under distressed paintwork.

"Distressed" Paintwork

● Mix 1 volume burnt umber japan color to 1/10 volume japan drier, and $\frac{1}{2}$ volume turpentine.
● Apply one coat of the above stain formula to raw or painted wood.
● Let dry overnight and then seal with two coats of diluted shellac.
● Apply two coats of flat or gloss oil-based paint to the object, allowing each coat to dry completely. Sand final coat with fine abrasive paper so the brush strokes are removed.

● Pour jelly or pasty consistency paint remover into a flat container and load the tip of a No. 8 hog bristle brush. Deposit the paint remover on edges, moldings, carvings, in small patches, especially at the base where you might expect wear. Aim for irregular, uneven edges [24].

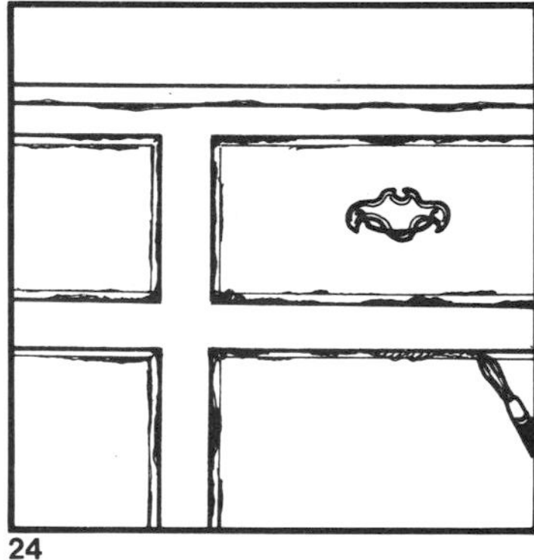
24

● Use a wooden meat skewer to push the paint remover into crevices and jagged edges [25].
● When the paint wrinkles, hit the area with a piece of towelling to lift the paint and stop the action of the paint remover—before it gets to the brown coat underneath. Don't ever wipe just the paint remover off, dab it!

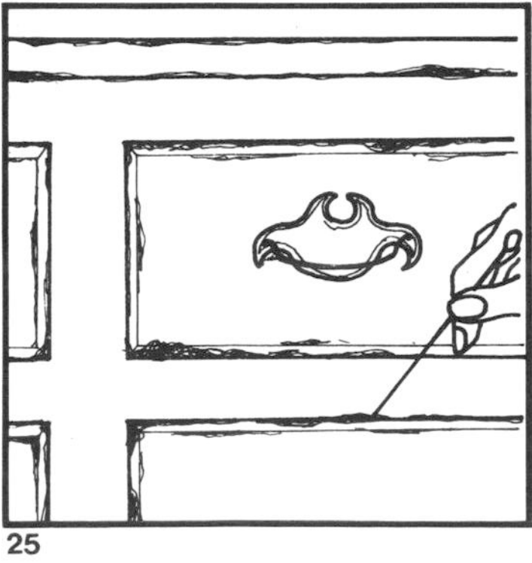
25

● Rinse off any remaining paint remover with water. Apply striping etc. if you wish, but rub this down (and nearly off) with fine abrasive paper.
● Finally protect the distressing with a high gloss varnish and "antique". (See previous pages, 92-3).

DECOUPAGE

The supplies needed for découpage are few:

- Curved scissors (cuticle 3″, 7.6cm)
- Water-soluble white glue with a resin base, and brush for applying it.
- Sponge
- Mat knife or scalpel
- Sealer and brush
- Turpentine
- Furniture wax
- Varnish and white bristle varnish brush
- ½″ (13mm) oxhair brush for small areas
- 1″ (2.6cm) oxhair brush for large areas

Often découpage decoration gets dented or damaged over the years—the glued-on motif loosens and tears, and eventually disappears, so the restorer must often find a suitable replacement print. The best sources are museum copies of prints, old damaged books with clean prints as illustration, magazines, old wallpaper books, old catalogues and facsimiles of Victorian and other early books.

● Remove the chosen page carefully with the knife; alternatively, photocopy an unremovable one.

● Occasionally the print will seem too thick; if so, wet the back with a sponge dipped into a solution of three parts vinegar to one part of water and gently peel off as many layers as necessary. The same mixture can be used to soften glue holding an old fabric backing [26].

26

● Repair the surface of the object, if it is damaged. Here, photographs show how a nursery screen was restored, but prints could be applied to virtually any household object in this way.

● For a three-dimensional effect use printed pictures, or shade black-and-white prints yourself with pencils or watercolor paint.

● After tinting, spray with aerosol fixative [27] or apply your own with a small brush, made from one half shellac and one half denatured alcohol (methylated spirits).

Cutting: Don't begin to cut until the fixative has dried.

27

● To cut out the selected print, use well-made, sharp cuticle scissors about 3″ (7.6cm) long, holding the scissors in one hand and turning the paper to feed the scissors with the other. This method of cutting causes the edges to turn under slightly and eases gluing [28].
Hint: the tips of the scissors should only be used for the corners.

Gluing

● Apply a water-soluble white glue with resin base, using an old clean brush, starting in the middle and working out [29].

28

29

● Let the glue get tacky before placing the print on the object [30].

● After the glue has dried for 24 hours cover the print with one part shellac, one part denatured alcohol (methylated spirits) to protect it.

● Let this dry for 12-24 hours, then rub down with the finest steel wool.

● Dust with a lintless cloth (clean old tights will do) and apply flat (mat) varnish thinned with the recommended solvent. Stroke it on, working in one direction. Apply ten thin coats but watch for runs, bubbles and streaks. Let each coat dry completely before applying the next. (Work until you can't feel the print at all.)

● If you drop it, scratch it or the cat walks by after varnishing, wipe the object with the varnish solvent and begin again. Hint: always apply varnish in good light.

● Finally sand with the finest wet-and-dry paper, followed by the finest steel wool; then dust. Optional: apply a furniture wax with a soft cloth, working in small circles until the desired shine is reached.

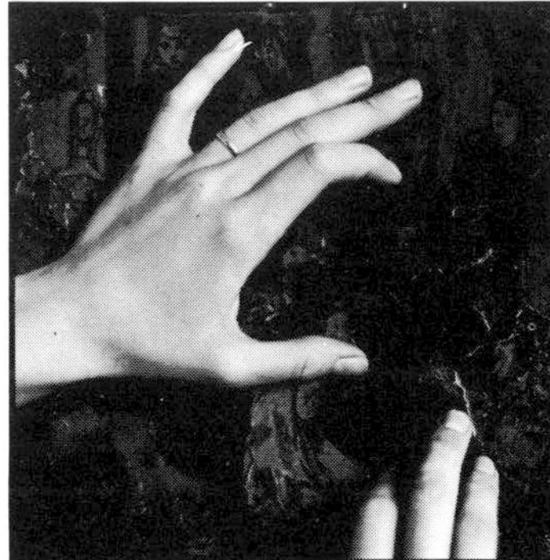

30

GILDING

To clarify, gilding is the process of covering an object with any kind of metallic-like finish, including pure gold. "Gold leafing" on the other hand is more specific and means covering a surface with thin sheets of gold, called leaves. When restoring, it is generally advisable to treat only the surface which once was gilded, but if infatuation with the shimmer overcomes you, the complete process is outlined below. Remember though, small highlights are often more effective than large areas. Entire objects are rarely gilded, with the exception of picture frames.

Cleaning: Use slightly soapy water or denatured alcohol (methylated spirits). (Undiluted vinegar will clean very dirty gilding but always rinse well, and dry). Rinse and polish with a soft cloth. Caution: don't use alcohol or methylated spirits near lacquer work.

Repairing Picture Frames

● Make sure the piece is in good condition, filling in holes, chips, etc. See the section relating to the material concerned elsewhere in the book.

- Use the T-square to see if the frame is "square" [31] and keep the inner liner and outer frame separate.
- Remove all remnants of gilding with paint remover (or formula given below) brushing into crevices with an old toothbrush or stencil brush [32].

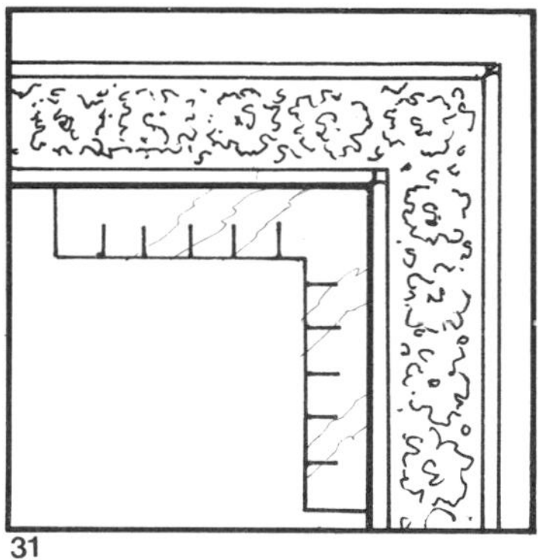

31

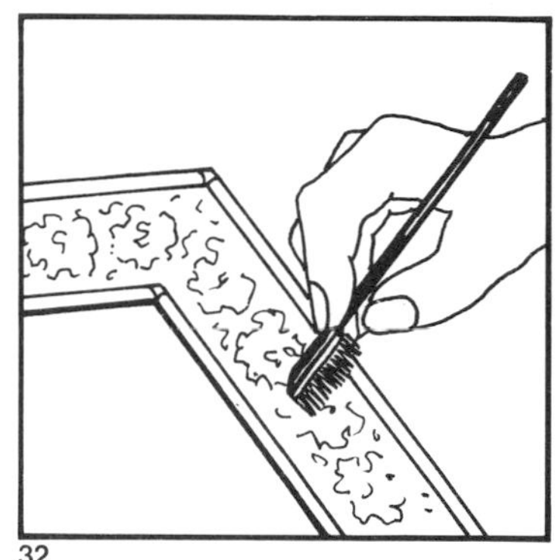

32

Removing Gilding: Add $\frac{1}{2}$ - $\frac{3}{4}$ oz (10-20gms) bicarbonate of soda and the same amount of detergent to 1qt (1 liter) of water.

Stir well and rub the solution onto the gilded surface with sponge. A wooden object, if small enough, can simply be immersed in the liquid. Use an old toothbrush to remove stubborn "gilt".

- Wipe or dust off the excess and rinse with denatured alcohol (methylated spirits), then for wood, sand with medium fine abrasive paper; for plaster, with a slightly finer grade. For the hard-to-get-at areas, use the finest steel wool rolled into a point; or typewriter pencil erasers [33]. Hint: for sanding concave areas evenly cut the same shape from a piece of wood or molding.

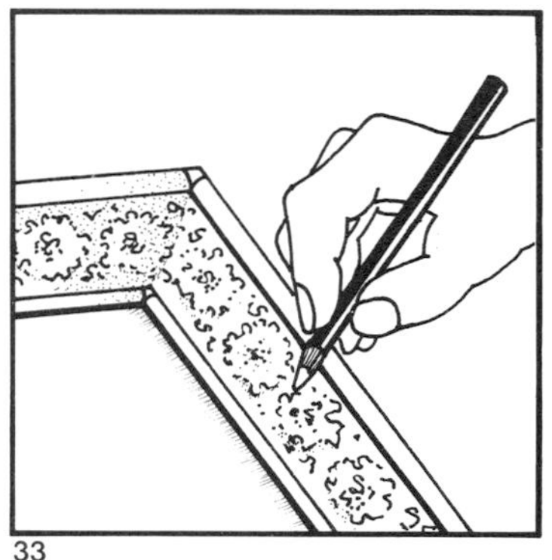

33

Metallic Powders

- Purchase the best quality pulverized metals—gold, silver, bronze.
- Prepare a glass-smooth surface by sanding as above and then applying gesso as follows:
- Gesso is sold today in powdered form and replaces the whiting used for centuries. (Do not confuse it with the modern polymer gesso used for priming artists' canvases.) Mix with cold distilled water in a glass jar [34] until the consistency of cream and allow to stand overnight.

34

- Place the jar in a pan of hot water and stir until the gesso is warm and slightly thicker. Keep it in this warm water while applying.
- Pour out some gesso into a ceramic cup, place that in a pan of hot water and stir every few minutes as you apply it [35].
- Apply thin coats with a flat soft oxhair or sable brush [36] (thin with distilled water if necessary).

35

36

● Apply two coats, waiting at least two hours between coats and smooth with the finest abrasive paper to remove brushmarks between coats.

● Apply twelve, yes twelve, more coats, allowing three hours for drying between coats. Sand with the finest abrasive paper, then the finest steel wool. Dust with soft cloth or blow with reversed vacuum cleaner.

● Apply one coat of shellac thinned with denatured alcohol (methylated spirits).

● Apply quick-drying purchased gold size (oil-type).

● Dust powder carefully over the wet size with ¾″ (20mm) oval or round camelhair dusting brush [37]. Hint: keep brush well filled with powders and let hairs hardly touch the tacky surface working on 2″-3″ (5-7.6cm) at a time.

● Let the object dry for at least twelve hours.

37

● Remove excess powder with feather duster or reversed vacuum cleaner [38]. Hint: touch up with gilt paint if necessary—blending to match the shade of the powder [39]. Let dry.

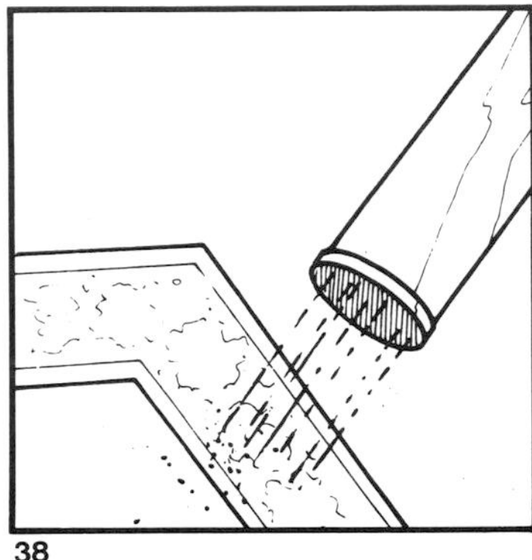
38

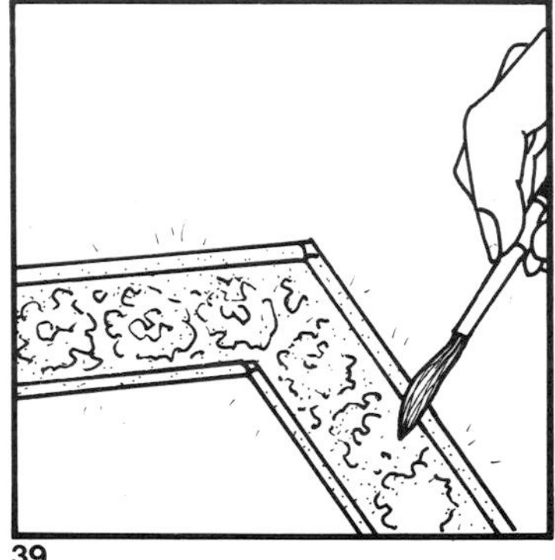
39

● Fix with a clear acrylic varnish in an aerosol can [40].

● Let this dry. Then brush on at least one coat of thinned shellac but apply three to five coats if object will be in general use.

40

Alternative: These powders are available not only in gold, silver and bronze but also in tints like red, green, blue. These are only for the really adventurous. Of course, different powders can easily be mixed before applying, for a very unusual effect.

Alternative: You can use liquid gilt after the shellac, but this really looks rather cheap and dull soon after application, and is only good for small areas. DON'T buy an ordinary commercial metallic gold paint. Try to get a high quality variety that is sold in art stores. After application protect the paint with varnish or shellac. Then polish the piece where possible with a good furniture polish.

Hints: Tap the back of small objects lightly to facilitate the spreading of the gesso.

Clean the brushes used for applying the powders or paint (see solvent bottle for relevant information), then wash them in soap and warm water before storing.

Some experts smooth the gesso, while applying, with a palette knife; you can also use your fingers.

GOLD LEAFING

Records show that in England before 1770, gold was ground in honey to make it stick! The following instructions are less organic but very time-consuming. Gold leafing is not for beginners at working with their hands but the patent leaf is easier to apply than the thinner, precious leaf. To begin, follow the first nine steps as above, remembering that when applying gold leaf it is more crucial that the surface be sanded glass smooth between each coat of gesso. (Use only the finest abrasive paper, followed by the finest steel wool as instructed.)

Optional: Perfectionists can tint the gesso with dry pigments; dark red-brown is usually used. After mixing it with the distilled water apply tinted gesso for the last two or three coats.

Finally decide whether you want the finished surface to be very shiny gold (burnished) or more dull (mat) or a combination. For picture frames the ornaments and convex, concave and other burnished surfaces are laid down first and polished so that the rubbing action does not disturb the mat parts.

For a Shiny (Burnished) Effect

- Purchase "gold size", really a fine clay called "bole". This is available in several shades, although red is the most commonly used. Stir well before using as this helps the leaf to adhere.
- Pour 1 cup/$\frac{1}{2}$ pint (0.3 liters) cold distilled water into a tall glass and add $\frac{1}{2}$ oz (14gm) rabbit skin glue grains. Stir with a spoon and let it stand overnight.
- Place the glass in pan of hot water (not steaming) and stir the mixture well until the glue granules dissolve [41]. Keep this mixture warm, not hot, by adding hot water as necessary to the pan.

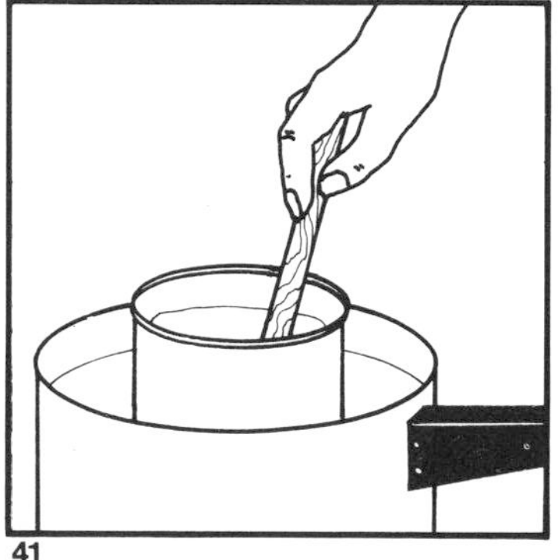

41

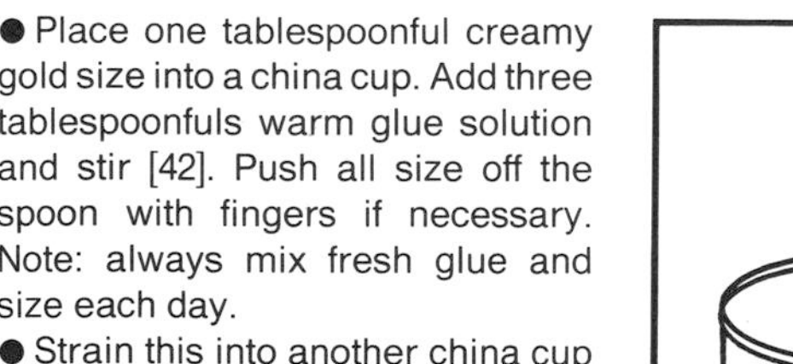

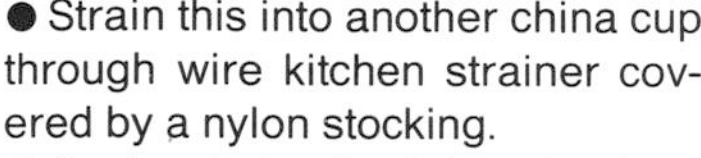

- Place one tablespoonful creamy gold size into a china cup. Add three tablespoonfuls warm glue solution and stir [42]. Push all size off the spoon with fingers if necessary. Note: always mix fresh glue and size each day.
- Strain this into another china cup through wire kitchen strainer covered by a nylon stocking.
- Apply strained mixture to dust-free object. Hint: work in a warm, dust-free room, using flat $\frac{5}{8}''$ (15mm) sable brush [43]; don't wipe the excess from your brush on the edge of the cup but on newspapers.
- Apply size in small even strokes in one direction. Let it dry for half an hour and apply five or six more coats allowing at least the same time between. Smooth after third and sixth coats, sand with the finest abrasive paper and then dust with a feather duster or reversed vacuum cleaner.

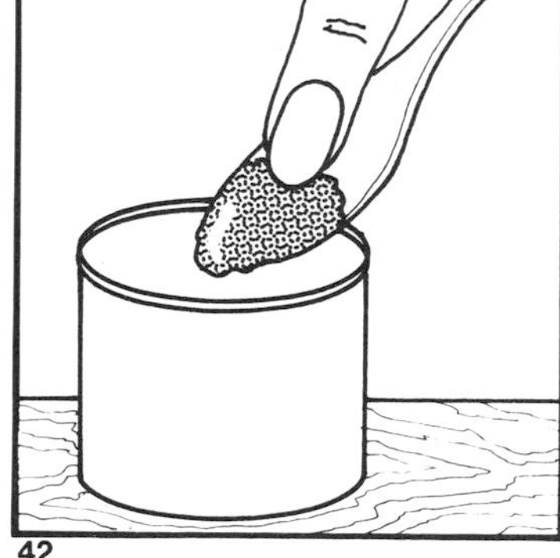

42

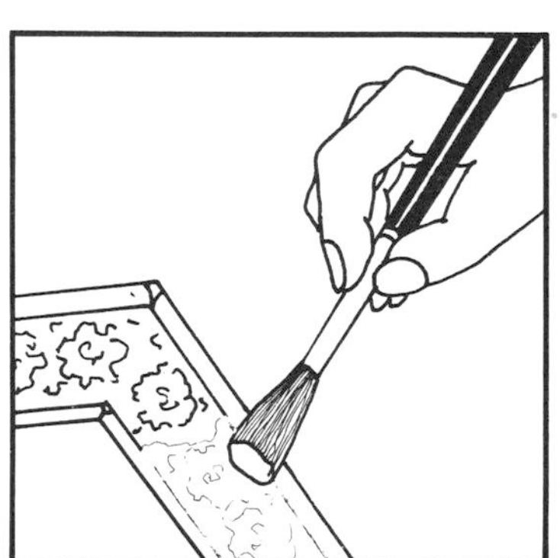

43

● Sand the final coat with gentle pressure using the finest abrasive paper. Do not rub through the red coats or the gold leaf will not adhere, although you can touch up any places where this happens with the mixture.
Apply loose-packed gold leaf as follows. This is usually sold 20-25 leaves to the book, measuring $3\frac{3}{8}''$ (8.5cms) square. Each leaf should be separated by tissue paper and should not be touched with fingers.

● Cover work surface with clean newspapers, and dust your fingers with talcum powder to discourage sticking.
● Cut off binding edge of the leaf book with scissors. Rub the cut edge afterwards to smooth any crumples [44]. Try to keep this firmly held while cutting, to prevent the leaves from sticking to each other.
● Use a new sharp paring knife with a 4″ (10cm) thin blade to lift off the cover from the book. There should be a tissue underneath, protecting the top leaf. Slip the knife under the first four leaves and lift them off [45], leaving a gold leaf exposed.
● Take the first four leaves in turn between tissues and tear very slowly in half, about $\frac{1}{4}''$ (7mm) at a time [46]. Then tear in half again. (Don't be tempted to simply cut—you'll crimp all the edges.)
● Keep the four stacks in a separate place, moving them by slipping the knife under the bottom tissue. They will be used for small areas.

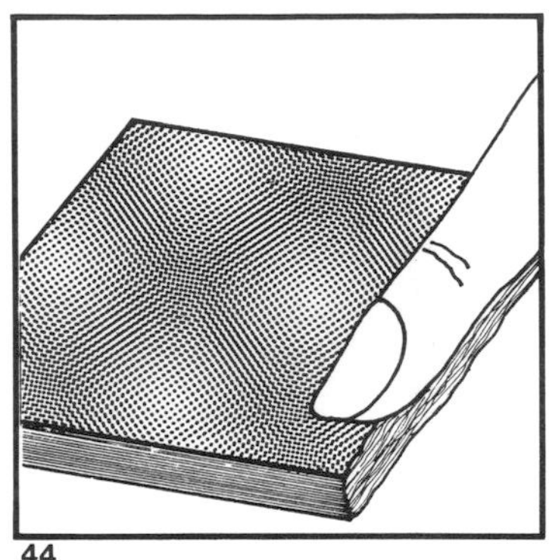
44

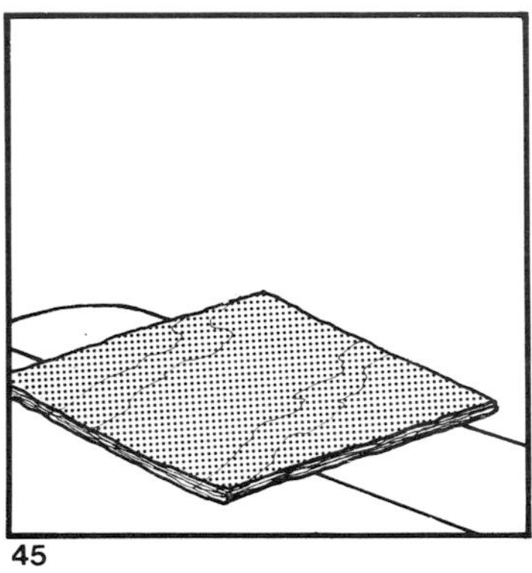
45

46

● Mix "gilder's liquor" in ceramic cup—seven teaspoonfuls distilled water with three teaspoonfuls denatured alcohol (methylated spirits). Move a gilder's brush, called a gilder's tip, lightly across your hair or trousers or skirt to magnetize it.
● Lift corner of top tissue with paring knife [47].

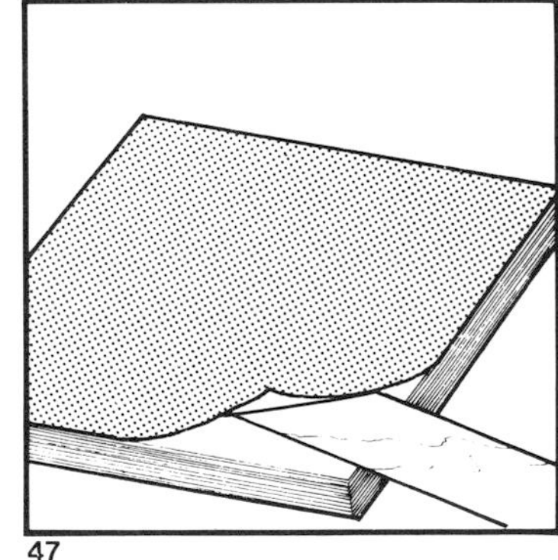
47

● Pick up the gold leaf by laying $\frac{1}{4}''$ (7mm) of the tip over the leaf [48]. Transfer tip and leaf carefully to the other hand.
● Dip round sable brush in the mixed "liquor", brush this onto the spot where the leaf will go. (Make this area wet with a single stroke: re-wet only when thoroughly dry.)
● When tacky apply the loose leaf [49]. To test for tackiness, touch the area with a knuckle of a bent finger—a "click" means the surface is ready to be leafed.

48

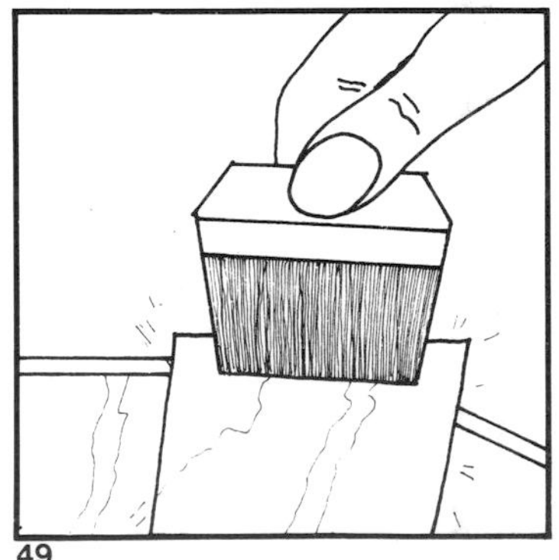
49

● When leafing small areas, use the torn pieces you have piled up separately.

● Pick up leaf with tip and lay pieces on the sized surface one by one, overlapping $\frac{1}{8}''$ (3mm). Lower them down with the tip, but don't let fingers or tip touch the size. If the leaf falls or crumples, re-magnetize (see opposite) the tip and pick up another piece of leaf before the "size" dries. If the size gets onto the wrong area and is left uncovered by the new leaf it will dull the already-applied leaf. Hint: on really curved parts, tear ribbon-shaped pieces of leaf and lower the hanging end in [50].

50

● When the sized surface has been entirely leafed, use the camel-hair dusting brush to remove the loose bits of leaf [51].

● Don't touch surface for twelve hours, then polish with pieces of absorbent cotton or cotton wool; don't rub hard as this type of leaf hardens slowly.

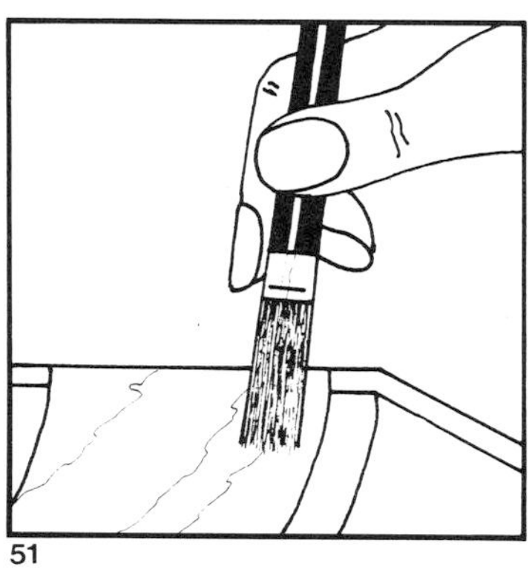
51

Hints

● Lay the leaf, working from the top of the object towards you.

● Tilt the work surface slightly if possible.

● If a drop of the size gets trapped under the leaf and makes a bulge, blow on the bulge to force it out. Don't press it out with fingers or brush.

● Don't touch a dried sized surface with your fingers.

● Don't touch a wet surface with anything but gold leaf.

● If a bare spot is exposed after dusting, tear bits of leaf of the approximate size and apply the leaf as before, but with a diluted size containing one part denatured alcohol (methylated spirits) and seven parts distilled water.

● Avoid wearing clothing made of wool or rayon because of their static-producing property.

● Don't attempt to gold leaf the inaccessible areas—they will have to be painted with liquid gilt.

Burnishing or Polishing Gold Leaf

● Wait at least six hours and then burnish the gold leafed surface with a curved agate burnisher [52]. This is a polished agate fastened to a wooden handle, replacing the dog's tooth used for centuries.

● Grasp the burnisher near the agate tip and rub the broad curve of the tool back and forth in left-to-right strokes or in circles depending on the area.

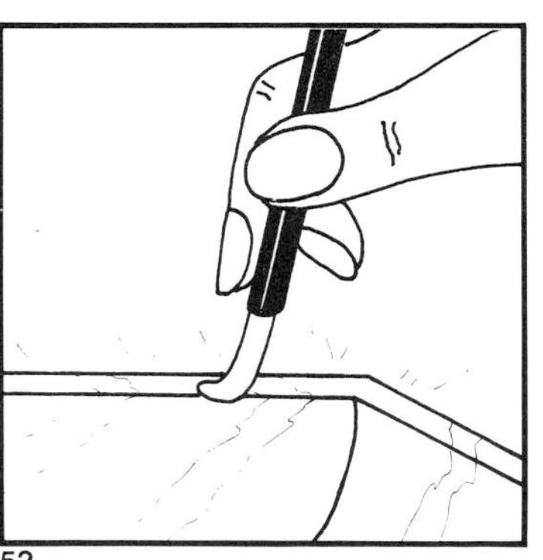
52

● Work slowly to avoid dull, unburnished lines between strokes. If any of the laid leaf tears or is damaged, relay a new piece on top and burnish it immediately.

● Wait 48 hours and burnish any raised areas to a brilliant polish.

For a Mat or Dull Effect

- Follow the first eight steps under Metallic Powders (pages 101-2).
- After final smoothing and dusting, apply sealer made from two parts orange shellac and one part denatured alcohol (methylated spirits) [53].
- Apply two more coats leaving at least two hours to dry between coats. Smooth with medium steel wool to remove brush marks as these will mar the surface. Dust the final surface as before. Remember the shellac mixture must not touch the parts to be burnished.
- Pour $\frac{1}{4}$ cup, $\frac{1}{8}$ pint (0.05 liters) of quick drying oil-based size into china cup and then apply it evenly with $\frac{5}{8}''$ (15mm) sable brush—sizing only the area you hope to cover with gold leaf in one hour, probably 2″-3″ (5-7.6cm) when beginning.
- Apply loose-packed gold leaf as described on pages 103-5 under gold leafing For a Shiny Effect, but do not burnish.

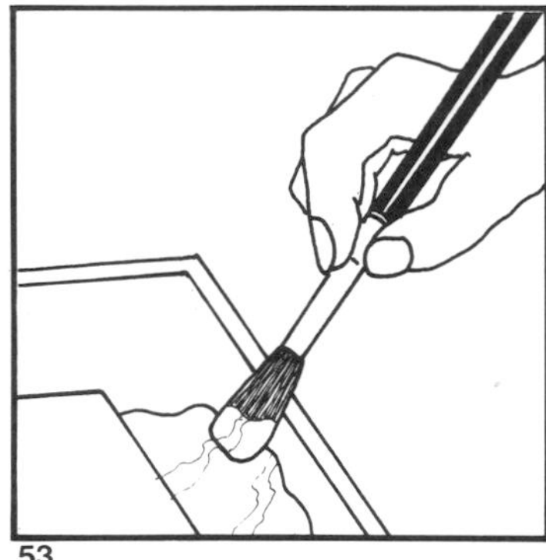
53

To Apply Patent Leaf

This type is perfect for flat surfaces and simple convex or concave shapes. It is less difficult to apply because the edging paper can be touched with fingers.

- Open book of leaf and remove four leaves plus backing one by one with kitchen paring knife or palette knife. Place gold side up on working surface. Touch only the back or margin of tissue with fingers if necessary.
- Cut leaves to required size with scissors and place the cut pieces near the object to be leafed [54].

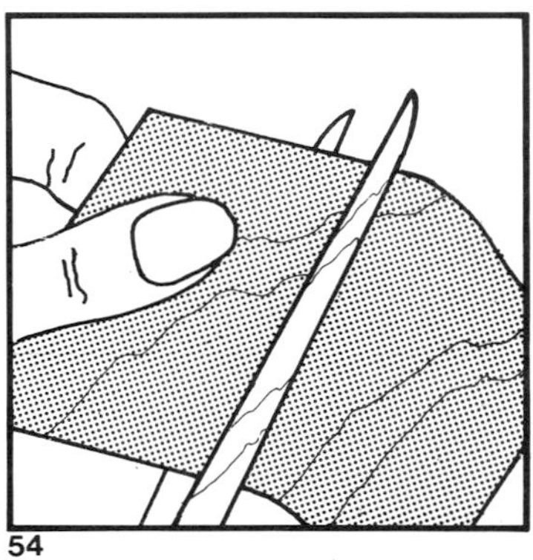
54

- Apply quick-drying size (oil-based) and test with knuckle for tacky "click" sound.
- Slide the knife carefully and slowly under the leaf edge and pick it up by the tissue margin [55], then turn it upside down, placing the gold side down upon the sized area.
- Rub a finger over the back of the tissue to press the leaf underneath completely down [56].
- Lift the tissue carefully off and lay next sheet over the first with an overlap of $\frac{1}{8}''$ (3mm).

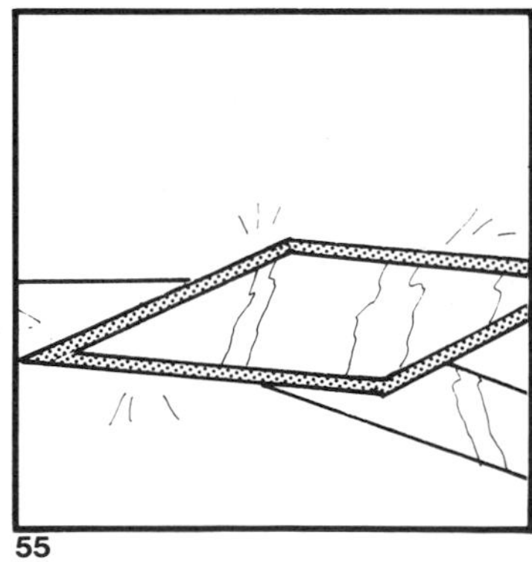
55

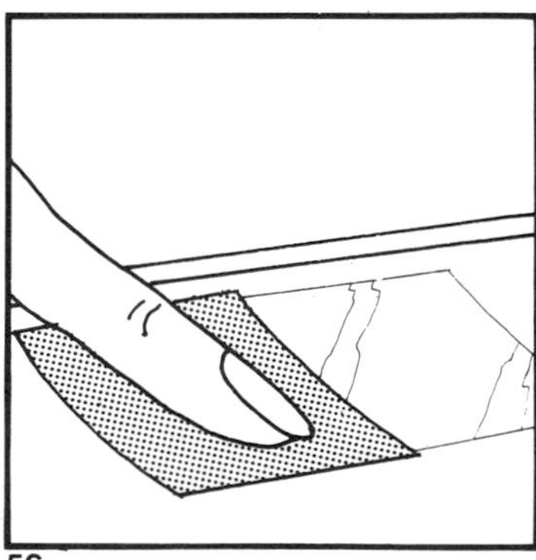
56

Hint: If the leaf cracks upon application, patch later as directed. On the other hand, if you seem adept at cracking it, perhaps you should accept that as your style—some professionals work for these cracks to produce a more "antique" effect.
Alternative: Change the commonly used red size to burnt umber.

Alternative: Silver leaf (slightly cheaper) varnished over gives a similar but less yellow effect. Varnish is not necessary over gold leaf unless to age it, although on a piece of furniture it may be advisable to protect much used support legs with varnish.

Alternative: After varnishing, take a pinch of metallic gold powder on your first finger and blow lightly towards the varnished surface so that the dust sticks. Try to work evenly—this is the difficult part.

An 18th-century gilt-wood mirror from the reign of George III—note the figures on each side: the king on the left represents Europe, the feathered chieftain on the right represents America.

TEXTILES AND

Textiles have been woven probably for as long as 5,000 years. Bits of bark cloth and simple weaving tools have been found at some of man's oldest dwelling sites, and these early fabrics were not just crudely woven burlap or sacking. Their texture and variety are truly amazing, and it is clear that decorative weaves and applied patterns, along with subtle and delicate vegetable dyes, were part of our earliest heritage.

Cotton has always been one of the most important and versatile fabrics available, especially in India where early weavers could produce cloths of surpassing beauty as well as simple straightforward textiles for everyday use. The secrets of manufacture in India, China and Egypt were soon carried by the traders of the Middle East to new customers in southern Europe. Later the Moors brought cotton to Spain, and the market for fine muslins and calico seemed inexhaustible.

The great Indian civilizations in Mexico and Peru also had a highly developed tradition of textile weaving, using brilliant dyes and boldly-handled patterns.

In Europe, the gradual spread of cotton weaving engulfed first the northern European countries and then, through emigration and export, the American colonies newly established in Virginia. The United States became the leading producer of both raw and manufactured cotton, especially after the invention of the cotton gin. That is still the case, with India a close second.

Wool is the second most important textile, but probably the first to be manufactured. Scarcely-domesticated sheep may have provided the early shepherds with tufts of long tangled down caught in thickets of thorn bushes, and its special qualities of warmth and durability must have been obvious pretty quickly. Fragments of woolen fabric have been found in the tombs and deserted sites of Babylon and Nineveh, in the oldest British burial mounds and, with cotton, in the remains of the great Peruvian civilizations.

Manufacture of wool spread quickly along with the improved sheep strains pioneered by the Romans, and the great flocks found a happy home in England, encouraged and helped by every early English King.

America developed her sheep farms early—George Washington was only one of many landowners who didn't like the high taxes imposed by the homeland, and he imported sheep and looms. Eventually sheep rearing was confined to the west, and the actual manufacture of wool was concentrated around New England. These woolen mills are still an important part of the American economy, but the raw wool comes from all over the world; Australia and New Zealand in particular are very important producers. Some special goat hairs are classed as wools—vicuna, camel, angora and cashmere.

True silk is the thread spun by the silkworm to enclose itself in a cocoon, and its first mention is in an ancient legend about a Chinese princess who was interested in the worms and the possibility of removing the fine-spun thread in pieces long enough for weaving. There are about 2,500 feet (750 meters) of thread in a single cocoon, and it must be twisted with four to ten strands together to make a thread sturdy enough for handling. Although the silk mills of China and Japan produced heavenly brocades and stiff embroidered silks for their nobility, it wasn't until the Renaissance that travelers

UPHOLSTERY

managed to slip out through the Chinese borders with silkworms, and the seeds of the mulberry tree on which they feed.

Italy and France developed a silk culture industry, and the silk mills of Lyons and Venice have been famed for their luxurious velvets and brocades ever since, but silk has never been produced to any notable extent in northern Europe or America.

There have been periods of activity—silkworms were bred in Spitalfields, London, during the 17th century, and later in Georgia during the 18th century; cocoons were bred and shipped back to England to be spun and woven. Italy and southern France, though, found the problems were less difficult to solve in their Mediterranean climate, and they still produce and weave raw silk in fair quantity, and of superb quality.

Silk can be made into many types of fabric, from rich brocades and velvets to simple taffetas, twills and failles, and delicate organzas. Today modern chemical additives and mixtures have made a "silk-type" fabric available in a wide range of qualities and prices, but pure silk is still worth saving, cherishing and repairing where you can.

Linen is made from flax, a natural fiber much valued throughout history. By the 15th century BC it was being used for ceremonial and religious cloths, as well as for robes and clothing, especially in Egypt. Hebrew and Phoenician traders took bolts of linen with them to all major Mediterranean ports. The Romans as usual were quick to scent a new market, and they began growing and exporting flax to the various cities in the Empire. When the Empire collapsed, the soldiers and citizens went home, but the flax fields went on producing such good flax that linen became the principal European textile throughout the entire medieval period. By the 11th century, Flanders exported its creamy fine thread along with its weavers, and they settled most happily in Ireland, which is still the largest producer of linen cloth, in every weight from sail-cloth to fine lawn. Unfortunately linen doesn't adapt well to modern fabric-spinning techniques—the thread is too inelastic, and it breaks too easily in the huge machines which now dominate the modern textile mill. Nonetheless, its special qualities are still highly valued—it stays cool to the touch even in very hot weather, it has a deep luster which adds richness to the finished product, and it is very strong.

Most of the fabrics you will come across in repairing and restoring are used as upholstery, hangings, or small pieces of embroidery or decorative work on bags and pictures. Before you begin, try to think about exactly how and where the finished piece will be used.

Anything used constantly should be carefully considered beforehand, and you will probably find it more practical to find a similar modern fabric to replace the old one. Always keep pieces of old fabric—sometimes pictures or pieces of patterned fabric can be used decoratively under glass—as long as you don't cut them up or damage them. Some day you may find your pretty but frail beaded bag was made by your great-great-grandmother's cousins, and it would be a pity to have nothing left but a frame and tatters.

And more important, the original, though faded and worn, may help to teach you about period design and fabric manufacture.

TAPESTRIES

One of the most beautiful and useful coverings, tapestries are also hard-wearing and marvelously strong. There are two basic kinds of tapestry; a true tapestry which is woven on a loom, and a needlepoint, which is worked in wool on a canvas base, but both are cleaned in the same way.

Cleaning

When removing a tapestry chair cover, be particularly careful not to catch the threads in any old nails or splinters.

- First shake it out briskly, unless the piece is very damaged—this should be done outdoors or at least out of a window. Then examine closely for moth holes.
- Select a softwood board as large as the opened-out tapestry and tape a piece of plain paper onto the board.
- Lay the cover on top of the paper stretched out flat, tape in place [1], and trace around it with a pen or pencil. Be as accurate as you can, for this is your guide to make sure the cover retains its shape.
- If the cover is very dirty or very valuable it will need to be washed or cleaned by a specialist. Take it with the tracing for an estimate, but if you decide to do the job yourself, keep the paper on the board, and tack the cover on top, wool side down.

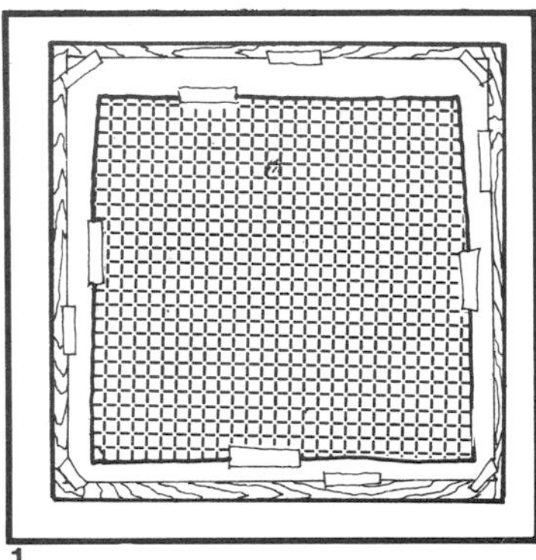

1

- Using a small hand vacuum cleaner, or a large one with a hose attachment, gently brush over every part of the back. This should remove much of the grit and dust.
- Let the cover rest for a few hours, and repeat the treatment.
- If the cover is very dirty, distilled water or softened water and soapflakes can be applied with a soft sponge. Brush the sponge gently over the back, trying to wet the cover as little as possible. Alternatively a dry-cleaning liquid can be used on most non-colorfast or delicate modern fabrics, but apply it as sparingly as possible. Test a small inconspicuous area first to make sure it doesn't stain or leave "tide marks".
- When dry, spray the covering with a moth repellent. When this has dried remove the cover and re-tack wool side up.
- Brush carefully with a very soft brush, and go over it once more with the vacuum cleaner, keeping the nozzle a few inches away from the surface and using the lowest suction. For persistent spots use the dry-cleaning liquid again, with only light pressure.

Damaged Tapestry: Holes and pulled yarn can be repaired quite easily—the real problem is matching the faded tones on the original. There are some weavers who make their own yarn and dye with traditional vegetable mixtures—these are much softer than modern aniline dyes, though they may not be fade or wash-proof.

When repairing a really valuable piece, using these hand-dyed yarns is worth the effort—if the right shade is difficult to find, dye your own wool or cotton yarns with some of the new dyes available for home use—the range is wide, and different shades can be easily mixed to give you just the right match. Use the ordinary basic needlepoint tent stitch, which will appear when finished as in Fig. 2. The top of Fig. 3 illustrates working the stitch from left to right; the bottom shows a diagonal pattern, working from the base, up and across. On woven tapestry follow the original pattern as far as possible. After the cleaning and repairing, replace as described in re-upholstery, pages 114-21.

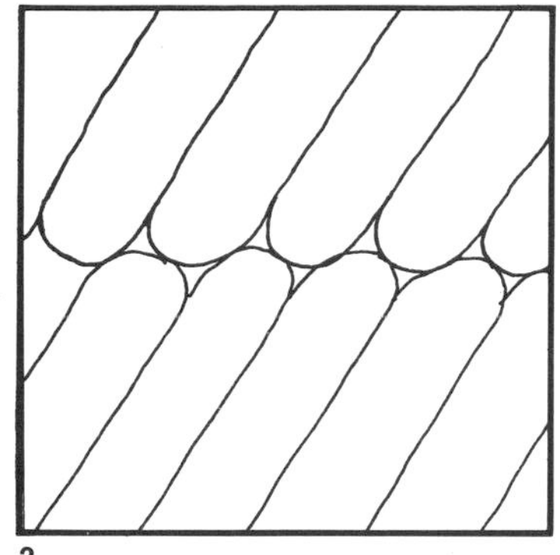
2

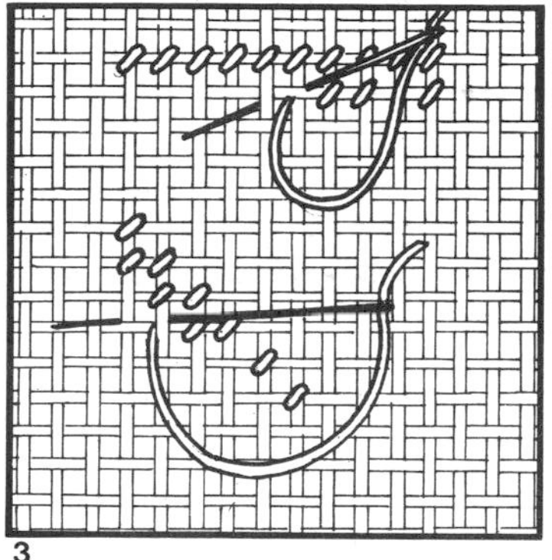
3

Other Upholstery Fabrics: After removing the loose dirt, remove all identifiable stains, consulting the stain removal chart on pages 121-3. Have the loose covers dry-cleaned if you are not sure they are washable. But if they are washable you can machine-wash them in warm water and soap powder and rinse thoroughly. Do not wring or spin as this tends to set creases and wrinkles. Chintz and linen fabrics will probably require ironing; do so when they are nearly dry. Glazed cottons should always be ironed on the wrong side. Dry-cleaning is advisable for most velvets used in upholstery, but velvet is *never* ironed. You can raise the nap by steaming it over a boiling kettle so that the steam passes from the wrong side to the right side of the fabric; alternatively a steam iron used on the wrong side of the fabric over a pressing cloth will have a similar effect [4].

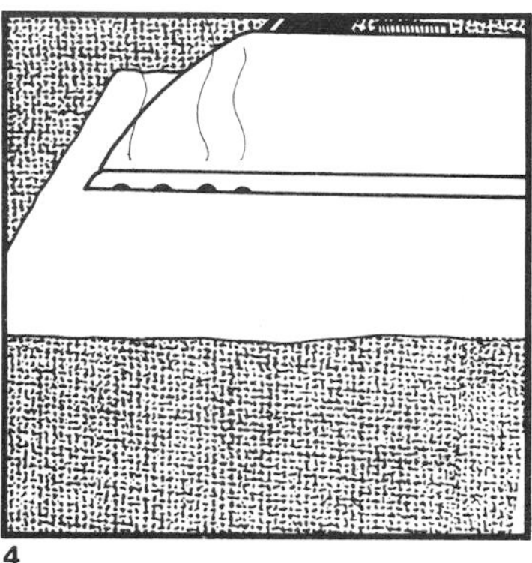
4

FINE LINENS, COTTONS AND EMBROIDERY

Many lovely old sheets, curtains and spreads are made of linen, which can be plain or embroidered (crewel embroidery was often worked on a linen ground). Badly damaged fabrics must be sent to professionals—they have the space and the equipment to handle large bulky pieces. This is especially true of curtains which take a very long time to dry, and should be dried flat, but sheets and smaller pieces may be treated at home.

Cleaning

First examine the piece carefully to see if there is any damage to the fibers.

● Make a note of the damaged places by using tiny safety pins to mark the spots as you find them [5]. On a large curtain or spread you can see holes one minute and lose them again by just picking up the next fold. Most linen can be washed at home. Use only distilled or softened water, as the minerals in ordinary mains water may leave brown marks which are impossible to remove.

● Let the fabric rest in clean lukewarm water for an hour or so, then drain off the water, taking away the surface dirt, and add fresh soft water with a good measure of pure soap flakes.

● Lift the fabric and turn it over and over, pushing the soap through, but never squeezing, rubbing or wringing.

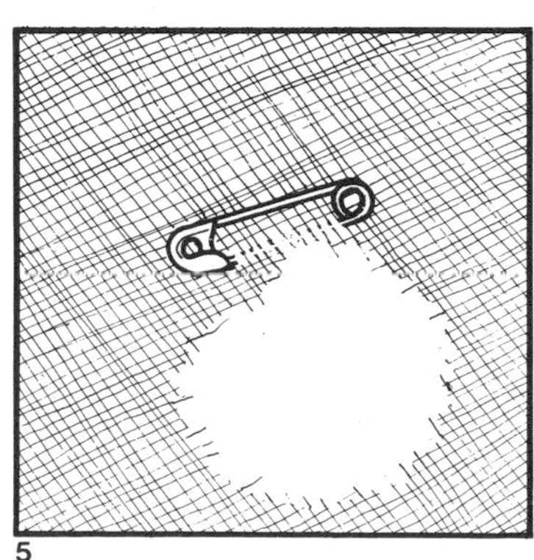
5

● Drain off the water again, rinse in clean lukewarm soft water; if the linen still seems dirty, repeat. Caution: Yellowed linen cannot really be whitened successfully; exposure to sunlight will affect the flax, and bleach, especially the chlorine type, is likely to weaken the fibers even more. In any case, that soft ivory tint is part of the charm! Brilliant white is characteristic only of cotton or man-made fabrics.

● Dry only where the item can be laid flat. Lay any embroidery face down so it doesn't get snagged by a careless fingernail.

● Iron on the wrong side when it is still slightly damp, using a pressing cloth for protection against scorching and a warm to hot iron.

Repairing Cotton and Linen

Repair after cleaning, so that you will be able to see more clearly what repairs are necessary. Remember to match your thread to the fiber and buy real linen thread if possible—or cotton for cotton material. If you can't find the right shade of off—white, then dye unwound white thread in a little cold tea [6], checking the strands every few minutes so it doesn't become too dark.

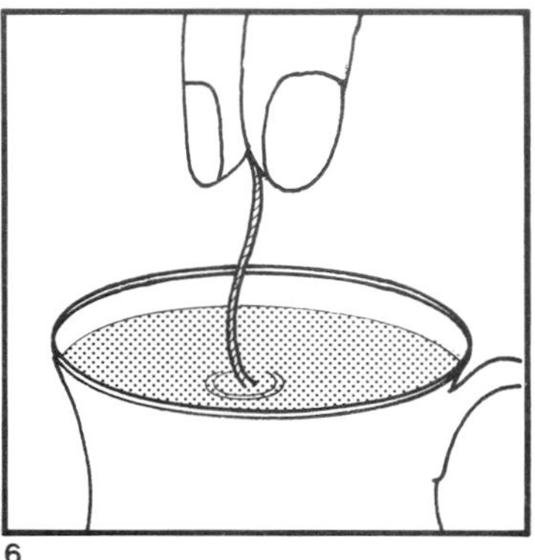

6

● Small holes can be repaired by cross darning. Hint: Never put your needle in just at the edge of the tear, you will probably add to the damage by pulling more threads loose.

● If it doesn't look as if your stitches will be fine enough, make a patch with a matching cotton or net, tacking it on from the back, and lift up as few fibers as possible so it doesn't show. Then, using thread dyed to match both old fabric and new patch, weave around the broken threads, going in the same direction. If you are careful and use tiny stitches, the result will barely show [7].

Patching: There is a right way and a wrong way to patch a hole in fabric. The photograph [8] shows both the incorrect method of simply sewing a patch in place on top of the hole, using the overcast stitch, and a better way, much more sensitive, and less noticeable.

● First turn under the raw edges and baste them in place.

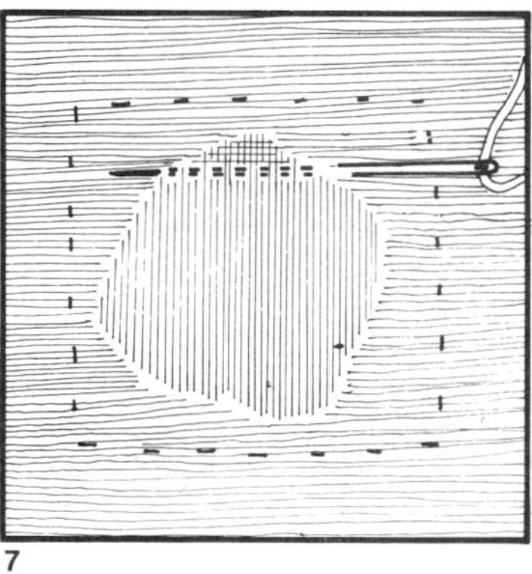

7

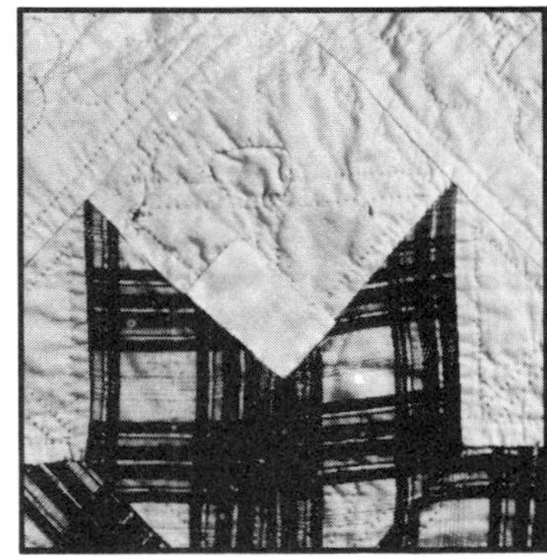

8

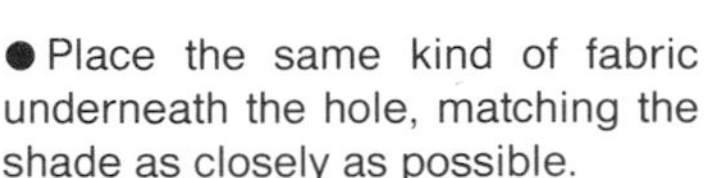

● Place the same kind of fabric underneath the hole, matching the shade as closely as possible.

● Pin in place.

● Stitch as shown.

● When repairing patchwork, also re-do the top stitching either by hand or by machine, depending on the original method.

Repairing Embroidery: When repairing missing embroidery, the hardest part is matching the faded dyes. (See under tapestries.) If you can find a piece of old material in the same tone, unravel it to use the thread [9]. Make an extra stitch on the back with a contrasting thread when you start; if you discover your shabby old curtains are 18th century crewelwork, you will want to know where your repairs begin and how much of the original remained.

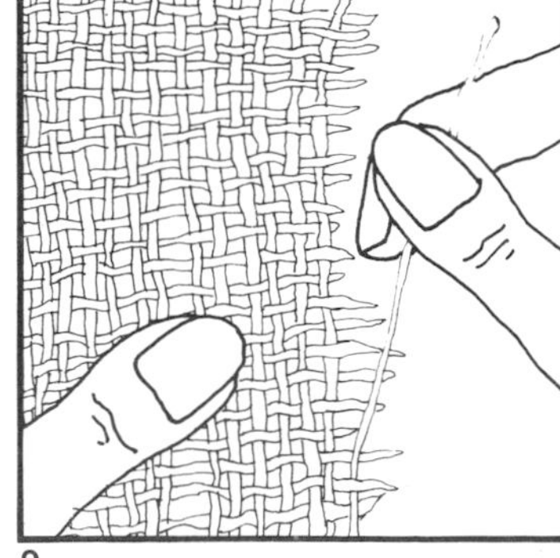

9

LACE

Fine lace is found as trimming on costumes, clothing and table linens, and also as individual pieces, used as flounces, collars, ruffles, handkerchiefs and shawls.

Cleaning

- If the lace is mounted on another fabric and it needs washing and repair, then it should be removed as carefully as possible. For light materials wash the fabric separately in lukewarm water and plenty of rich soapsuds, being careful not to tear it.
- Damp-dry, wrapped in a towel or laid flat, away from direct heat, and iron when slightly damp under a protective layer of cloth.
- If the fabric is velvet, brocade, or heavy wool or silk, have it dry-cleaned by a specialist firm—it's *not* a four-hour express job. Take it to a cleaner who specializes in fragile materials and fine costumes. If in any doubt, or if there is none listed in the telephone book, call your local museum.
- The lace itself will be white, écru or black—handmade lace is seldom any other shade. If it was originally white but has yellowed with age, then it will never really be pure white again—strong bleaches may do the trick, but they will also destroy the threads and weaken the knots which form lace patterns. Trace the length and width of your lace on clean brown paper. Wash in lukewarm softened water and pure soapsuds, followed by a rinse in plenty of clean soft water. Do not wring, rub or twist. Wrap in a white towel and damp-dry.

Repairing

Bobbin lace is knotted from long threads wound on spindles, called bobbins. It is not too difficult for the expert to pick up the pattern and weave in replacements for badly torn or damaged sections. But the amateur is better off doing needle repair with a matching thread. For ivory or yellow tones you may find it easier to dye a hank of cotton thread to match—cold tea is often a quick solution, but be careful it doesn't stain the thread too brown. Remember all wet thread or fabric will dry out a slightly lighter shade.

- Mount any wet lace on a board over paper and pull gently until it reaches the correct size. Tack into place using plenty of pins or tacks so that the edges sewn to the fabric are even and straight [10]. Let it dry away from direct heat or sunlight.
- Thread for bobbin lace comes in various weights. Traditionally made in linen or silk, it is also found in cotton. There are lace-suppliers all over the world in the major cities, and a good yarn store should be able to put you in touch with the nearest retailer if they don't carry a stock of it. Other kinds of lace, crochet, knitted, needle weaving, needle, and network can use almost any thread from heavy wool and macramé string to crochet thread, etc. The most important point is matching the shade and texture: for example, if you are dealing with thick wool lace, darn with matching wool, unraveled if necessary, and using one strand at a time.

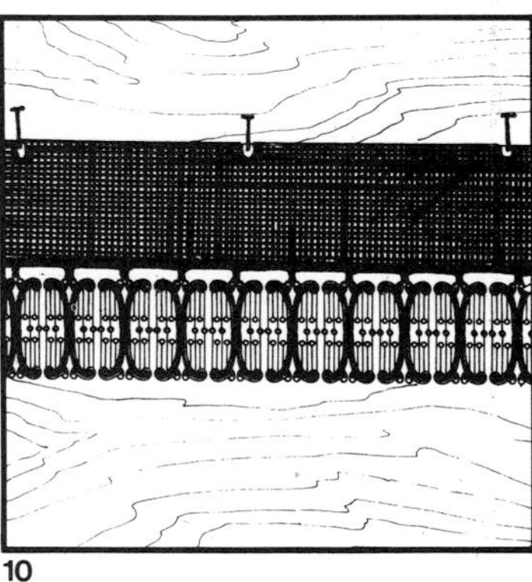

10

● Lace will tear most often at the top edge if it pulls away from the fabric, and along the seams where lengths were mitered or hemmed together. Darn with the finest thread you can find, using tiny stitches [11].

● For holes in the pattern try faking it with "bridges" of linen thread in the right shade, sewn with a needle. Try to follow the basic lines of the pattern. For a heavier look slip the needle around and around the new threads. Even better, use buttonhole stitching on the threads—this resembles many woven and crochet lace stitches. Some laces are made of lengths of braid or linen sewn into net. These can be repaired with matching or similar fine braid bought by the yard, or bias binding.

● Lay the lace flat, face down.

● Sew a patch of fine net over the hole or torn part, turn over and sew down the braid or binding, trying to match up the general lines of the pattern.

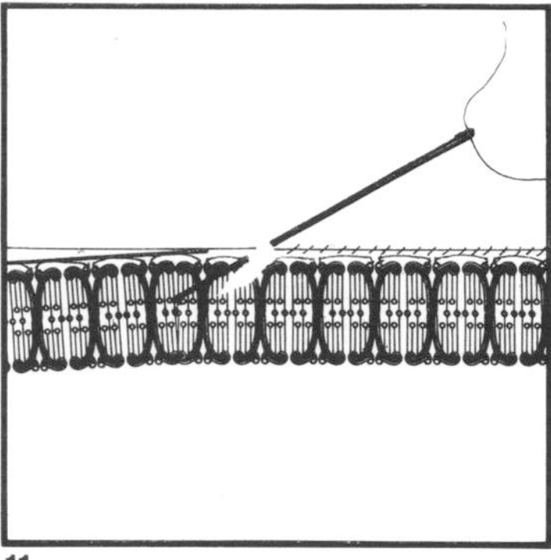

11

● Then repeat the "bridges" as above, to link up the scrolls where indicated [12]. Whatever you do, avoid pulling the thread too tight, because it will distort the lace and make the repair too obvious.

● Sew back onto fabric along the edge with tiny slip stitches, using the finest thread.

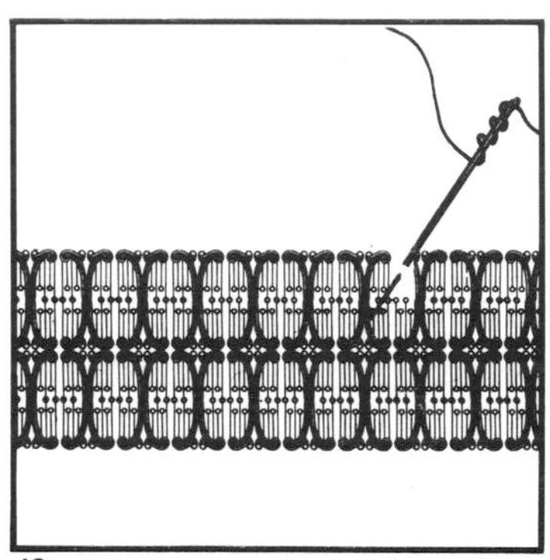

12

UPHOLSTERY

The history of upholstery surely began when someone tossed an animal skin over a rock or log to make it more comfortable to sit on. Over the centuries this softer seat has been refined but the purpose is the same. Today it is undoubtedly cheaper to re-upholster an old chair or sofa than to buy a new one and happily over the last few years the range of textiles has increased enormously, so that virtually every kind of color, texture and motif is available.

On the other hand, in the midst of the nostalgia wave of recent years, you may simply prefer to clean that 1940's chintz. So if it is simply grimy, remove the loose dirt with a clean stiff brush and vacuum cleaner. Then remove all stains before cleaning, consulting the stain removal chart on pages 121-3.

After cleaning look carefully at the piece and if the covering seems worth saving, mend the tears and patch the holes with fabric cut from the skirt, if there is one, or the back, if it will be placed against a wall. If there are exposed wooden parts that need attention, refer to the Wood chapter; be sure to refurbish these before re-upholstering.

The Old Covering

If the old upholstery fabric is beyond repair, first remove all the visible tacks or staples with a screwdriver or blunt chisel and mallet and then carefully remove the stitches, holding the old covering and stuffing, piece by piece. This old covering is used as a pattern when cutting, so remove it intact if possible!

● Turn piece upside down and remove tacks and old covering from the underneath [13].

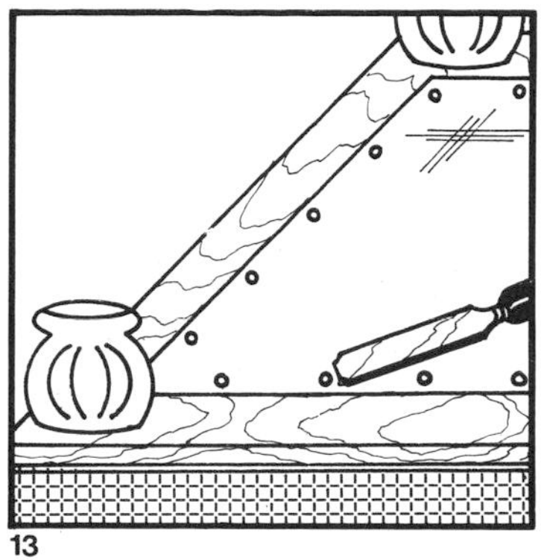
13

● Turn right side up and remove tacks and/or stitches from the covering, first removing any loose cushions or buttons [14]; then continue in the order shown—back of bottom, inside back, outside arms, inside arms, front border and/or panel on front arms, seat.
● Remove padding and/or stuffing —see illustration [15] for a cross-section.
● Make a note of the way the top covering is attached, the number of springs and strips of webbing and the height of the original padding.
● Dismantle only the materials that seem damaged—you may find that the springs and webbing are still good, in which case you leave them in place.
● Treat the wooden frame for woodworm (see pages 31-2) and fill old tack holes with wood filler (page 32) [16].
● If the springs are damaged, save them anyway for matching with a new, non-rusting variety of the same size.

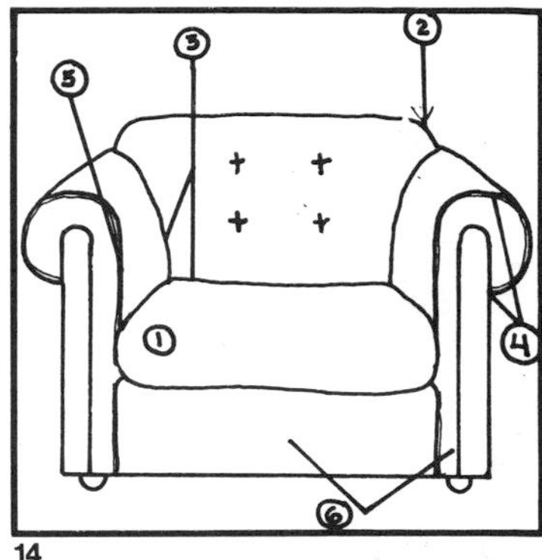

14

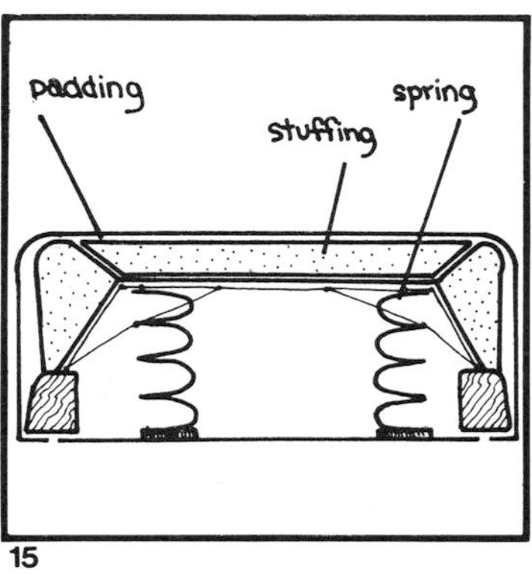

15

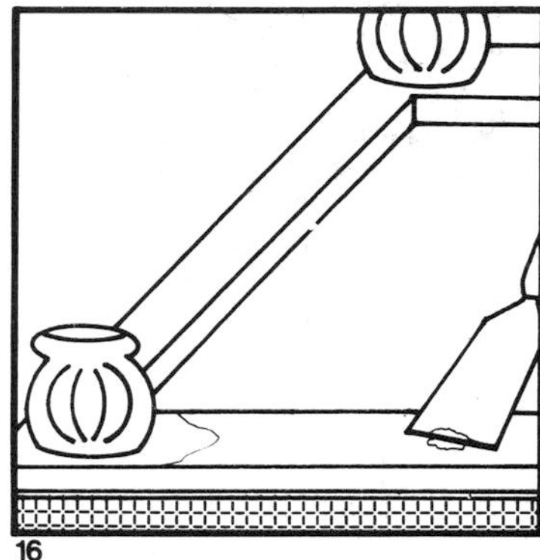
16

The New Fabric

When choosing the new fabric, purchase a material of the proper upholstery weight and consider a patterned material if the piece will get lots of use—patterns seem to hide spots and wear better than plain colors. A rough approximation of fabric required is: two-seater sofas, 10-15 yards (9-12 meters); armchairs 5½-8 yards (5-7 meters). Calculations depend on the width of the fabric, whether stripes or pattern must be matched, and whether a skirt at the bottom is desired. The assistant in the upholstery department will be able to calculate more exactly, providing you have all dimensions of the piece you want to recover.

Supplies

● Upholstery fabric and thread to match. (Old un-worn curtains, often of velvet, can sometimes be purchased cheaply from a second-hand store—make sure they have been cleaned before working with them.)
● Stuffing—real horsehair is classically recommended, but it is difficult to find and very expensive. Instead purchase Algerian fiber (a palm grass), curled hair (an animal mixture) or rubberized hair. Sometimes the old stuffing can be salvaged—hand-wash it in soapy water and rinse well; tease it out before re-using.
● Webbing—measure the lengths you have removed and purchase twill webbing or upholsterer's rubber webbing. The best grade of twill is black and white, made of 100% flax. As a guide, a chair seat will take 3-4 yards (2.75-3.65 meters) of 2″ (5cm) wide webbing.
● Webbing stretcher
● Twine—a special strong, smooth thread of flax and hemp, used for holding the stuffing in place, and for securing the springs. Sometimes labeled No. 252.

- Canvas, burlap or hessian—heavy upholsterer's variety, used over the springs and cut to the same size as the seat, plus 1″ (2.6cm) all around.
- Carpet tacks—No. 3 for thin fabrics, No. 4 for heavier fabrics, No. 7 for webbing.
- Scrim—a gauzy material for covering the first layer of stuffing. Allow enough to cover the seat plus 6″ (15cm) all round.
- Unbleached cotton—for covering second layer of stuffing, and cut slightly larger than the scrim.
- Wadding, sometimes called batting—used over the cotton and cut the same size.
- Needles—darning, mattress (or upholsterer's), upholsterer's regulator or one thin knitting, half-circle (or spring) and sacking.
- Magnetized upholsterer's tack hammer.

Renewing the Webbing

- The wooden frame of the piece should now be exposed, so the first step is to renew the webbing if necessary, as it is the basis for the rest of the upholstery. To fix the webbing turn the piece upside down on the work surface, preferably at table level. To stretch the webbing, you will need a webbing stretcher. You can buy one from a specialty store or you can easily make one, as shown, from a piece of wood 2″ × 1″ (5cm × 2.6cm) with a deep "V" cut at one end—use a coping or jigsaw. Use it as a lever when stretching the webbing before tacking [17].

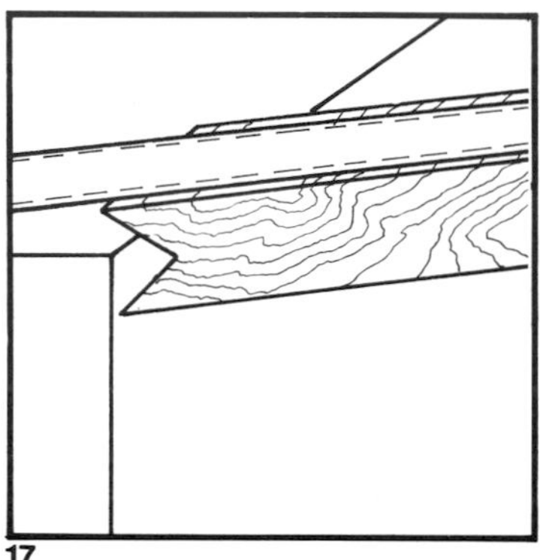
17

- Using the webbing straight from the roll, fold under ½″-1″ (13mm × 2.6cm) of webbing and center on the back rail so that the cut edge is up and ½″ (13mm) away from outer edge of frame. Tack down with five tacks staggered in a "W" as shown [18]. (Use finer tacks if wood splits).
- Using a webbing stretcher, lever the stretcher down, stretching the webbing taut. Use a cotton pad under the stretcher to prevent damaging the chair frame.

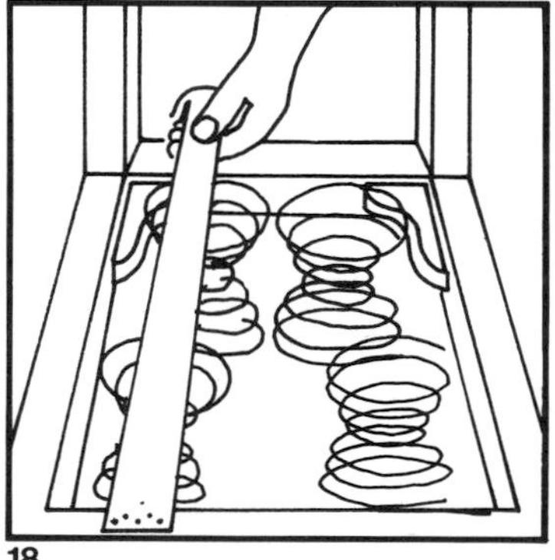
18

- Tack down with three tacks in a row, cut off webbing 1″ (2.6cm) from tack, fold over this cut end and tap in two more tacks between the first three.
- Attach the rest of the webbing in the same way, referring to your notes about the number of strips, the distance between each and number of crossed-over webbing strips. Try to center the crossed-over webbing above the springs as shown in illustration no. 19.

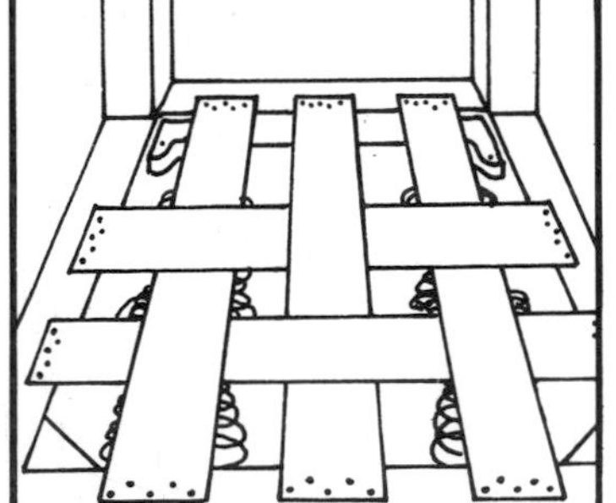
19

The Springs

The springs must be securely sewn to the webbing on the base and then lashed in place with the half-circle needle and twine, positioning them squarely over a place where the webbing crosses [20]. Hint: don't cut the twine as you move from spring to spring but move along to next one with needle and twine and come up from the underside to "lace in" the spring.

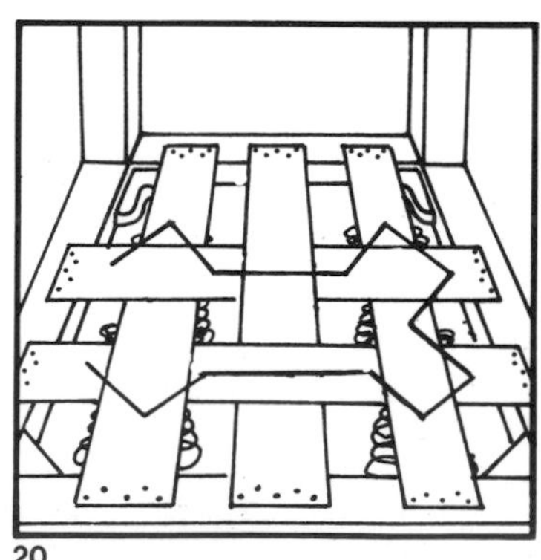
20

● Each spring is secured in at least three places to the double thickness webbing as shown. Make a knot after each stitch and pull the twine taut as you go along.

● Turn the piece over and align tacks on the frame with the rows of springs and hammer them in halfway.

● Cut enough twine (some people prefer a heavy type of cording) to go once around the frame and tie it around the front side of a front spring, leaving a tail 8″ (20cm) long. Wrap it around the tack and hammer the tack in to secure the twine.

● Take the main length of twine to the nearest spring at the back, knot it around the spring, take it through the center of the coil, and knot again at the front side of the spring (using a clove hitch knot).

● Move onto the other springs in the row and "lash" together in the same way, not pulling too tight so that the distance between the top and bottom of each spring remains the same. When all springs have been lashed up, tie the twine around the tack on the back rail and hammer the tack in.

● Repeat until all the coils in each row are lashed together, first one way, then the other.

● To give a rounded upward shape in the center, leave the 8″ (20cm) again tie the spring nearest each tack so that these springs tilt down slightly toward the frame. See illustration 21 for knotting and degree of tilt.

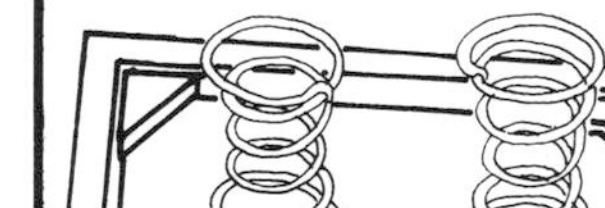

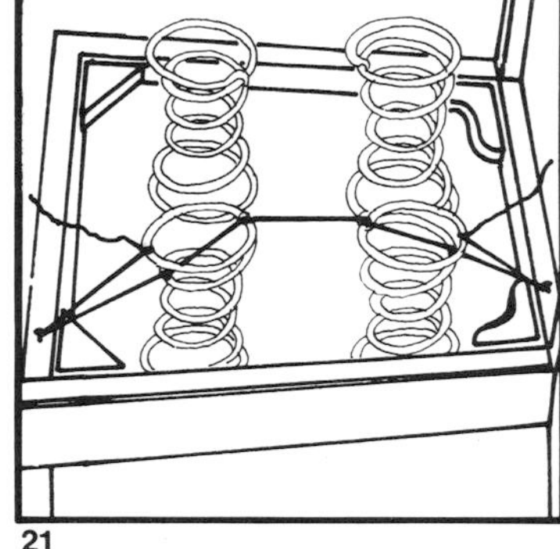

21

The Main Stuffing

● Center the canvas, hessian or burlap over the springs; fold over 1″ (2.6cm) on the back edge and tack this down on the back frame, spacing the tacks 1″ (2.6cm) apart. Fit it neatly around any back uprights or clip ¼″ (7mm) at a time to fit.

● Pull this canvas straight to the front rail, keeping it taut [22], and tack it to the front rail with tacks halfway in through a single thickness of canvas.

● Smooth it to the side rail and temporarily tack in place again [23].

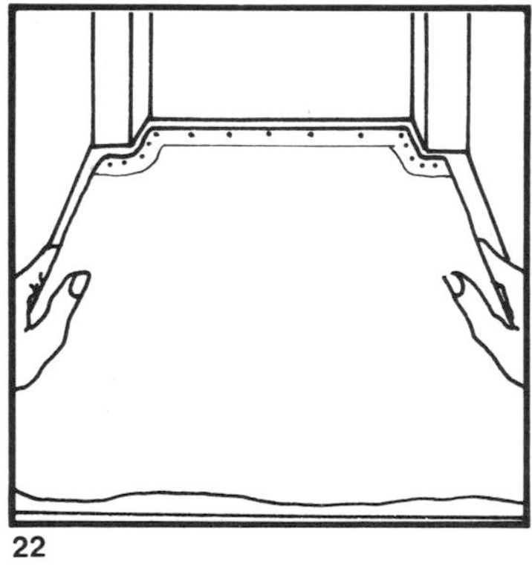

22

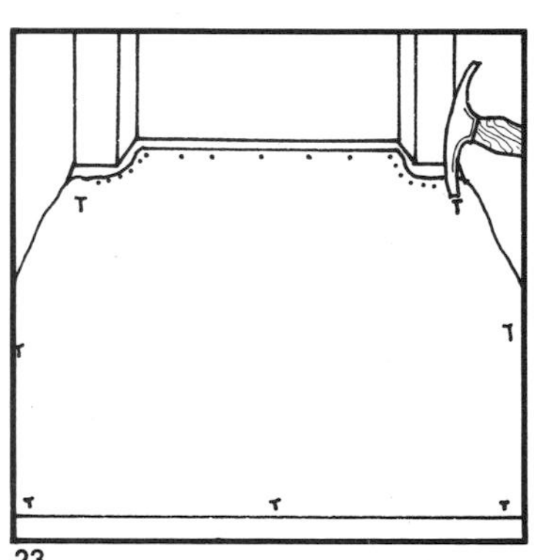

23

● Look closely, and if the canvas lies smooth and straight, hammer the tacks in completely. Trim off excess canvas leaving 1″-1½″ (2.6-3.75cm), which is folded up and over the first tacks and then secure with tacks spaced at 2″ (5cm) intervals [24].

● Using the half-circle needle again, stitch the top of the springs to the canvas, again making a knot after each stitch [25].

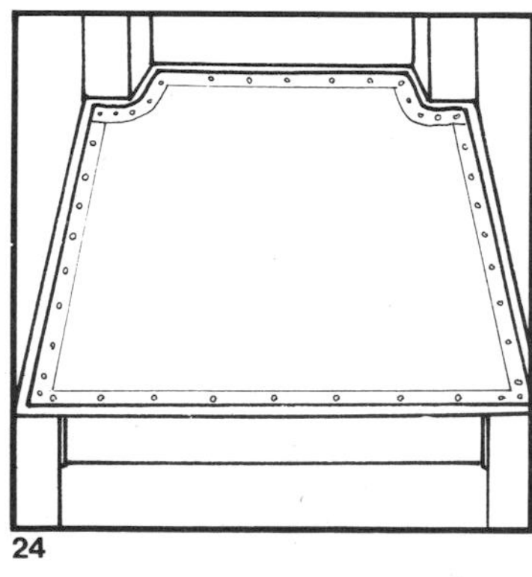

24

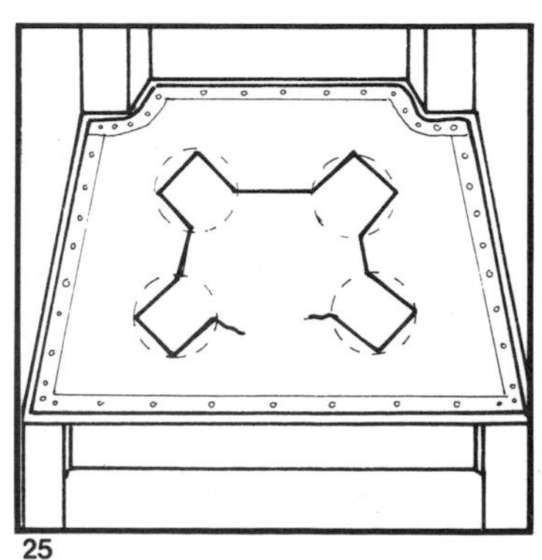

25

The Bridle Ties

(These are back-stitched loops about 3″ (7.6cm) from the chair's edge for holding the stuffing in place.)

● Thread needle with a length of twine to go around the chair $1\frac{1}{2}$ times.

● See drawing [26] for bridle stitch detail and work around the edge of the chair in this way making sure a 1″ (2.6cm) stitch is made at each corner [27]. Note: there should be about 4″ (10cm) between these loosely worked stitches.

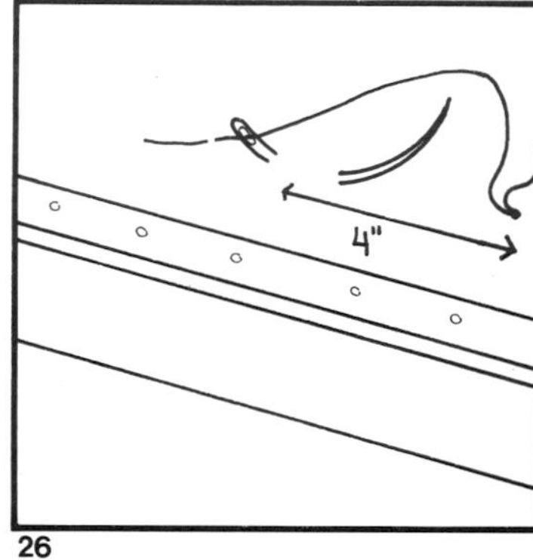

26

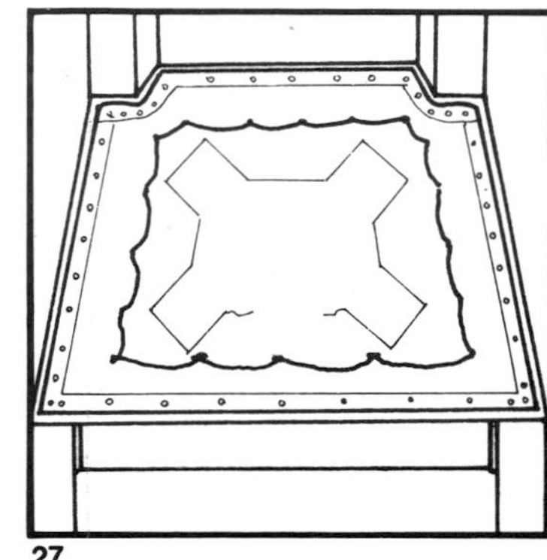
27

● Take a handful of stuffing, tease it out, removing any lumps, and place it under the bridle ties [28] and then fill up any space left in the middle, keeping it evenly distributed.

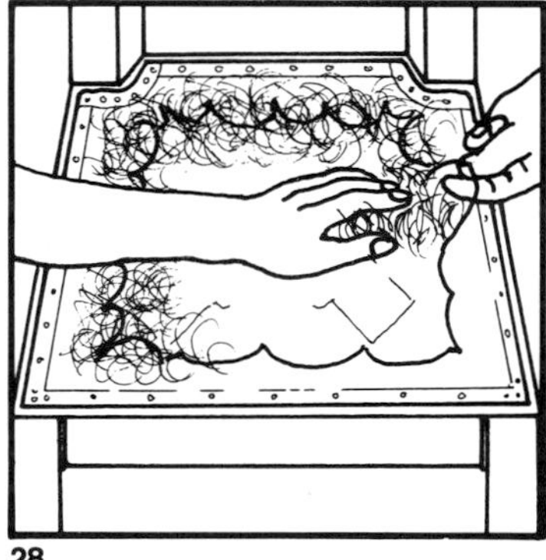
28

The Scrim

● Place the piece of scrim centrally over the stuffing and tap in tacks halfway on each side to hold it in place.

● Thread a large-eyed needle, like the upholsterer's needle, with 1 yard (1 meter) of twine and stitch through the scrim to the canvas making a rectangle or square shape, usually about 3″ (7.6cm) from the edges of the seat [29].

● You will be pulling the needle out between the webbing on the underside, and leaving a 7″ (18cm) tail on top, and then pushing it back up, resurfacing, and making a stitch about 3″ (7.6cm) long and then back down. Hint: Pull the twine tightly so that the scrim is pulled down. Try not to catch the springs with the needle or thread as you go through the center.

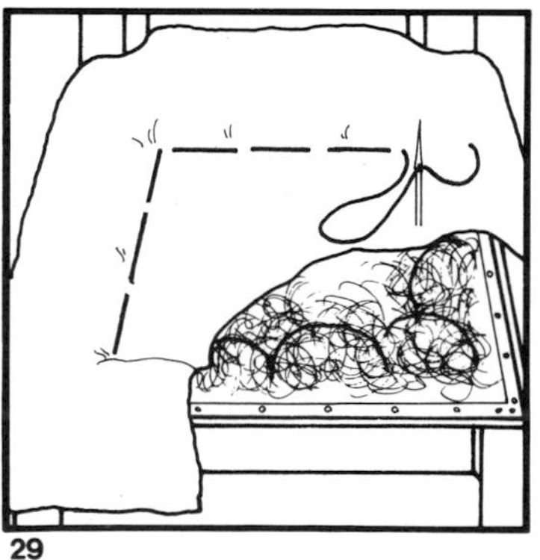
29

● Remove the temporary tacks on the chair frame and even out the stuffing underneath the scrim if necessary.

● Add more stuffing under the scrim so that it protrudes slightly beyond the edge of the frame.

● Tuck the raw edge of scrim under the hair, and tack the folded edge to the chamfered edge of the frame—but don't pull this too tightly [30].

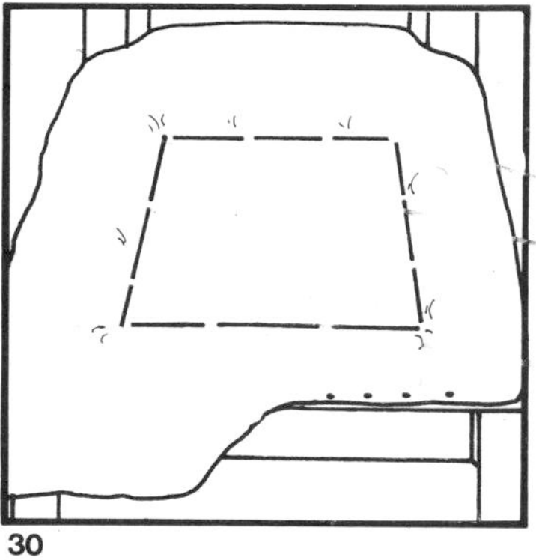
30

Stitching the Edge

● Thread the upholsterer's needle with a yard (a meter) or so of twine and insert the end into scrim just above the tacks and $1\frac{1}{2}''$ (3.75cm) from the corner. Insert the needle at about 45 and pull the needle through on top about 2″ (5cm) from the edge, but stop before the eye is visible. This is called blind stitching. (see close-up illustration [31]), which pulls some of the stuffing to the edges and holds up a firm edge.

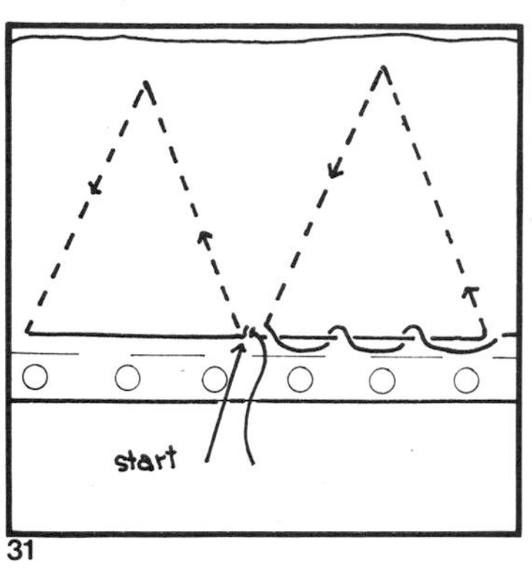

31

● Then push the needle back into the stuffing again and down, making a V-shaped stitch or triangle in the stuffing.

● Knot after this first stitch and begin the second blind stitch 2″ (5cm) along, going in again at 45° and coming back out along the row of tacks but wrapping the bottom thread to secure as shown.

● After working around one side of the base in this manner put the needle into the center top temporarily. Hold the stuffing edge and top with your left hand as shown, and pull on the twine with your right hand. Wrap the twine around your fingers or hand to get a good hold. You should feel the stuffing being pulled toward the edge [32].

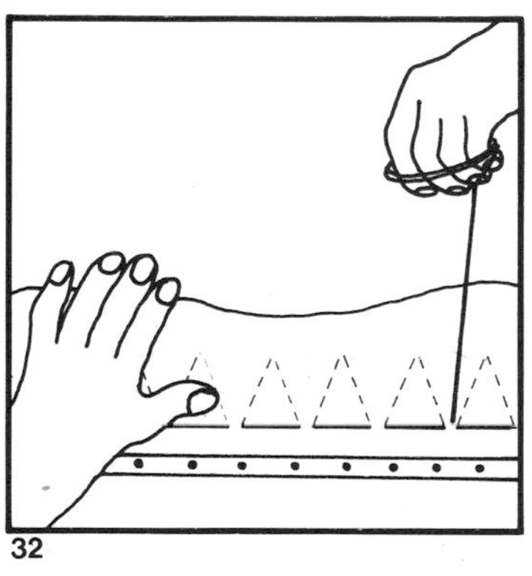
32

● Work around the chair in this manner, making the triangular blind stitches and then pulling the stuffing toward the edges. Knot the twine tightly when finished.

● Correct any unevenness you feel with the regulator or a long thin knitting needle by poking it through to the stuffing.

Top Stitching

This is the second stage, similar to blind stitching, only the needle is drawn completely through on top of the stuffing so that a complete stitch can be made.

● Thread the upholsterer's needle with a long length of twine and start in a corner, placing the needle vertically into the scrim $\frac{1}{2}$-1″ (13mm-2.6cm) above the blind stitching and pushing it through so that it emerges about 1' (2.6cm) from the top edge.

● Re-insert the needle 1″ (2.6cm) to the left of this point and push through through so it comes out 1″ (2.6cm) to the left of the start. Wrap the twine around the needle to knot, and insert again 1″ (2.6cm) away toward the top, emerging so that the next top stitch forms a continuous line parallel to the chair edge (see illustration [33] and profile illustration [34] of the two stitches).

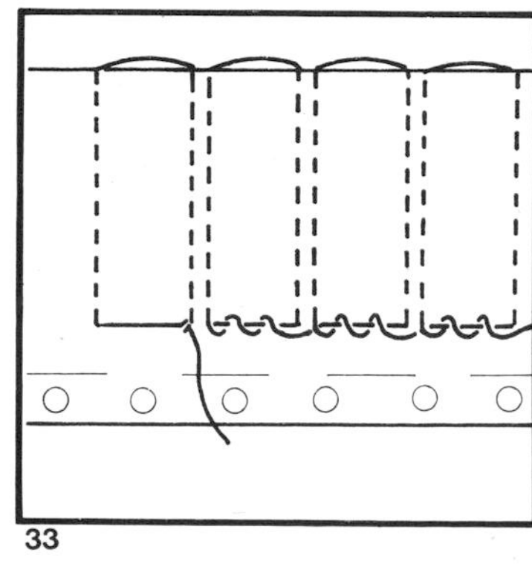
33

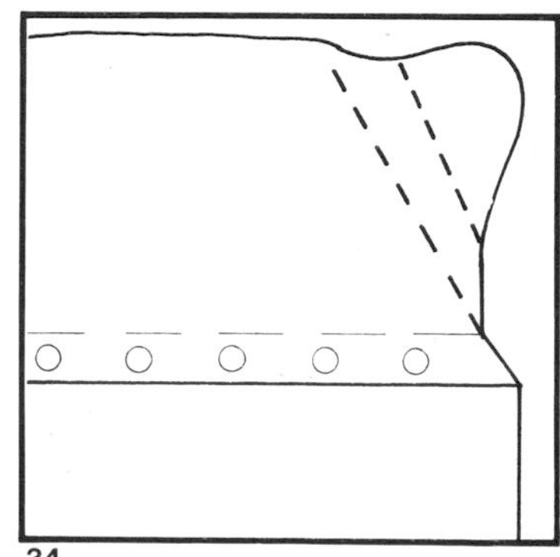
34

The Second Stuffing

● Make bridle ties on the scrim as before.

● Fill the ties and cavity in the center with more stuffing [35].

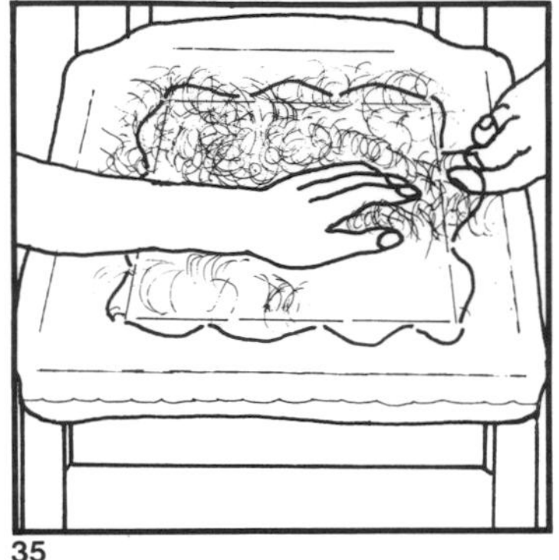

35

● Cover this with a piece of unbleached cotton cut to size and tacked temporarily in place at the front, then the back and finally at the sides, spacing the tacks 2″ (5cm) apart. Smooth any bumps or sags by readjusting the stuffing before tacking the cotton in place. Miter corners as shown to get around any awkward places.

● Sink the tacks only after satisfactory positioning of the cotton, making sure that the grain lies straight.

The seat should now look smooth and full and is ready for the final covering [36].

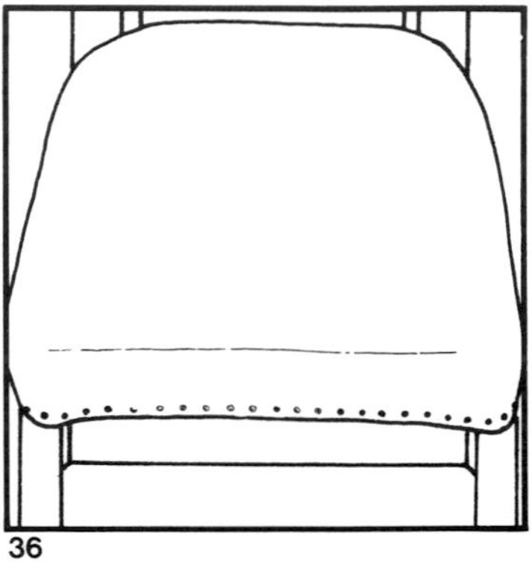

36

Top Covering

● Cover the unbleached cotton with cotton wadding, sometimes called batting, to prevent the stuffing from working through. Again tack in place, spacing tacks ¾″ (2cm) apart.

● Cut a piece of the new upholstery fabric, using the original piece as a pattern. Keeping the grain straight, temporarily tack it in place through a single thickness, starting at the back. Miter or pleat corners as necessary.

● Trim off excess and finish by tapping in the tacks when the fabric is straight and smooth [37].

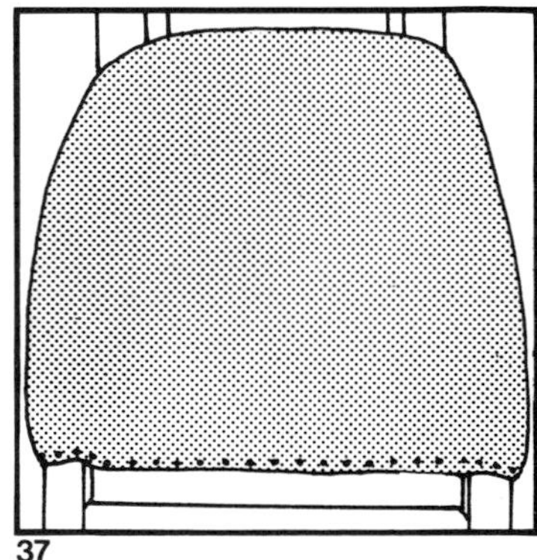

37

● The tacks and raw edges can then be covered with gimp or braid which is glued in place with a latex adhesive, working 6″ (15cm) at a time. Don't apply too much glue or the excess will mark the gimp and upholstery fabric. Miter the braid at the corners as illustrated [38].

Alternative: Instead of gluing the gimp in place, you can use tacks with rounded brass heads to hold the gimp [39]. This treatment seems especially suited to leather-covered and heavier furniture styles.

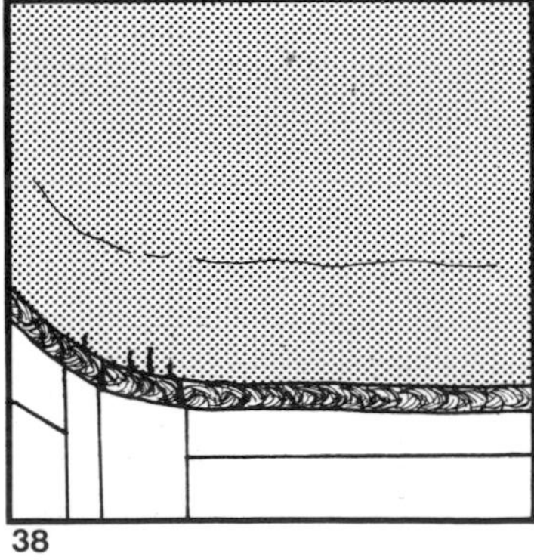

38

39

Hints

- Begin with a piece you can easily dismantle—avoid deep buttoning, as on Chesterfields, when doing your first piece.
- Remove all old tacks in the wooden frame and fill the holes with "plastic wood", or your own filler made according to recipes on page 32.
- To economize, use cotton twill webbing and make your own webbing stretcher as shown.
- Don't cut the webbing into lengths before stretching.
- Don't use foam rubber (sometimes called rubberized foam)—it is a short cut and doesn't wear especially well as upholstery. However, it is all right when used for cushions.
- When upholstering a sofa, first do the back, then the arms.
- If the fabric is not wide enough to cover the sofa back, center the width and "piece" at both edges, carefully matching grain, nap and pattern.
- When upholstery meets wood on arms, use a cardboard piece to hold the fabric at the wooden edge, tack in place, and fold the fabric over the cardboard.
- Spread tacks far apart on a piece of light paper so that it is easier to pick them up one at a time.
- For the wings of wing chairs use the thickest cotton batting or wadding before applying the upholstery fabric.
- Optional cording for box cushions: cut bias or crosswise strips from upholstery fabric 2″ (5cm) wide and sew several together making a continuous piece. Lay the cording, $\frac{1}{4}$″ (7mm) diameter, down the center of the strip, fold the fabric over it and stitch with zipper foot or cording foot. Tack in place before fitting final upholstery fabric. This will then have to be blind stitched in place.

STAIN-REMOVAL, GENERAL ADVICE

When trying to remove a greasy stain just saturate the area with liquid detergent and then launder. A cleaning fluid can also be used before or after laundering. Sponge non-washable fabrics with a cleaning fluid, allowing it to dry between applications perhaps with the aid of an absorbent fabric placed underneath.

To remove non-greasy stains from washable fabrics sponge immediately with cool water, then later soak in cold water for 30 minutes or overnight. On non-washables try cool water, followed by diluted white spirit (2:1). For combination stains (greasy and non-greasy mixtures) like soup, treat the stain first as a non-greasy one, using cool water and liquid detergent and then treat any remains with a cleaning fluid. A bleach can sometimes be employed for all kinds of stains but test on an inconspicuous area first if possible; the reactions of bleach with certain textiles is uncertain.

Always try cool water first and enzyme detergents on washable material. Never iron over a stain.

Kind of Stain	Method of Removal
Greasy marks	Washable materials: liquid detergent, cleaning fluid Non-washables: cleaning fluid
Oil, heavy grease	Eucalyptus oil
Adhesive tape	Cleaning fluid
Alcohol	Turpentine substitute
Black coffee or tea	Pour boiling water over the area from a height of a few feet and not directly on heat-sensitive textiles

TEXTILES AND UPHOLSTERY

Kind of Stain	Method of Removal
Blood	Cold water for washables, for stubborn stains diluted ammonia, wash in detergent, on thick textiles and carpets use absorbent
Candlewax	Scrape away as much as possible with dull knife, place area between paper towels and press with warm iron. Sponge traces left with cleaning fluid
Chewing gum	Rub area with ice and pick off hard bits; then saturate with cleaning fluid
Clear liquid glue or aircraft cement	Acetone (test on small area first)
Cosmetics and crayons	If washable, try liquid detergent and if not, use a cleaning fluid
Eggs	Cold water or cleaning fluid
Fruit	Cool water immediately followed by boiling water; never use any soap at first
Grass, flowers, foliage	Use turpentine substitute, tested on small area first; alternatively liquid detergent and bleach
Gravy	Cold water followed by a wash; use cleaning fluid on non-washables
Ink	Acetone or amyl acetone on synthetic fibers
India ink	Cool water followed by liquid detergent; don't let it dry out
Iodine	Moisten with water and place it on warm radiator or in steam from a kettle Non-washable; use diluted turpentine substitute
Iron rust	On washable white fabrics use bleach or pure lemon juice; difficult to remove from non-washables
Metallic stains	White vinegar, or lemon juice and rinse with water; do not bleach
Mildew	Sun and air are best treatments and preventions. Wash area with soapsuds and rinse.
Mustard	Cool water, then liquid detergent. Cleaning fluid on non-washables. Difficult to remove from plastics.
Pencil	Try erasing the area, or liquid detergent
Perspiration	Enzyme detergents for fresh stains, old stains respond to wiping with white vinegar and rinsing. Always remove before ironing.
Scorch	Sponge area with hydrogen peroxide and rinse. If serious, on wool brush with fine sandpaper, impossible to remove if fibers of textiles have been burned.
Shoe polish	Turpentine substitute, cleaning fluid.
Soft drinks	Sponge immediately with cool water.
Wine	Sprinkle salt on stain and pour boiling water.

General Stain-removers

Absorbent:	Oatmeal, cornflour, powdered chalk, talcum powder, fuller's earth, french chalk
Bleaches:	Chlorine, hydrogen peroxide, sodium perborate, color remover
Other chemicals:	White vinegar, ammonia
Solvents for greasy stains:	Non-flammable carbontetrachloride
Solvents for non-greasy stains:	Acetone, pure amyl acetate, white spirit

LEATHER

Animal skins were used by early man to supply many needs: tools, thread, shoes, clothing and pouches. In the dry climate of the Middle East, examples of leatherwork have been preserved dating from 5,000 BC. The skins were simply scraped clean of flesh and hair, spread to dry in the sun and rubbed with salt or just earth, to cure or preserve them. Roman shoes have been found perfectly preserved in peaty soil, complete with the maker's name.

In England, the Stonyhurst Gospel (687 AD) is the earliest surviving example of leather bookbinding, but by this time the curing process was done with oak bark. Later oil oxidation was used and then "tawing", a mineral process incorporating alum, which reached Britain about 900 AD. Medieval society depended on leather for protective clothing, weapons, boats, breeches, gloves, saddling, shoes and containers for all sorts of products. Then, as now, Spain was noted for her leatherwork, with 11th century Cordoba the manufacturing center for leather panels and wall hangings. This fashion later spread to Flanders, France, Holland and Italy, and by the 13th century, wealthy noblemen displayed gilded leathers on their walls. Such hangings were important as draft-excluders and were much more durable and heat-retaining than fabric. There were also leather carpets and bedspreads, tooled and printed in marvelous medieval and Renaissance patterns.

There is an old story that Henry VIII built a manor house for Anne Boleyn with a tower room hung with gilded leather. (Around 1800 the unappreciative owner had the hangings burnt in order to recover the gold leaf, which turned out to be worth very little.) But most "gilded" leather was actually covered in thinly beaten silver or tin and coated with layers of yellow varnish.

The process of leather-working grew more complicated with its development from the Tudor period onwards until the end of the 19th century, and with the use of different types of leathers. Fine ornamental skins with lovely, close-grained surfaces were scraped until they were very thin, dyed in bright shades, and then washed and stretched until they were as soft and supple as silk. These skins were used for the elegant caps and hats worn by the wealthy, and for men's breeches and women's slippers. Gloves were a special delight, embroidered and bejeweled in a rainbow of delicate tints. The passion for scented gloves in the court of Queen Elizabeth I in England was echoed in all the major capitals of Europe, and later a fashionable Regency beauty would have a pair of gloves for every outfit, often numbering hundreds.

A special thick leather was often used for the various objects and containers, which formed such an important part of household equipment—"Black Jacks" (jars holding about a gallon of liquid), fire buckets for the fragile wooden houses, boxes and caskets to hold precious personal possessions, knife sheaths, lanterns and work clothing.

Many such objects were made by the misleadingly named *"cuir bouilli"* (boiled leather) method. After being tanned with vegetable dyes, the thick leather was softened in cold water, then shaped over a core of wood, clay or wet sand. When the leather had been stretched tight it was decorated by tooling, punching different shaped holes, incising or simply burnishing—rubbing the surface with a bone until it took on a glossy finish. Then it was dried as quickly as possible, a process helped by dipping the leather for a second in boiling water, which is perhaps where the term "boiled leather" came from. When thoroughly dried, the leather set as hard as wood and could even be mounted with metal frames and hinges. Jars were made waterproof by a lining of molten pitch or resin swirled around inside as soon as the setting was complete.

There were many other uses for leather. Thicker hides came to be used for folding chairs, or for durable, deep-buttoned Chesterfields and wing chairs. Of course leather had always been used for harness and saddlery, following the patterns of places and time—simple bits and reins for the Normans, medieval jousting saddles with high panels and sharply slanted backs (which strangely enough appeared again in the American West as cowboy saddles), litters and coaches made of leather hide, sometimes stretched over a wooden framework, like the leather paneling on old trunks.

The protective qualities of leather have always been a special advantage for hard-wearing clothes too, from riding boots, Indian moccasins, and shirts to aprons etc.

Recently so many cheaper cloth and plastic substitutes have been developed that real leather has become a luxury once more, kept for the finest bookbinding, expensive clothes and only the very best upholstery. But its qualities of pliability, durability and natural beauty are still there, and many craftsmen and amateurs have discovered the pleasures of working with this ancient and highly prized material that mankind has always found so useful and decorative.

RESTORING LEATHER

Old leathers crack, peel, split and powder as they dry out, so the restorer's chief job is to replace the natural organic oils. The instructions below apply to any leather object unless stated otherwise. Before applying any of the substances mentioned, test in an inconspicuous spot for color fastness—most leather has been dyed.

Cleaning

● The leather must be cleaned by gently dusting with a soft cloth or feather duster. If it seems very dirty, clean with slightly soapy water (not detergents) and a soft cloth, or better still saddle soap (sold in a can and worked to a foam with a small damp sponge) [1].

● Oily spots can previously be removed with a few drops of dry cleaning fluid, lighter fluid, sal-ammoniac, or a mixture of equal quantities of vinegar and warm water [2].

1

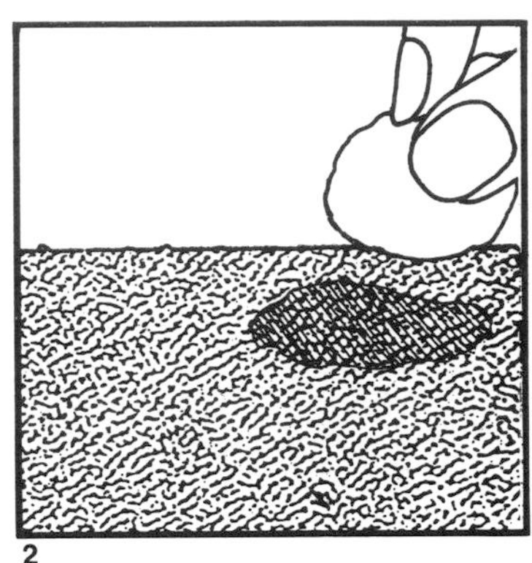
2

Restoring Cracked Leather

● Apply lanolin or castor oil with a soft cloth, first warming the oil in a glass over a pan of warm water [3].

● Let the oil soak in for 24 hours, then buff with a soft cloth and repeat. Neatsfoot oil will not produce a sheen unless mixed equally with one of the other oils. Use it mixed with petroleum jelly on light-colored leathers and patent leathers, but be warned: it has a tendency to become rancid.

● If leather is very brittle spray or paint on lanolin mixed in equal quantities with petroleum spirit. Warm leather and emollients to room temperature before applying.

3

Putrid and Decaying Leather

● Cover the object with a solution of dilute denatured alcohol (methylated spirits) adding a small quantity of carbolic acid. Leave for ten minutes.

● Follow by immersion in a bowl of melted Vaseline, which should restore the suppleness and sheen.

● If it still looks in bad condition dip it in melted paraffin wax, which will act as a preservative against further decay.

● You can also make your own leather polish, but you will need a thermometer to get it just right.

● Purchase: $1\frac{1}{2}$oz (45gm) stearic acid, $\frac{1}{8}$oz (3.5mg) triethanolamine, $\frac{3}{4}$oz (21mg) carnaubawax and $\frac{1}{3}$pt (70ml) pure turpentine. Add the first two to just enough water to dissolve, and boil. Separately melt the wax in the turpentine by heating both in the top part of the double boiler [4].

4

● When this mixture has reached a temperature of 158°F (90°C) [5], combine the two solutions, remove from heat and stir until cold.

5

● If the leather has become powdery, paint it with a mixture of 60% castor oil and 40% denatured alcohol (methylated spirits) and again in 24 hours with pure castor oil [6].

6

Leather Attacked by Insects

Apply a fine spray of mercuric chloride (corrosive sublimate) dissolved in denatured alcohol (methylated spirits) [7]. This mixture is extremely poisonous. Have it prepared by a professional pharmacist, if possible in a disposable plastic spray bottle.

7

Stitching that is Corroded or Missing

This can be replaced with an appropriately sized needle and a wax-coated thickish thread. Sometimes re-piercing the holes with the needle before starting makes re-sewing easier [8] but, in any event, use a thimble to protect your "pushing" finger. Obviously you must remove all old thread before starting [9].

8

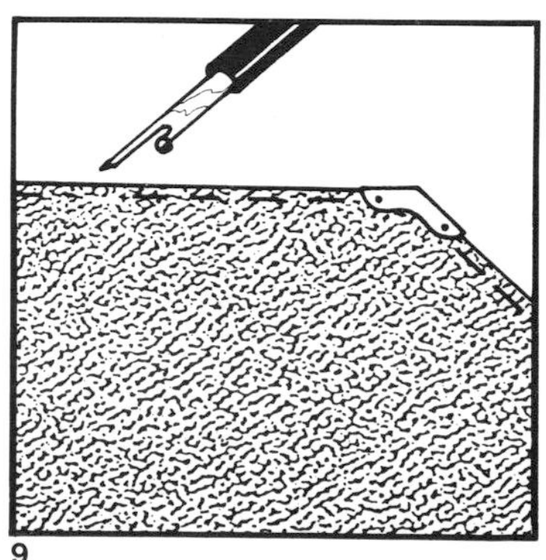

9

REPLACING LEATHER

● Rip off old, damaged leather.
● Wash off old glue and remaining bits of leather with warm water [10]. Avoid getting the surrounding wood wet, if possible.

10

● Smooth the surface of the table with successively finer pieces of abrasive paper, until a medium smoothness is achieved [11]—a slight roughness gives the glue something to grip. Obviously, fill any dents or splits with wood filler—they will only show through on the new top.
● Dust and wipe with white spirit after sanding. Cut new leather a little larger than the space to be covered, and always keep leather at room temperature or warmer while you work.
● Apply double strength wallpaper paste to the table top with an old brush [12]. Build up a few layers, until it is gummy. (Be careful not to get too much glue on the surrounding wood. If you wish, the ever-useful masking tape can be used with sheets of plastic to protect it.)

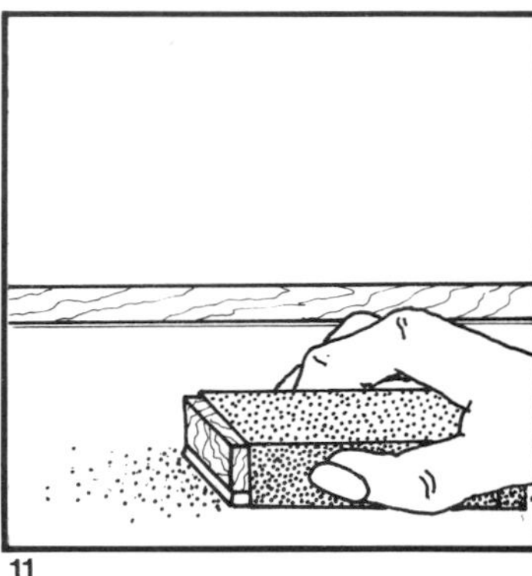
11

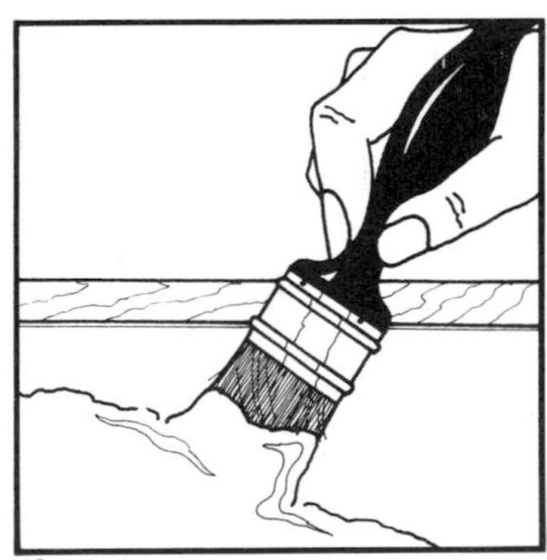
12

● Position the leather on the table top (get help from a friend with this if the area is large).
● Smooth out wrinkles and puckers with a cork pad or rounded piece of softwood, even the heel of your hand will do, starting in the center and working towards the edges [13]. It may help to use wax paper or tracing paper under the leather, easing the paper out as you stick the leather into place. This is recommended especially when laying large pieces.

13

● Continue stroking until the leather lies flat. Then let it dry for one hour and cut the excess off carefully and slowly with a sharp knife with replaceable blades and a straight edge [14].

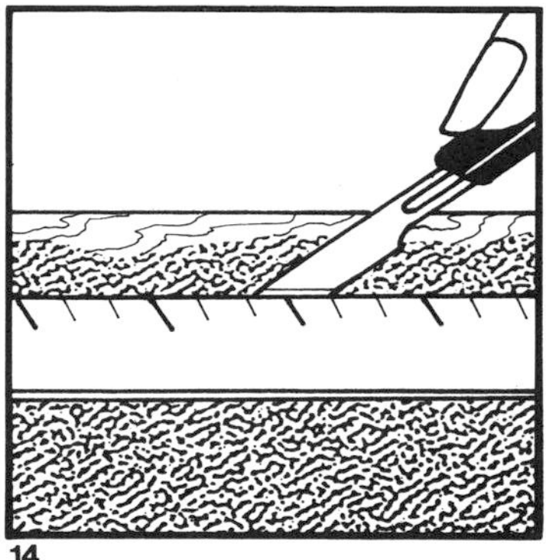
14

● Seal the leather at the edge by running along a warmed brass embossing wheel (something like a pastry cutter) which gives it a nice finish. This wheel has to be heated to about hand-hot temperature; if the wheel is too hot the leather will shrivel. Illustration 15 shows, left to right, polishing iron for polishing the gold, embossing wheel, and wheel for tooling single lines.

15

Embossing with gold is a very skilled job, not for beginners. But if you want to try, purchase a roll of gold leaf. You feed this out with one hand while the other hand follows with the embossing wheel. Rock the wheel from side to side to make sure that both edges of the leaf are sticking firmly, and move back and forth to complete the transfer, at the same time traveling parallel to the edge of the table.

If this sounds too tricky, there are some specialist craft suppliers who will sell leather cut and gold-stamped to your specifications. When applying leather supplied in this way, it is easier to cut the piece to fit and then lay and glue in place.

Parchment, the skin of sheep and goats, and vellum, the skin of calves and birds, require different treatment. NEVER use water to clean either, as they will swell and deform; instead use petroleum spirit to clean very dirty and oily spots, but the best advice is to keep articles made of either kind of leather well dusted.

CAUTION: do not confuse imitation parchment with the real thing.

CARPETS

From the earliest appearance of settled communities, floor coverings have been the mark of domestic pride. Beaten earth was covered with strewn rushes, and some kind of dried grass woven into a basketweave pattern was probably the first floot mat. Even such a simple and primitive arrangement was an improvement on bare ground, and much more comfortable than the stone or brick floor which was the next stage. Grass mats can be surprisingly decorative—no early ones have survived, but some fragments of basket work show that both geometric and figurative designs could be made with the simplest materials.

Another early floor covering used by nomadic tribes was animal skins, probably used for transportation during the day, and laid flat as bedding during the night; we can assume that the sheepskins in Mongolian tents and the sealskins in Eskimo igloos today have prehistoric ancestors. The first carpet that is datable (to c.500 BC) was found in an Anatolian tomb, dyed in rich tones, and appliquéd with brilliant and charming motifs. Carpets also appear on Assyrian stone reliefs, and are mentioned in other ancient writings, although so far no actual pieces have been found.

The Middle East craftsman has been the source of many of our precious works of art, but in most crafts (glass, pottery etc.), his influence is a matter of historic fact rather than present reputation. Not so with carpets; the Persian rug has been acclaimed as the finest in the world and in spite of intervening fashions and modern mechanical inventions, it remains so today.

Historically the rudiments of carpet weaving were practised in almost every Middle Eastern country, and by the 7th century AD the Persian kingdom of Chorosoes had achieved the greatest reputation for rich and luxurious furnishings. Pattern-makers, dyers and weavers worked together creating finer and finer knotting techniques, to depict complex images and symbols. Competitions were held to encourage designers, and to produce works of art for the king and his nobles to contemplate.

Enormous sums were spent on special wools from carefully bred sheep, and on beautifully laid out gardens for the plants needed for dyeing. A great achievement was the Spring Garden Carpet, the first of many to create an allegory of Paradise. To a desert people surrounded by arid sand, water is the true gift of the gods, and the carpet reflects this in its design of a central pool, long canals, thick greenery, lush growing flowers, and ripe fruit trees.

But even this vision wasn't enough, and the carpet was re-embroidered with solid bands of emeralds for the meadows and sapphires for rippling water. All fragments of this legendary creation have disappeared, supposedly torn up and distributed as spoils of war when Chorosoes was destroyed in the 9th century, and all that is left is the description, and the vision of peace and coolness which is still an essential part of every Persian garden carpet design.

Except for scraps here and there, the earliest carpets still in existence date from the 16th century, and the great Persian schools of weaving which flowered under the benevolent hand of Shah Abbas. They used patterns and techniques which are still part of many modern designs, but the quality of workmanship has never since been surpassed—the Ardebil carpet has 320 knots to the square inch, while a modern broadloom or Persian handwoven rug may have anything from 35 to 60! Nonetheless,

.ND RUGS

although such workmanship has probably gone forever, there are still many fine pieces to be found. Most were probably made no earlier than the 18th or 19th centuries. Some have thick velvet piles, others have flat surfaces like the Soumak and Kelim carpets which have brilliant large-scale designs strikingly similar to the Indian designs of North America.

In Europe the Dutch took over the eastern tradition of using carpets over low tables as well as on the floor. Many contemporary portraits show how luxurious these cloths were, and there is still a tearoom in Rotterdam with carpeted tables for its patrons.

During the 18th century the English textile industry also developed rapidly; woven and needlework carpets were made at Spitalfields and Moorfields, some imitating Persian designs, but many with distinctive English appeal. Factories in the Midlands developed the larger looms which were used at Wilton and Axminster, utilizing the sturdy English wool and modern chemical dyes. At first, the looms were merely expanded versions of the old hand-worked frames, but gradually the need for mass production outweighed tradition, and the last hand looms were taken out of the factories around 1910.

In France, the Persian designs were soon discarded in favor of Baroque and then classical motifs, especially scrolls, flowers, shells etc. The Savonnerie factory was a royal project, and at Aubusson fine tapestries and carpets were made, using different techniques adapted from the Soumak carpets, for the French taste. Great halls and salons were designed with matching plasterwork on ceilings and walls, and motifs were repeated on furniture, hangings and specially made carpets. Both factories continued to serve the aristocratic world, although Aubusson was always just a little less fashionable, and certainly less expensive.

American rugs began humbly: at first the lack of materials and imports meant that small scatter rugs on simple wooden floors were very popular, and rugmaking at home improved and adapted many traditional techniques. Hooking and braiding were extremely convenient for scraps and left-over fabrics and wools. Designs were simple and charming, especially on hooked rugs; braided rugs depended more on subtle stripes and bars of related earth tones made with vegetable dyes.

In the later 1800's, as the country prospered, the need for "leftovers" became less and many variations of embroidered and knitted rugs were made using new wool in bright, "Berlin"-style patterns.

It was left to the New World to revolutionize mass modern carpet manufacture, with machines to make broadloom quickly and cheaply. The easy-to-live-with, wall-to-wall, long-pile carpets and textured monotones have become a 20th century symbol of luxury and sophisticated taste. Strangely enough, this almost universal use of neutral or unobtrusive background carpeting has revitalized the hand-made rug. Looms are now a basic fixture in art and craft schools. Squares for sewing into needlepoint rugs are featured in magazine pages, and hooking kits complete with wools and canvas are bringing one of the simplest techniques back into everyday use.

The family loom also has come back into use in the West, and even though the design may be closer to modern painting than to the Spring garden of Chorosoes, the symbols and rich patterns carry on the same tradition of carpet weaving.

GENERAL ADVICE

As with all fine things (and textiles in particular) carpets and rugs should be maintained in good condition, since grime, dirt and stains can destroy even the heaviest pile, if left long enough without cleaning. Badly stored rugs in unventilated conditions will also encourage moths to feed gratefully and happily during the warm summer months.

If your rug is encrusted with the accumulated deposits of years of hard use, grayed with dirt and dust, beg, steal or borrow a garden or a backyard in which to begin renovation. If possible, put up a very strong clothes line, sufficiently high to let you whack the dirt out of the backing and pile. The rug should hang freely with one end as near the line as possible, to let you beat from the back [1]; never beat the pile as it drives the dirt back into the knots, and embroidered or finely woven surfaces may be damaged. A real old-fashioned carpet beater is still the best tool for the job [2]. They are still made in the Middle East, and in one of the ethnic stores which import traditional basket-work you may be lucky enough to find one.

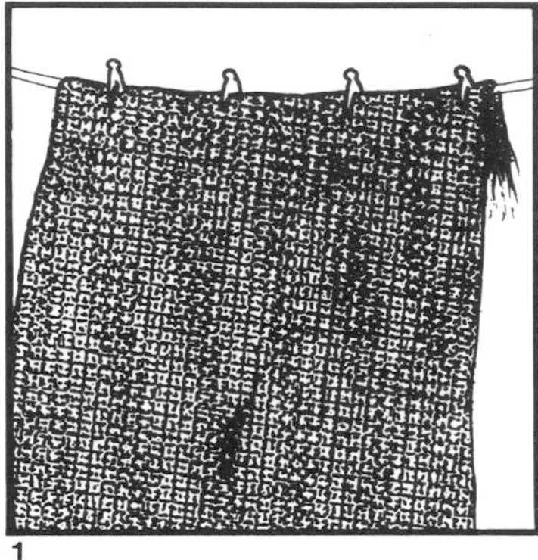
1

2

A possible alternative is the shag rug comb, or rake, which can be used with the tines pointing away from the back of the carpet. Or try a cheap plastic garden rake, the kind with splayed-out tines used for gathering.

Choose a dry day with not too much wind. Cover your hair with a scarf, and wear an old washable dress or a nylon overall. It's unbelievable how much dust, dead insects and dried up debris can accumulate in a neglected carpet. Ordinary woven carpets, even valuable Oriental rugs, can be given fairly hearty wallops. Even if all the dirt doesn't fall out, it will be considerably loosened, and easier to remove; but be much more gentle with embroidered and knotted rugs—you must be particularly careful not to catch stitches on the back if you use one of the rakes.

Never beat hooked or knitted rugs.

After the dirt has stopped rising, pull the rug over the line so that the other end now hangs free, and beat as before from the back [3]. Never leave a rug hanging overnight—dew or sudden showers may dampen the fabric, which will take days to dry out. After beating, it is best to vacuum a large rug with the curtain cleaning hose attachment of your vacuum cleaner, while it is still hanging free—you may need a long extension cord [4].

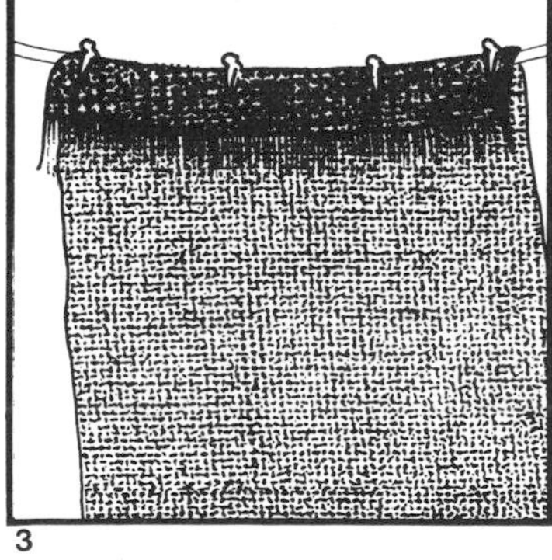
3

4

Start at the back as before, using medium suction for heavy canvas or light for finer backings.

After the back is done, work on the front. Try to keep the nozzle or roller moving always in the direction of the pile. Working the other way will let you get at the base, but it may dislodge threads and leave the surface ragged and tangled. Flat embroidered carpets of course have no pile, so work up and down along the length of the stitches with very light suction.

If the rug is very fragile, or you cannot take it outside, then spread a thick layer of brown paper on the floor and lay the rug face or pile down. Do not use newspaper—the ink may be absorbed by the fibers. An old sheet will do, but obviously it will have to be washed afterwards. Hit the back gently with the beater, shaking the whole rug from time to time to let the dirt fall out onto the paper. When finished, wrap up the paper carefully and toss out. Vacuum the back carefully, using light or medium suction; for very dirty rugs, you may find a nozzle is better than the wide brush since it can get into corners and seams; but do not use the nozzle on knitted or crocheted rugs as the wool will be pulled out of the stitch surface.

The pile, when brushed the right way, lies flat and even, covering the backing, and in Oriental rugs it will have a glossy sheen. Brushing the wrong way will leave threads untidy and spots of backing showing in long-haired rugs, and make the pile look dark and rough in short pile ones.

Knitted, crocheted and fine hooked rugs must always be handled very carefully. Keep a look out as you work for pulled threads or loose stitches. It's a good idea to keep a needle threaded with bright contrasting wool at hand—when you see a damaged spot, put a basting stitch there with the bright wool and leave a long tail showing [5]. This will make finding the damage quick and easy, especially with large pieces.

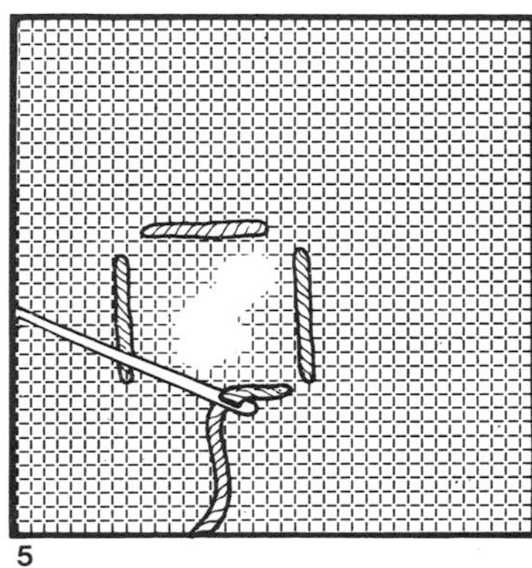

5

Cleaning

Now that the preliminary cleaning has been done, take stock of the condition of the backing. The following pages give cleaning instructions for the various types of rug. After any repairs, maintain your carpet in good condition by regular and gentle vacuuming, and immediate removal of stains.

As a general rule, remove stains quickly and wet the rug as little as possible. A good dry-cleaning fluid is suitable for most rugs, and will remove greasy food stains, gum etc., and oily dirt effectively and easily.

For organic and food stains (egg, coffee, blood, etc.) a useful cleaning solution is one teaspoonful *white* vinegar and one teaspoonful pure mild soap flakes, in a quart (1 liter) of lukewarm water. Stir until the soap has dissolved, and use when cool. Sugar and alcohol stains respond well to plain warm water, applied on a sponge that's lightly wrung out. Double-sided rugs or braided rugs should be turned often so that they wear evenly, although rugs are designed to take a good deal of wear.

Storing

To store your rugs, keep them flat, enveloped in brown paper and plastic sheets (remembering never to store a rug in plastic unless it's bone dry).

Rugs too big to lie flat can be rolled around a light pole, with the pile turned in [6]. It's usually suggested that fine hooked rugs be rolled pile out—but sound, sturdy examples will be safe either way.

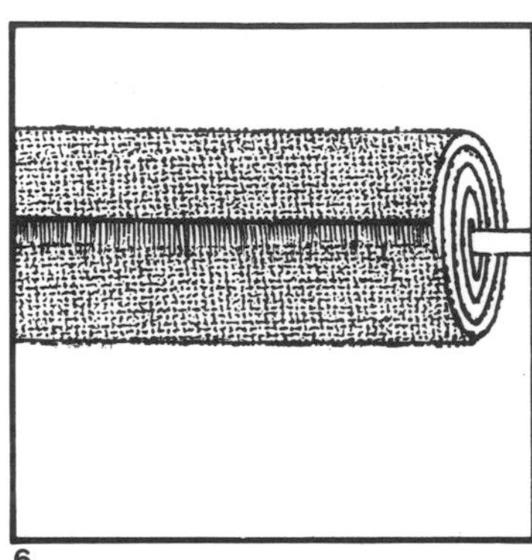

6

Note: All fine rugs should be repaired by experts, and this is particularly true of woven rugs. So make sure your rug is correctly valued before you begin to tinker with it. However, tears and fraying should be stopped at once, even if really "invisible" repairs must wait until you become an expert yourself or can afford to pay for one!

BRAIDED AND RAG RUGS

Cleaning Braided and Rag Rugs

These are sturdily made, from hard-wearing fabrics for family use. Since they are reversible, it is difficult to find a spot for testing carpet cleaners or shampoos, so begin with a mild solution. Remember that old braided rugs may have a number of different fabrics, so to be really sure test each one before washing in warm water soapsuds. Use the suds instead of the water to prevent the rug from getting too wet. Rinse with a moistened sponge, making sure all the soap is removed.

Note: Really fine antique rugs over 150 years old were made with vegetable-dyed wools and fabrics. These have usually faded to muted "earth" shades of terracotta, blue and brown, and although liable to run if too much water is used, their mellow appearance is softer and more appropriate with antique furniture than the fast, but harsher, aniline dyes of today. Be sure to dry these flat, away from direct heat, in a warm, even temperature.

Repairing Braided Rugs

Old braided rugs can suffer from two main problems: the outer length of braid wears away, or the lacing may come undone and break off. If the wear is very bad, consider replacing the worn strip with a new one. Match the predominant shades as best you can, in a similar fabric. Unpick the outside braid and cut away the worn parts sewing on new strips [7]. Try to stagger the cuts so the change is gradual and unobtrusive. Rebraid, following the original pattern as best you can—most rugs are braided with three strips. Work as much as you need, lace together and tuck the ends under. After repairing you can protect the outer edge with a strip of bias binding in the same shade as the rug [8]. Tack stitch in place. Lacing can easily be replaced, using an upholstery needle and matching thread. Follow the pattern on the rest of the rug.

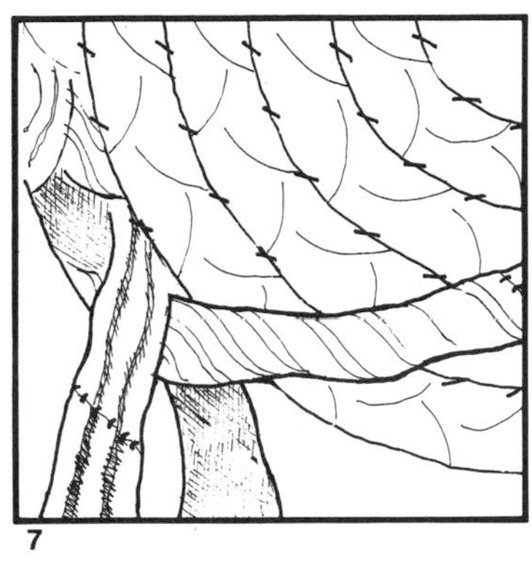
7

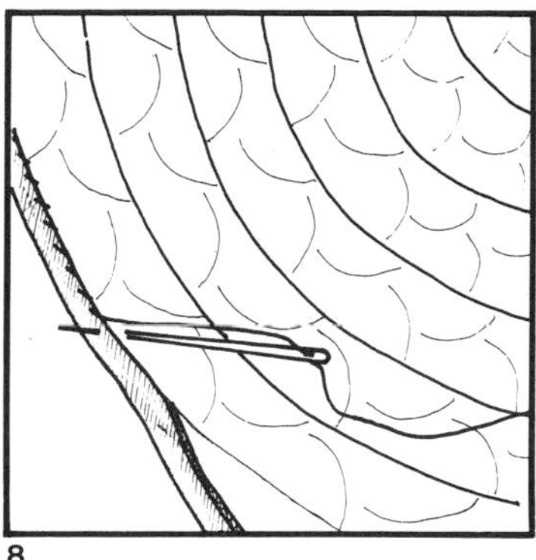
8

Repairing Rag Rugs
Most rag rugs are made with a kind of braid. The rags are cleaned and joined into strips, then braided and laced together in the usual way. Care and repair follow the instructions on braid above. Some rag rugs are strips of fabric woven on coarse fabric or canvas. To replace worn bits, unpick the damaged area, find a matching fabric and restitch, using a rug needle. If your rags are too thick even for that, then make a "needle" by wrapping Scotch tape round and round an end until it makes a sharp point.

CROCHETED AND KNITTED RUGS

Cleaning Crocheted and Knitted Rugs
These are small enough to wash like a wool or cashmere sweater. Measure the rug for length and width. Use a commercial wool-cleaning liquid (follow the directions on the bottle) and let the rug soak for a little while until rinsing leaves clean water. You may have to rinse the rug over and over again, but do not let it soak for long or the wool will lose all its natural oil and body. Roll in towels until almost dry, then block by stretching gently all around until it regains its size [9]. Dry off while flat, checking now and then to make sure the stitches haven't pulled out of shape. Never dry over a clothes line, because the weight of wet material will pull the rug out of shape.

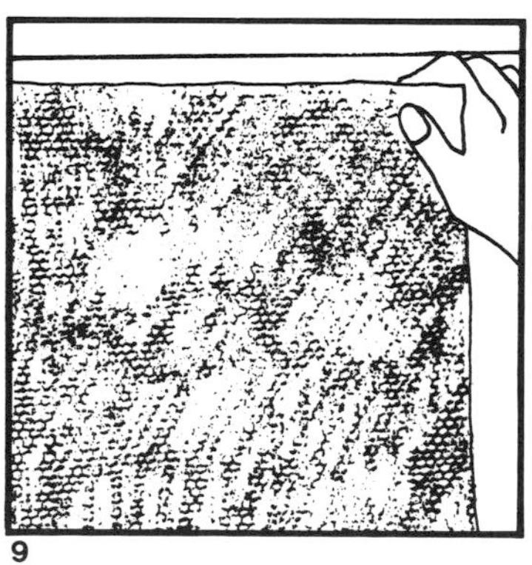
9

Repairing Crocheted and Knitted Rugs

If the rug was worked as a single piece you need to be a bit of a needlewoman to repeat or replace a pattern, but it can be done. Before you attempt it though, see if you can simulate the effect with a needle and thread or wool, much like darning a sweater.

It's amazing what a little careful stitching can do. Start with a canvas patch big enough to cover the affected part with a good margin to spare. Baste this to the back [10]. This will keep the area flat while you work.

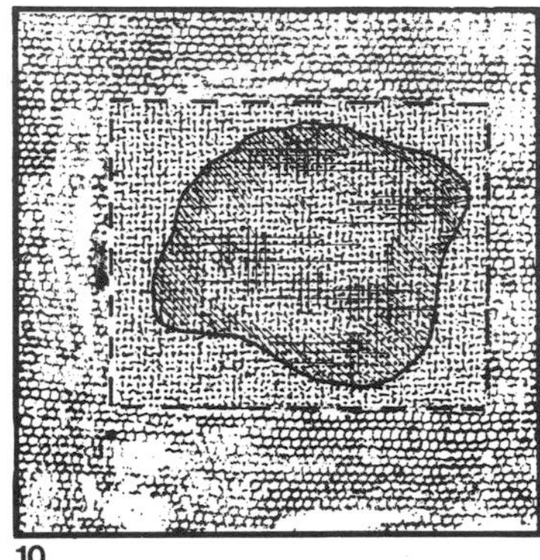

10

Then splice a loose end of wool from the top of the damaged area to new matching wool. To do this, unravel a small part of each end into its separate plys [11], snipping each ply a different length and twisting together as shown [12]. Thread a needle onto the new wool [13], and starting at the top, cross the damaged area back and forth. Then weave vertically until all the hole is darned.

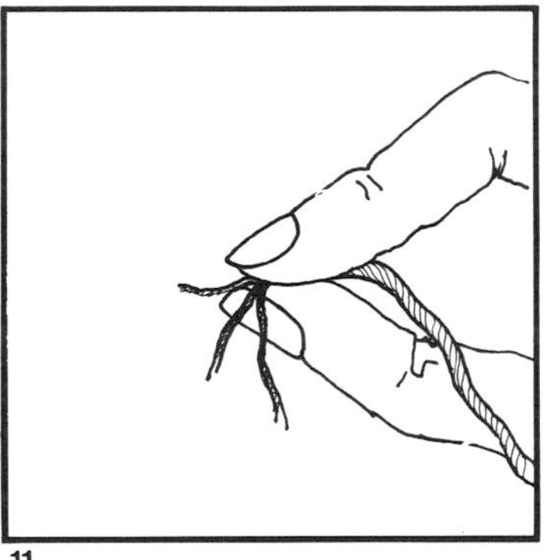

11

12

Be sure to catch all the damaged threads up as you go—as you start each crossing place the needle about $\frac{1}{4}''$ away from the damaged area; and, of course, as you cross make sure you do not darn through the temporary backing.

13

To incorporate another shade, work on top of the first darning; to simulate an irregular texture, use a suitable thread worked into the darning to create the effect of tufts. After the repair is complete, snip away the basting stitches from the patch and remove it. Remember that all repaired rugs need very careful handling.

FLAT EMBROIDERED RUGS

Cleaning Flat Embroidered Rugs

Most larger examples were worked in squares and put together much like a chess board, and you must be particularly careful if the joining was badly done, or the seams have been damaged—a beautiful room-sized carpet can fall apart into little mats! If there's any sign of weakness, sew a backing onto the entire piece. Use strong open-weave burlap or hessian, machined to the right size. Hem and slipstitch to the outside edge of the rug.

Small embroidered rugs can be gently cleaned with carpet cleaning fluid, or washed with the foam or soap suds, but they may need blocking to retain their correct size. Measure before cleaning, rinse with a moist sponge, and tack down to the right shape on a wooden floor or large board.

Repairing Flat Embroidered Rugs

If the stitching has worn away, unpick the damaged area, keeping the edges irregular. Tuck the wool ends through stitches on the back to keep them from unraveling. Match the wool as best you can. There are a few nationally available brands of embroidery wool which have an incredible range; ask for a sample card or write to your nearest supplier. Take snippets of the worn wool with you. Then rework in the same stitch. If a large section of a repeated motif is missing, mark the pattern with embroidery markers as you remove old bits so that you can follow it later when re-sewing [14]. (These markers are sold in most craft stores; do not use ordinary felt tips as they will run and stain the wool.) Otherwise, copy the pattern from an undamaged place and rework the bare canvas in matching wools.

If the canvas itself is damaged, then unpick the stitches around the hole or tear, going at least an inch (2.6cm) in every direction. Let the threads hang down from the back. Cut a new piece of canvas slightly larger than the damaged area, lining up the holes if you can. With embroidered side up, thread the old wool through an embroidery needle, and begin working at the top putting the needle through both thicknesses of canvas [15]. Work all around the area, making sure the patch lies flat. You will probably find there isn't enough old wool to cover the patch completely, but match with shades as near the original as you can find.

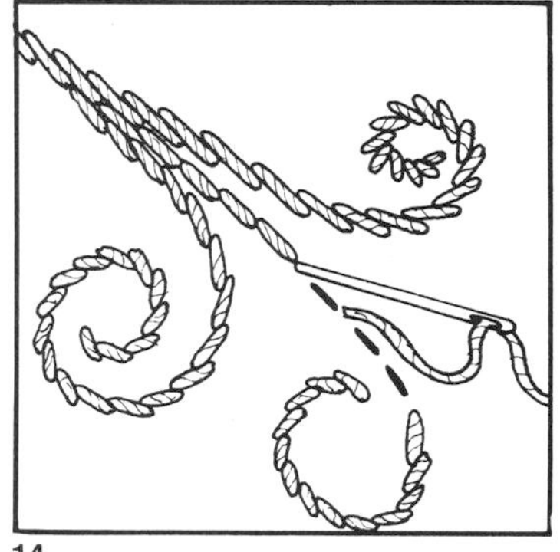
14

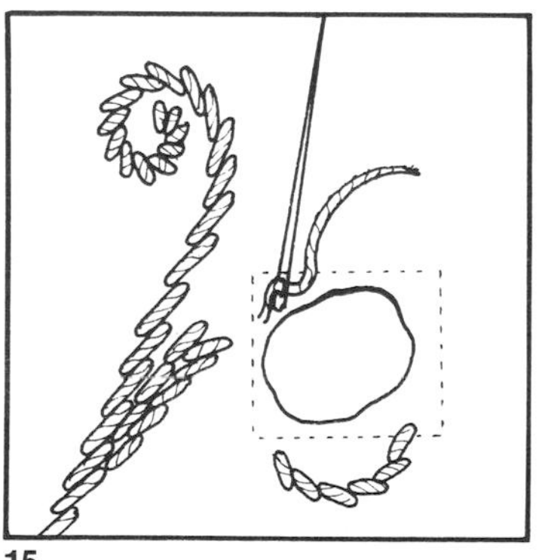
15

If the canvas seems to be an odd size then use a really fine petit-point canvas—it has so many holes you are certain to find one at nearly the right spot to make your new stitches the same length as the old. With all repairs, do not pull the thread too tight or the rug will never lie flat.

HOOKED RUGS

Cleaning Hooked Rugs

Handle these very carefully; you can remove a lot of dirt by vacuuming from the pile side, but only when the rug is flat on the ground, and using the lowest suction.

Before you embark on any more serious cleaning, test all the different fabrics for fastness—the printed patterns were generally bought by the yard, but many plain shades were dyed at home and will run easily. Use a mild soap solution with plenty of cool suds, and work with these suds only. Gently brush a sponge over the surface, but be very careful not to soak the backing. Vacuum gently when thoroughly dry.

Repairing Hooked Rugs

These are fairly easy to repair since the worn or damaged stitches can usually be pulled out without trouble. Also remove the odd stitch around the damaged area, so that the new material will appear less obvious. When purchasing new fabric try to match the texture as well as the shade.

- Cut a patch of new backing material larger than the damaged area, and baste to the original backing.
- Turn face side up and hook through both old and new backing. The easiest tool is an old-fashioned hooker, which pushes through the fabric from above and catches a loop which you hand guide underneath. Pull through to the correct height to match the other pile, and release. Push through a little way along the line, keeping spaces and loop height the same as the original [16]. Since the lengths are more irregular than counted embroidery, the hooked patch will seldom stand out as long as the general effect of new and old fabric is the same.
- When repairing badly worn edges, undo the braid, and pull out stitches evenly all the way around, until you reach sound work.
- Turn under the backing and rebind with fresh braid.

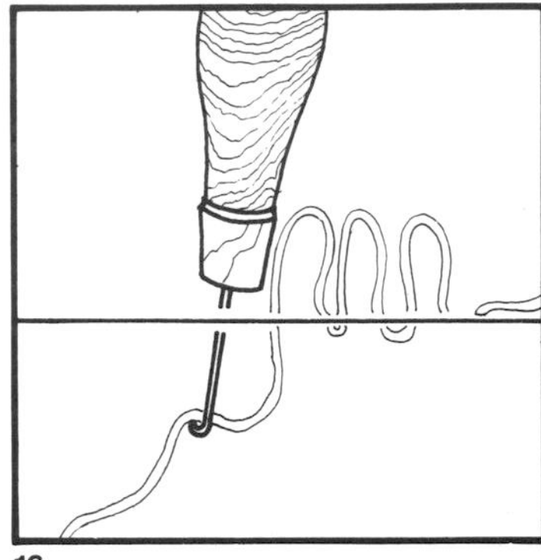

16

WOVEN RUGS

Cleaning Woven Rugs—Short Pile, Orientals and Long Pile

These are usually the hardest-wearing rugs of all. Clean with a good carpet cleaning liquid (follow manufacturer's instructions carefully) poured on a sponge and brushed over the nap, going the right way. Don't use too much liquid or you will soak the backing.

Shampoo vigorously, using a fairly stiff brush or a special carpet shampooer. Early Orientals and other woven carpets were also made with vegetable dyes, but almost all "modern" examples are aniline. If you think you have an old piece, check for fastness before shampooing. It may be worth having it cleaned professionally. Short pile rugs remain damp for a deceptively long time. Do not brush or vacuum until it is dry. If you have removed the furniture, do not replace it until the carpet is bone dry or you may make permanent marks. At least put a thick pad of foam rubber under the legs of each object [17].

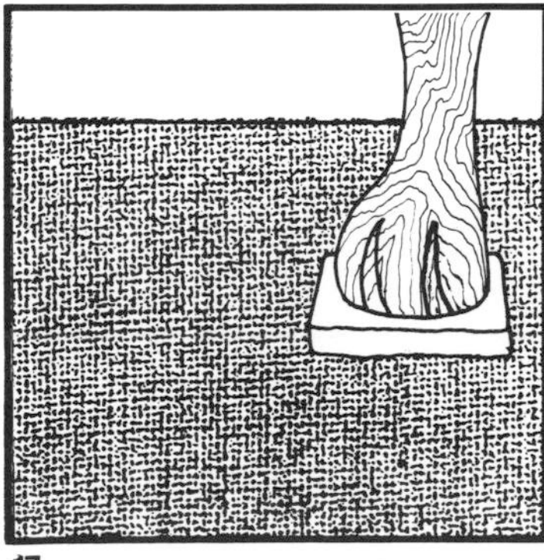

17

Repairing Woven Rugs

The most common repairs necessary are to torn fringes and edges, and "reweaving" small damaged spots, often caused by cigarette burns.

To "reweave" the latter cut away the blackened pile, and examine. You may find that once the dark scorch has gone, the shorter pile is scarcely noticeable, but if the burn goes right down, use tiny pointed scissors to cut the knots which tie each loop.

Use a needle threaded with matching wool to make tiny new stitches; knot and cut off at the same height. There are two basic knots in oriental carpets, the Ghiordes, or Turkish knot on the right of illustration 18, and the Senneh, or Persian knot on the left. Variations of these are used for all woven rugs.

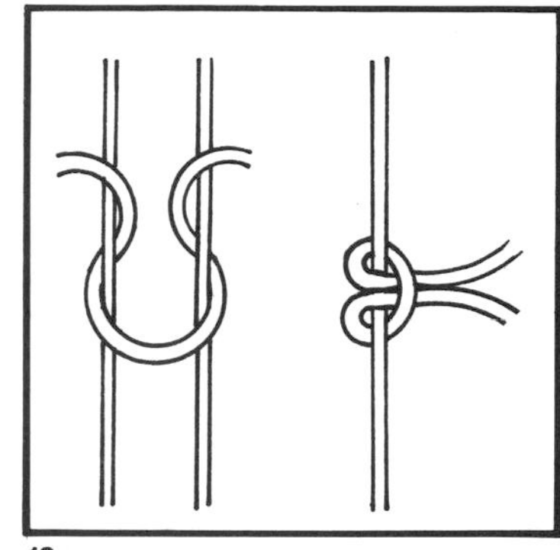

18

For badly damaged areas of any size, have the repair done professionally unless you are willing to spend a lot of time. It isn't difficult, but the knots are tiny, and it takes a lot of stitches to fill up a very small area. Mistakes can be quickly snipped out, but most rugs have a complicated pattern which is slightly irregular, anyway, and long pile rugs will hide mistakes in their depths as long as the general effect blends into the original.

Fringes at the end are made from the warps; if they pull away at the corners then the warp may be damaged, and need to be replaced. Lay the corner face up on a slanted board. Buy matching warp threads, and splice to the old ones, letting them run out at least two inches longer than the existing fringe. Then splice [11 and 12, page 136] a new weft thread to an old one at the lowest inside part of the damaged area. Weave this weft in and out of the new warp threads with a large rug needle until you come to the side edge of the rug. At this point, wrap the weft around a pin pushed into the board; let the weft thread hang free.

The Knots: Look carefully at an existing knot to see what kind it is [18]. For repairing short-pile rugs use pre-cut wool strands; for long-pile, cut the skein to the appropriate length.

Naturally, attempt to match the original shades as closely as possible. Each length is then knotted by hand around the warp thread doing one knot at a time, working from the inside of the rug to the edge. When you have completed one row of knotting, pick up the weft and weave back into the rug above the knots until you reach the old pile. Then work the needle through the old backing to link the new section to the old, ending with the needle on top of the rug ready to work another weft row. Now make another row of knots; next pick up the weft thread and weave it back to the edge of the rug as before, pushing each weft thread down to hold the row of knots firmly in place. Go on alternating rows of knots and wefts until you reach the top edge and the last row of knots. At this point there is usually a firm binding of weft threads. Duplicate the depth of this, catching the undamaged binding into each row; then pull the end of the weft through and secure with a knot on the back. Finally knot the warp threads at the top to match the existing fringe and then clip the new fringe to the correct length.

GLASS

Of all the substances and objects covered in this book, glass is unique—for against all appearances and common sense explanation, it is not a solid. Scientifically, the description of glass is a liquid in suspension, or sometimes a super-cooled liquid—very appropriate when we think of tiered chandeliers with long drops swaying and glittering like so many icicles. This extraordinary fact is reflected in the pattern of glass manufacture—it requires some knowledge of chemistry and an enclosed kiln to create the necessary temperatures. Almost all primitive societies had some form of pottery, and usually metal working as well, but glass-making has a selective history. The first glass was probably made by accident, in one of the 18th dynasty ceramic workshops in Egypt, as a turquoise glaze used on pottery beads.

However it began, glass-making developed very quickly to a fine art; the ingredients were tinted to resemble semi-precious stones such as lapis lazuli, jade or turquoise, and melted together in small pots. After they were cooled, the blocks of glass were cut, chiseled, rubbed, engraved and polished. Patterns were made with small bits of glass laid together in the kiln, which fused together during firing. Such pieces were produced throughout the Greek and Roman periods, especially in Alexandria, which continued to provide carved and cut glass for the luxury trade until the collapse of the Islamic empires.

Sometime around the 1st century BC, glass blowing was discovered, probably in Syria. Blown glass involved more than just a different technique; an almost entirely new material became possible, thin, transparent, and above all, infinitely adaptable. Soon all kinds of objects were exported throughout the entire Roman trade area. Bottles and jars were used for oil, wine, cosmetics and food; they were pale green, fairly transparent, and surprisingly light in weight, although it may be that centuries of burial have destroyed some of the original thickness. The greenish tinge comes from the iron oxide in the sand—the process of purification used for clear glass was developed only gradually through the centuries, and in any case was never considered necessary for storage or everyday cheap items.

During the Middle Ages, elaborate designs disappeared, except for the "forest" glass of Northern Europe. Sometimes clumsy and rough, the best cone beakers are quite elegant, and the rather heavy Teutonic style has always had some influence. But farther south, Venetian Guilds revolutionized glass production in their city, and in all Europe. A great period of research and experimentation had begun when the Guilds were moved out of Venice to Murano in 1348. Their work in mosaics for Byzantine churches had continued throughout the dark period, and by the 15th century they were blowing stylized drinking glasses, ornamental plates, dishes and cups, all richly tinted and intricately decorated with enamels and even jewels, or engraved like the precious stones they resembled. Eventually a new chemical formula resulted in an almost transparent glass, easy to work, very flexible, light, and breathtakingly fragile. For the next two centuries Venetian cristallo was exported everywhere. In spite of severe penalties, workers slipped away to establish rival glass houses in many other cities, especially in Altare, Antwerp, Paris and London. Cristallo and all other glass before 1670's was made of silica, soda, and lime; silica is found as sand, the soda is a flux to allow the sand to liquify, and the lime acts as a stabilizer, albeit a sometimes imperfect one.

A new glass was needed, stronger, more stable, and capable of standing up to everyday use by the rapidly expanding middle classes. English chemists worked on a new mixture using lead oxide as the flux, and by 1700 glass of lead, sometimes called flint glass, had almost replaced cristallo. Today it is often called lead crystal and this deep-glowing material, heavier and far better at reflecting light than soda glass, remains the finest product of modern factories. It is as suitable for cutting in elaborate facets as for the fluid, sculptured shapes of modern Scandinavian design. No other glass is used for fine tableware, and mirrors, stained glass and even modern Venetian decorations are all variations on a basic theme.

The advent of pressed glass, pioneered by American factories as the answer to the mass market, created a whole new art form. Some pressed glass merely copied blown and cut glass, but the best was individually designed and worked for the special qualities of that medium. Today early pressed glass, with lacy patterns and sculptured ornaments, is widely collected, and equally widely faked—since genuine and fake are both mass produced, it is quite hard for the beginner to tell the difference, so do your homework, consult a local expert and beware of unbelievable bargains. Paperweights are a fairly modern idea, invented by French stationers around 1850 as a pretty toy for desks. They were made by the great French factories such as St. Louis and Baccarat, but today they are among the most expensive forms of glass collecting. Little slices of millefiori-patterned glass rods and fantastic lace and animal figurines in the best Venetian tradition were enclosed in clear domes, and sometimes cased again in red or blue layers with windows cut to show the little scene inside.

France kept its supremacy for a long time, but English, Scottish and American glassmakers have all challenged their position, and created individual and delightful paperweights and doorstops. But beware of imitations—sometimes clumsy and obvious, but not always—and too many pretty weights turn out to be plastic.

The interior of a glass-blowing factory hasn't changed much, although the kilns are probably electric. The tools are traditional, a blowpipe to make the first bubble, a heavy flat surface of metal or marble to roll the bubble into shape, metal or wooden shapes to help make uniform designs for each glass, shears to cut off the lip, and a solid iron pontil rod to hold the glass by the foot while it receives the final touches. The work is usually done in a team and the master craftsman is called the gaffer. As with many modern crafts studio glass is also made by individuals, working on special decorative pieces with techniques adapted from every glass tradition.

Today glass has the widest appeal it has ever known; you can choose from a banana shaped baby bottle or a pressed glass flask with a patriotic symbol, the iridescent shimmer of Art Nouveau lamps by Tiffany or the petals of an early Steuben vase, a cut-glass bowl from Ireland, a simple Central European decanter with painted hearts and flowers, or a geometric mirror in an Art Deco frame. Even the impurities typical of soda glass can be deliberately created—Mexican glass, bubbly and fluid, is a new interpretation of Venetian swirls where the bubbles and uneven tints add to the decorative effect. Whatever kind of glass you have treat it gently, care for it well, and remember that modern inventors have not yet produced anything that begins to equal the importance of glass in domestic life.

GLASS

Cleaning

Washing in warm soapy water followed by a clear rinse is the best method for cleaning dishes or glasses. Always dry glass gently with a clean, dust-free cloth, or water spots will remain.

Ornamental glass can be cleaned with water and ammonia, or water and white vinegar, or with one of the commercial window cleaning fluids. Follow the manufacturer's instructions, then rub gently to give a high gloss. This method is particularly good for mirrors and glass tables. Alternatively make your own cleaner:

Mix $\frac{1}{4}$ pint (140ml) denatured alcohol (methylated spirits)
$\frac{1}{4}$ pint (140ml) household ammonia
$\frac{1}{2}$ pint (285ml) water

Try not to rub painted or gilded glass—instead pat it dry gently and polish around the design if desired.

The intricate glory of late-18th-century cut glass: far left, double star motif within circle of leaves and swirl flutes; left, large diamond composed of smaller ones, with leaf patterns at each end. This was a peak period for English and Irish cut table-glass. Pieces of such quality should normally be repaired by qualified experts.

Repairing

Repairing badly broken glass is really a job for a craftsman, and with a few exceptions it is impossible to join fragments of clear or pale-tinted glass invisibly, since the light will be reflected at the break. Experts can do surprisingly effective work, sometimes replacing broken bits with new pieces, re-cutting to cover up a bad scratch or making a whole new glass to match eleven of your set. Certainly for anything of value it is worth taking the pieces to a specialist before throwing them away.

Nonetheless, there are some simple repairs that can be done at home. Work in a warmish room at an even temperature and avoid handling the pieces roughly or applying too much pressure. Glass is not a solid—it's a liquid in a suspended state. The tensions set up by working molten glass and annealing or cooling are delicately balanced, and glass will shatter without an obvious blow (Fig. 1 illustrates the parts of a stemmed glass). Repaired glass should be washed with extra caution, and dried very carefully. Try to be as relaxed as possible when repairing or even cleaning fine glassware. The pressure of your fingers on a thin glass stem can cause it to snap. For that reason, it's a good idea to learn to hold drinking glasses by the foot, or near the heavier base of the stem, even when using them on the dinner table.

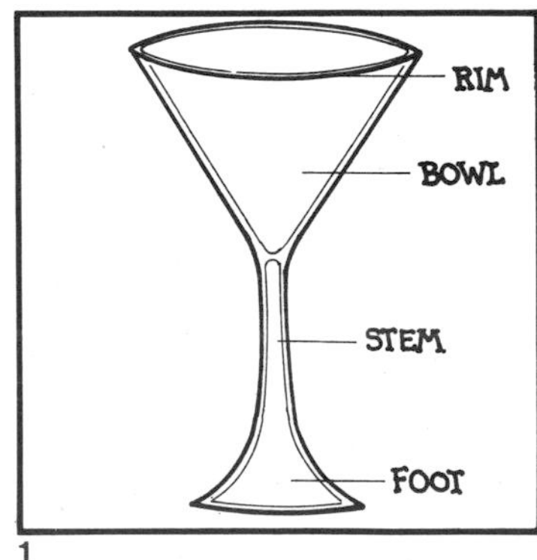

1

Mending Broken Stems: This is one of the commonest repairs, and the hardest to fix if the break is in the middle, but fortunately the bowl usually snaps off cleanly.

● First wash both pieces carefully in water with a little ammonia, then dry with a dust-free cloth. Make sure the glass is absolutely dry before you begin work.

● Turn the bowl upside down. Move the stem until it is in the correct position. If the stem is broken into two or more pieces, join the part nearest the bowl first.

● Take a small glob of plasticine, and make a roll about an inch (2.5cm) long, thick enough to support the stem [2].

● Push one end firmly but not too hard onto one side of the bowl, just below or to one side of the break.

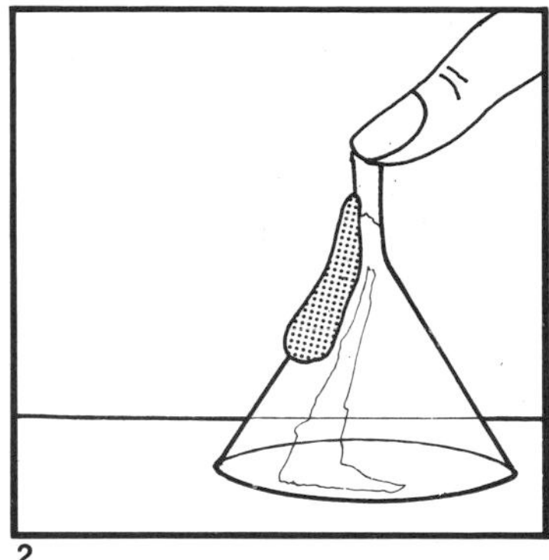

2

● Coat both surfaces of the break with a little synthetic-based glue—choose one that's transparent and waterproof. Try not to let the glue slip onto the sides of the stem. (A wooden matchstick is a very useful applicator if you have lost the pin or spreader) [3].

● Now fit the stem in place on the bowl again. Hold it firmly in place for a minute, and while keeping the stem straight with one hand, push the plasticine against the top part with the other [4].

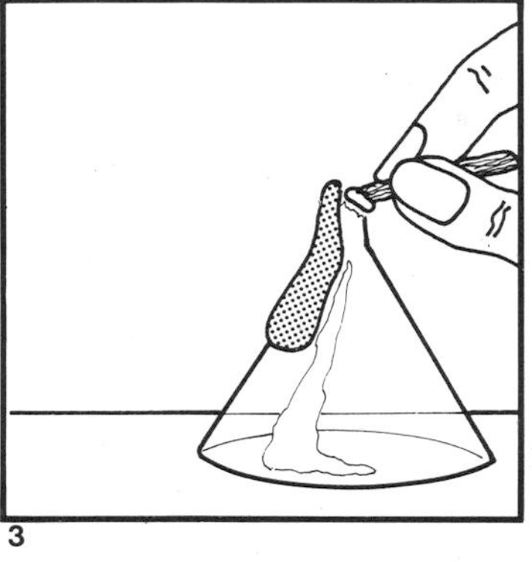

3

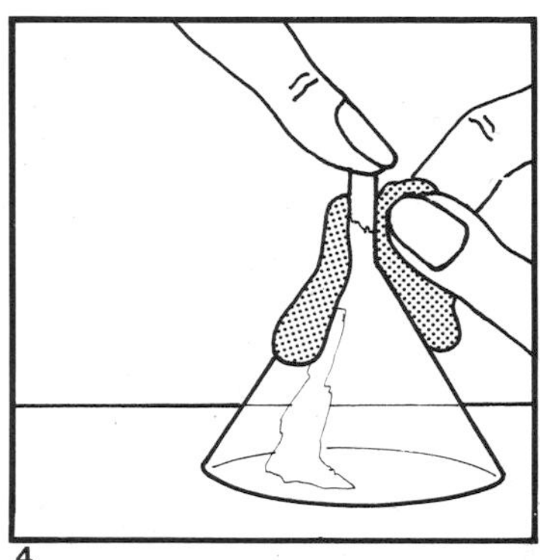

4

● For a very straight break which doesn't balance well, or a heavy stem, use additional plasticine on the other side, but be sure you don't push the top of the stem out of place. For breaks near the foot, the plasticine will probably have to be a little more generous so that the "cartwheel" balances [5]. Leave the glued glass in position for at least 24 hours. (You shouldn't work at the same table for five to six hours unless the glue instructions indicate a very quick setting time.) Check at the beginning to make sure passing cars or slamming doors haven't made the glass vibrate and move. The same procedure can be followed for large chips and broken pieces of all kinds.

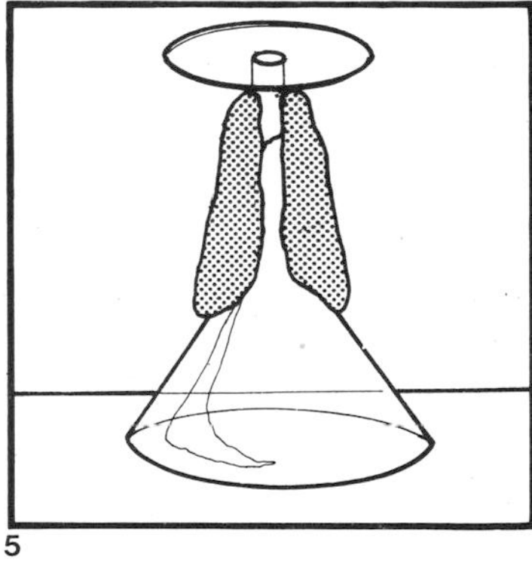

5

Alternatively you can also use masking tape to hold the pieces in place [6]. Tape from unbroken glass right across the end down the other side. With a multiple break work on one piece at a time, leaving 24 hours at least before you add the final fragment.

6

Chips: A small chip can be smoothed over with abrasive paper—use a medium grade wet and dry paper wrapped around a pencil or stick of wood so that it can rub down the edges evenly [7]. You can have a little taken off the top all around the rim, by a professional glass cutter, but it may change the appearance of the glass considerably. However, it's worth doing when the chip is really bad, or there are radiating cracks which may break off even more pieces.

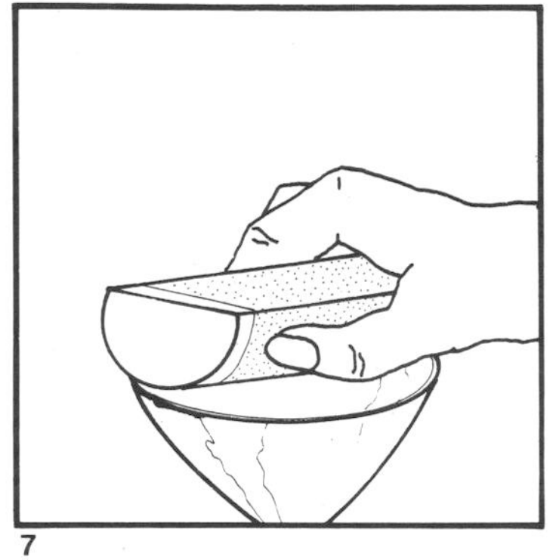
7

Have the cut made below all the damage. Thicker glass may be cut with one of the home bottle cutters which are available in many large stores, but fine glass requires professional attention.
After cutting, the rim must be smoothed. In the glassworks this would be done by slightly melting the rim, but at home stick to abrasive paper. There will be a slightly frosted effect, but if you change to finer and finer grades, and then polish it well, the clouding should be minimal.

Scratches: Theoretically glass can be made to flow enough to cover small scratches. If you have the time and patience, take a chamois cloth and rub in one direction only, until the scratch fades [8]. It will probably take weeks, but having a slightly warmed glass would help.
Scratches on the base of any glass piece should never be erased or ground away unless they disfigure the object. Such markings are the sign to any valuer that the glass is old and has survived a certain amount of wear and tear.

8

Painting and Gilding: During the past 100 years the craft of home decoration was very widespread and American women were particularly good at enriching plates, glassware and other *objets d'art*. Many little vases and lamps made from milk, or pale tinted, glass were adorned with bouquets of flowers and classical designs. These were seldom fired, and the paints were not very permanent, so you may find faded or flaky examples which need restoring.

- Hold the glass up to the light [9]—paint usually leaves a slight residue of oil and you should be able to trace the missing parts easily, using a sharp brush or felt-tipped pen.
- Paint over the markings in the same shades that are already on the glass. It's best to use special glass paints, also used for painting on china. If they are not available, acrylic or enamel paints will do. No paint that is not fired or semi-permanent will resist much washing and daily use—so it's better to keep such decoration for ornamental articles.
- Use a very small brush and try to work as evenly as possible. Do one shade at a time, letting the paint dry completely between each coat.

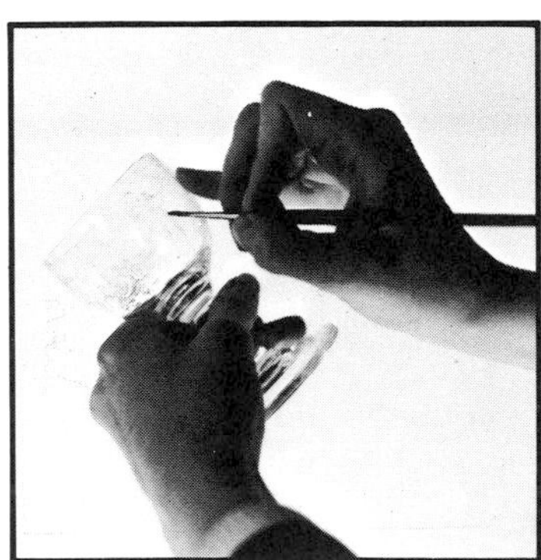
9

Regilding presents the same problems as re-painting—no gilding will be even semi-permanent unless it's fired in a kiln or oven. China can be treated in this way but glass is too fragile. However, re-gilded and re-painted glasses can be used as candy or nut dishes, and rinsed out quickly by hand.

For step-by-step instructions on painting a new motif or design, see page 87. If you choose a pattern from a straight-sided glass and want to put it on a funnel bowl, it will need adapting. It's best to start with fairly simple, freehand designs [10], but avoid geometric borders as such patterns are very difficult to control for the beginner, and show up clumsy brushwork immediately. For badly placed strokes, dip a cotton swab in paint remover, and wipe off at once.

10

Chandeliers: Most of the damage to chandeliers is in the metal parts and these can be replaced at a good lamp store. The crystal drops are also available in various shapes and sizes—take each shape to the supplier to match accurately. Beware of modern plastic imitations, which can be surprisingly good. Real crystal has an "oily" feel and a brilliant appearance when cut and polished.

Do not rewire a chandelier yourself unless you are an electrician.
To replace the rings which let the drops hang freely, buy fairly thin, pliable wire, cut into lengths of about an inch (2.5cm), and thread through the hole at the top of the drop. Try to match the color of the original wire.
Pinch the ends together but keep the ring shape (as on the left side of Fig. 11). If the rings are closed too tightly (as on the right side of Fig. 11) they will not turn or twist in the air and it is this movement which makes a chandelier sparkle. Sometimes the ring on the top of the drop will hook onto the chandelier itself as in [12].

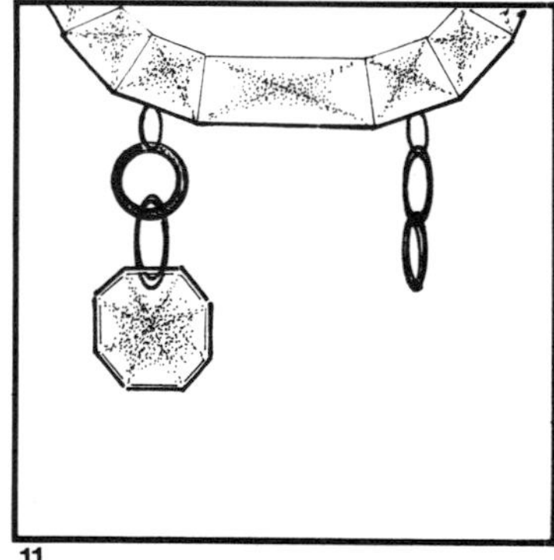
11

Broken nozzles and drop pins can be replaced by old ones, or new ones made to match. Remember any good chandelier comes apart into dozens of pieces which can usually be matched in an antique shop or re-made into a smaller version. All the glass bits and pieces can easily be cleaned, with denatured alcohol (methylated spirits) or the formula mentioned on page 142.

12

GLASS

Reversed Glass Paintings: The skill needed to paint these pictures on glass is considerable; they are worked on the reverse side of the glass, and must be painted with the foreground details first, background last. A face, for example, would have to have eyes, nose, mouth and shading painted before the shape was filled in. Restoration is very precise and infinitely painstaking—unless you are an experienced artist, take your painting to an expert, and preferably to someone who has at least worked on miniatures before.

- Very often it is the backing which has become damaged, and allowed dirt and grime to collect on the glass. Remove the frame by prying up the nails.
- Take off and discard all the old board or fabric unless it is in good condition.
- Wash the picture very gently in warm soapy water, not rubbing on the painting at all.
- Rinse carefully, and let it dry in a warm room.
- Clean the frame itself and then cut a board to the size of the old piece. Remember you will see one side through the glass so choose your piece of board carefully—white or light-tinted backgrounds are usually best, but it depends on the painting.
- Place the glass gently into the frame, put in the board, and push down the nails until they press the board flat against the glass.

Mirrors: Old mirrors in their original frames have a lovely, speckled charm which is completely destroyed by re-silvering. If the marking is very bad, use the mirror as an ornament and put modern mirrors in bathrooms, etc., for utility. Or replace the glass, but keep the old piece well wrapped up so that you can restore it to its proper home one day. (Modern glass in an old frame has much less value than the original.)

If the silvering has really worn away, try spreading a thin layer of metal foil on the back, taped in place, and smoothed down to lie flat [13]. One of the best reasons for not using new plate is the fine beveling which is characteristic of all old mirrors and is so expensive today.
A very effective way of cleaning mirrors is to rub the surface with a ball of soft paper dampened with denatured alcohol (methylated spirit). Follow by rubbing with a duster sprinkled with a little whiting and finally polishing with a chamois.

13

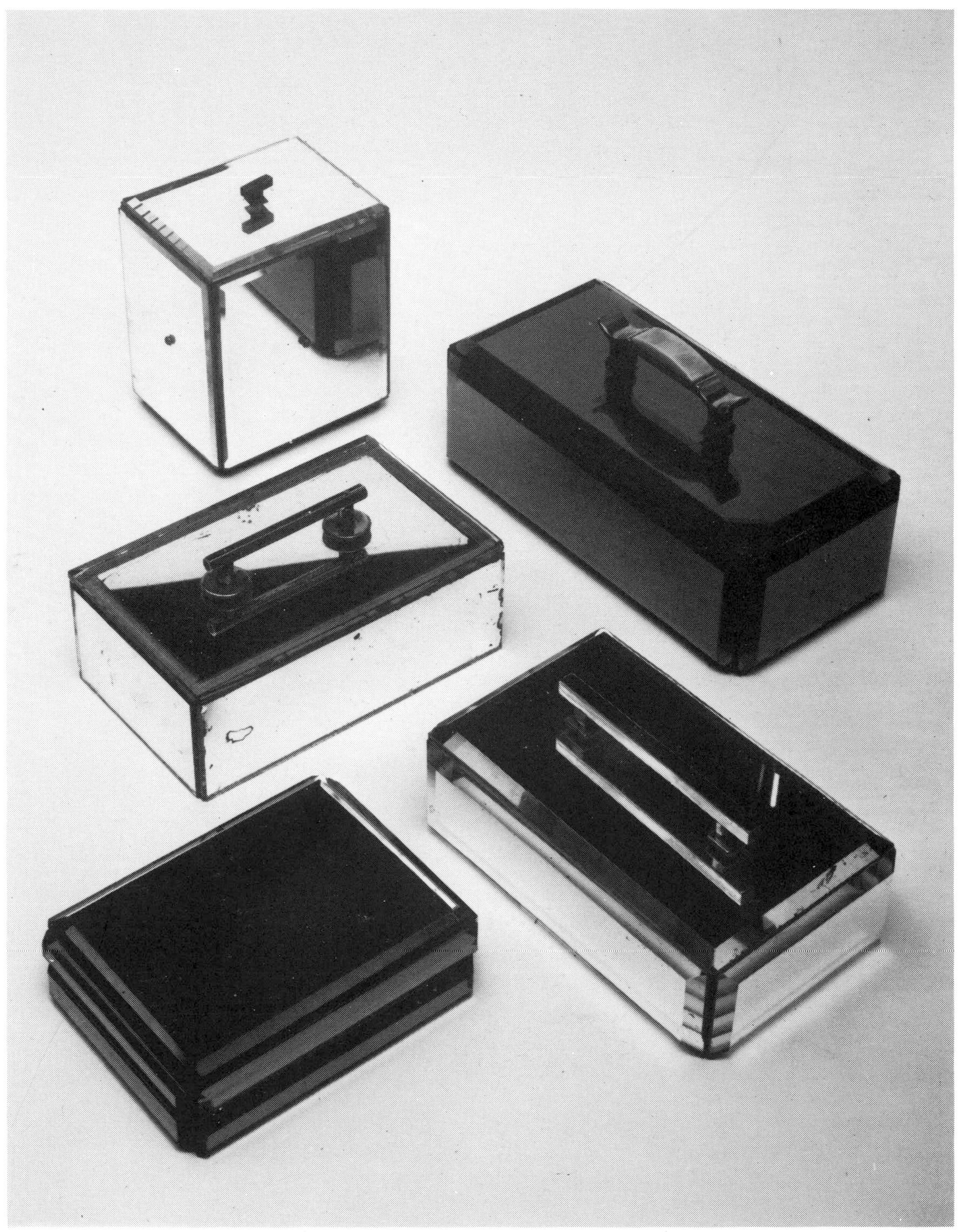

Five mirror-glass boxes in the Art Nouveau style dating from the early part of this century—an interesting variation for glass-collectors and box-collectors alike.

POTTERY AND

Billions of years ago, as the earth's crust cooled, extreme temperatures, wind, storms, ice floes and heavy rain all took their toll of the surface rock. Over thousands of millions of years the different rocks broke up into smaller and smaller particles, and the surface became covered with a deep layer of soil—pure sand, solid clay and every possible mixture in between.

The first settled communities found lumps of different muddy clays, mixed with stones and bits of debris, but sticky and cohesive enough to retain the footprint of an animal. Perhaps after a long, dry, hot spell a hunter realized that the same footprint was still there, but now hard and almost permanent, and capable of retaining liquids.

Surprisingly enough, this is the basis of all pottery, whether ancient or modern; clays are dug out of the earth, dissolved in water to wash away the impurities, then drained, pounded and kneaded like dough until smooth and malleable, and finally shaped and baked. Clays vary in their mineral content and the type of clay determines the texture and tint of the finished pot, which can be from pure white through brown or yellow, and the various reddish shades we usually refer to as terra cotta.

The Chinese were the first to develop refined and sophisticated techniques for making pottery. They used clays with a high proportion of kaolin and petuntse—china stone which, blended in about equal proportions, could be fired at a much higher temperature than ordinary clay and became glasslike or vitrified all the way through. The fired body is very hard and impervious to liquid. This true porcelain was the envy of the world, and the first pieces brought back to the Middle East and then to Europe inspired many attempts at imitation. It was a long time before the West could emulate the achievements of the East but still, we owe much beautiful work to these early experiments.

European potters were a little more successful—first Italy and then France produced a mixture of kaolin and glass ingredients to make a type known as soft paste, but Meissen in Germany was the first place where the true, hard-paste porcelain was made. It was first produced in 1718, and is very finely textured, translucent and brilliant white. This technique remains the basis of all European and American porcelain. In England, towards the late 18th century kaolin and petuntse clays were mixed with calcified animal bone to produce bone china, slightly softer and creamier than hard-paste, but more durable. Bone china is one of England's best loved creations, and English factories, like Wedgwood and Crown Derby, are household names in many Western homes.

One of the attempts to make sturdier and more durable pots resulted in stoneware, a vitrified semi-porcelain that is completely waterproof. Stoneware often has a roughish texture and German potters, who made huge quantities of pots and tankards, found that throwing common salts in the kiln during firing left a thin hard film with an "orange peel" surface which was pleasant to handle and gave an extra gloss. Salt-glaze is still made in studio potteries, although commercially its place has been taken largely by the development of oven-proof china.

Glazes developed together with the different bodies, as ovens and kilns replaced the

PORCELAIN

irregular heat of the sun. In Egypt, sand and soda were used to make a thin, glassy coat on the pot during the firing, and the addition of copper gave a beautiful translucent green or blue tint. This is the earliest known form of glass, found on a string of beads dating from the 18th dynasty (c.1400 BC). Other glazes were soon in use, particularly those using lead oxide. When powdered over the clay and fired, the lead fused with the sand or silica to make a rich honey-syrup coating, waterproof and sturdy. Lead glaze can be stained with iron (yellows and browns), cobalt (blues), copper (greens), or manganese (reds and purples). One of the most popular glazes relied on a mixture of manganese and iron to make a glossy black surface. Lead-glazed wares were the most common products of small potteries everywhere, from Rome to 19th century America. Tin oxide added to clear lead glaze makes a beautiful opaque white coat, completely hiding the clay, and forms a perfect background for decoration. Tin oxide made ordinary ware look something like Chinese porcelain, and its use spread through Spain and Italy, leading eventually to the development of the rich painting and fanciful decoration of majolica, the charm and lightness of French faience, and perhaps most popular of all, the blue and white "oriental" wares of Delft and other pottery workshops in Holland.

Early pottery was decorated before it was fired, and the paints were restricted to those which would not burn away in the intense heat—the colors were mostly blues, reds, and purples and greens. Later, more elaborate decoration was done with glassy enamels—these had to be fired a second time on top of the glaze, but at a much lower temperature; the widest range, including pinks, turquoises and bright reds, gradually developed with improved technology.

Transfer printing meant cheap, cheerful ware for everybody. Engraved copper plates hold the paint in a design which is transferred to a thin piece of paper. Laid on the fired, glazed pottery, it is pressed down and then the paper soaked off, leaving the print to be fired in a low-temperature kiln. The cheapest and most common designs were in monochrome (blue, black or copper-red) since only one printing was required.

Identifying your object is important—ceramics are difficult for a beginner to date accurately unless there is a fairly recent, well-known mark. China doesn't aquire a patina like wood or metal, and fake early marks are all too easily printed or painted on. Letters stamped or cut into the clay before firing (called impressed marks) are harder to imitate because they are covered with the original glaze. Reproduction plates and dishes are the hardest to spot, so much depends on subtle differences in shape and decoration. Items such as the popular Meissen and Dresden figurines are somewhat easier to identify, since genuine ones were beautifully modeled with crisp, sharp details and edges, whereas copies are almost all clumsy and round-edged.

If you think you do have a rare or valuable piece, take it to an expert. Learn to know the features of different kinds of ceramics, so that you can enjoy your growing collection even more.

IDENTIFYING POTTERY AND PORCELAIN

Hard-paste Porcelain: First successful European imitation of Chinese fine porcelain made in the Meissen factory. Very hard, pure white body. Continues in production up to present day.
Soft-paste Porcelain: English and French attempt to copy Meissen, produced until the development of bone china in the 19th century. Softer than hard-paste type because of differing constituents; has a creamy body.
Soaprock Porcelain: Another attempt to produce hard-paste, made in a few English factories in 18th century. Often decorated in blue and white patterns.
Bone China: Great English contribution to ceramic development in 19th century. Originally made with calcified bone ash, resulting in durable, fine porcelain, slightly creamy body, and capable of taking glazes and intricate decoration.
Parian Porcelain: Biscuit or unglazed porcelain, made in imitation of Parian marble. First developed by Copeland in England, it was also made by Spode, at Bennington, Vermont, and elsewhere.
Stoneware Basalts: Wedgwood experimented with many kinds of clay and developed the first really popular basalt. It was left unglazed, the body itself being stained with manganese. The texture was very fine and although the ware was so hard it could be polished or engraved on a lathe, it was not vitrified to the point of porcelain.
Jaspers: Another Wedgwood development, a fine stoneware which was tinted blue, lilac, green, yellow or black. Decoration was usually ready-cast classic motifs in white. Blue jasper was often used to make medallions for furniture and ornaments, ring pins, bracelets and so forth.

American Parianware pitcher of around 1860. Note the ears of corn faithfully represented on the side.

Pottery

Maiolica: Early Italian tin-glazed wares, with luster decorations; heavy shapes, greens, purples, blues and yellows. Do not confuse name with 19th century majolica, a William Morris term for tiles and wares in dark monochromes and flowering designs.
Stoneware: An early and very popular form of non-porous ware, heavier than earthenware; semi-vitrified stoneware vessels can be used for almost any liquid.
Salt-glazed Stoneware: Common salt thrown in the kiln during firing produced a rich, orange-peel texture and a glossy finish. First used by Rhenish potters in medieval times, still popular on "natural" forms and modern studio pottery.
Earthenware: Ceramic name for porous, non-vitrified pottery—sometimes distinguished by body type (red ware, yellow ware, white ware etc.). The earliest and still the most common glaze is of lead oxide, clear or tinted, such as the familiar black or brown glazed teapot.
Creamware, Queen's Ware: A very fine cream-bodied earthenware developed by Wedgwood and imitated all over Europe, England and maybe America. Particularly adapted to pierced designs.
Red Stoneware: Fine stoneware made to imitate Chinese ware, mostly in Chinese designs. Based on a red body, the finish is almost always unglazed and mat.
Delftware: Earthenware of every kind with a tin glaze, originally made in Delft and other Dutch towns, to copy the blue and white Chinese porcelain shipped from the Dutch East Indies. Delft potters often added their own very European idiom (tulips, windmill scenes), and were copied in turn throughout England and America. Blue and white remains one of the most popular forms of decoration ever developed, but orange Delft was also made, as well as polychrome ware, sometimes with black background and gilded decoration.

REPAIRING

Pottery

Although pottery includes as a generic term all baked earth products, current accepted usage confines it to those ceramics which are fired in a low temperature kiln (below 100°F or 38°C) and which therefore never become vitrified, remaining soft and porous in varying degrees. Its general characteristics are a porous body, which must be glazed if required to be waterproof, and a rather crumbly texture when broken; it absorbs liquid easily, and is quite fragile and easily scratched. It is also rather heavy in comparison with porcelain. The edges of broken pottery are seldom neat—there is often a lot of flaking which can make repairs very difficult and almost impossible to conceal..

● Broken glazed pottery shows this distinct layering of body and glaze [1], one of the marks that distinguish it from stoneware or porcelain.

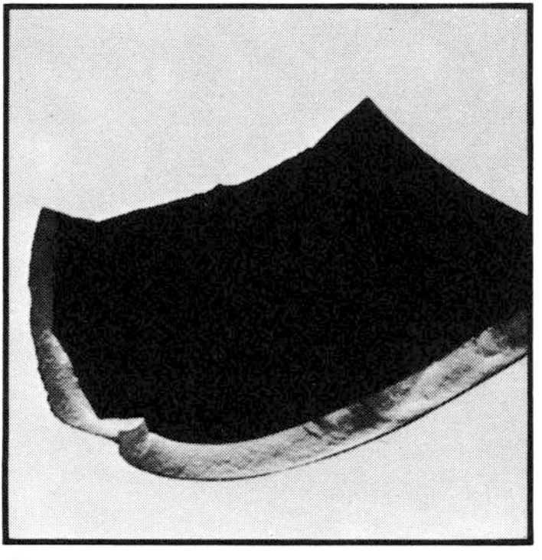

1

● When glazed pottery breaks try to keep as many of the bits as possible, collecting them in cotton or a soft clean rag and store in a box until you are ready.

● Make sure the pieces are as clean as possible.

● If the damage is new, wash around it with a swab keeping the water away from the porous body showing along the break. Liquid will soak through the body and seep under the glaze, remaining damp for a long time so that the glue will not set properly.

Even if it's very dirty try to clean the grease off with a soft rag, perhaps dipped in alcohol. If you obtain a marvelous plate or platter for nothing because it is broken, then wash as quickly as possible in warm soapy water. Do *not* use a strong solvent or bleach—it will remove years of grime, even encrusted growths in a trice, but probably take away the glaze and decoration as well!

Gluing

● Fit the pieces together gently until you see where the attachments should be made. Pottery usually breaks into a number of small pieces, and the edges may be difficult to match up.

● Work from the bottom up, and let each section dry completely before adding the next. A plate or dish is usually easier to work on upside down—the rim makes a fairly stable base.

● Curved parts or handles can be supported in a heap of flour or fine sand, but make sure you use as little glue as possible, or you will find a line of glued flour adhering to the break.

● As you get better at working quickly use an instant bond, but remember it cannot be moved once the sides touch, so put it on right the first time.

● Use a matchstick or thin plastic knitting needle to apply your preferred cement—make sure it is heat and waterproof, and really transparent. Remove bits of glaze on earthenware, and keep them aside. Coat both edges to be glued very thinly, press together according to the directions on the container [2].

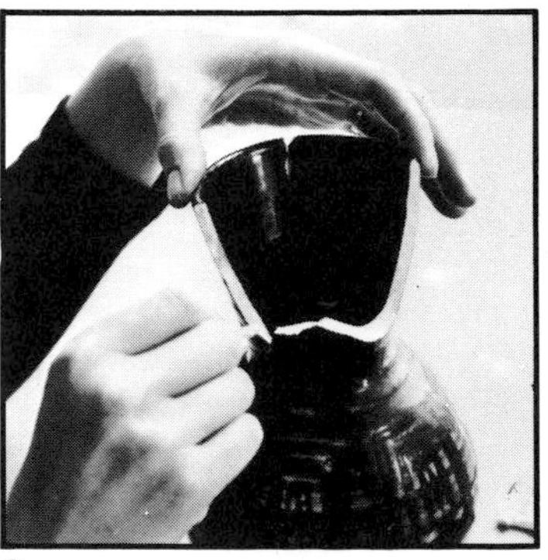

2

● Leave to dry. Wipe off any excess as soon as the piece has set fairly firm, using a very light touch. Add piece by piece until the object is whole again [3].
● Glue down any flakes of glaze which you have rescued.

3

Replacing Broken Parts: Missing pieces which are lost can often be replaced by the new waterproof fillers. Plaster of Paris, which in the past was used for this purpose, will not be really waterproof.

● Follow directions for mixing a small quantity.
● Lay a double thickness of oiled paper or plastic wrap on the dish, covering the gap.
● Tape firmly to object [4].

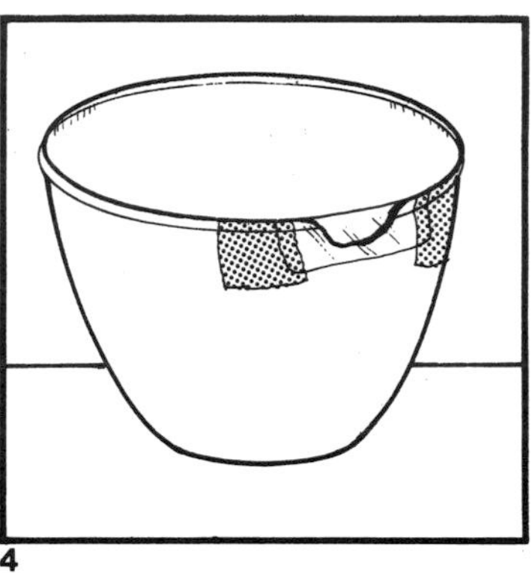
4

● Using a small palette knife, fill the gap carefully, smoothing filler into place [5].

5

● Use the minimum of filler, but be sure to match the thickness of the object and follow the contours as carefully as possible.

● Leave to set. When absolutely dry, remove paper, and sand surface with very fine abrasive paper [6], but do not go over onto the real china or the glaze will be damaged. (An emery board or typewriter eraser may be useful).
● The filler may be painted to match the background. Use paints and gilding made for decorating china and follow the rest of the pattern as best you can.

6

Alternative: If necessary, use powdered pigments to tint the filler to match the background shade.

Porcelain

The most important difference between pottery and porcelain, when it is a question of repairs, is that the glaze on porcelain pieces does not show up as a separate layer (compare with Fig. 1); the break will expose a smooth, glassy, non-pourous texture all the way through. In practical terms this means that it is possible to wash a broken piece of porcelain thoroughly—water will not be absorbed, and repaired pieces will show no tell-tale signs of broken glaze along the fracture.

When the repair is made, carefully remove excess glue from the visible surfaces. Most fine porcelain is valuable, and should really be repaired by an expert.

Retouching:

After the whole piece is absolutely dry, you may be able to touch up the decoration and hide some of the damage with new, slightly translucent acrylic paints suitable for china, which have the appearance of glazed enamel. Otherwise use modelmakers' enamels which are available in small cans. A transparent lacquer coat on top will give the appearance of glazed ceramic to the filled area.

Caution: Pottery should never be used for food after a break, since once the glaze is broken, germs and bacteria can accumulate under the surface. So only use repaired pieces for wrapped candies, cigarettes, pins, display etc. Porcelain however is like glass—the break is as hygienic as the surface, so repaired porcelain *can* be used for all normal purposes. *But* no repaired china should be put into a dishwasher, no matter what the glue manufacturers say!

Pennsylvanian salt-glazed stoneware butter crock; around 1840. Salt-glazed stoneware is still popular on "natural" forms of modern studio pottery.

STONE

Ever since peoples of the earliest civilizations made rough incisions on pieces of rock, stone and other kinds of naturally occurring material have been prized by sculptors and craftsmen. A vase; a tiny seal; a huge chimney piece; a rough chiseled cannon ball for a doorstep, or a delicately chased bowl which would break if handled carelessly—all these are examples of a wide range of objects worked and prized by man.

Although treatment and care will vary according to the material, there are certain characteristics which all stone objects share. To begin with, stones are distinguished by their geological origin. All are shaped and sometimes flawed by the forces of nature.

The beauty of such formations has inspired many imitations, but modern methods of analysis make it easier to screen out the more obvious substitutes—particularly important where the piece may have considerable value. And some imitations have achieved their own identity—Venetian glass of the 14th and 15th centuries was used to imitate almost every valuable stone, and today can be worth as much as or more than the material copied so beautifully.

Museums, sale rooms, and good antique stores are full of various types of stone. Marble, for example, has been used since very ancient times and to see examples of its variety, you might visit a local museum displaying, perhaps, a few simple carved figures from the Cycladic period (c.3000-1100 BC); a Roman Venus chiseled out of the beautiful white marble of Mount Pentelicus; a Renaissance *bas relief* of Carrara marble, or a floor of richly veined black, white and green marble squares. A reasonably good antique store may have a bracelet made around 1850 of marble mosaic, or a French sidetable with a Siena marble top. Specialists in rocks and minerals often keep a stock of dozens of small, many-hued pieces from many parts of the world. Many ordinary homes can find a place for a Victorian washstand or a modern coffee table made from a slab of marble. Other common marble objects are ashtrays, floor tiles, lamps with a marble base to add weight, a thick slab of marble for rolling out pastry, or a small marble egg tucked into the sewing basket to keep hands cool.

Veined marbles are quarried in many parts of the world. Italy, France, Spain and Germany produce variations of rose-pink, red, green and gray marble while New England (especially Vermont), New York, Tennessee, Alabama and Missouri have quarries producing every kind of marble, from the black stone used mostly for memorials and tombstones to the clouded grays and yellows with a sheen like watered silk.

British marble is seldom pure white, but variegated marbles are found in great abundance and many public buildings in England are decorated with bluish green limestones from the Purbeck quarries and deep blue and gray tinted stones from Derbyshire and Yorkshire.

The more precious stones like jade were just as versatile, but far more expensive and therefore today most likely to be found as small pieces and carvings—pierced tokens to wear as good luck charms; tiny Buddhas to hang from the ears; small delicate carvings of Oriental gods and goddesses. Strangely enough, raw jade is not found in China. The Chinese aristocracy were so delighted with every kind of jade work that huge quantities were imported, practically absorbing the world's production. Some of the greatest jade pieces were the result of Chinese artisans' skill responding to the sophisticated tastes of their clients.

Identification is the key to the best care and treatment of stone and stone pieces, because of the many possible substitutes. Most stone is highly polished, and this makes it comparatively easy to substitute a smooth-textured plastic or cheaper stone dyed to the right shade. It is vitally important not to damage the surface while you are trying to establish what lies underneath that glossy coat. Antique stone has a patina as valuable and rich as the lovely dark glow on bronze or old wood. It also acts as a shield against absorption of dirt and destructive pollution in the air. So always try to find an inconspicuous part to test, then repolish afterwards for protection.

The scientific tests for various stones are based on hardness and gravity, or density. The diamond will scratch all the others, while alabaster can be damaged by a sharp fingernail. There are a few other materials, besides stones, which are treated in a similar manner; that is, they are carved and polished and used in the natural state, either on their own or as inlay or decoration on other materials. These also may cause you problems by the number of modern substitutes, particularly plastics. With a small highly carved piece of work such as a tiny pierced ivory ring or a florid amber seal, it may be impossible to detect fakes easily. Always take these to an expert. If in any doubt do the minimum cleaning and store in a plastic bag to prevent further deterioration until obtaining a professional opinion. Until then, don't repair breaks unless absolutely necessary—your expert needs to be able to see the basic material beneath the polished surface.

Unlike many objects dealt with in this book, stones, once restored and repaired, need almost no care except a very occasional cleaning. Above all, keep your pieces where you can see and handle them as much as possible—the pleasure they can bring you is more than adequate compensation for a very little effort in restoring them.

MATERIALS

Stones and Natural Materials

Agate
Alabaster (Lime carbonate)
Basalt
Diorite
Feldspar (Aventurine)
Granite
Hematite
Jade: Jadeite and Nephrite
Jasper
Jet
Lapis Lazuli
Malachite
Marble (hard limestone)
Obsidian
Onyx
Quartz
Rock Crystal
Sardonyx
Serpentine
Soapstone (Steatite)

Animal Materials

Amber
Bone
Coral
Ivory
Horn
Mother-of-Pearl
Tortoiseshell

MARBLES

There are two basic types of marble; the fine, close-grained pure white limestone, which is used for statues and ornamental carvings of all kinds, and the variegated type where the limestone has become impregnated with minerals and deposits producing rich veining and subtle patterns in the stone.

White marble is found mostly in Italy and the finest comes from the quarries around Carrara. However, other areas have produced fine quality marble: American quarries, especially in the New England area have some first-class deposits. Indian craftsmen working for the great Shahs and Maharajahs were able to rely on considerable quantities of beautiful marble from Rajputana and Jabalpur.

White Marble—Cleaning

White marble can usually be cleaned with pure soap flakes and careful scrubbing. Small pieces can be placed in a plastic bowl in the sink. Large slabs and tabletops may be separate, or attached to a piece of furniture.

● When cleaning separate pieces, lay a very thick layer of newspaper on a waterproof floor or cover the floor first with a plastic sheet or tarpaulin and stand the slab on it, resting the top against a cabinet or bench [1].

1

● Start scrubbing at the top, and gradually work downwards, mopping up as you go.
● Rinse off immediately and wipe dry with a chamois or clean rag.
● After the first washing, examine the piece carefully for chips or stains. Tabletops often have rings and food stains, particularly from fruit juices, where the acid has eaten through the polish and dissolved the surface of the stone. If the damage is slight then careful polishing will usually restore the shine. Use powdered chalk, pumice powder or tin oxide, rubbing energetically in circles with a slightly damp chamois or a thick clean rag [2].
● When the surface feels smooth, rinse off the powder with clear water and dry thoroughly.

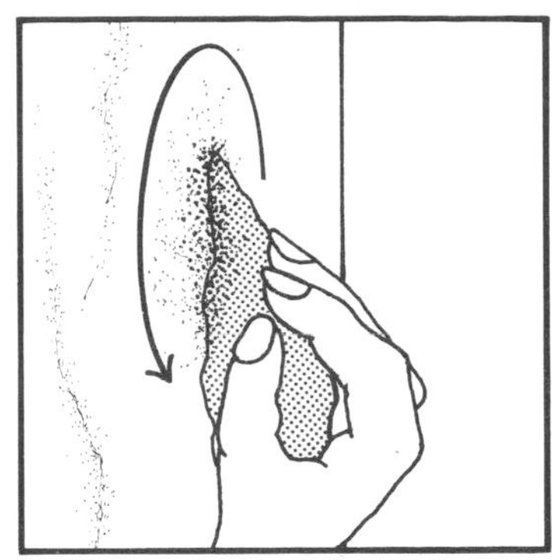
2

Removing Oil and Grease: Oil and grease have a slightly different effect. The liquid seeps through the surface and stains the marble, without actually damaging it. You must draw out the grease absorbed by the stone. A series of poultices should do the trick, as follows.
● Make up a small quantity of paste with powdered kaolin and benzene, or dampen a piece of white blotting paper with alcohol or acetone. If possible, lay the marble flat at a comfortable working height.
● Place the paste or the paper over the stain, and cover with a piece of plastic wrap to keep the poultice from drying out too quickly [3].
● After about half an hour, remove and check the condition of the stain. It may be necessary to repeat this a number of times with fresh poultices. If you are working on marble built into a wall, or lining a fireplace then tape the poultice in place firmly with adhesive tape.

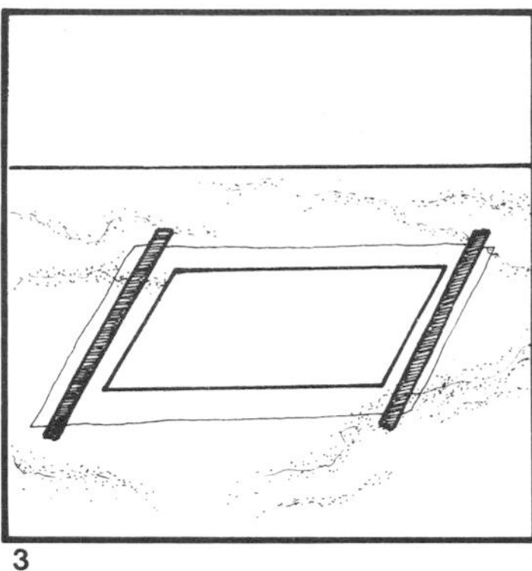
3

Removing Stains: For almost all other kinds of organic or deep stains, the easiest solvent is hydrogen peroxide in a 35 percent solution.
● Lay the stained marble flat, and carefully pour about a teaspoonful of the solvent onto the stain [4].

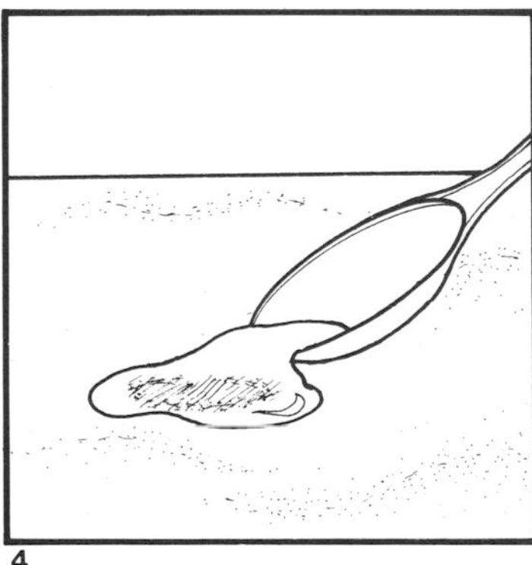
4

● Immediately sprinkle a very few drops of ammonia on top—the peroxide will start to bubble [5].
● When the bubbling stops rinse at once with clear water, two or three times.

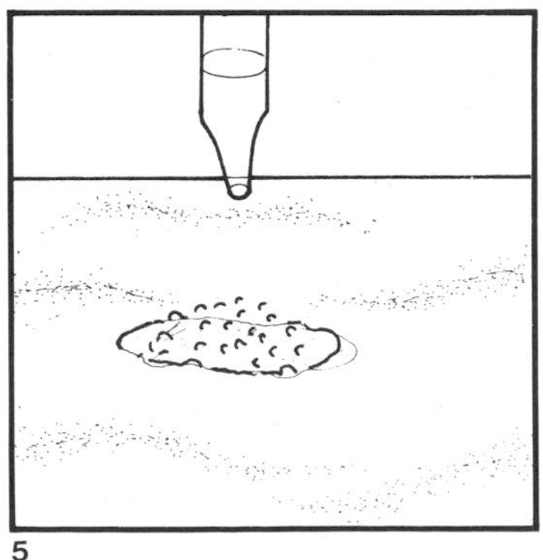
5

● Repeat if necessary.
● On vertical surfaces make a poultice with a clean piece of rag moistened with the peroxide and tape into place as before. There are a number of commercial marble stain-removers on the market almost all based on the same principles. Most are perfectly reliable but always try a new product on the underside first.
Badly stained marble can be cleaned quite satisfactorily in the following way, but any surrounding wood or metal must be thoroughly protected from the solution.
● Cut a bar of ordinary soap into chips and place in a saucepan [6]. Add enough water to cover the chips. Boil until the soap has completely dissolved and then pour into a measuring jar and make a note of the quantity.
● Pour into an old, clean bowl. Put on a pair of rubber gloves, and then with great care add the same measure of caustic potash, and then the same measure again of quicklime.

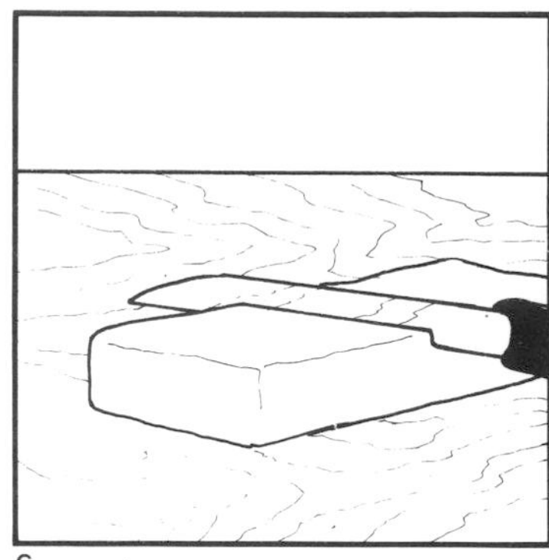
6

● Using an old, clean brush, paint on to the marble and leave for two or three days [7].
● Wipe off with paper towels or a rag and rinse with clear water. Repeat if necessary. Throw away the solution and the rag if you used one—and rinse the sink at once with plenty of running cold water.

7

Variegated Marbles

Variegated marbles are formed by a combination of limestone minerals and silicas, and are found in bewildering variety from dark veined forest green to palest blush pink or yellow. Since the markings add enormously to their beauty such marbles are used in large pieces where the patterning can be appreciated; for example in wall and floor tiles, columns, tabletops, etc. However, small bits are found in furniture inlays, while the tiniest chips are set in mosaic designs. These were very popular around the turn of the century for bracelets and necklaces. Marble tabletops of a single shade may be inlaid with an enormous number of variegations, making chessboards, pictures, or abstract designs. Sometimes precious stones like lapis lazuli and turquoise were also used, but these are rarely found except on the finest furniture.

Cleaning: Variegated marbles are sometimes damaged by strong stain removers, so even if you have successfully used a product on white marble, test it again to make sure. Do not use the strong caustic solution recommended for white marble.
Repolishing: For a fairly simple piece of marble an adequate finish can be achieved with powdered chalk, pumice powder, or another fine abrasive. Rub with an even, firm pressure, using a slightly damp pad or cloth or felt. Eventually a soft shine should develop. Rinse off the powder and polish dry. There are many special polishes available on the market. Silicone-based ones impart a definite shine, but never use anything with tinted resin or shellac. For a badly damaged piece, it is best to take it to a marble finisher who will have polishing wheels for use with fine abrasives, taking minutes rather than weeks of handwork.

ALABASTER

Alabaster is very similar in appearance to fine marble, but it is much softer. Antique alabaster, often used for beautifully translucent vases, is a lime carbonate—most modern alabaster is a lime sulphate which is much more fragile, easily damaged and—especially important for the restorer—soluble in water. Never leave alabaster figures to soak in water, even if they are badly stained.

Avoid alabaster ashtrays, which are very difficult to keep in good condition because the black marks caused by stubbing out cigarettes or cigars will eventually penetrate the rather soft surface, leaving rough patches difficult to clean and repolish. It's better to use them for desk clutter, or to hold nuts and candies.

Cleaning: The method is the same as for marble, except that you should try to restrict the use of soap and water as much as possible. It is much better to use one of the vaporizing solvents—denatured alcohol (methylated spirits), benzene or lighter fluid. Apply with a clean, soft brush or rag and wipe dry immediately [8].

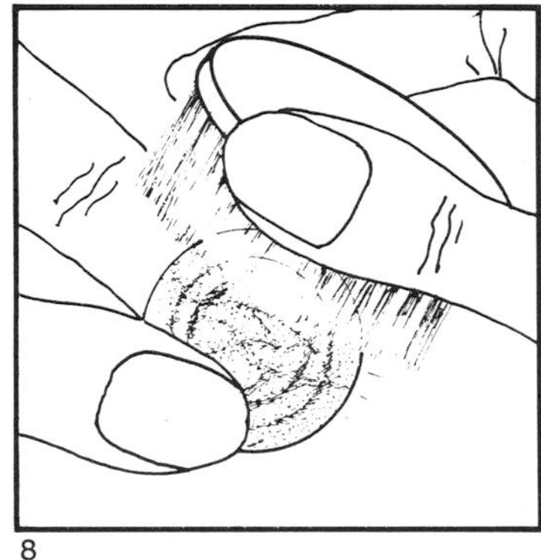

8

JADE: JADEITE AND NEPHRITE

The stone we know as jade is actually two slightly different minerals—jadeite and nephrite. Shades range from pure white to dark green, and every delicate one has its special beauty. Objects found on prehistoric sites in Europe, Asia, New Zealand and Mexico indicate that jade was highly prized, and used for both utilitarian and religious purposes. The Chinese, acknowledged as the greatest jade workers, had to import all their raw material from Burma and India. The carvers searched for years looking for a special piece, and may have spent an equally long time on the work itself. Today you may find jade used for simple, cheap beads, or for intricately carved necklaces with a hundred interlocking rings. Jade found in Mexico is quite distinctive, and always rich green. Interesting discoveries include religious ceremonial axes weighing 10 pounds (4.5 kilos) or more, fantastically carved masks of terrifying appearance, and ordinary beads, tokens and decorative household articles which may have been part of everyday life. The source has not yet been found, although there are thought to be deposits in Alaska and British Columbia.

Cleaning: When properly polished, jade seldom needs more than a thorough wash with warm water, pure soap and a medium soft brush. Jadeite has a very glossy look when polished, nephrite a somewhat oily, softer sheen. Jade is a hard composition usually carved and cut, like glass, on a wheel. It will also scratch a piece of glass [9], and this fact is very useful these days because there are literally dozens of jade substitutes which are almost impossible to identify without a microscope or instruments to check gravity. Jade carvings should never be repolished by an amateur, although they can be well cleaned, but inexpensive jade beads or solid pebbles can be given a lovely glossy finish in an inexpensive tumbler now sold in most craft stores for pebble and rock collectors.

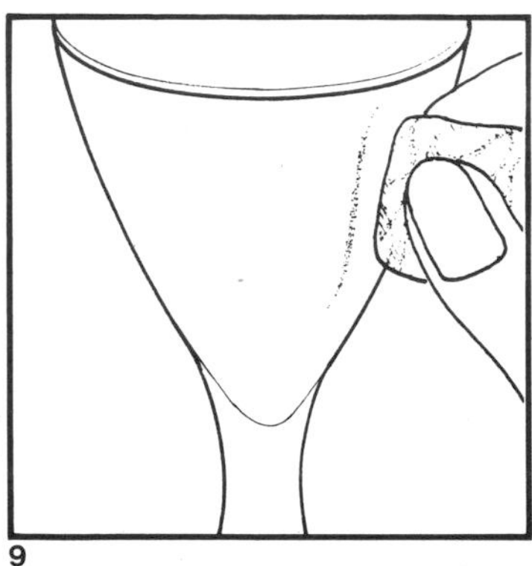

9

Fakes

Sometimes other stones have been left in aniline dye to absorb the more popular jade greens—a damp white rag rubbed firmly in the deeper parts of the carving will show traces of dye that have not been absorbed. Another kind of fake jade is made of glass. This technique became very popular in the 19th and early 20th centuries in America when the craze for Art Glass swept the country, and glass was made to look like opaque porcelain, jade, amber, aventurine or tortoiseshell, among others. Other favorite substitutes include quartzes, silicates and other minerals, most being much softer than jade and often dyed to achieve the rich greens so highly prized by collectors. Pale tones are harder to imitate and therefore are not used so much by forgers.

SOAPSTONE (STEATITE)

Soapstone is the softest of all minerals, used for carvings and decorative work. An ordinary steel knife will cut it fairly easily, and a piece of soapstone is far too soft to scratch glass. Try it and you will see a kind of chalk mark, like soap, on the glass surface, hence its popular name. Because of its extremely fragile surface, soapstone must be handled very carefully. Wash it only with soap and water and a soft brush. Soapstone will not take a high polish and the surface will crumble away under rough abrasives, but gentle circular rubbing with one of the finer abrasives (jeweler's rouge, putty powder) will usually result in a pleasant sheen.

ASSORTED STONES

Aventurine: A feldspar rock, containing flecks of other minerals which catch the light under the surface. Aventurine was always a favorite subject for glassmakers. Don't confuse the true stone with the glass bowls and dishes made especially popular during the Art Glass period, 1850-1920.

Basalt: Black, glossy rock mostly used for vases and memorial objects. Black basalt, a pottery imitation, has been made by Wedgewood since the 1770's in styles which reflect the Classic Greek and Roman taste.

Obsidian: Black volcanic glass, very, very hard, used for ceremonial knives and ornaments, especially in South America. Takes a very high polish. Not imitated too often, but the usual substitute is black glass. This is one case where the imitation has the same degree of hardness, since obsidian is only a naturally occurring glass.

Malachite, Serpentine: Both are minerals. Malachite contains copper and is always a deeply veined, marvelously rich green. Serpentine is silica-manganese and ranges from green to black. Often used as a substitute for jade, since unlike malachite it is mottled rather than veined.

Hematite: Iron ore, dark red to blackish in color, found and worked in small pieces.

Feldspar: An important silicate, valued not only for its decorative varieties (aventurine among others) but because it decomposes into china clay (kaolin) and china stone (petuntse) which are both important ingredients in the production of fine porcelain.

Quartz: The generic name for silicas from crystalline deposits of all kinds: rock crystal, amethyst, onyx, cornelian, chalcedony are all varieties of quartz and share the same basic structure. The variation is the result of different impurities in the silica solution. Quartzes are often used as substitutes for more precious stones, and in their own right as finely carved ornaments or decorative inlays. Coromandel screens with lacquer backgrounds, and pictures worked in pieces of hard stones are always very popular, and missing pieces can often be replaced with similarly marked quartz chips.

Cleaning and Polishing

Although these various stones have different degrees of hardness (see page 155), in general they may all be treated alike—clean only with soap and water, avoiding bleaches or any acids which will eat through the surface. If properly polished, stains are unlikely; most dark marking, if not natural, is caused by dirt collecting in hidden cracks or tiny fissures—a good stiff toothbrush is the best for dislodging it [10]. Most hardstone carving is done on a wheel and cannot easily be copied at home. Small areas can be repolished with a fine abrasive such as jeweler's rouge, but be careful not to press down too hard unless the piece is carefully supported on a cushion. This is particularly true of the fine parts of a carved figure or bowl. Single pieces can be smoothed and polished in a rock or pebble tumbler.

Broken pieces can be repaired with the same glues and using the same procedures as for porcelain. Clean thoroughly, dry, coat the broken areas with a transparent cement recommended for glass and china. Tape the pieces together with masking tape and let dry for around 24 hours. Remove the tape by dipping the object quickly in warm water and pulling it off carefully.

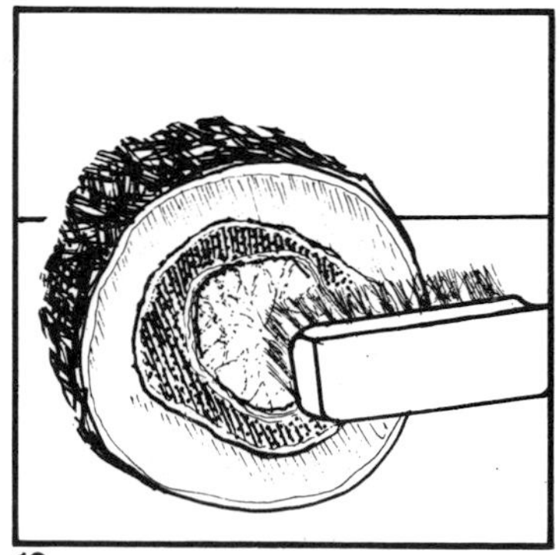

10

STONE

Caution: For stones which are mounted on furniture, in lacquer-work or as personal ornaments remember that at all times you must treat the stone carefully without damaging its setting. For example, marble tops that cannot easily be removed from their wooden base must be washed very carefully so that water does not seep into the wood [11]. All bleaches must be used with caution. A good idea is to mask off everything around the stone with several layers of masking tape and/or plastic sheeting.

11

OTHER NATURAL SUBSTANCES

Coal fueled the Industrial Revolution, bringing us soot, dirt and great factory chimneys polluting our atmosphere. But there is one kind of coal, which is very similar to an especially hard kind of anthracite which can be cut and polished like stone. Britain is extremely rich in jet deposits, and the coast of Yorkshire provided beads, for ornament and religious uses, rings and buckles since perhistoric times.

Most jet ornaments found today will be very much newer—dating from its most popular period which began around the mid-19th century. When Prince Albert died, Queen Victoria plunged the whole country into mourning, and jet ornaments became the only possible way of combining decoration with decorum. For about fifty years jet was commonly used for beads, buttons, hair ornaments, combs, filigree, bracelets, bangles, lockets, cameos and every possible kind of small piece. It was usually faceted to give extra sparkle and often mounted in gold or silver.

Cleaning: Unmounted jet can easily be cleaned with mild soapsuds and water, but be careful not to damage strings or clasps. A safer way to remove dirt is to pull out the inside of a few slices of soft bread, crumble lightly and then rub into the crevices and corners of carved jet pieces [12]. The crumbs will gradually absorb the dirt and grease and can then be easily brushed away with a soft old toothbrush. This is particularly useful for mounted jet, where washing may loosen the cement, and for beads, where grease collects in the pierced holes and cannot be removed by washing without fraying the thread.

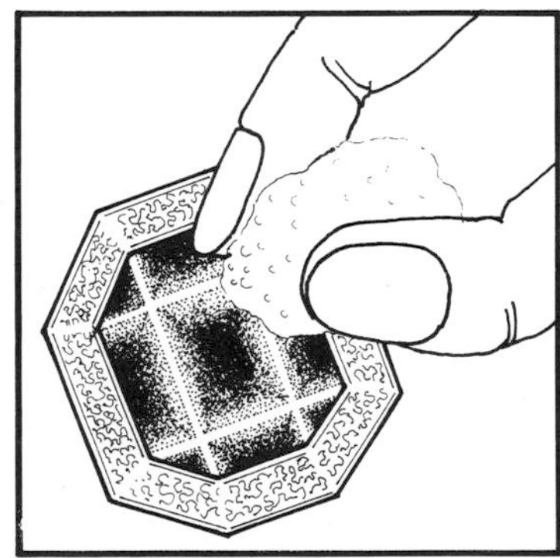

12

Mother-of-Pearl

Shells have always been regarded as both ornamental and useful since the earliest civilizations. Apart from their decorative uses many peoples have used them as money. Some shells have been made into cameos; craftsmen take advantage of the fact that the larger shells are often built up in layers shading from pure white to dark brown. Such cameos are most often mounted in gold or silver as personal ornaments. A number of species make a deposit of iridescent, nacreous material inside their shell and this can be detached in layers and used as mother-of-pearl, also called nacre. It is the same material which forms around a foreign substance in the mollusc to make real pearls, and fine mother-of-pearl has the same light refraction and luster. Individual pieces are mostly quite small, and almost always used as inlay or for small carved objects, especially fine buttons on men's shirts and children's dresses, and the handles of fruit knives and forks. In Victorian times, mother-of-pearl was often inlaid into papier mâché: small chips of varying shades were used to make up huge bouquets of flowers, or borders of simple floral design.

Repairing: Mother-of-pearl itself is not easy to repair, but since the chips seldom break, it is usually a question of replacing and/or regluing them onto the background. You can buy pieces of abalone at rock shops and if thin enough, it could be used to replace missing sections of mother-of-pearl. Use a transparent cement. Scratches sometimes mar the iridescent surface and unfortunately these will not polish out.

Cleaning: Never use ammonia or any acid on mother-of-pearl. Mild soap and water should take off any dirt, and rubbing with a chamois will keep them glossy. Never let cutlery soak in water (it will loosen the glue) or wash in a dishwasher. Care of cutlery is dealt with also in the Metalwork chapter.

Horn and Tortoiseshell

Both horn and tortoiseshell are gelatinous substances; horn is a product of wild or domestic cattle, tortoiseshell is made from the back of the sea-turtle. Horn, much cheaper, has been used largely for everyday things like shoe horns, small boxes, handles, buttons etc. Tortoiseshell has more beautiful and distinctive markings, and is generally more precious. It is used for combs and ornaments of all kinds; it is mounted in silver and gold, inset with gold dots and stars and inlaid with brass and bronze in French boulle work. Both substances can be shaped with heat and under pressure; they are fairly flexible and, when cut into thin sheets, almost transparent.

Repairing: Cutting is done with knives or fine saws. Missing sections can be replaced by pieces cut to size from a sheet [13]. Use a template as if you were replacing a bit of marquetry (see p. 58). Fine abrasive paper will smooth any rough edges. Broken shoehorns can be glued together with an epoxy resin but are unlikely to be of any practical use afterwards—the same is true of combs. Sometimes broken pieces can be mounted by an expert in silver or gold and riveted into place, but such work would cost far more than replacing the shell, unless it is a very special piece.

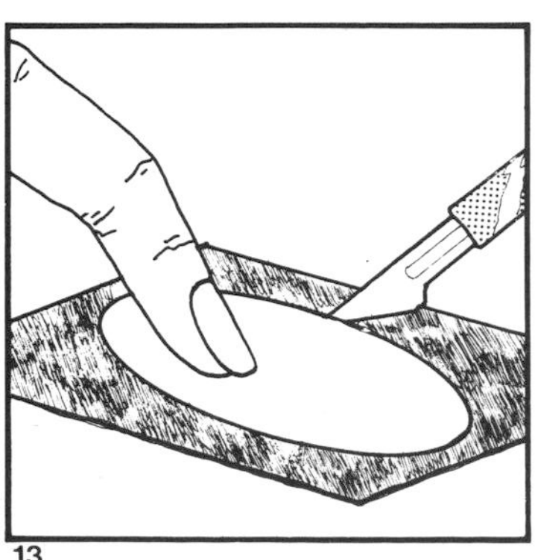
13

Cleaning: Use a very fine abrasive to polish the surface. Whiting or jeweler's rouge used on a buffing wheel is best.

Coral

Natural branch coral is made of the skeletons of thousands of sea organisms which flourish in the waters of the Mediterranean, and other warm areas, mainly in the Pacific Ocean.

The most common variety is deep pink coral. Coral was believed to have the power to ward off evil and so it has always been popular for children's pieces—tiny bracelets, armlets, teething rings and so forth. Finer pieces are in all shades of blush pink and white. Coral beads and lockets are always popular, sometimes intricately carved, sometimes plain. It takes a high polish, and really needs cutting and polishing by an expert. However, it should be kept clean and free from dirt, which collects around the mountings and on the strings of beads. Clean these, like jet, with bread, or wash quickly in warm soapsuds. Never scrub any threaded beads—the hard stone edges will fray the string.

Bone

Bone, similar to ivory in appearance and treatment, is simply the cleaned and often polished skeletal structure of any animal, fish or bird. Early sewing tools were sharpened bones, used as needles of all kinds. Gradually techniques improved, and many useful tools and ornaments were made—pins, knives, combs, hooks, etc. Until the present century bone was commonly used for inexpensive carvings, toys, buttons, toggles, knitting needles, lace bobbins, and model making; the bone ship models made by French prisoners of war during the Napoleonic period have been eagerly sought by collectors for a long time.

Remember to handle bone very carefully, especially when wet; it is quite soft. It can be polished lightly like ivory, with jeweler's rouge and a soft cloth, but the surface is too fragile to take a really hard gloss.

Amber

Amber is a fossil resin, which can be pale yellow or the deepest brown. Translucent, glowing with light, it often contains plant or animal fossils which were trapped in the sticky, slowly hardening mass. This characteristic has been exploited by scientists interested in dating the formation of our earth, and rather more decoratively by craftsmen in the 19th century, who made ornaments of amber centered around the delicate fossil tracings. Today amber is used mostly for small ornaments, beads and the mouthpieces of fine cigarette holders and pipes.

Cleaning and polishing: Amber is quite soft, easily scratched and is usually simply carved and polished. Soap and water are the best cleaning agents, as amber dissolves easily in alcohol and most other common solvents—at one time amber was even used in furniture varnish together with linseed oil or turpentine. Amber-colored glass or plastic are both used for imitations, but the texture is quite different. Pressed amber is harder to distinguish: broken bits and small chips of amber are heated until malleable and then compressed under enormous pressure. Amber can be lightly polished with a very fine abrasive, such as jeweler's rouge, but it must be carefully done. Finish with a soft cloth or chamois.

Ivory

Our own teeth contain material which is very similar to the ivory tusks which some large mammals carry. Most commercial ivory is made from elephant tusks, although walrus ivory carvings are common among the Eskimos and Indians of the north. Because of today's greater awareness of the need for wildlife protection, ivory is becoming progressively rarer.

The texture of ivory is so close and smooth that the most finely detailed carvings can be made. Handle these very carefully, as old ivory is very brittle. This is one case where soap and water is not really recommended because ivory grows in layers and soaking may cause the layers to swell and separate. However, if the carving is really very dirty, make a lukewarm solution of mild soap with as little water as possible and brush quickly with a soft toothbrush. Rinse under clear water and dry immediately. For less drastic cleaning, a gentle wipe over with a soaped sponge and then a damp, clean sponge should do the trick.

For adding luster, ivory can be polished lightly with jeweler's rouge or a very fine abrasive powder. Rub gently in circles until the surface glows, then clean off excess powder with a soft rag.

Ivory will yellow more quickly in the dark, so don't lock it away. Leave the piano keyboard cover open. Smooth-surfaced, uncovered objects which turn very yellow can be scraped down by an expert to a light-cream color, but the brilliant white piano keys and billiard balls (another important product of the ivory carvers) have been specially bleached. Eventually this wears off and cannot be repeated. Fine ivory carvings are increasing in value every day so do not even try to repair them without the advice of an expert. Broken pieces can be carefully glued together using a clear-drying cement, but use only the minimum necessary. Craftsmen can make the most delicate repairs with tiny pegs of ivory and these should always be used for any valuable piece. Ivory is often found as an inlay in furniture, as key-hole surrounds or as knobs on the smaller pieces of furniture, and as handles for silver tea and coffee pots and for sets of cutlery. When the ivory is mounted in this way, it is important to try and keep the furniture or metal polish from staining the edges.

There may be tiny fissures and cracks around the join. Fill these with wax or polish. Masking tape will keep the ivory clean while you work on the metal [14].
Loose cutlery handles can be reglued but it is very important to see that all the old glue is removed first.

14

- Don't try to squeeze extra glue into the joint, but first remove the handle completely if you can by applying glue remover with a small brush. Let it work for a few minutes, loosen it a bit more by hand, and repeat the application until the handle comes away [15].
- Then clean off all the old glue. To get into the inside of the handle, use a small bottle brush dipped in solvent [16].

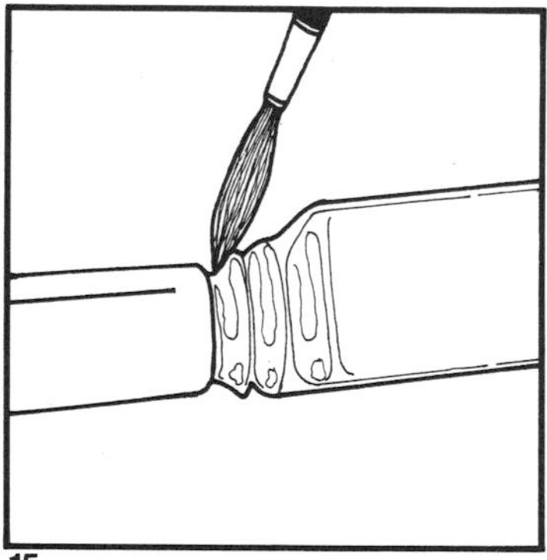
15

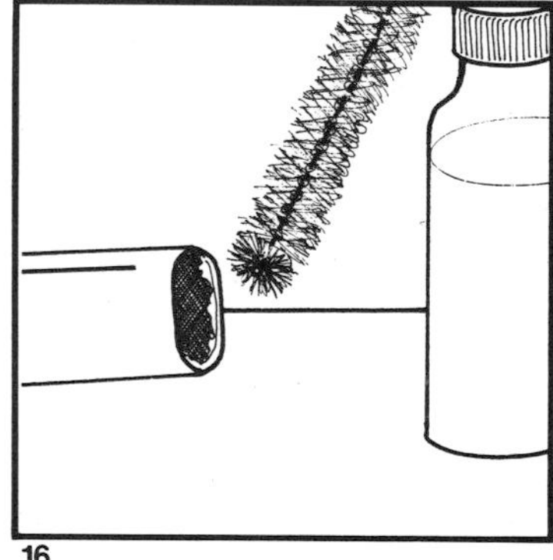
16

- Rinse out in clear water and let it dry thoroughly.
- Finally, re-apply one of the newer all-purpose transparent cements, replace the handle and hold together with masking tape until absolutely set.
- Note: *Never* put ivory, or bone (or mother-of-pearl) handled cutlery in the dishwasher, or leave it to soak in water. Instead, wash it quickly and thoroughly and dry gently without too much pressure. Sometimes handles are held in place by screws or rivets—this is particularly true of kettles and knobs of all kinds. Remove the screw if you can—if the thread is rubbed down, wrap a few layers of thin gauze soaked in glue around the screw [17], and screw back into place. Riveting should be done professionally.

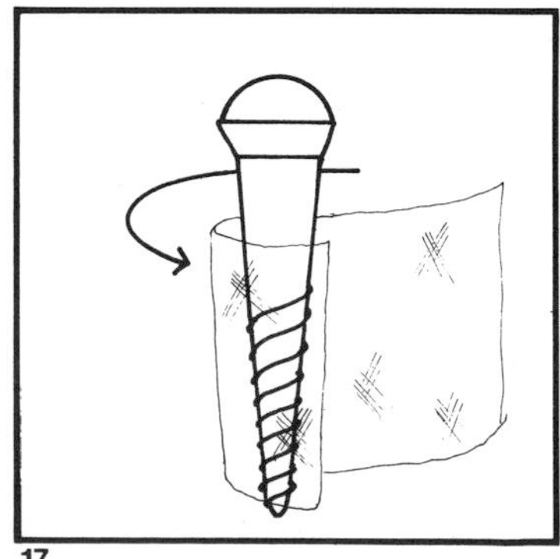
17

ALL KINDS

Metal working is an ancient craft—and many modern techniques only represent refinements and developments of the processes and tools used thousands of years ago. Strangely enough the word metal itself is almost meaningless. There is no single definition of it, as there is of wood or ceramics: it only has a collection of properties or characteristics; for every property generally applied to metals, there is an exception—they are usually solid (but not always), liquefy when heated (but not always), etc. So each metal is really a story on its own.

Let us begin with the simplest and most versatile, iron. Iron is found almost everywhere in the world, and its strength and adaptability have been highly valued since the first forged weapons were made, around 3-4000 BC. There are two basic forms—wrought iron is made at the forge, using hammer and anvil to shape iron bars into a variety of objects from simple farm gates to elaborate scrolled chandeliers.

Cast iron was not really developed until the 17th century, and proved particularly useful for kitchen pots, stoves and utility items. In the 19th century techniques improved enough to allow crisp detail and decorative ornamentation to be mass produced—fenders, candlesticks and lighting fixtures, delicate railings, balconies and garden furniture were all made of cast iron.

Copper has a lovely reddish-gold sheen which is sometimes applied to other metals as a decoration. This was very popular during the Art Nouveau period, when hammered copper was often used in conjunction with other metals for a multitude of objects. Most often though, tin-plated copper was found in the kitchen in the form of kettles, bowls, and saucepans. In the past thirty years or so, however, tin has been largely replaced by stainless steel and numerous plating processes, such as chrome and nickel.

Pewter is a lovely alloy, but very variable in quality and weight. Early pewterware was made from tin alloyed with copper, which together are harder than either component on its own. Lead was added to make the alloy even stronger, with a low melting point that made casting very easy.

As an art metal, c.1900, pewter by Liberty was burnished to a beautiful sheen and often set with turquoise to produce a distinctive look. But usually plates, dishes, tankards, mugs and candlesticks follow the silver patterns of before the turn of the century. The finest early pewter was marked by the craftsman so that his work could be identified. However, the increasing use of silver plate diminished the pewter market considerably, and for a long period pewter almost disappeared. Today the revival of simple shapes and dark woods have made it fashionable again.

Silver is one of the softest metals—in a pure state it is too soft to be worked alone. Its lustrous and rich appearance has added beauty to important objects throughout history. It was comparatively rare in medieval times until the Spanish explorations in Mexico and South America discovered veins of ore already being mined by the advanced Indian cultures, and huge shipments of ingots were sent back to Madrid.

Standards had been established in 1300 for the composition of silver metal, and the English hallmark system was devised whereby the date and place of manufacture could

OF METAL

easily be determined. This is, of course, a boon to present-day collectors. Unfortunately other countries did not always follow suit, and so the dating of Continental, or eastern silver must depend on an expert knowledge of techniques and designs. In America, the "sterling" standard was adopted from the English in the 19th century.

Bronze is certainly the oldest alloy known to man, made from the same ingredients as pewter but in different proportions. Copper is the main ingredient (usually about 75%) but tin and lead and sometimes zinc were added in various proportions during the centuries; older pieces are likely to have a higher proportion of tin.

Bronze can be very hard to work by hand, and is almost always used as a cast metal because its melting point is so low, although it is often finished by hand and the quality of this work can determine the value of antique bronze. When molten it has great fluidity, so that even the most complicated and convoluted details can be reproduced sharply. Its contraction upon cooling is very slight, so there is little distortion.

Brass, an alloy of copper and some form of zinc, has been made since pre-historic times, and has proved an invaluable asset to many civilizations. Its appearance is similar to the harsher forms of gold, but it is much stronger and, of course, much cheaper. Some scholars insist that trumpets described in the Old Testament as brass were the earliest known examples, but others date the use of brass to the late Roman era. Most early objects were made with calamine (which is mainly zinc oxide) instead of pure zinc. In the medieval period, much work came from Germany and Flanders, and some domestic utensils were cast for the wealthier households. Production began to expand enormously towards the end of the 17th century. The traditional Dutch chandeliers were first made then, and are still popular today, with their simple round globes in the center, and lovely S-curved arms. By the 1800's zinc had been purified and the resulting improvement in the new brass gave it qualities more suitable for casting processes; Birmingham (England) became almost a generic name for brass articles of all kinds, which were sent round the world. Some fine brass castings were gilded or even plated with silver and then varnished to prevent tarnishing. Today many of these articles are made in lighter, newer alloys, and the once-ordinary brass bedsteads and doorknobs have become valuable luxury items.

Ormolu is one of those misleading words, derived originally from the French *or moulu* (literally, "ground gold"), but used for bronze coated with gold initially in an amalgam with mercury; this was applied to the surface, then heated, the mercury being given off as a vapour. Unfortunately many craftsmen were poisoned by the mercury vapor, and this technique fell from favor. Today the term usually implies a fine type of brass alloy, using equal parts of copper, zinc and tin, or copper and zinc alone. It is easy to cast, and is usually associated with elaborate French furniture and metal parts made in the 18th and 19th centuries.

Never be tempted to buy an expensive bit of metalwork unless you know the dealer or have done some homework. Precious metals don't always cost a fortune but don't be fooled by reproduction silver and gold.

Repairing by Soldering

Soldering is fairly simple. It is a way of joining or seaming two pieces of metal, or repairing small holes or gaps. Practise on pieces of scrap metal or old damaged pieces until you learn to calculate the amount of solder needed, and the length of time for which heat needs to be applied. You will need:

Silver solder: This is available in three grades—easy, medium, and hard. Easy solder melts at the lowest temperature and gives a good joint, but with reasonable strength. Medium is slightly stronger and melts at a higher temperature. Hard solder melts at the highest temperature and it is also the strongest. The three grades are primarily designed to enable successive solderings on a single piece without melting the previous joint. In such cases a start is made with hard, the next joint is soldered with medium, and finally easy is used. For this reason repair work is usually done with easy, especially when other joints may be at risk.

Flux: This prevents oxides from forming under heat, and helps the solder to melt more readily. It is painted on the joint before soldering.

Soldering iron or blowtorch: It is best to use a small propane blowtorch that you can handle easily without danger to surrounding areas. Never use a torch with flammable liquids or fabrics lying nearby. Keep a small fire extinguisher handy in case of accidents.

Types of metal	*Solder and flux to use*
silver brass copper nickel	silver solder and flux, which is usually made by grinding a borax cone with a little water in a borax dish.
gold	gold solder, and flux as for silver.
cast iron	special brazing solder and special flux made from cuprous oxide.

Clean the piece thoroughly. Smooth out any dents. If you are working on a seam which has opened, gently hammer the sides down until they lie flat together; rub the edges to be soldered lightly with a file or abrasive paper to give the solder a grip. Paint the seam with the flux, covering the entire area you intend to solder. Put several small panels of solder on the seam, and apply the flame, first heating the whole piece and then moving it to and fro along the seam. When the solder melts, it will run towards the flame.With experience this characteristic can be used to encourage melted solder to flow evenly along the entire joint. Only experience will tell you how much solder to use.

Cleaning Iron

The worst enemy of iron is rust which, in time, can completely destroy a heavy iron piece and, even after a short time, may leave the surface pitted and flakey. So the first and most imperative task is to get rid of every trace—even the slightest rust left inside a crevice or under a bit of decorative riveting will gradually eat its way through the metal. A commercial rust remover will do (ensure it will not corrode the metal beneath the rust), or even plain soap and water, but whatever liquid you use, make sure the iron is scraped absolutely clean.

Wrought iron is heavier and corrodes more easily than cast iron, which is quite resistant. It is distinguished by its strength and solidity. The metal is worked when hot, so it is fairly well tempered, and comparatively easy to repair. For actual riveting of new collars or welding, it is best to go to a forge if you are lucky enough to know of one (believe it or not there is one in New York City), or to a workshop which handles such restoration work. Consult the classified section of your telephone book. Old wrought iron was fashioned with simple tools at the open fire, and the modern electric and acetylene torches for welding and riveting leave different marks and if used, may ruin the value of a genuine old piece. This applies to all wrought iron made in the traditional way, even to modern products.

● Scrub the chinks and crevices with a metal wire brush [1], the flat surfaces with fine steel wool pads or silicone carbide abrasive paper.

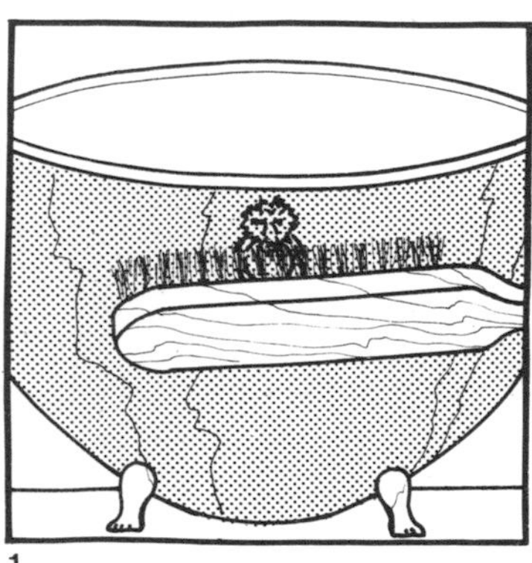

1

● If there are any hidden places that you feel are too deep or too curved for the brush to penetrate, use a spray rust remover [2] and follow instructions for small objects. For engraved surfaces which may be damaged by rubbing, let the entire object sit in a plastic bucket or bath of rust remover. Some rust-removers may etch the surface of the metal—be sure to check first.

2

● After thorough cleansing, rinse off in clear water, and dry as quickly as possible, since prolonged exposure to even dampish air may start the rust forming again.

Simple Repairs to Iron

Some simple repairs can be done at home—spikes and ornaments pushed out of position can be gently hammered back, and for small or delicate pieces a vise or a pair of pliers can be used to hold the piece straight while you work [3]. But be sure the rust is removed first, so that you can see if the metal is strong enough at the damaged part to stand the strain of repair. If it is not, it may be necessary to remove the part down to the nearest join and replace it with a new section. See your expert! Missing ornaments and whole sections can easily be copied at the professional forge.

3

Among the commonest finds are old wooden boxes bound with iron straps and secured with massive iron locks and keys. If the key is stuck, do not force it in any way. Spray rust remover in the keyhole [4], wait as instructed, and try again. If it seems to move a little, then spray again, wait, and so on. Eventually the key should move fairly easily. If you are adventurous, you can try dismantling the lock yourself, very carefully, cleaning the parts and putting them back together again, after lightly greasing with oil.

Many locks are actually quite simple but even so they are precision-made, and too energetic handling, particularly of old iron, can break off or damage important working parts. So either learn something about locksmithing, or remove your lock and key intact and take it to an expert. Do not take it to an ordinary locksmith unless he knows something about antiques—old pieces need very careful handling, and were often dated and signed by craftsmen proud of their work.

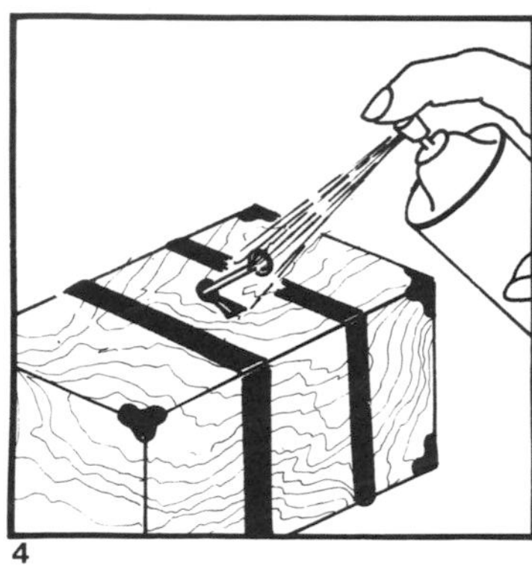

4

Iron Finishes

When the shapes have been straightened, loose handles or pieces re-riveted and re-welded, your ironwork is ready for finishing. Natural wrought iron has a lovely dark glow that is especially suitable for display pieces or indoor use.

If you are going to handle the object often, use a little Vaseline oil, or furniture wax, and renew regularly. For cooking utensils, keep spoons and ladles hanging up so they dry thoroughly, and never leave them lying in damp pools of water near the sink. Iron kettles and other pots and pans may be tinned inside (copper pans must be). Andirons, firedogs, and irons, tongs, etc., are often made of wrought iron. These if used in a fireplace will seldom get rusty, but they will accumulate layers of soot and wood ash, so scour regularly with a wire brush or coarse steel wool [5]. They are best left in their natural finish, although blacking, which is also used on old ranges and stoves, can be used for old cast iron firebacks. Do not use common paints on any fireplace or kitchen equipment—there are paints made especially for iron.

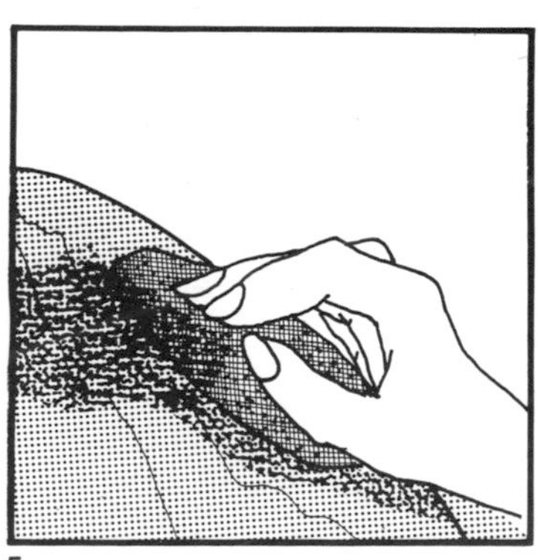

5

Other objects can be painted—traditional black or white, sometimes highlighted with a little high quality gilt paint. After any rust has been completely removed, wash, dry, and paint with one or two coats of rust-preventative paint—this is usually a pompeian red shade. Then paint with two or three topcoats. Make sure the paint is applied as thinly as possible, so it doesn't accumulate in the decorative curves and make the design look clumsy and thick.

Cleaning Copper

Copper, like pewter, often acquires a lovely patina from years of gentle polishing so try not to destroy this finish by using harsh abrasives. Copper sheeting was often used for wall plaques, candle sconces, etc., and was decorated with repoussé work which was hammered out from the back. This can easily be dented by too much pressure with steel wool or a brush. Remember all metalwork should be thoroughly dried as quickly as possible after cleaning.

Note: Certain foods affect copper so that enough of the metal may be dissolved to poison the contents. All cooking vessels made of copper must therefore be lined with tin.

Copper does not rust, but it does become green from a deposit called verdigris, which is often difficult to remove. However, it does yield to careful cleaning with very fine steel wool, but do not use a wire brush as copper is too soft. For less affected pieces commercial copper cleaners are available, and most are easy to use. You can also make your own paste from 1oz (30mg) iron oxide, 3oz (85gm) ground pumice stone (pumice powder) and enough oleic acid to form a paste. Apply this to the surface with a soft cotton pad or shaving brush [6], avoid scratching and wipe off with a clean dry cloth. Copper can also be lacquered with a special clear gloss lacquer for metals. This prevents tarnishing but can only be done with articles not used for preparing or serving food.

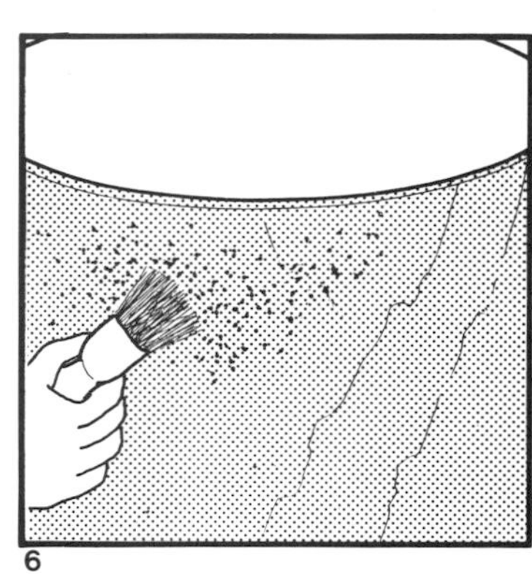

6

Cleaning Pewter

Pewter doesn't rust as some other metals do, but it does become coated with an oxide film which darkens and dulls the finish. Usually this can be cleaned off with ordinary metal polish but if the piece is old and has been badly neglected, a heavy black "crust" may have developed, which is very difficult to remove.

- Soak the piece in scale remover, a lye solution, or in a solution of 10% ammonia, 90% water.
- Rinse off after an hour and dry thoroughly.

Lye, or sodium hydroxide, is an old-fashioned, very strong alkali, used today most often as a drain cleaner. It must be treated with extreme caution, as it eats its way through almost anything, given time. Do not let it touch your skin, face, or eyes, and keep children and pets well away. For pewter, add a cupful of lye to an enamel bucket of water deep enough to cover the object completely. Immerse it for fifteen minutes. Rinse thoroughly in running water, wearing protective gloves, and scrub with a bristle brush. Repeat if necessary.

Old pewter has a lovely, dark patina—do not polish it so brightly that it loses this attractive character. Once the pewter has been cleared of the oxide it is preferable to wash it only in mild soap and water, and polish with a mild abrasive like rottenstone or jeweler's rouge mixed with enough olive oil to make a paste. Wash again, rinse, and dry. Happily, there are also proprietary pewter cleaners on the market.

Repairing Copper and Pewter

Copper can be repaired fairly easily as is is a very soft metal, but it should therefore be treated carefully. It can be soft soldered easily at home, but the results will probably be unsightly and articles of any merit should be done professionally. Joins can be disguised with copper paint, but this is not recommended and may flake off quickly.

Old copper and pewter kettles are often badly dented, and you will need to find some sort of rounded shape to use as a form. If you think you will be doing enough work, then a silversmith's shape made of heavy wood is a good investment. Otherwise get a block of any hardwood about a foot (30cm) long and six to nine inches (15-25cm) square. Turn it on end, and plane away the edges to make a rounded pillar. For solidity, screw it down on to an old table. This can be used for any metal piece that needs reshaping and is sufficiently wide at the neck.

A smaller piece about three inches (7.6cm) square is good for small pieces such as creamers. Slip the piece over the rounded top, holding it so that the dent or the damaged piece rests on the top, and using a ball or soft-face hammer with repeated very light blows, gradually encourage the metal back into its proper shape. Use many light blows instead of one heavy one, and if the metal can be lightly warmed first, so much the better. Particular care must be taken with hard, brittle metal; cast metal is much more easily broken than wrought or sheet metal, and the hammer head should be wound around with cotton rag strips for extra protection. Pewter is heavier and stronger than either tin or copper, so if you are repairing pieces of different metals at one session, remember to adjust your hammering accordingly.
Dented spouts, feet, covers and so forth can be treated in the same way, on various pieces of wood. Small shapes can be cut out of solid wood or planks to the exact size you need. Special parts should be kept in a box, because you will find a use for the same shapes, over and over again. Holes in kettles and pots can be patched with slugs which expand with heat to make a waterproof seal. Unfortunately they will never match the original so it is best to have most repairs on fine work done at a forge.
Unfortunately pewter is very difficult to solder at home because the alloy mixture varies so much and the exact tone required is often difficult to match. It's best to have old pewter repaired by an expert.

There are now modern flatware (cutlery) patterns made in traditional "country" styles with pewter handles. These should be repaired as silverware (see page 176). Forks and spoons can easily be straightened, but the pewter should be protected at all times from the vise and a wooden mallet should be used in preference to a ball hammer.
Bad spots of corrosion or dirty marks of all kinds can be removed, but be careful—good pewter is quite soft. Use a fine steel wool or abrasive paper, dampened with a little olive oil [7]. This will take off the marks and prevent tiny surface scratches.

7

Cleaning Tin
Tin may be cleaned in the same way as iron, but it is always much thinner and lighter than iron—do not use a wire brush except very carefully, and avoid coarse grades of abrasive paper. If the tin has been painted on the exterior and the paint has almost all disappeared, it is better to remove as much as possible with a commercial paint stripper or fine abrasive paper. On the other hand if remnants of a hand-painted tôle motif remain and you would like to restore it, refer to the chapter on Lacquer.

Bronze
When cold, cutting edges of bronze can be tempered by hammering, which sharpens and strengthens them.

Bronze ages beautifully with care, acquiring a deep glowing patina and adding marvelous shadows and textures to the piece. Craftsmen in bonze could also achieve this effect deliberately—a process called patination. Never remove this patina unless absolutely necessary—that's why strong cleaners or excessively bright polishes should be avoided.

Cleaning Bronze

● Wash with mild soap and water, rinse well, and wipe very thoroughly with a soft cloth.

● For badly encrusted small objects, coat the object in paraffin wax, let it set, then lower it gently into a very strong solution of nitric acid. Wear rubber gloves without any holes, and conduct the operation in a plastic container. Try not to touch the acid at any time. You must watch the object carefully; as the thickness of the crust will vary, so the time needed to remove it varies. Note that it is easy to render old coins valueless by cleaning them—if there is any question of their having real worth, it is generally best to leave them untouched. Museums have their own special techniques for dealing with the problem.

● Use wooden tongs to lift the piece out, and while still holding it with the tongs, rinse under running water and then dry and polish with a very light furniture wax.

Cleaning Brass

Old brass often has a dark sheen which is very pleasant, but don't confuse this with tarnish or dirt—it comes from the impurities and other ingredients used in its manufacture. But sometimes varnish on the old brass may have worn away, leaving a dull film everywhere.

● Remove the film with acetone or commercial paint remover and the finest steel wool, and then wash the piece carefully in mild soap and hot water or water and household ammonia (20:1).

● Any underlying corrosion will show up then, and can be removed by rubbing hard with a good brass polish.

● Badly tarnished pieces may require a real effort—you may have to use a very fine steel wool, or silicone carbide abrasive paper which is sold especially for metal working. Do not rub in a circular motion as the texture of the metal runs straight and it may create serious scratches.

● For really badly corroded small articles that do not have delicate inlays or incorporate other materials, boil in water containing a cupful of vinegar and a spoonful of salt.

● The easiest way to polish brass is with a good metal polish—they do vary, so follow the makers' directions. Leave the darker crevices alone—they contrast well with the gleam of polished areas.

● Wash again in soap and water after polishing to remove any acid deposit, and polish finally with a clean, dry, soft cloth.

Alternatively, an old recipe recommends rubbing the brass with an equal mixture of vinegar and fine salt followed by polishing with tripoli powder, jeweler's rouge, or pumice powder and olive oil. Brass that is not used for cooking or near the fire should be protected with transparent metal lacquer; this comes in liquid or spray form, and you must be careful not to let the lacquer accumulate in ugly, thick deposits. Large pieces, such as brass beds, or fine lamps, for example, should for preference have the lacquer applied professionally. Lacquered brass will keep its bright appearance with regular dusting and the occasional rinse in warm water and mild soapsuds.

Repairing Brass

Brass is a very hard alloy, and the repair of broken brass pieces is probably best left to a foundry which specializes in restoration.

For replacing broken bits of Boulle-work or other brass inlays of simple design (very popular on Regency and Empire furniture), sheet brass can be cut to match. Use a piercing saw, smooth the edges with abrasive paper, polish, and glue in place with great care using a general purpose glue. Pieces of more complicated design and the larger pieces which are sometimes held in place with tiny brass screws, can often be copied for you by the specialist craftsmen.

Ormolu

Repairing ormolu casting is a professional job, but ormolu objects can easily be cleaned.

- First remove any traces of old varnish or lacquer with acetone—which usually dulls the appearance considerably.
- Then scrub with soap and water or water and ammonia. Scrub because all ormolu castings are elaborately textured with crevices, curves and hatched surfaces absolutely hungry for dirt. Use a stiff nail brush (not a wire brush!) or an old tooth brush, to remove all the dirt.
- Rinse when clean but do not polish—polishing would highlight the shadows and rough surfaces which give ormolu its distinctive appearance.

Caution: For porcelain vases or lamps, mounted in ormolu, be careful the acetone doesn't get into the joints which are often reinforced with acetone-soluble glue.

Chrome

Chromium is a rare metal, found only ih other compounds, and is used for our purposes in two forms. It is an element in the chromates which are used as dyes (chrome yellow, black, red, orange and green), and in its manufactured metallic state it is used as plating for other metals, when it forms a non-tarnishing brilliant coat with a mirror-like surface.

Repairing as such is impossible, since the coating is deposited by an electro-plating process. So if it becomes badly scratched or gouged, then the object will have to be professionally replated. But chrome plating can be easily cleaned with a damp cloth, followed by a dry rub. Abrasives of any kind should never be used; they will mark the finish indelibly. Soap and water is best for very dirty, gummy chrome, or a small quantity of fine liquid or cream silver polish can be used on bad spots. Never leave salt on chrome, as it will corrode the plate very badly.

Britannia Metal

A very variable alloy of tin and copper, plus bismuth or antimony. This was made especially for working from thin flat sheets of metal, which were seamed, shaped, and finished on the lathe. Pewter itself was far too soft for this mechanical treatment; the added ingredients made a much harder metal. It can be repaired, but it is far harder to work than pewter and much more brittle, so treat carefully. It can be polished to a high gloss similar to silver.

"German" Silver or Argentine

This was commonly manufactured until the early 1900's and is an alloy of tin, copper and antimony. Like Britannia metal, it is hard, brittle and difficult to work. German silver was often used for cast pieces, and these are very difficult to repair at home; small dents can be removed with a wooden mallet, but be very careful—make sure there is a wooden block underneath. Cracks or broken seams are difficult to repair because of the matching problem, so take these to an expert.

Cleaning Silver

Old or neglected silver acquires a heavy, ugly tarnish which can be very stubborn. Remember that the surface, particularly of engine-turned or engraved silver, cannot be scraped like harder metals. And repoussé or chased silver must be cleaned without pressure. So drop the article into a solution of ammonia and water—a bad case of corrosion may take a day or two of soaking. Rinse under running water immediately after removing and polish. For polishing itself, there is really no substitute for time and loving care. Silver is one metal which actually seems to improve as it is used, cared for, and polished regularly. It acquires a mellow glow that cannot be reproduced in any other way. Other methods are faster and sometimes more convenient, but they often damage and spoil that sheen. So find enough time—the results are worth it.

You will need a good polish made especially for silver, a number of soft dry cloths and a silver brush, purpose-made for getting into cracks and crevices without scratching. You can also make your own paste for cleaning from 1 oz (30gm) levigated chalk and 1 oz (30gm) soldium thiosulphate. Wear rubber gloves to protect your hands.

- Wash the silver gently in very warm soapsuds, rinse thoroughly with warm water.
- Apply the polish in fairly small quantities with a cloth, rubbing fairly firmly up and down, not in circles [8].
- Use the brush to make the polish reach areas not easily accessible, but remember that many patterns are designed to hold some tarnishing in the recesses, to give the contrasts of light and shadow.

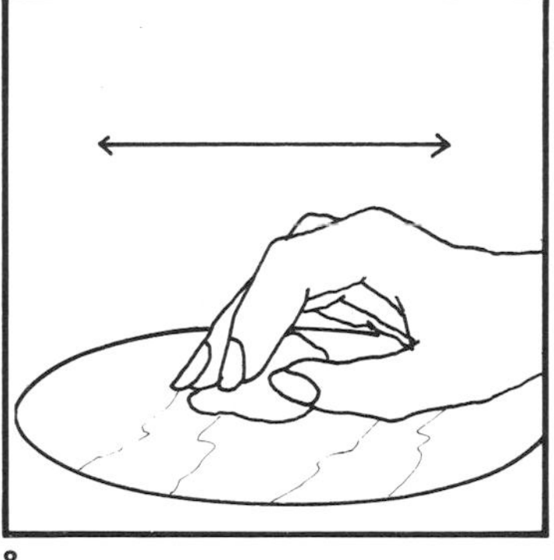

8

- Rub with a clean cloth to remove all traces of polish—the silver should now be clear and bright. Wash again.
- Don't wrap it up and put it away—silver responds to being handled and used, so make the most of your possessions. If you must put it away, wrap it in sealed plastic bags to discourage tarnishing.

Repairing Silver

Although silversmithing is not physically difficult, the metal being so soft and malleable that it responds quickly to all metalworking techniques, good silverware is very valuable, and should really be repaired by a silversmith.

This advice is to prevent you from ruining a potentially valuable piece, and if you find yourself truly interested then take a short course on the rudiments of silver smithing. Otherwise stick to simple tasks such as the careful straightening of feet or finials and other unobtrusive areas. Use wooden mallets and hammers especially made for such work, and always handle the metal lightly.

- Wooden shapes described under copper repairs (page 171) are a great help for dented spouts and sides. Move the silver constantly so that each blow is on a slightly different area, checking all the time to make sure you are not distorting the basic shape.
- Other unplated or stainless steel knives can be re-edged with a sharpening stone, and this also removes small dents and nicks. Never try to sharpen a serrated-edge knife at home though.
- Spoon bowls can be hammered very gently back into shape, again using a wooden rounded shape such as suggested under copper repairs.
- The easiest way to straighten forks is by putting all four prongs in a vise and clamping gently until they line up correctly [9].

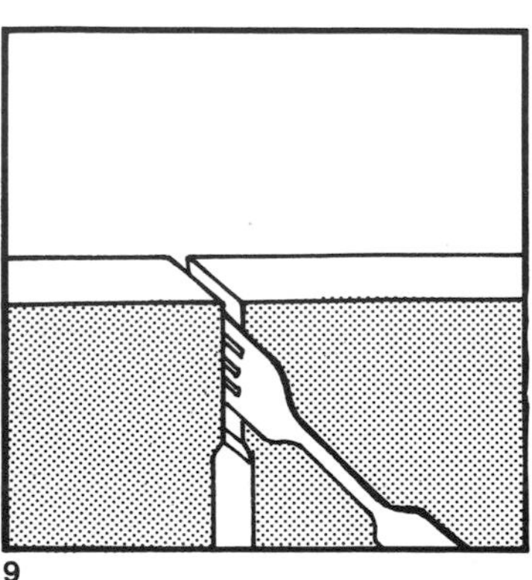
9

- Handles which snap off knives and forks can usually be soldered on, though a home repair is likely to be unsightly—cast silver, like cast iron, is more brittle than the wrought metal. A simple break can be mended with one of the instant-bonding epoxy resin glues. Follow directions. Sometimes the metal part is fixed to the handle in pitch, and any heat applied to this in an attempt to solder will only make matters worse. Spoons can be gently straightened, but be very careful—if they have been bent before, the strain of moving back and forth will often make the metal break off at the weak point. For that reason, spoons which have been bent around to make rings will probably break if you try to reform their shape.
- Modern silver boxes are often made of thin sheet metal over a wooden frame—if this becomes dented, then the whole sheet must be lifted off, the metal flattened and replaced—a repair for an expert!
- For very thin spouts at the end of tea or coffee pots which have become dented, try inserting a dowel or even a pencil into the spout to act as a cushion before hammering.

Silver Plate and Sheffield Plate

Sheffield plate was made in the 18th century as a substitute for hallmarked silver. A sheet of silver was fused to a sheet of copper, usually on both sides. Sometimes an added layer of nickel alloy was used between the silver and copper on the outside. After the sheet was ready, the article was made up in the same way as pure silver, by handwork and fine craftsmanship. For this reason, real Sheffield plate is very much in demand. After 1850 however, the electro-plating process was developed, which is still used today for silver plate. In silver plating the completed base metal article is placed in a solution of silver which is deposited in an even coating over all its surface.

Care and Repair: Care for plate is the same as for silver, except that repairs are more difficult, since the base metal may show through any poor joints. Also the surface silver may wear thin after years of use; but a really worn coating can be replated by a craftsman, using the electrolysis method. Do not have Sheffield plate replated, since it ruins the patina and value.

PRECIOUS METALS AND MOUNTINGS

Gold

As gold is too soft to be used in its pure state, other metals are added to it to increase strength and deepen the tint of the pale yellow gold. (The fineness of gold is expressed in karats—absolutely pure gold is 24 karats).Copper is added in small quantities to make pink gold, in larger quantities to make red gold. Nickel and/or palladium or platinum are used to make white gold, which has a shine somewhere between the glowing dark luster of silver and the bright hard glitter of platinum itself.

Platinum, Palladium

These are modern metals of brilliant white appearance which are much harder than gold and won't tarnish. Platinum is quite heavy while palladium is much lighter. Settings made of these metals for jewelry are much thinner and lighter than those of any other metal, and are now used extensively for fine diamonds and other precious stones; they should be seen by an expert if in need of repair.

Care of Precious Metals and Mountings

Cleaning: All small pieces of metal can be routinely cleaned by commercial jewel-cleaning preparations which are very effective and are usually sold in small bottles or kits. Follow the directions on the container for best results.

Warm water and soapsuds are actually better for cleaning silver, which the commercial dip may leave flat white. Use an old, medium-grade toothbrush to scrub gently into all the crevices, links, etc., but don't rub so hard that you bend any small, delicate parts. Rinse in clean water, again brushing well with a soft, clean toothbrush until all the soap film has dissolved. If the surface has dulled, polish with jeweler's rouge and a dry soft cloth but be careful not to touch engraved surfaces. It was often the craftsman's intention that some areas were to be left mat in order to contrast with highly polished parts; so look at the piece carefully before you change its appearance.

Another design technique to watch is press or stamp work: this was a way of creating a depth of pattern with only a very fine layer of metal Victorian locket bracelets are often made like this, and the hollow links, which are also stamped out mechanically for mass production, can be very fragile. Don't press when cleaning or the links will dent.

Repairing Precious Metals: Home repair or even cleaning of precious metals and stones is not advised—these jobs should always be taken to an expert. The advice given below is for work on more modern pieces, but if you do not have the patience, even these could be badly damaged so proceed carefully. Links can be repaired with wire rings, made at home or bought from a craft supplier. Use tiny pliers made especially for delicate work.

For a simple missing link, cut a piece of matching wire and bend into a hook [10]. Place the ends of the hook in the chain across the gap, putting a finger on top to hold in place, and turn over carefully.

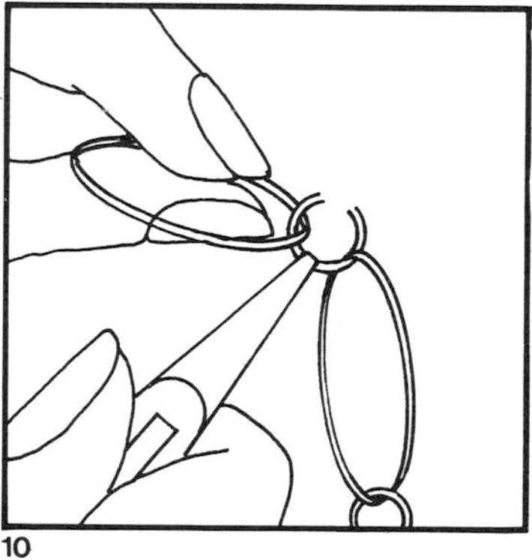

10

Join the ends of the "hook" together; use the pliers to press the wire from either side until the ends meet [11]. Tangled chains are usually slip-knotted together. Lay flat on a table, use a needle fine enough to slip into the knot and shake gently. You may need to use two needles, to pull gently in opposite directions until the knot loosens. Don't pull too hard or you will merely tighten the knot somewhere else or break the chain.

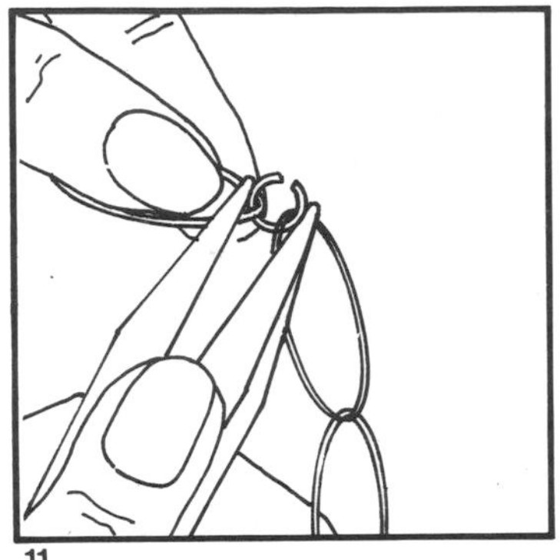
11

Try to keep chains and necklaces hanging from a peg—it saves hours of aggravation. Otherwise they should be opened out and wrapped in a piece of plastic wrap.

Box-snap clasps can be tightened simply by inserting the edge of a spatula (you can buy one designed for sauce-making) or make a chip yourself from a scrap of wood. Raise the togs slightly—this should increase the "spring" and tighten the hold.

Hinge pins can be replaced by bought ones. For emergencies, take a piece of gold or silver wire of the right thickness, and cut it slightly longer than the hinge section. Slip it through the holes, and with the pliers bend over each end until it is hooked firmly down (in a real emergency a fine hairpin or even a needle with sturdy yellow thread will keep a bracelet together).

For mounted stones cleaning must be adjusted to the stone (see Stone chapter). Rubbing with a brush may loosen the prongs of the mount. The best treatment for some mounted pieces is a quick dip in special jewelry-cleaning liquid but SEEK EXPERT ADVICE FIRST, as certain materials—pearl is one—are liable to dissolve! Dry off very carefully with a soft dust-free cloth.

Bent claws of mounts can be straightened [12], but remember that bending metal back and forth greatly weakens it, so if a stone is very valuable and persistently loose, take it to a professional craftsman. Until the late 18th century stones were sometimes backed with foil—as indeed are modern cheap stones—you can replace modern backing with a little gold leaf (page 103) applied to the underside, or a piece of silver foil. If necessary keep the stone in place with a thin coating of absolutely clear cement. Chipped or broken stones must be professionally repaired or replaced.

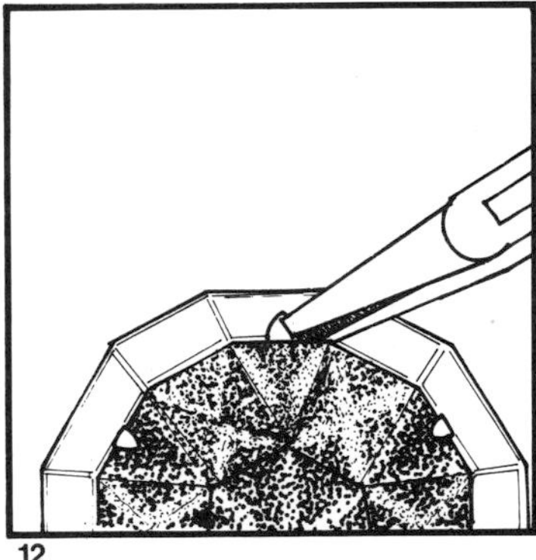
12

Bent pins can be hammered straight with a soft-face or wooden mallet. Place the pin on a flat surface and tape in place so that it doesn't roll over when you try to tap it straight with the hammer [13].

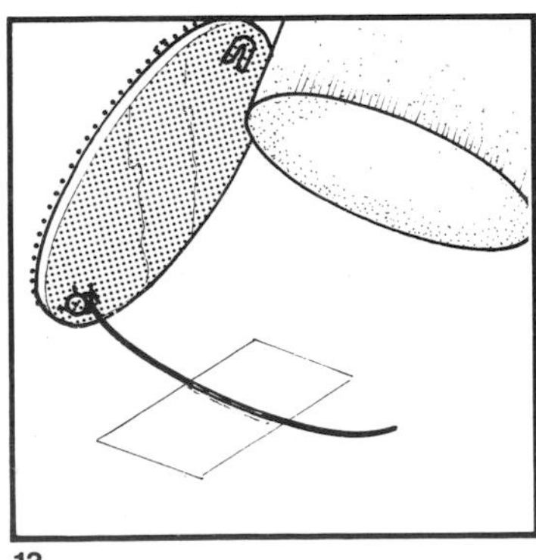
13

A set of brass kitchen scales dating from the end of the 19th century.

MISCELLANEOUS

CLOISONNÉ

An unusual form of metal work, cloisonné developed because early enamels had a tendency to run together in the kiln during firing. So Chinese artisans separated the enamels with strips of fine copper (or gold) soldered onto a bronze base. Then the spaces were filled with glass enamels, and fired. Eventually very fine cloisonné was worked into intricate pictures and patterns.

Unfortunately the enamel sometimes chips, but it can be repaired by placing a little translucent acrylic or enamel paint onto the area with a fine brush—it gives a similar effect to the original without firing. You can also use the china and metal enamels which can be fired in an oven, and are available from most craft stores; but the fine metalwork must be restored by experts.

Chinese cylindrical box with cloisonné enamel decoration; mid-19th century.

PLASTER OF PARIS

This is a mixture of gypsum (hydrated lime sulphate) and water, and it can be bought in different grades, coarse for rough work, medium for single plaster casts or filling work, and the finest quality for work that is very detailed, with crisp edges and intricate patterns. Always add the powder to the water and mix immediately. Caution: it will harden fairly quickly—in about a quarter of an hour.

Plaster casts are extremely useful for the restorer, and particularly useful for pieces of elaborate carving which have parts lost or damaged. Corners of picture frames are particularly vulnerable, and providing one corner is intact, duplicates can be made for the other three.

Plaster can also replace small parts of wooden carving, but of course the object must be gilded or painted after. Alternatively the plaster may be tinted with powdered pigments to match the wood but it needs to be "grained".

Taking a Cast

- Begin with a corner that is complete and cover more than the area you need with a thin layer of wax, Vaseline or oil. Make sure the surface is really covered, including all the crevices, since this layer protects the original, and lets you slip off the cast after it hardens.
- Mix plaster and water to a fairly thick consistency, and place it over the damaged area with a trowel, being careful not to extend beyond the oiled area. Also make sure there are no air bubbles.
- Apply the mixture to a depth of about $\frac{1}{2}$″-1″ (13mm-2.6cm), depending on the size of the damage; obviously the larger the area, the thicker the coat.
- When the plaster has set absolutely hard, it should lift off without any trouble.
- Now lay the cast down, hollow side up, and oil the inner surface thoroughly.
- Mix some more plaster and water, and trowel into the hollows, stirring carefully to get rid of any bubbles or spaces.
- Smooth over the top, and let it set.
- Turn the outer cast over, and you should be able to lift the first casting out without any difficulty.
- When it is absolutely cold and set hard, glue into place on the frame, cutting away to fit the wood on either side, and finish to match.

GESSO

Basically gesso is a variety of plaster-gypsum mixed with glue. It is used as a fairly thin liquid, and sets as a ground for wall paintings, a stiffener for canvas, and a coating over cheap wood to take gold leaf or gilt paint decoration.

Today gesso can be bought as a ready-mix powder, or made at home with equal proportions of gypsum, glue, water or size, and zinc white.

Apply with a brush thinly, allow to dry and sand smooth. Brush on another coat, dry, sand, and so forth.

Although traditionally gesso was used under gold leaf and lacquering it is also very useful for coating wood pieces to which you want to give a very high gloss, since it makes an absolutely non-porous base.

You would be very fortunate to own a gesso piece as fine as this 18th-century gilt chest. Needless to say, the care of such an example should be left to the experts. Nowadays gesso is often used as a base for gloss finishes.

PLASTICS AND ACRYLICS

Plastics and acrylics, including perspex and lucite, can sometimes be repaired if they are handled gently; remember they are fairly brittle and liable to snap under stress.

Broken Edges

Use a tenon or coping-saw for basic work, although a fretsaw may be necessary for complicated pieces. (Use water to lubricate the saw if it heats up). Trim the broken edge back to a usable shape, making sure you are cutting off any cracks or fissures. After cutting, deal with the edge—it should be filed down to match the other edges on the piece—either square, rounded or angled. Use the smooth end of a metal file, and finish off with finer and finer grades of abrasive paper.

Cracked Corners

Modern cube tables often crack at the corners, or at a join, and a piece may break off. If the piece is small and not noticeable, put it back on with a clear-drying synthetic glue.

Scratches

The most common problem with plastics, especially clear and smoky ones, is the proliferation of scratches. Re-polishing acrylics is almost impossible to do, except by gently heating the surface, and rubbing in one direction across the scratch, over and over again, so the softened plastic will flow into the mark. This can be done fairly easily with small pieces like trinket boxes, by letting them soften on an electric hot-plate, covered by an asbestos mat.

Do a little smoothing at a time—the plastic curls over quickly, and yet it mustn't get warm enough to lose its shape and melt the glue. For a very badly scratched surface, there is really nothing you can do except rub it all over with abrasive paper to make a frosted effect.

Cleaning Plastic

Use a window or glass cleaner, wipe or spray on, and rub off with a dry clean cloth. Or wash in warm soapy water, rinse and buff dry.

Polishing

There are a few commercial polishes for fine acrylic furniture and hardware such as door knobs, often available as two liquids. Follow directions, being very careful not to use dirty cloths—even the slightest dust or grime may scratch a plastic surface.

TUBULAR FURNITURE

Not to everyone's taste, the spare lines of tubular furniture are too often associated with municipal halls and hospitals. But if you find yourself attracted by its simplicity the renewal and renovation of the rusty metal and tattered canvas is not difficult.

- First remove the canvas. To do this you will have to unscrew the bars holding it in place. Place bars, nuts, bolts and old canvas aside [1].
- Smooth all rusty patches on the frame and bars with medium-grade steel wool or emery paper.

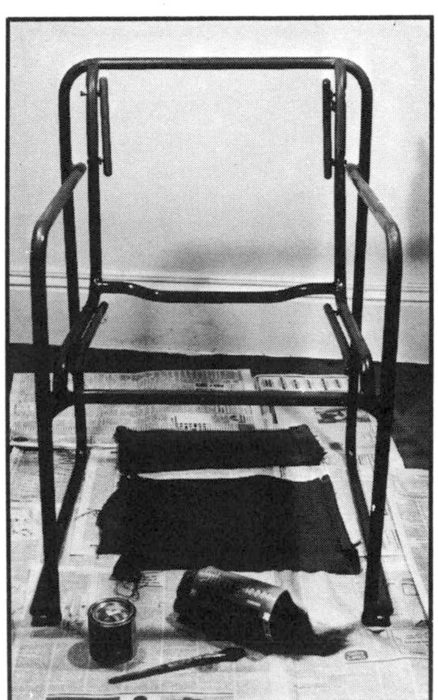

1

- Paint the entire frame and support bars with a rust-preventer. These are also available in aerosol cans but obviously this method of application is wasteful. (On the other hand applying the preventer with a paintbrush is tricky—be careful not to overload your brush).

● Then apply two coats of gloss paint designed to go over the rust preventer—some enamels are not suitable [2].
● Cut new "upholstery" from any strong washable fabric using the old pieces as patterns—here unbleached canvas was selected to contrast with the white frame.
● Secure the new upholstery with the nut and bolt attachments as before.
● Cross stitch the loose ends in place as shown [3].

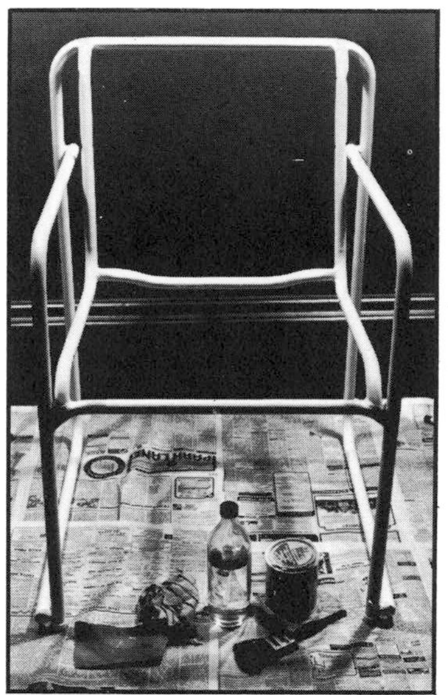

2

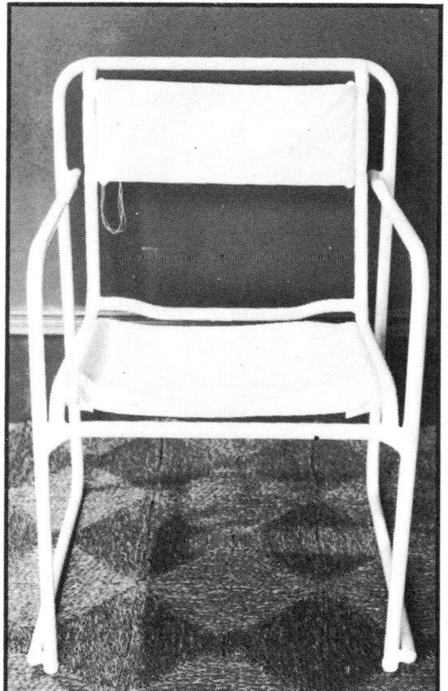

3

BIBLIOGRAPHY

W.M. Adam *A History of Italian Furniture* Vol. 2, New York, 1919

J. Aronson *Encyclopedia of Furniture* London and New York, 1966

M. Amaya *Tiffany Glass* New York and London, 1968

R. Austin and K. Ueda *Bamboo* New York, 1970

C.L. Avery *Early American Silver* 1930, reprinted New York, 1968

A. Bealer *The Art of Blacksmithing* New York, 1969

J. Bedford *All Kinds of Small Boxes* London, 1964, New York, 1965

Suzanne Beedell *Restoring Junk* New York, 1971, London, 1972

E. Bemiss *The Dyer's Companion* New York, 1973

O. Benson and G. Tod *Weaving with Reeds and Fibers* New York, 1976

S. Bing *Artistic America, Tiffany Glass and Art Nouveau* Cambridge, Mass., and London, 1971

E.H. Bjerkoe *The Cabinetmakers of America* New York, 1975

L.A. Boger *The Complete Guide to Furniture Styles* New York, 1959

F. Bradbury *A History of Old Sheffield Plate* Sheffield, 1968

W. Buckley *The Art of Glass* London, 1939

J.T. Butler *American Furniture 1607–1914* London, 1975

R. Campbell and N.H. Mager (eds) *How to Work with Tools and Wood* New York, 1965

M. Campana *European Carpets* London and New York, 1969

C. Cennini *The Craftsman's Handbook* New York, 1933

W. Chaffers *Chaffer's Handbook to Hallmarks on Gold and Silver Plate* 9th ed., London, 1966, Alhambra, Calif., 1967

R.J. Charleston (ed.) *World Ceramics* London and New York, 1968

R.J. Charleston *English Porcelain 1745–1850* London and Toronto, 1965

R.J. Christoforo *How to Build Your Own Fun* New York, 1965

F.J. Christopher *Basketry* New York, 1952

P. Clabburn *The Needleworker's Dictionary* London and New York, 1976

M. Clayton *The Collector's Dictionary of the Silver and Gold of Great Britain and North America* London and New York, 1971

P. Collingwood *Techniques of Rug Weaving* London, 1968, New York, 1969

H.H. Cotterell *Old Pewter, Its Makers and Marks* London, 1929, reprinted Rutland, Vt., 1963, London, 1968

E.G. Couzens and V.E. Yarsley *Plastics in the Modern World* Harmondsworth and Baltimore, Md., 1941, 1956, 1968

S. Crompton (ed.) *English Glass* London, 1967

J. Culme and J. Strang *Antique Silver and Silver Collecting* London and New York, 1973

J.P. Cushion *Ceramic Tablewares* London and New York, 1976

J.P. Cushion and W.B. Honey *Handbook of Pottery and Porcelain Marks* 3rd ed., London and Boston, Mass., 1965

J.P. Cushion *Continental China Collecting for Amateurs* London, 1970, Alhambra, Calif., 1971

BIBLIOGRAPHY

J.P. Cushion *Pocket Book of French and Italian Ceramic Marks* London, 1965
J.P. Cushion *Pocket Book of German Ceramic Marks* London, 1965
D.C. Davis *English and Irish Antique Glass* London, 1964
Jo Anne C. Day *Pennsylvania Dutch Stencils* New York, 1976
J.W. Dean *Leathercraft Techniques and Designs* Bloomington, Ill., 1949
E. Delieb *Silver Boxes* London and New York, 1968
M. Doerner *Materials of the Artist* revised eds., New York, 1962, London, 1969
D. Eyles *Royal Doulton* London, 1965
D.A. Fales, Jr *American Painted Furniture 1660–1880* New York, 1972
F. Fontana *Patchwork Quilt Designs for Needlework* New York, 1976
Sir H. Garner *Oriental Blue and White* London, 1964, New York, 1971
C. Gere *European and American Jewelry* London and New York, 1975
E.V. Gillon *Picture Sourcebook for Collage and Découpage* New York, 1975
G. Groneman *Leather Tooling and Carving* New York and London, 1950
G. Grotz *The Furniture Doctor* London and New York, 1969
J.E. Hammesfahr and Clair Stong *Creative Glass Blowing* San Francisco, 1968
E.B. Haynes *Glass Through the Ages* Harmondsworth and Baltimore, Md., 1959, 1969
H. Hayward *World Furniture* London and New York, 1969
L. Henzke *American Art Pottery* Camden and New York, 1970
K. Herberts *Oriental Lacquer: Art and Technique* London and New York, 1963
Louise C. Hoefer *Leathercraft Instruction* London, 1945
P. Hollister *The Encyclopedia of Glass Paperweights* New York, 1969, London, 1970
J. Holtzapffel *The Principles and Practise of Ornamental or Complex Turning* New York, 1974
W.B. Honey *Dresden China* London, 1934
Hugh Honour *Chinoiserie—The Vision of Cathay* London, 1961
House & Garden Dictionary of Design and Decoration London, 1973
G. Hughes *Modern Silver* London, 1967
H. Huth *Lacquer of the West* Chicago 1971
Marguerite Ickis *The Standard Book of Quilt Making and Collecting* New York and London, 1949
B. Jacobs *Axminster Carpets (Hand-made) 1755-1957* Leigh-on-Sea, 1970
Harriet Janis and R. Blesh *Collage: Personalities, Concepts, Techniques* London, 1967, revised ed. Philadelphia, 1972
Japan Woodwork Catalogue 1701 Grove Street, Berkeley, Calif. 94709
J.G. Jenkins *Traditional Country Craftsmen* London and New York, 1965
R.S. Jenyns and W. Watson *Chinese Art* London and New York, 1963
S. Jenyns *Ming Pottery and Porcelain* London and New York, 1953
S. Jenyns *Later Chinese Porcelain* London, 1951
W.D. John and Anne Simcox *Pontypool and Usk Japanned Wares* Newport, Isle of Wight, 1966
R.W. Johnston *The Book of Country Crafts* South Brunswick, N.J., 1964
E. Jones *Old Silver of Europe and America* 9th ed., London, 1966, Alhambra, Calif., 1967
F. Kayama and J. Figgess *Two Thousand Years of Oriental Ceramics* New York, 1960, Tokyo, 1961
A.F. Kendrick and C.E.C. Tattersall *Hand-woven Carpets, Oriental and European* London, 1922

BIBLIOGRAPHY

R.P. Kinney *The Complete Book of Furniture Repair and Refinishing* New York, 1971, London, 1972

E.F. Kronquist *Metalwork for Craftsmen* New York and London, 1972

A. Lane *A Guide to the Collection of Tiles* 2nd ed., London, 1960

L.I. Laughlin *Pewter in America: Its Makers and Their Marks* vols 1, 2, 3, Barre, Mass., 1969

Alma Lesch *Vegetable Dying* New York, 1971

J.S. Lindsay *Iron and Brass Implements of the English and American House* Boston, Mass., 1964, London, revised eds. 1970

Jean Lipman *American Folk Decoration* New York and London, 1970

R. Lister *The Craftsman in Metal* London, 1966, Toronto and Cranbury, N.J., 1968

H. and G.S. McKearin *American Glass* New York, 1948

D. Macnamara *A New Art of Papier Mâché* London, 1963

C. Mahler *Once Upon a Quilt* New York, 1973

L. Margon *Construction of American Furniture Treasures* New York, 1973

H. Maryon *Metalwork and Enameling* 4th ed., New York and London, 1971

E. Meigh *The Story of the Glass Bottle* Stoke-on-Trent, 1972

R. Metz and A. E. Fanck *Precious Stones and Other Crystals* London, 1964, New York, 1965

R.F. Michaelis *Antique Pewter of the British Isles* London, 1955, 2nd ed. New York, 1971

K. Middlemas *Continental Coloured Glass* London and New York, 1971

J.F. Mills *The Care of Antiques* London and New York, 1964

Modern Plastics Encyclopedia P. Box 430, Hightstown, N.J. 08520

C. Munsey *The Illustrated Guide to Collecting Bottles* New York, 1970

J. Norbury *The World of Victoriana* London, 1972

W.M. Odom *A History of Italian Furniture* vols 1, 2, New York, 1919

G.H. Oelsuner *A Handbook of Weaves* New York, 1975

Isabel O'Neil *The Art of the Painted Finish for Furniture and Decoration* New York, 1971

C.S.M. Parsons and F.H. Curl *China Mending and Restoration: A Handbook for Restorers* London, 1963

G. Petersen and E. Svennas *Handbook of Stitches* (trans. Anne Wilkins) New York and London, 1970

P. Phillips (ed) *The Collectors' Encyclopedia of Antiques* London and New York, 1973

A.U. Pope (ed) *A Survey of Persian Art* 13 vols, London and New York, 1939, revised ed. 1965

M. Praz *An Illustrated History of Interior Decoration* London, 1964

D. Rainwater *American Silver Manufacturers* New York, 1967

J. Ramsay *American Potters and Pottery* New York, 1947

E. Rawlings *Découpage: The Big Picture Sourcebook* New York, 1976

S. Reed *Oriental Carpets and Rugs* London and New York, 1967

Nancy Richardson *How to Stencil and Decorate Furniture and Tinware* New York, 1956

A. Rose and A. Cirino *Jewelry Making and Design* New York and London, 1967

G. Savage *Porcelain Through the Ages* Harmondsworth and Baltimore, Md., 1954, 1970

G. Savage *Pottery Through the Ages* London, 1958, New York, 1963

R. Scharff *Complete Book of Wood Finishing* New York, 1956. London, 1968

I. Schlosser *European and Oriental Rugs and Carpets* London, 1963

E. Sloane *A Museum of Early American Tools* New York, 1964

J. Spargo *Early American Pottery and China* New York, 1926, 1948

J. Stalker and G. Parker *A Treatise on Japanning and Varnishing*

1688, reprinted Chicago 1960, London, 1971
K. Swezey *Formulas, Methods, Tips and Data for Home and Workshop* New York, 1969
R.W. Symonds *The Present State of Old English Furniture* London, 1921
E.H. Tangerman *Whittling and Woodcarving* New York, 1936
J.H. Toulouse *Bottle-makers and Their Marks* Camden, N.J., 1971
A. Tuer *Japanese Stencil Designs* New York and London, 1968
K. Ullyet *Pewter Collecting for Amateurs* London, 1967
H. Walton *Home and Workshop Guide to Sharpening* New York and London, 1970
P. Wardle *Victorian Silver and Silver Plate* London, 1963, New York, 1970
J. Waring *Early American Stencils on Walls and Furniture* New York, 1937, reprinted 1968
L.W. Watkins *Early New England Potters and Their Wares* reprinted Hamden, Connecticut, 1969
L. Watkins *American Glass and Glassmaking* New York, 1950
D.B. Webster *Decorated Stoneware Pottery of North America* Rutland, Vt., 1970.
Leslie Wenn *Restoring Antique Furniture* London, 1974
N. Whitlock *The Decorative Painter's and Glazier's Guide* London, 1827
R. Wilkinson *The Hallmarks of Antique Glass* London, 1968
C.P. Woodhouse *The Victoriana Collector's Handbook* London, 1970, New York, 1971
A Wooster *Quiltmaking* London, 1974
D. Young *Encyclopedia of Antique Restoration and Maintenance* London, 1974

PICTURE ACKNOWLEDGEMENTS

The photographs were specially taken for this book by Alwyn Bailey with the exception of the following, for which grateful acknowledgement is made (the numerals are page numbers):

By courtesy of the Birmingham Museums and Art Gallery: 180. Mrs. M. Cole, photo by Neville W. Smith, Stratford-upon-Avon: 56 (left). Cecil Davis Limited, London: 140-1, 142 (both). Dan Klein Antiques, London, photo by A.C. Cooper Limited: 147. Phoebe Phillips, photo by A.C. Cooper Limited: 179. Phillips the Fine Art Auctioneers, London: 124-5. The Smithsonian Institution, Washington D.C.: 150, 153. Sotheby Parke Bernet, London: 107. Crown Copyright, Victoria and Albert Museum, London: 88, 181.

The wood samples on pages 26 and 27 were kindly supplied by The Art Veneers Company Limited, Mildenhall.

The line drawings are by the author.

INDEX

INDEX

INDEX